Soc. Coop a r.l.
Editrice Minerva Assisi
Vicolo degli Archi 1 — Assisi — Italy
ISBN: 88-87021-53-8

PILGRIM'S COMPANION TO FRANCISCAN PLACES

Dedicated to our beloved
brother and friend,
John Wojtowicz, O.F.M.,
who completed
his pilgrimage
into eternal life on
March 8, 2002

FRANCISCAN PILGRIMAGE PROGRAMS

MISSION STATEMENT

The Franciscan Pilgrimage "Experience"

is a cross-cultural journeying together

in the spirit of Francis and Clare

in order to nurture an encounter

with Jesus Christ

through the spirituality of place.

We commit ourselves

to serve

as sisters and brothers,

fostering conversion

to a deeper Gospel life

and promoting the future vitality

of the Franciscan heritage.

TABLE OF CONTENTS

THE TAU CROSS
AND PILGRIMAGE LOGO

The *scallop shell* was recognized prior to the Middle Ages as a symbol of Christian pilgrimage and became the emblem of every pilgrim. One of its purposes was to scoop water to quench thirst.

The *Tau* was a symbol used by Francis of Assisi as his signature. It was also the symbol of many hospital orders dedicated to caring for the sick, poor, and lepers. Pope Innocent III used this symbol as his personal signature when announcing the Fourth Lateran Council in 1215.

Today people wear the *Tau* as a declaration of commitment to on-going conversion, which is at the core of Francis' spirituality. This particular *Tau* centered in the scallop shell is reputed to have been made by Francis' own hand on a windowsill in the chapel of St. Mary Magdalene at Fonte Colombo. Francis also marked the sign of the cross on trees, pathways and other places, perhaps recalling his own *Prayer before the Crucifix:*

Most High,
glorious God,
enlighten the darkness of my heart
and give me
true faith,
certain hope,
and perfect charity,
sense and knowledge,
Lord,
that I might carry out
your holy and true command.

CHRONOLOGY OF ST. FRANCIS OF ASSISI

1182   Giovanni (John) di Pietro di Bernardone was born and baptized in Assisi. Later he was renamed Francesco (Francis) by his father, Pietro, after a business trip to merchant fairs in France.

1198   Innocent III was elected pope.

1198   Francis participated with citizens of Assisi in razing the Rocca Maggiore, the center of imperial power in Assisi.

1198–
1200   Civil war raged in Assisi, a *comune* intent on independence from both papal and imperial power. Noble families fled to the city of Perugia, the archrival of Assisi.

1202   Francis engaged in the Battle of Collestrada, between Assisi and Perugia, was captured and imprisoned in Perugia.

1203   Pietro ransomed Francis from prison. A long illness tempered Francis' desire for glory and knighthood.

1204   Francis set out to enlist with Walter of Brienne in Apulia in order to become knighted through participation in the Fourth Crusade. En route, a vision at Spoleto directed Francis to return to Assisi to seek God's will. Francis' return caused Pietro great consternation and confusion.

1205   *(Spring)* The gradual process of conversion began. Francis gave generously to poor beggars who came to his father's cloth shop; he embraced a leper and "that which seemed bitter to me was changed into sweetness."

1205   *(Fall)* Praying one day before a large Syro-Byzantine crucifix in the dilapidated church of San Damiano, Francis heard a directive, "Go, repair my house which, as you see, is falling completely to ruin." Francis took cloth from his father's shop, sold it in Foligno and gave the money to the priest at San Damiano for church repair. Pietro took Francis before the bishop of Assisi, demanding public recompense. Francis stripped himself before the bishop, returning all his clothes and renouncing his inheritance. This formally began his religious life as a "Penitent of Assisi." He left Assisi and went to Gubbio.

1206   *(Spring)* Francis made a pilgrimage to Rome, exchanging clothes with a beggar.

1208   Francis began nursing lepers and begging for stones to repair the churches of San Damiano, San Pietro and the Porziuncola.

1208   *(February 24)* At the Porziuncola Francis heard the Gospel for the Feast of St. Matthias. Inspired by the words of Scripture, Francis discovered his vocation: to imitate Jesus Christ perfectly and to preach penance and peace.

1208   *(April 16)* Bernard of Quintavalle and Peter Catanii joined Francis.

1208   *(April 23)* Giles joined them.

1208   *(Summer)* Three new members, one of them named Philip, joined the young fraternity.

1208   *(Late)* Seven members went to Poggio Bustone and preached throughout the Rieti Valley. A new member joined, and they went two by two on a preaching mission.

1209   *(Early)* The eight returned to Assisi. Four more members joined.

1209   Francis composed a brief Rule and went to Rome with his companions to seek approval from Innocent III. Innocent granted approval and the "brothers" returned, staying for a short time near Orte, then settling in a little hovel outside Assisi named Rivo Torto.

1210   Displaced by a farmer who demanded space for his

donkey, the brothers moved to the Porziuncola, a small church located in a swamp outside Assisi. The church was donated to them by the Benedictines in return for an annual basket of fish.

1211 Francis planned a mission to Syria (Muslim territory), but his ship was detoured by heavy winds.

1213 *(May 8)* Francis received as a gift from Count Orlando a mountain in the Tuscan Valley called La Verna. Francis frequently visited this hermitage seeking solitude in the midst of his preaching activity.

1213 Francis attempted a missionary journey to Morocco; he got only as far as Spain and returned home because of illness.

1215 Francis was in Rome for the Fourth Lateran Council. Inspired by the canons of the council, Francis began his "Eucharistic Crusade," writing letters exhorting reverence for the Blessed Sacrament.

1216 *(July 16)* Pope Innocent III died in Perugia. Two days later Honorius III was chosen to replace him. At this time Francis probably met Archbishop Jacques de Vitry.

1216 *(Summer)* In Perugia Francis obtained from Pope Honorius *Il Perdono (The Pardon)* to commemorate the consecration of the Porziuncola.

1217 *(May 5)* All the brothers, now numbering in the thousands, convened in a Chapter at the Porziuncola. Francis sought volunteers to preach in Germany, Tunis, and Syria. Eventually brothers also traveled to Spain. These were the first missioners to cross the Alps and the Mediterranean. Francis planned to go to France, but Cardinal Hugolino met him in Florence and persuaded him to stay in Italy.

1219 *(End of June)* The first brothers were martyred in Morocco. Francis, longing for martyrdom himself, left from Ancona to attempt to convert the Sultan, Al-

Kamil, from Islam to Christianity.

1220 *(Spring and Summer)* Alerted to the difficulties occurring within the order during his absence, Francis returned to Italy with Peter Catanii, Elias, and Caesar of Speyer. Pope Honorius III wrote a papal bull requiring Francis to establish more discipline for errant friars and to develop a "year of probation" for those new to the Order. Recognizing his lack of administrative skills, Francis resigned as Minister General and chose Peter Catanii to replace him. At Francis' request Pope Honorius designated Cardinal Hugolino as Protector of the Order.

1221 *(March 10)* Peter Catanii died. Elias was designated as Vicar General.

1221 Since the earliest days many single and married men and women desired to follow Francis' teachings by living simply and peacefully and caring for the poor. Francis preached and someone wrote down "the words of life," which became the basic directive to guide these followers.

1221 At the request of Hugolino, Francis traveled to the hermitage of Fonte Colombo to incorporate his way of life into a more formal rule.

1221 *(May 30)* The General Chapter received the first written Rule for Friars Minor. This text never received canonical approval.

1223 At Fonte Colombo, during the early part of the year, Francis composed a revision of the Rule, which was discussed in General Chapter in June. Pope Honorius III approved it on November 29.

1223 *(December 24–25)* Exhausted and ill, Francis went to Greccio in the Rieti Valley. There he reenacted the Christmas story. It was from this event that the tradition of the Christmas crèche developed.

1224 First friars arrived at Canterbury, England.

1224   *(August 15–September 29)* Francis retired to La Verna to celebrate Lent in honor of St. Michael. On September 14 or 15 he received the stigmata.

1224   *(October and early November)* Francis returned to the Porziuncola, passing by Borgo San Sepolcro, Montecasale, and Città di Castello.

1224/
1225   *(December to February)* Riding a donkey, Francis undertook a preaching tour through Umbria and the Marches.

1225   *(March to May)* Francis' eyesight worsened; nearly blind, and at the insistence of Brother Elias, he spent some time at San Damiano where Clare and her sisters cared for him. He underwent treatment, but there was no improvement. In the midst of these sufferings, he was assured of eternal salvation and composed *The Canticle of the Creatures.*

1225   *(June)* Francis added a verse to *The Canticle* and effected the reconciliation of the bishop and the *podestá* ("mayor"). Receiving a letter from Cardinal Hugolino, Francis left San Damiano for the Rieti Valley.

1225   *(Early July)* Francis was welcomed to Rieti by Cardinal Hugolino and the papal curia; he went to Fonte Colombo for eye treatment (cauterization) recommended by Cardinal Hugolino. The treatment was delayed until Elias arrived.

1225   *(September)* Francis went to San Fabiano near Rieti; another doctor treated him. While Francis was there, the crowds ruined the vineyard of the poor priest. Francis prayed and the harvest was restored.

1226   *(April)* Francis was taken to Siena for a new treatment.

1226   *(May or June)* Francis stayed at Le Celle in Cortona, where he began to dictate his *Testament.* He later returned to the Porziuncola.

1226 *(July/August)* During the summer's heat, Francis stayed at Bagnara, in the mountains near Nocera.

1226 *(Late August or early September)* His condition worsening, Francis was returned to Assisi, passing through Satriano. There he stayed in the bishop's palace.

1226 *(September)* Sensing that his death was near, Francis insisted on going back to the Porziuncola, the birthplace of the Order. He composed a final verse about "Sister Death" for his *Canticle*.

1226 *(Saturday evening, October 3)* Francis died at the Porziuncola. The next day he was buried in San Giorgio, the parish church were he had attended school.

1227 *(March 19)* Cardinal Hugolino became Pope Gregory IX. John Parenti became Minister General of the friars in May.

1228 *(July 16)* Gregory IX canonized Francis in Assisi near San Giorgio. Thomas of Celano was commissioned to write a life of St. Francis.

1230 *(May 25)* The remains of Francis' body were transferred from San Giorgio to the new Basilica of San Francesco constructed in his honor.

GENEALOGY OF ST. FRANCIS

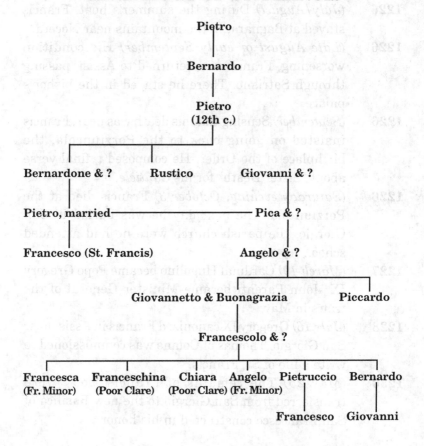

Pietro

Bernardo

Pietro
(12th c.)

Bernardone & ?　　　Rustico　　　Giovanni & ?

Pietro, married———————————Pica & ?

Francesco (St. Francis)　　　　　Angelo & ?

Giovannetto & Buonagrazia　　　Piccardo

Francescolo & ?

Francesca　　Franceschina　　Chiara　　Angelo　Pietruccio　Bernardo
(Fr. Minor)　　(Poor Clare)　(Poor Clare)　(Fr. Minor)

Francesco　Giovanni

Adapted from *Francis of Assisi,* Arnaldo Fontini, [New York: The Crossroad Publishing Company, 1981], and *Naked Before the Father: The Renunciation of Francis of Assisi,* Richard C. Trexeler, [New York: Peter Lang Publishing Inc., 1989].

CHRONOLOGY OF ST. CLARE OF ASSISI

1193/
1194   Clare was born in Assisi, the eldest daughter of Favarone and Ortolana di Offreduccio.

1199/
1200   Clare's family moved to Perugia as a result of civil war in Assisi.

1205   The family returned to Assisi.

1210/
1211   Clare met with Francis to hear his exhortations about Gospel life and her own vocation.

1212   *(March 18–19)* On Palm Sunday night, Clare joined Francis and the friars at the Porziuncola.

1212   *(March 19)* Clare began her stay at San Paolo delle Abbadesse, a Benedictine monastery of women in Bastia.

1212   After a few days at San Paolo and a few weeks at Sant' Angelo in Panzo, Clare moved to San Damiano.

1212   *(April 3–4)* Clare's sister Catherine joined her at Sant' Angelo. Because of the intense suffering she endured, she was renamed Agnes.

1212–
1215   Francis dictated a "form of life" (of which we have a portion), which governed life at San Damiano as others joined Clare and Agnes.

1213   *(Summer)* The miracle of the flask of oil occurred.

1215   The Fourth Lateran Council issued a decree forbidding any new religious orders.

1215   *(End of 1215 or beginning of 1216)* Clare accepted title as abbess.

1217   *(March)* Cardinal Hugolino arrived in Tuscany as papal legate.

1218–
1219   The Rule or Constitutions of Hugolino were imposed on San Damiano.

1218	The Cistercian Ambrose, the chaplain of Cardinal Hugolino, became visitator for the sisters.
1219	Clare's sister Agnes was sent as abbess to Monticelli near Florence.
1219–1220	Brother Philip was appointed as visitator for the Poor Ladies.
1220–1223	The Cistercian Ambrose, after an intervening term of Brother Philip, was again visitator.
1224	The severe, long illness of Clare began.
1226	*(Before April 13, 1226 to 1228)* Brother Pacificus was visitator.
1226	Clare's mother, Ortolana, entered the community at San Damiano.
1226	Francis spent six weeks at San Damiano because of his illnesses.
1226	*(September to the beginning of October)* Francis sent his last exhortation to Clare and her sisters.
1226	*(October 4)* The body of Francis was brought to San Damiano on the way to burial.
1227	*(March 19)* Cardinal Hugolino became Pope Gregory IX.
1227	*(December)* Gregory IX, in the bull *Quoties Cordis* gave the care of the Sisters of St. Clare to the general of the Friars Minor—John Parenti.
1228	A monastery for the Poor Ladies opened in Pamplona, Spain.
1228	*(September 17)* Gregory IX issued the *Privilege of Poverty*.
1228–1246	Brother Philip was visitator a second time.
1229	Clare's sister Beatrice joined Clare and her mother, Ortolana, at San Damiano.
1230	After Gregory IX's letter *Quo Elongati* was promulgated, Clare protested against its prohibition

that no brother could enter the monastery as chaplain without permission. Her response was to stage a hunger strike after dismissing the questing brothers. Soon Gregory relented.

1232–
1233 The Child Jesus appeared during a sermon by Brother Philip.

1234 *(Before June)* Clare wrote *The First Letter to Agnes of Prague.*

1235–
1237 The Order sent sisters to Germany and Bohemia.

1234–
1239 Clare wrote *The Second Letter to Agnes of Prague.*

1238 *(June 8)* The Sisters of San Damiano appointed Oportulo di Bernardo as their syndic and procurator for the sale of a piece of land.

1238 The miracle of the multiplication of the bread occurred.

1240 *(September)* The Saracen invasion of Assisi ended at the entry to San Damiano due to Clare's intercession in prayer.

1241 The city of Assisi was liberated from Vitale d'Aversa.

1241 Sister Balvina of Corano was miraculously healed.

1247 *(June–August 23)* The Rule of Innocent IV was made obligatory for all enclosed women. Clare did not accept this Rule and after August 6 began work on her own rule.

1249 A woman was miraculously freed from five evil spirits.

1250 *(November 11)* Clare became critically ill.

1251 *(September)* Sister Benvenuta of Madonna Diambra was miraculously healed.

1252 *(June–July)* Sister Cristiana was miraculously healed.

1252 *(September 8)* Cardinal Rainaldus visited Clare, who petitioned him for the approval of her *Form of Life.*

1252   *(September 16) The Form of Life of Clare of Assisi* was approved by the cardinal protector, Rainaldus.

1252   *(December 25)* By means of a miraculous vision, while bedridden at San Damiano, Clare joined with the friars and her sisters at the Basilica of San Francesco to experience the divine liturgy.

1253   Tradition recognizes this date for the composition of *The Testament* of Clare.

1253   Clare's sister Agnes returned to San Damiano and was present at the death of Clare in August.

1253   *(April 27)* Pope Innocent IV arrived in Assisi.

1253   *(Soon after April 27)* Innocent IV visited Clare the first time.

1253   *(A few days before August 11)* Innocent IV visited Clare the second time.

1253   *(August 8)* Clare saw a vision of the King of Glory. In the evening Sister Benvenuta of Madonna Diambra saw a vision of the Mother of God with the heavenly court at the deathbed of Clare.

1253   *(August 9)* Pope Innocent IV approved the *The Form of Life* with the bull *Solet Annure*.

1253   *(August 10)* A friar brought the bull of approval to Clare from Perugia.

1253   *(August 11)* Clare died at San Damiano.

1253   *(August 12)* Clare was buried in San Giorgio in Assisi, the church were Francis had initially been buried.

1253   *(October 18)* Pope Innocent IV commissioned Bishop Bartholomew of Spoleto to conduct an inquiry into the life and miracles of Clare. This initiated the process of canonization.

1254   *(November 24–29)* Testimony of the witnesses was taken for the process of canonization in the monastery of San Damiano and in the monastery of San Paolo in Assisi.

1255   *(August 15)* St. Clare was canonized by Pope

Alexander IV (formerly Cardinal Rainaldus) at Anagni, a city south of Rome.

1260 The community of sisters moved from San Damiano to the new convent inside the city walls. The monastery and the Basilica of Santa Chiara were built around the Church of San Giorgio, where the bodies of Francis and Clare had rested. Clare's body was transferred to the new basilica built in her honor.

1850 *(August 30)* The coffin of St. Clare was found under the altar of the main church.

1872 *(October 3)* St. Clare's body was placed in the newly erected burial chapel of Santa Chiara where the people could now pray at her tomb..

1893 The original *Form of Life* was found after having been lost for centuries.

GENEALOGY OF ST. CLARE

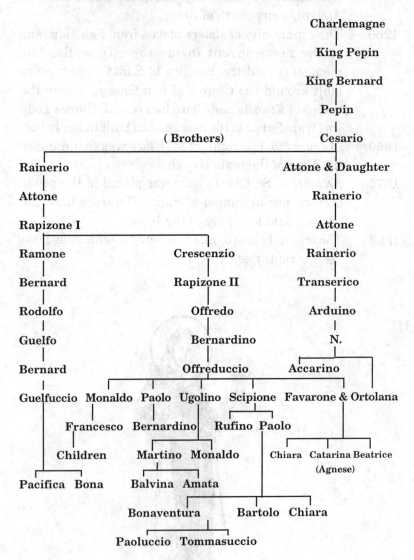

Adapted from: Gemma Fortini, "The Noble Family of St. Clare of Assisi."
Franciscan Studies, 1982. Vol.42, pp. 48-65.

ABBREVIATIONS FOR
FRANCIS OF ASSISI: EARLY DOCUMENTS

Writings of St. Francis

Adm	The Admonitions
BlL	A Blessing for Brother Leo
CtC	The Canticle of the Creatures
CtExh	The Canticle of Exhortation
1Frg	Fragments of Worchester Manuscript
2Frg	Fragments of Thomas of Celano
3Frg	Fragments from Hugh of Digne
LtAnt	A Letter to Brother Anthony of Padua
1LtCl	First Letter to the Clergy (Earlier Edition)
2LtCl	Second Letter to the Clergy (Later Edition)
1LtCus	The First Letter to the Custodians
2LtCus	The Second Letter to the Custodians
1LtF	The First Letter to the Faithful
2LtF	The Second Letter to the Faithful
LtL	A Letter to Brother Leo
LtMin	A Letter to a Minister
LtOrd	A Letter to the Entire Order
LtR	A Letter to Rulers of the Peoples
ExhP	Exhortation to the Praise of God
PrOF	A Prayer Inspired by the Our Father
PrsG	The Praises of God
PrsH	The Praises To Be Said at All the Hours
OfP	The Office of the Passion
PrCr	The Prayer before the Crucifix
ER	The Earlier Rule (*Regula non bullata*)
LR	The Later Rule (*Regula bullata*)
RH	A Rule for Hermitages
SalBVM	A Salutation of the Blessed Virgin Mary
SalV	A Salutation of Virtues
Test	The Testament
TPJ	True and Perfect Joy

Franciscan Sources

1C	The Life of Saint Francis by Thomas of Celano
2C	The Remembrance of the Desire of a Soul
3C	The Treatise on the Miracles by Thomas of Celano
LCh	The Legend for Use in the Choir
Off	The Divine Office of Saint Francis by Julian of Speyer
LJS	The Life of Saint Francis by Julian Speyer
VL	The Versified Life of Saint Francis by Henri d'Avranches
1–3JT	The Praises by Jacopone da Todi
DCom	The Divine Comedy by Dante Alighieri
TL	Tree of Life by Ubertino da Casale
1MP	The Mirror of Perfection, Smaller Version
2MP	The Mirror of Perfection, Larger Version
HTrb	The History of the Seven Tribulations by Angelo of Clareno
ScEx	The Sacred Exchange between Saint Francis and Lady Poverty
AP	The Anonymous of Perugia
L3C	The Legend of Three Companions
LP	The Legend of Perugia
AC	The Assisi Compilation
UChL	An Umbrian Choir Legend
1–4Srm	The Sermons of Bonaventure
LMj	The Major Legend by Bonaventure
LMn	The Minor Legend by Bonaventure
BPr	The Book of Praises by Bernard of Besse
ABF	The Deeds of Saint Francis and His Companions
LFl	The Little Flowers of Saint Francis
KnSF	The Kinship of Saint Francis
ChrTE	The Chronicle of Thomas of Eccleston
ChrJG	The Chronicle of Jordan of Giano

Taken from: *Francis of Assisi: Early Documents Volume II—The Founder,* edited by Regis Armstrong, O.F.M. Cap., J. A. Wayne Hellmann, O.F.M. Conv., and William J. Short, O.F.M. [New York: New City Press, 2000], p. 26.

ABBREVIATIONS FOR
CLARE OF ASSISI: EARLY DOCUMENTS

1LAg The First Letter to Blessed Agnes of Prague
2LAg The Second Letter to Blessed Agnes of Prague
3LAg The Third Letter to Blessed Agnes of Prague
4LAg The Fourth Letter to Blessed Agnes of Prague
LEr The Letter to Ermentrude of Bruges
RCl The Rule
TestCl The Testament
BCl The Blessing
UltVol The Last Will of Saint Francis Written for the Poor Ladies
Proc The Acts of the Process of Canonization
Leg Cl The Legend of Saint Clare

Taken from: *Clare of Assisi: Early Documents*, revised and expanded by Regis J. Armstrong, O.F.M. Cap. [St. Bonaventure, NY: Franciscan Institute Publications, 1993], p. 395.

THE
ASSISI
EXPERIENCE:
INTRODUCTION

FRANCISCAN PILGRIMAGE PROGRAMS

THE ASSISI EXPERIENCE: INTRODUCTION

WELCOME!

Dear Franciscan Pilgrim,

Peace be with you! You are soon to begin a pilgrimage that you may have dreamed about for years. We welcome you and pledge ourselves to your service. Since we are traveling in the spirit of St. Francis and St. Clare, we turn to their words to seek "form" for our journey:

> Wherever the brothers [and sisters] may be and meet one another, let them show that they are members of the same family. Let each one confidently make known his [her] need to the other, for if a mother loves and cares for her son according to the flesh, how much more diligently must someone love and care for [a brother or sister] according to the Spirit! When any brother [or sister] falls sick, the other brothers [and sisters] must serve him [her] as they would wish to be served themselves. (LR VI: 7–9)

> Wherever the brothers [sisters] may be and in whatever place they meet, they should respect spiritually and attentively one another, and *honor one another without complaining.* Let them be careful not to appear outwardly as sad and gloomy hypocrites but show themselves *joyful,* cheerful and consistently gracious *in the Lord.* (ER VII: 15–16)

> I counsel, admonish and exhort my brothers [and sisters] in the Lord Jesus Christ not to quarrel or argue or judge others when they go about in the world; but let them be meek, peaceful, modest, gentle, and humble, speaking courteously to everyone, as is becoming. (LR III: 10–11)

What you hold, may you [always] hold. What you do, may you [always] do and never abandon. But with swift pace, light step [and] unswerving feet, so that even your steps stir up no dust, may you go forward securely, joyfully, and swiftly, on the path of prudent happiness, not believing anything, not agreeing with anything that would dissuade you from this resolution or that *would place a stumbling block* for you on the way, so that you may offer *your vows to the Most High* in the pursuit of that perfection to which the Spirit of the Lord has called you. (2LAg 11–14)

This is a sample of our demanding call. Unlike ordinary tourists, we do not set out as "privileged" people, for we are simply "pilgrims and strangers." Those who are privileged have power and expect to be served; those who are little recognize themselves as servants and try to "carry one another's burdens." A pilgrimage is not exactly a vacation; it is a moving out of one's known environment into another, and at the same time a moving out of one's ordinary mind-set into another in order to know Christ Jesus. So, be ready for self-discovery; be ready to "do penance," to see new possibilities for your life, new ways of acting, new joy and peace. Our journey will not necessarily be easy, but we can make it light by bearing one another's burdens. Any other spirit will vitiate the pilgrimage.

To be a pilgrim—in one sense—means to be guided by another. Our ancestors in faith, the Israelites, were led by Yahweh, at times as a pillar of fire, at other times as a pillar of cloud. We, your guides on this pilgrimage to Rome and Assisi, Rieti and La Verna, welcome the challenge to lead you. To help us on our journey we have put together this special companion book. Pilgrims in the past often expressed a desire to have copies of prayers we used or references to citations quoted. Others wished they could carry back home some visible memento of places where they visited and prayed. Why not have a pilgrim's manual that might serve, in some ways, to meet a few of these needs? And so, the book you now hold in your hands provides a collection of readings, descriptions of places, prayers and songs to be used for Eucharist, prayer, study and reflection.

Though by no means a substitute for our personal presence to you as your guides, this book, nevertheless, will serve as a useful companion and a handy reference to all that will take place during our days together.

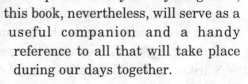

We go forth in peace and in prayer for each other.

The Pilgrimage Staff

The Assisi Experience of "Spirituality of Place" *

"Does geography have anything to do with spirituality?" Keith Warner recently asked. In Franciscan spirituality, he answers, it does.[1] The late Eric Doyle had also addressed the issue when he wrote that in addition to the writings of St. Francis and the early written sources about him and his message, "there remains still one more source: the city of Assisi itself. It is one of the holy places of the earth."[2] Additionally, Doyle proposed that anyone who wanted to "penetrate the mystery of St. Francis, ... really ought to visit Assisi."[3] For modern Franciscans, the journey to such a holy place means making *pilgrimage.*

In the fall of 1986, a group of pilgrims participating in The Assisi Experience made their way through San Damiano; the presence of thirteen Poor Clares among them made this a historic visit. Moving slowly through the monastery, the group eventually came to the large dormitory of St. Clare, where a cross and fresh flowers always mark the place where the Lady

Clare met Sister Death. As the pilgrims entered the room, no explanations were given, no comments were made by the Pilgrimage directors. As the Poor Clares found themselves standing in this sacred place, which up to that moment they had envisioned only in their imaginations, the majority of the sisters were in tears. They had connected with a *sacred place*.

The directors of The Assisi Experience programs have for [many] years predicated their work on the concept of the "spirituality of place." In these programs, *sacred places experienced in the context of pilgrimage* form the foundation of a profound religious experience. ...

Pilgrimage

The concept of *pilgrimage* informs the entire Franciscan story. We know that in Francis's understanding of the Gospel, "Jesus was a traveler, a pilgrim on the way. . . . Francis uses the expression 'follow the footprints of Christ' five times in four writings." Other writers have likewise commented upon the Scriptural picture of Jesus as pilgrim; Kajetan Esser held that this theme was at the heart of Francis and of Franciscan spirituality.[4] The Gospels themselves (Lk. 2:41-42; Jn. 2:13; 5:1; 7:10) show us Jesus observing Jewish law concerning pilgrimages.[5] And we know from various sources that Francis made pilgrimages to Rome and to the Holy Land (1C 8; L3C 10; LMj 1:6 for Rome; 1C 55; LMj 9:5-9 for the Holy Land). Francis and the early companions visited the tomb of Peter after they received approval of the primitive Rule, and Brothers Bernard and Giles journeyed to the shrine of St. James at Compostela (1C 34; 1C 30). St. Clare's mother Ortolana made pilgrimages to Rome and to the Holy Land (Proc 1:4; Leg Cl1); Bishop Guido of Assisi was on pilgrimage to the shrine of St. Michael at Gargano when Francis died (2C 220). Pilgrimage is undeniably embedded deeply in our Franciscan roots.

In tracing the history of the phenomenon of pilgrimage, one learns that the idea of a holy journey precedes both Jewish and Christian traditions of pilgrimage. In classical terms, the Latin *peregrinus* denoted "a foreigner without citizenship"; later it referred to "one on a journey to a holy place or shrine."[6] The earliest attestation of a Christian pilgrim identifies Alexander, bishop of Cappadocia, as going to Jerusalem to "pray and know the holy sites." After 313, the year of civil recognition of Christianity, the Holy Land journey became the source for all other devotional journeys.[7] In the patristic era, becoming a pilgrim was considered on a par with the monastic state; in the following centuries *peregrinatio* acquired heavy connotations of an "ascetic wandering of the earth in exile, seeking a heavenly homeland."[8] By the time of Gregory the VII (d. 1085) it had been deepened to include an inner desire and subjective experience, according to Warner.

Benedictinism and Bernard of Clairvaux moved the idea of pilgrimage to a journey one undertook in the heart and a need to keep oneself unentangled from the snares of the world. Irish monks proposed pilgrimage as a penance for sins.[9] By the eleventh century, the notion of pardon had been attached to visiting a specific shrine. "When Francis exhorted his brothers to live as pilgrims and strangers in this world, he summoned images of Abraham, Jesus, and the holy men and women of the early Christian tradition."[10] Indeed, the idea of pilgrimage to the Porziuncola in Assisi each August 2nd for the feast of The Pardon (*Il Perdono*) is built upon the larger Christian context of pardon for one's sins.

Francis did not conceive of pilgrimage as exclusively an inner journey, but as "an inner journey which corresponded to an outer one."[11] In the understanding of the late Joseph Doino, O.F.M., pilgrimage is "extroverted mysticism," and mysticism is "introverted pilgrimage. Pilgrimage is prayer of the feet while mysticism is interior footwork."[12] Doris Donnelly, a contemporary

Catholic writer, further expands our notion of pilgrimage when she writes:

> Most pilgrims who undertake physical pilgrimages understand that it is their own interior incompleteness that leads them to seek contact with holy places and persons to do for them what they cannot do by themselves: to deliver them from fragmentation and effect a glimmer of wholeness which invariably opens unto God.[13]

There are five ways in which pilgrims and tourists differ. The distinctions between tourist and pilgrim are worthy of consideration here.

1. Pilgrims perceive an internal dimension to pilgrimage, while tourists are concerned with the external journey alone.
2. Pilgrims invest themselves; tourists avoid personal commitment. ·
3. The focus for the pilgrim will be affected by the pilgrimage. Tourists seek to remain untouched on a deep level by their experiences.
4. Both the journey and the arrival are important to thepilgrim, while only the arrival matters for the tourist.
5. Community is formed for pilgrims; community is not a desideratum for tourists.[14]

It seems that a deeper understanding of pilgrimage would serve well the People of God of the post-Vatican II era: our life is a Christian spiritual journey, we are a Pilgrim Church (Lumen Gentium 48).

Sacred Place

Beyond the notion of pilgrimage, a second concept holds our attention in The Assisi Experience. Recalling the 1986 visit of the Poor Clares to the dormitory at San Damiano, we see an instance of immediate apprehension of and encounter with the sacred place they had entered—the place where St. Clare slept, where she had spent many days and nights in convalescence from illness, and where she was embraced by Sister Death on 11 August 1253. These events and the place coalesced into a most powerful moment for the Clares; their tears gave witness to the depth of their experience with the spirituality of sacred place.

James Postell, teacher and architect, provides a rich explanation of sacred place: "**Sacred** has to do with both an inner and an outer presence—a spiritual power, an intersection of Heaven and Earth. **Place** implies human significance, human action derived from history, belief, ritual, and everyday ... activity."[15] According to Postell, sacred places are **perceived as sacred** and serve to mark "important geographic, cultural, political, and religious transitions involving spiritual power. As such, their presence requires an attentive eye and open mind and heart.[16]

One of the first lectures presented to pilgrims in The Assisi Experience explains the focus of the pilgrimage—the spirituality of place. In bringing the pilgrims to so many places associated with the lives of St. Francis and St. Clare, the directors invite the pilgrims into an experience of the spirituality of these sacred places. Each pilgrim has a copy of *The Pilgrim's Companion*, a book containing excerpts of Franciscan sources as well as prayers, rituals, Eucharistic celebrations, and historical background on each Franciscan site in Rome, Rieti, Assisi, and LaVerna. Equipped with *The Pilgrim's Companion* and guided by the staff, pilgrims are invited to participate in an unfolding process at each of the sanctuaries. First, there is the historical visit: upon arrival at one of the sanctuaries, a staff member guides the pilgrims on an extensive historical visit of the sacred place. This is followed by the prayer experience: in each sanctuary the pilgrims are called to participate in prayer through celebration of the Eucharist or another ritual, or through a morning or evening prayer service. Thirdly, there is reflection time: personal time for reflection on the meaning of the particular sacred place is provided for the pilgrims. Always, the pilgrims are advised that the staff will be able to do the first two parts of the process with them, but the third part—the reflection—can only be done by the pilgrims themselves. It is precisely in reflection that the spirituality of the sacred place unfolds and is experienced.

Dr. Ewert Cousins writes of what he calls the "mysticism of historical event." During the Middle Ages there was in Western Europe an immense transformation in popular devotion, with a new focus on devotion to the humanity of Christ and the historical events of Christ's life. "Religious sensibility" of the era desired to "imagine and re-enact these events and to imitate Christ in the concrete details of his earthly life." According to Cousins, it was Francis of Assisi, "more than any other saint or spiritual writer," who helped transform religious sensibility this way.[17] This use of imagination has consequences for a spirituality of place. For each pilgrim, the meaning of a given place is colored and shaped by her/his own personality type, just as it was for Francis. When one looks at the types identified in the Myers-Briggs Preference Indicator and attempts to apply them to St. Francis, it may be conjectured that Francis was probably an ESFP — extrovert, sensate, feeler, perceiver. He "exhibited all the marks of the SP temperament, which is characterized by an attitude of openness and willingness to go in any direction the Spirit calls."[18] As an SP, Francis was especially interested in the events, and therefore in the places, of Jesus' life. "The events surrounding [Jesus'] birth, his hidden life, his baptism, his miracles, his passion, death, and resurrection will hold special interest for the SP."[19]

When a modern pilgrim moves into the reflective stage of the process described above, she/he is already situated in a sacred place and is prayerfully pondering historical events that happened there. Cousins considers this type of meditation a form of mysticism, the mysticism of historical event—that is, "a distinct form of contemplative mystical consciousness whereby one attempts to enter into a significant event of the past in order to tap into its spiritual energies."[20] The events of Francis' or Clare's lives offer opportunities for each pilgrim to enter into a mystical experience. According to Cousins:

> How should one assess this form of meditation? Is it a mere exercise of imagination ... or is it rooted in deeper levels of the psyche and in the very structure of human existence? I believe that it is rooted in the very historicity of human existence and that it activates that level of the psyche whereby we draw out the spiritual energy from a past event.[21]

There are others whose work supports such a comprehension of reality. Historical events do not occur in a vacuum, they happen in places. Therefore, both event and place are conduits of spiritual energy—even in the post-modern world. A fine example of someone who experienced spirituality of place is Thomas Merton. In an insightful analysis of Merton's spirituality of place, Wayne Simsic maintains that Merton did not want simply to occupy a place, he wanted to be at home in it, dwell in it. "Through a solitude grounded in Christ, he discovered power and energy in the place itself. He found himself pulled toward places not so much out of emotional need or because he knew the place, but because the place knew him."[22] According to Simsic, Merton also remained "open to the energy of the earth."[23] This resonates with Franciscan spirituality, especially when one thinks of our Sister, Mother Earth (CtC).

Simsic identified two interesting elements in Merton's spirituality of place: the telling of stories and the enactment of rituals. Stories seem to trigger the release of the spiritual energies of a place. According to Simsic, Merton found that "people who live close to the land embody their wisdom in stories. Stories preserve their relationship with the land and with the natural order."[24] In fact, Merton's own stories connected with Gethsemani Abbey "reveal the sacredness of the place to him and act as a reminder of the spiritual landscape hidden within the physical landscape. . . .Stories knit his soul to the landscape, deepening his appreciation of and familiarity with it."[25] In a similar vein, The Assisi Experience makes constant use of stories from the rich storehouse of Franciscan sources. As the pilgrims move from place to place, they are encouraged to read these stories which recall the events of our larger Franciscan story.

Merton's rituals, according to Simsic, "anchored him in landscape" and "rooted him in the ground of Mystery" so that earth and sky stood within a deep primordial relationship with him. "Each gesture and action [of ritual] filled space with meaning ... and became signs of his relationship with sacred space."[26] The Assisi Experience incorporates ritual in visits to the Franciscan sanctuaries. Many times, the ritual itself facilitates the release of the spiritual energy of the place in a way that lectures, homilies, or historical input are unable to accomplish.

A word about the most significant Christian ritual of Eucharist. One of the strongest elements of Christian pilgrimage is "the centrality of the Eucharist as the ritual that commemorates the roots of the community and re-establishes the identity of pilgrims and companions — breakers of bread."[27] Over the years in which The Assisi Experience has matured, rituals — especially the ritual of Eucharist — has played an increasingly important role in the experience of the spirituality of place. Celebration of the Eucharist at the various holy sites helps sustain a focus on Jesus Christ, the heart of the pilgrimage. Staff members consciously allude to how the lives of Francis and Clare constantly and unwaveringly point toward and conform to the life of Jesus Christ. Among the sources cited, two stand out: Thomas of Celano describes Francis as "always occupied with Jesus; Jesus he bore in his heart, Jesus in his mouth, Jesus in his ears, Jesus in his eyes, Jesus in his hands, Jesus in the rest of his members" (1C 115). Bartholomew of Pisa, near the end of the fourteenth century, wrote the *Book of Conformities,* in which he describes how Francis was conformed to Christ. Assisi pilgrims come to understand that the deepest reason for their journey to Franciscan Italy lies in their ability to see how the lives of Clare and Francis point consistently to Christ. Every pilgrim is on the way to meet Christ and to discover the glory of God in the face of Christ, even the crucified Christ.

Conclusion

In light of all that has been said, if we return once more to the experience of the Poor Clares at San Damiano in 1986, it is clear that the events which occurred in that sacred place, especially the death of St. Clare, were already part of the meditation of these women before they entered the dormitory. The historical events that had happened in that room centuries before effected a release of spiritual energy in each of them, bringing them to a mystical experience. When they found themselved in the sacred room, the place itself released its own energy, which brought them to tears—the external expression of a powerful interior movement. I recognized this movement because at one time I was privileged to accompany the late Carroll Stuhlmuller, CP, on pilgrimage to the Holy Land. At the church called "Dominus Flevit," "The Lord Wept," (Lk 19:41), Stuhlmuller gave a lecture on the "Theology of Tears." In that lecture he proposed that in the experience of tears there is a movement of God. The Poor Clares at San Damiano underwent a profound experience of the spirituality of place, encountered a release of San Damiano's own spiritual energy, and entered into a mystical experience discerned by their tears.[28]

Each Assisi Experience eventually comes to an end. The pilgrims pack their luggage (usually a bit heavier than at arrival) for the return home. The biggest item taken home, however, is the collage of memories, which, in the words of Thomas Rossica, weigh nothing, go easily through customs, and can be enjoyed for a long time.[29] It is the memories of sacred events, sacred places and sacred experiences that will enliven the continuing pilgrimage through life toward the final "homeland."

André Cirino, O.F.M.

Endnotes

[1] Keith Warner, *Pilgrims and Strangers: The Evangelical Spirituality of the Early Franciscan Friars,* unpublished Master's thesis (Berkeley: Graduate Theological School) 1.

[2] Eric Doyle, "Select Bibliography on the Life and Message of St. Francis," in *Francis of Assisi Today,* Concilium Religion in the Eighties, ed. C. Duquoc and Casiano Floristán (New York: The Seabury Press) 74.

[3] Doyle, "Select Bibliography."

[4] Warner, 53–54, citing Kajetan Esser, "Studium und Wissenschaft im Geiste des hl. Franziskus von Assisi," in *Wissenhatt und Weisheit* 39 (1976): 28.

[5] Warner, 54.

[6] Thomas M. Rossica, CSB, "Towards a Biblical Spirituality of Pilgrimage," *Catholic International* (December, 1994): 569.

[7] Warner, 13, citing F. Raphael, "Le Pélerinage, approche sociologique," *Les Pélerenages de l'antiquité biblique et classique à l'occident médiéval* (Paris: Librarie Orientatliste Paul Geunther, 1973) 11–12.

[8] Rossica, 569–70.

[9] Warner, 73.

[10] Warner, 76–77.

[11] Warner, 78. Emphasis added.

[12] Warner.

[13] Joseph Doino, OFM, "Pilgrimage: Reality and Illusion," lecture delivered at the annual Assisi Pilgrimage Staff Meeting, San Antonio, Texas, 2 January 1991.

[14] Doris Donnelly, "Pilgrims and Tourists: Conflicting Metaphors for the Christian Journey to God," *Spirituality Today* 44 (1992): 23.

[15] Donnelly, 21.

[16] James Postell, "Making Sacred Places," letter to Margaret Carney, OSF, 28 July 1995. Emphasis added. The point of reference for the letter was the renovation of the motherhouse chapel of the Sisters of St. Francis of the Providence of God, Whitehall, Pennsylvania.

[17] Postell. He also cited the view of Mircea Eliade that sacred sites

have a single origin and function: they were the meeting places of heaven and earth, the sacred center through which heaven and the underworld are joined.

18 Ewert C. Cousins, "Franciscan Roots of Ignatian Meditation," in *Ignatian Spirituality in a Secular Age*, ed. George P. Schner (Toronto: Willrid Laurier University Press, 1984) 56.
19 Chester P. Michael and Marie C. Norrisey, *Prayer and Temperament* (Richmond: William Bird Press, 1984) 69.
20 Michael and Norrisey, 72.
21 Cousins, 60.
22 Cousins, 59-60. Emphasis added.
23 Wayne Simsic, "Merton's Spirituality of Place," *Review for Religious* (July–August, 1994): 572. Emphasis added.
24 Simsic, 575.
25 Simsic, 573.
26 Simsic, 574, 576.
27 Simsic, 576.
28 Donnelly, 33.
29 Rossica, 573.

The Cord 47, no. 1 [1997], 3–10. Reprinted with Permission.

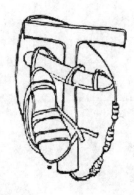

ROME:
WELCOME

FRANCISCAN PILGRIMAGE PROGRAMS

ROME: WELCOME

EVENTS
Going to Rome summed up a direction to which Francis always turned in his life. Assisi was secondary to and dependent on Rome.

Francis' visits to Rome are hard to trace. His first visit, as far as we are concerned, was a pilgrimage to the Tomb of Peter, an opportunity to get away from his relatives and acquaintances. In Rome he could do what he felt he had to do (L3C 10; 2C 8; LMj I:6). In 1205–1206 he needed anonymity. Thus Francis arrived in Rome on pilgrimage (cf. L3C 10 below).

SPIRITUALITY
Francis had to leave his home to respond to some new stirrings in his life.

Francis' journey to Rome was part of his conversion process. Our arriving here is another significant stopping-off point on our conversion journey through life.

REFLECTION
What does it mean to have left your hometown and come to Rome, like Francis?

ROME: THE ETERNAL CITY

Rome is the capital city of Italy, of the region of Lazio, and the province of Rome. It is located on the Tiber River near the coast of the Tyrrhenian Sea. For centuries Rome has been called the Eternal City because of its importance as one of the great cities of Western civilization, the capital of the Roman Empire, and the world center of the Roman Catholic Church. Today Rome's economy relies upon two activities, government operations and tourism. A number of international corporations and agencies, including the United Nations Food and Agriculture Organization, International Fund for Agricultural Development, and the World Food Programme, are headquartered here.

Long a major city of Europe, Rome has become an unparalleled repository of monuments of all periods, from the Etruscan era to modern times. The period of Rome's early history under Etruscan kings is represented by relatively few relics; the legacy of the following period, the Roman Empire, is extensive in comparison. Roman monuments range from the almost perfectly preserved Pantheon (founded 27 B.C.; rebuilt A.D. 118–128), considered one of the finest surviving temples of antiquity, to the still impressive—although partly destroyed—Coliseum (opened A.D. 80), a huge amphitheater that was the scene of gladiatorial combats and other spectacles. Ancient city walls, triumphal arches, great public meeting places, churches, and palaces are all found in Rome.

Foremost among these monuments are the Roman Forum and the Imperial Forum, ancient centers of commerce and religion; the Baths of Caracalla, built about A.D. 217 and until recently used as the setting for summer opera performances; the Catacombs, ancient tunnels beneath the city in which early Christians practiced their religion and were buried; and the Castel Sant' Angelo, built as a mausoleum for the Roman emperor Hadrian (A D. 135–139) and converted into a fort in the Middle Ages. The Basilica of St. John Lateran, the Cathedral of Rome, was founded in the 4th century and substantially rebuilt in the 17th and 18th centuries; the Basilica of St. Paul Outside the Walls was built in the 4th century and reconstructed after being destroyed by fire in 1823; and the Basilica of St. Peter in Chains, founded in the 5th century, was rebuilt in the 15th century and contains a sculpture of Moses executed by Renaissance artist Michelangelo.

Other popular points of historical interest include the Piazza del Campidoglio, a square containing a bronze statue of Emperor Marcus Aurelius completed during the 2nd century; the Piazza Navona, a square with three fountains, including the *Fountain of the Four Rivers* by the Italian sculptor Gianlorenzo Bernini; the Trevi Fountain, an 18th-century baroque fountain into which tourists toss coins while making wishes, and the Piazza di Spagna, where the famous Spanish Steps, built in the 18th century, ascend to the 15th-century church of the Trinità dei Monti. Perhaps the finest works of more modern times are the structures built for the 1960 Olympic Games, several of which were designed by one of Italy's leading contemporary architects, Pier Luigi Nervi. Across the Tiber River from the Olympic Stadium is the site of the first Islamic mosque ever built in Rome. It opened in 1995 after twenty years of construction and blends Roman and Islamic architectural styles.

Rome has been an urban center for more than two thousand years, and although monuments of most periods of the city's history still stand, the destructive impact of pollution and vibrations from heavy vehicular traffic is gradually leading to increased efforts toward preservation, including restrictions on cars and trucks in the historic center.

Adapted from the *Encarta Encyclopedia*, 1993-1998, s.v. "Rome (Italy)," 3–4.

FRANCISCAN READINGS

THE LEGEND OF THREE COMPANIONS 10

Francis' pilgrimage to Rome and experiences with the beggars

At this time he happened to go to Rome on pilgrimage. As he was entering the church of Saint Peter, he noticed the meager offerings made by some, and said to himself: "Since the Prince of the Apostles should be greatly honored, why do they make such meager offerings in the church where his body rests?" With great enthusiasm, he took a handful of coins from his money pouch, and threw them through a grating of the altar, making such a loud noise that all the bystanders were astonished at his generosity.

As he was leaving and passed the doors of the church, where there were many poor people begging alms, he secretly exchanged clothes with one of those poor people and put them on. Standing on the steps of the church with the other poor, he begged for alms in French, because he would speak French spontaneously, although he did not do so correctly.

After taking off the beggar's clothes and putting on his own, he returned to Assisi, and began to pray that the Lord would direct his way.

THOMAS OF CELANO, FIRST LIFE 32

Francis' return to Rome with his first companions

When blessed Francis saw that the Lord God was *daily increasing* their numbers, he wrote for himself and his brothers present and future, simply and in few words, a form of life and a rule. He used primarily words of the holy gospel, longing only for its perfection. He inserted a few other things necessary for the practice of a holy way of life. Then he went to Rome with all his brothers, since he greatly desired that the Lord Pope Innocent the Third confirm for him what he had written.

ORIENTATION TO ITALY

MATTERS OF PRACTICALITY

1. TIME

After 12:00 noon Europeans count 13:00, 14:00, 15:00 (thirteen hundred, fourteen hundred, etc.) for 1 P.M., 2 P.M., 3 P.M., etc. With regard to time we ask you to please be on time for all activities and departures as found in your schedule. Everyone is expected to take part in the program from beginning to end. Please stay with the group whenever we move as a group. Don't lag behind, for example, to buy souvenirs. *Riposo* "rest" time is urged for all.

2. WATER

Spigots are marked with a capital F for *freddo*, meaning "cold," and C for *caldo*, meaning "hot." All water is safe to drink except when you see the sign "acqua non potabile," which indicates "nondrinkable water."

3. PENSIONE

When away from the *pensione*, the practice is to leave all keys at the desk. Rooms are equipped with shades or blinds that can be raised or lowered by use of a canvas-like cord affixed to the wall. Ask for instructions if you do not know how to operate them. In the dining room bottled water, soda, wine, or beer may be purchased.

4. THE BAR

There are two ways to order at a bar: standing inside or sitting at table. Anything you order is cheaper while standing. If you sit down at a table, you can expect to pay a higher price. Bottled water is called *acqua minerale* or *acqua normale*. If you prefer carbonated water, ask for *"acqua minerale con gas."*

5. MAIL

Stamps (*francobolli*) can be purchased in Vatican City Post Offices or Italian (Nation) Post Offices. Vatican City stamps can be posted only in Vatican City; and letters and cards with Italian stamps, only at Italian post boxes. The two should not be mixed.

6. REST ROOMS

Rest rooms are found at most public places. If you need to ask for a rest room, use the following words: *gabinetto*, *bagno*, or the initials for water closet, *wc*. Occasionally people who clean the rest room will ask for a coin. This is their salary for their work. A sign will indicate how much. We encourage you to carry some tissues with you for use in public toilets.

7. STREET SIGNS

Avanti means walk. *Alt* means don't walk.

8. SECURITY

The art of purse snatching has been developed by a number of young men on motor scooters or motorcycles. One individual drives and the other snatches. So it is important to carry your purse or packages in the hand over the shoulder farthest from the curb and to keep a firm grip on whatever you carry. In bars and restaurants keep your belongings with you on your lap. Don't set things on another table while you are eating. Passports are needed only for the exchange of currency. They should be left in the pensione.

9. ROOM NUMBERS OF YOUR STAFF

_____   _____

10. ITALIAN WORDS

"Good morning"—*Buon giorno*. Use until riposo.
"Good afternoon"—*Buona sera*. Use after riposo until retiring.
"Good night"—*Buona notte*. Use when going to bed.
"Please"—*Per favore*.
"Thank You"—*Grazie*.

EUCHARIST

READING: GENESIS 12:1–7

A reading from the book of Genesis

Now the LORD said to Abram, "Go from your country and your kindred and your father's house to the land that I will show you. I will make of you a great nation, and I will bless you, and make your name great, so that you will be a blessing. I will bless those who bless you, and the one who curses you I will curse; and in you all the families of the earth shall be blessed." So Abram went, as the LORD had told him; and Lot went with him. Abram was seventy-five years old when he departed from Haran. Abram took his wife Sarai and his brother's son Lot, and all the possessions that they had gathered, and the persons whom they had acquired in Haran; and they set forth to go to the land of Canaan. When they had come to the land of Canaan,

Abram passed through the land to the place at Shechem, to the oak of Moreh. At that time the Canaanites were in the land. Then the LORD appeared to Abram, and said, "To your offspring I will give this land." So he built there an altar to the LORD, who had appeared to him. **The word of the Lord.**

RESPONSE: The Lord is my shepherd.

PSALM 23

The LORD is my shepherd,
I shall not want.
He makes me lie down in green pastures;
he leads me beside still waters;
he restores my soul. **R.**

He leads me in right paths for his name's sake.
Even though I walk through the darkest valley,
I fear no evil;
for you are with me;
your rod and your staff—they comfort me. **R.**

You prepare a table before me
in the presence of my enemies;
you anoint my head with oil;
my cup overflows. **R.**

Surely goodness and mercy shall follow me
all the days of my life,
and I shall dwell in the house of the LORD
my whole life long. **R.**

ALLELUIA: Come to me, all you that labor and are burdened and I will give you rest, says the Lord.

GOSPEL: LUKE 24:13–21, 25–35

A reading from the holy Gospel according to Luke

Now on that same day two of them were going to a village called Emmaus, about seven miles from Jerusalem, and talking with each other about all these things that had happened. While they were talking and discussing, Jesus himself came near and went with them, but their eyes were kept from recognizing him. And he said to them, "What are you discussing with each other while you walk along?" They stood still, looking sad. Then one of them, whose name was Cleopas, answered him, "Are you the only stranger in Jerusalem who does not know the things that have taken place there in these days?" He asked them, "What things?" They replied, "The things about Jesus of Nazareth, who was a prophet mighty in deed and word before God and all the people, and how our chief priests and leaders handed him over to be condemned to death and crucified him. But we had hoped that he was the one to redeem Israel. Yes, and besides all this, it is now the third day since these things took place."

Then he said to them, "Oh, how foolish you are, and how slow of heart to believe all that the prophets have declared! Was it not necessary that the Messiah should suffer these things and then enter into his glory?" Then beginning with Moses and all the prophets, he interpreted to them the things about himself in all the scriptures. As they came near the village to which they were going, he walked ahead as if he were going on. But they urged him strongly, saying, "Stay with us, because it is almost evening and the day is now nearly over." So he went in to stay with them. When he was at the table with them, he took bread, blessed and broke it, and gave it to them. Then their eyes were opened, and they recognized him; and he vanished from their sight. They said to each other, "Were not our hearts burning within us while he was talking to us on the road, while he was opening the scriptures to us?" That same hour they got up and returned to Jerusalem; and they found the eleven and their companions gathered together. They were saying, "The Lord has risen indeed, and he has appeared to Simon!" Then they told what had happened on the road, and how he had been made known to them in the breaking of the bread. **The Gospel of the Lord.**

EUCHARIST

FEAST OF ST. JAMES, PATRON OF PILGRIMS

READING: 2 CORINTHIANS 4:7-15

A reading from the second letter of Paul to the Corinthians

But we have this treasure in clay jars, so that it may be made clear that this extraordinary power belongs to God and does not come from us. We are afflicted in every way, but not crushed; perplexed, but not driven to despair; persecuted, but not forsaken; struck down, but not destroyed; always carrying in the body the death of Jesus, so that the life of Jesus may also be made visible in our bodies. For while we live, we are always being given up to death for Jesus' sake, so that the life of Jesus may be made visible in our mortal flesh. So death is at work in us, but life in you. But just as we have the same spirit of faith that is in accordance with scripture—"I believed, and so I spoke"—we also believe, and so we speak, because we know that the one who raised the Lord Jesus will raise us also with Jesus, and will bring us with you into his presence. Yes, everything is for your sake, so that grace, as it extends to more and more people, may increase thanksgiving, to the glory of God. **The word of the Lord.**

RESPONSE: The Lord is kind and merciful.

PSALM 126

When the LORD restored the fortunes of Zion,
we were like those who dream.
Then our mouth was filled with laughter,
and our tongues with shouts of joy;
then it was said among the nations,
"The LORD has done great things for them." **R.**

The Lord has done great things for us,
and we rejoiced.
Restore our fortunes, O Lord, like the watercourses in the Negeb. **R**.

May those who sow in tears reap with shouts of joy.
Those who go out weeping,
bearing the seed for sowing,
shall come home with shouts of joy,
carrying their sheaves. **R**.

ALLELUIA: I have chosen you from the world, says the Lord, to go and bear fruit that will last.

GOSPEL: MATTHEW 20:20–28

A reading from the holy Gospel according to Matthew

Then the mother of the sons of Zebedee came to him with her sons, and kneeling before him, she asked a favor of him. And he said to her, "What do you want?" She said to him, "Declare that these two sons of mine will sit, one at your right hand and one at your left, in your kingdom." But Jesus answered, "You do not know what you are asking. Are you able to drink the cup that I am about to drink?" They said to him, "We are able." He said to them, "You will indeed drink my cup, but to sit at my right hand and at my left, this is not mine to grant, but it is for those for whom it has been prepared by my Father."

When the ten heard it, they were angry with the two brothers. But Jesus called them to him and said, "You know that the rulers of the Gentiles lord it over them, and their great ones are tyrants over them. It will not be so among you; but whoever wishes to be great among you must be your servant, and whoever wishes to be first among you must be your slave; just as the Son of Man came not to be served but to serve, and to give his life a ransom for many." **The Gospel of the Lord.**

ROME:
BASILICA
OF
ST. PETER

FRANCISCAN PILGRIMAGE PROGRAMS

TOMB OF ST. PETER

EVENTS
Francis came to Rome on pilgrimage in order to visit and pray at the Tomb of St. Peter. The Tomb of St. Peter was a magnet that drew pilgrims from all over the world, and it was to this tomb that Francis would return again and again. Since Francis was called to the apostolic life, he had to live and die like the apostle Peter, as a missionary, as a preacher, as a martyr. This is what it meant to "follow the teaching and footsteps of the Lord Jesus Christ" (ER I: 1).

In the piazza in front of St. Peter's as it was in Francis' day, Francis changed clothes with a beggar and begged in the French language. It is at this point that Rome became important in his process of conversion.

SPIRITUALITY
Francis paid tribute to a place made special because the apostle Peter preached here and was martyred here.

Francis prayed at the Tomb of Peter and asked Peter to help him discover the treasure of Gospel poverty.

Francis, at the beginning of his conversion, exchanged clothes with a beggar and attempted to overcome shame (cf. 2C 8).

REFLECTION
What does it mean to overcome shame? How can this deepen one's spiritual journey?

What does it mean to share the faith of the apostles?

What is the meaning of a pilgrimage to the tomb of a saint?

How do you answer Christ's question to Peter: "Who do you say I am?"

ROME:
BASILICA OF ST. PETER

HISTORICAL NOTES

The largest and perhaps the most impressive basilica in the world rises over the pagan cemetery that flanked Nero's Circus. It was exactly on this spot in 67 A.D. that the Apostle Peter was crucified. Pope Anacletus, Peter's immediate successor, built a small chapel over the Apostle's tomb. It immediately became a place of pilgrimage for the early Christians despite the risk. Under the Emperor Constantine the persecutions came to an end and Christianity was legalized. In 326 Constantine leveled the hill and built a basilica over the entire cemetery with the main altar standing over St. Peter's tomb, which he left undisturbed.

After twelve centuries, however, the basilica naturally began to show the ravages of time. Restorations and repairs were of no use. Thus, in 1506, Pope Julius II, a Franciscan, was compelled to pull down the old basilica and laid the cornerstone of a new one. Construction and decoration lasted 120 years. Bramante was the first architect followed by Michelangelo, Raphael, and several others. Bernini was commissioned to decorate the interior. This church was to be a timeless image of heaven, thus the interior would have no materials that faded; there would be marble instead of wood, mosaics instead of canvas. The dome that was designed by Michelangelo was completed in a record 22 months. The entire structure was consecrated in 1626, exactly 1300 years after Constantine consecrated the first basilica.

FRANCISCAN READINGS

ST. BONAVENTURE, MAJOR LEGEND I:6

Francis and the beggars of Rome

With religious devotion he visited at this time the shrine of the Apostle Peter. When he saw a large number of the poor before the entrance of the church, led partly by the gentleness of his piety, encouraged partly by the love of poverty, he gave his own clothes to one of the neediest among them. Dressed in his rags, he spent that day in the midst of the poor with an unaccustomed joy of spirit, in order to spurn worldly glory and to arrive, by ascending in stages, at Gospel perfection.

THOMAS OF CELANO, SECOND LIFE 8

Francis and the beggars of Rome

Once on pilgrimage to Rome, out of love for poverty he took off his fine clothing and dressed himself in a poor man's clothes. He happily settled among the poor in the square in front of the church of Saint Peter, a place where the poor are abundant. Considering himself one of them, he eagerly ate with them. If his embarrassed friends had not restrained him, he would have done this many times.

THE LITTLE FLOWERS OF SAINT FRANCIS 13

On Francis praying at the Tomb of Peter for the treasure of holy poverty

Saint Francis said, "My dear Masseo, let's go to Saint Peter and Saint Paul, and pray to them to teach and help us to possess the immeasurable treasure of most holy poverty. ... So let us pray to the most holy Apostles of Christ, who were perfect lovers of this evangelical pearl, that they gain for us this grace from our Lord Jesus Christ: that by His most holy mercy he grant us to be considered worthy to be true lovers, observers and

humble disciples of most precious, most beloved and evangelical poverty."

And while talking this way they reached Rome and entered the church of Saint Peter; and Saint Francis placed himself in prayer in one corner of the church, and Brother Masseo in another. And as Saint Francis remained in prayer for a long time with devotion and many tears, the most holy Apostles Peter and Paul appeared to him with great splendor and said, "Since you request and desire to observe what Christ and the holy Apostles observed, our Lord Jesus Christ sends us to you to announce that your prayer *has been heard*: God most perfectly grants to you and your followers the treasure of most holy poverty. And further, on His behalf, we tell you that whoever by your example will perfectly follow this desire is assured of the blessedness of eternal life. And you and all your followers will be blessed by God." After saying these words they disappeared, leaving Saint Francis filled with consolation.

THE LEGEND OF THREE COMPANIONS 10

How Francis changes clothes with a beggar

He was so changed by divine grace that, although he was still in secular attire, he yearned to be in another city where, as someone unknown, he would take off his own clothes and, in exchange, put on the rags of a poor man. And he would try begging alms for the love of God.

At this time he happened to go to Rome on pilgrimage. As he

was entering the church of Saint Peter, he noticed the meager offerings made by some, and said to himself: "Since the Prince of the Apostles should be greatly honored, why do they make such meager offerings in the church where his body rests?" With great enthusiasm, he took a handful of coins from his money pouch, and threw them through a grating of the altar, making such a loud noise that all the bystanders were astonished at his generosity.

As he was leaving and passed the doors of the church, where there were many poor people begging alms, he secretly exchanged clothes with one of those poor people and put them on. Standing on the steps of the church with the other poor, he begged for alms in French, because he would speak French spontaneously, although he did not do so correctly.

After taking off the beggar's clothes and putting on his own, he returned to Assisi, and began to pray that the Lord would direct his way. He did not share his secret with anyone.

FRANCISCAN POPES

Pope Nicholas IV
Friar Jerome Masci of Ascoli
pont. 1288–1292, Italian

He advanced missions into Asia, promoted Catholic–Orthodox reunion and commissioned his confreres Jacopo Torriti and Jacopo Camerino to mosaic the apses of St. John Lateran and St. Mary Major, Rome. He commissioned the first notable book of medicine in the West. In 1289 Nicholas formally approved the Rule of the Third Order.

Pope Sixtus IV
Friar Francesco della Rovere
pont. 1471–1484, Italian

He founded the first public library and the first foundling hospital and established the Vatican archives. He constructed the Sistine Chapel, named after him. Sixtus IV officially introduced the feasts of the Immaculate Conception and St. Joseph, as Husband of Mary. He was titled *"Restaurator urbis"* for renovating medieval Rome into a Renaissance monument.

Pope Julius II
Friar (novice) Giuliano della Rovere
pont. 1503–1513, Italian

He spent many years expelling foreign domination from the Papal States, refusing to be subservient to secular monarchs. He commissioned Bramante to begin the present St. Peter's Basilica and commissioned Michelangelo to fresco the Sistine Chapel. He founded the Vatican Museum and the Swiss Guard and called the Fifth Lateran Council.

Pope Sixtus V
Friar Felice Peretti
pont. 1585—1590, Italian

He reorganized the entire administration of church government. He founded the Vatican Press and founded or enlarged many colleges. The dome of St. Peter's was completed in a record twenty-two months under his guidance; he constructed new aqueducts to bring water to many parts of the poorer sections of Rome. This Sixtus assisted the poor with loans and established schools for poor girls. He was titled: *"Restaurator urbis"* for renovating Renaissance Rome into the baroque monument of today.

Pope Clement XIV
Friar Lorenzo Ganganelli
pont. 1769–1774, Italian

He negotiated with King George III of England for Catholic emancipation. He also received the patriarch of the Nestorian schism into union with Rome. Clement XIV founded the Vatican Museum of Antiquities, as well as the present Lateran University, Rome. Because of tremendous pressure from European monarchs, he was compelled to suppress the Society of Jesus in 1773. (The Jesuits were restored in 1814.)

Note: Several popes in recent history were also Secular Franciscans. In fact, every pope between 1846 and1963 was a Secular Franciscan: Pius IX, Leo XIII, Pius X, Benedict XV, Pius XI, Pius XII, and John XXIII.

EUCHARIST

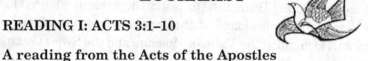

READING I: ACTS 3:1–10

A reading from the Acts of the Apostles

One day Peter and John were going up to the temple at the hour of prayer, at three o'clock in the afternoon. And a man lame from birth was being carried in. People would lay him daily at the gate of the temple called the Beautiful Gate so that he could ask for alms from those entering the temple. When he saw Peter and John about to go into the temple, he asked them for alms. Peter looked intently at him, as did John, and said, "Look at us." And he fixed his attention on them, expecting to receive something from them. But Peter said, "I have no silver or gold, but what I have I give you; in the name of Jesus Christ of Nazareth, stand up and walk." And he took him by the right hand and raised him up; and immediately his feet and ankles were made strong. Jumping up, he stood and began to walk and he entered the temple with them, walking and leaping and praising God. All the people saw him walking and praising God, and they recognized him as the one who used to sit and ask for alms at the Beautiful Gate of the temple; and they were filled with wonder and amazement at what had happened to him. **The word of the Lord.**

RESPONSE: Their message goes out through all the earth.

PSALM 19

The heavens are telling the glory of God;
and the firmament proclaims his handiwork.
Day to day pours forth speech,
and night to night declares knowledge. **R.**

There is no speech, nor are there words;
their voice is not heard;
yet their voice goes out through all the earth,
and their words to the end of the world. **R.**

READING II: GALATIANS 1:11–20

A reading from the letter of Paul to the Galatians

I assure you, brothers and sisters, the gospel I proclaimed to you
is no mere human invention. I did not receive it from any human
person, nor was I schooled in it. It came by revelation from Jesus
Christ. You have heard the story of my former way of life in
Judaism. You know that I went to extremes in persecuting the
church of God and tried to destroy it; I made progress in Jewish
observance far beyond most of my contemporaries, in my excess
of zeal to live out all the traditions of my ancestors.

But the time came when the One who had set me apart before
I was born and called by his favor chose to reveal Jesus, the
Holy One, to me, that I might spread among the Gentiles the
good tidings concerning him. Immediately, without seeking
human advisors or even going to Jerusalem to see those who
were apostles, I went off to Arabia: later I returned to Dam-
ascus. Three years after that I went up to Jerusalem to get to
know Cephas, and with whom I stayed fifteen days. I did not
meet any other apostles except James, the brother of the Lord.
I declare before God that what I have just written is true.
The word of the Lord.

ALLELUIA: You are Peter, the rock on which I will build my Church, to last for ever.

GOSPEL: MATTHEW 16:13-19

A reading from the holy Gospel according to Matthew
Now when Jesus came into the district of Caesarea Philippi, he asked his disciples, "Who do people say that the Son of Man is?" And they said, "Some say John the Baptist, but others Elijah, and still others Jeremiah or one of the prophets." He said to them, "But who do you say that I am?" Simon Peter answered, "You are the Messiah, the Son of the living God." And Jesus answered him, "Blessed are you, Simon son of Jonah! For flesh and blood has not revealed this to you, but my Father in heaven. And I tell you, you are Peter, and on this rock I will build my church, and the gates of Hades will not prevail against it. I will give you the keys of the kingdom of heaven, and whatever you bind on earth will be bound in heaven, and whatever you loose on earth will be loosed in heaven." **The Gospel of the Lord.**

ROME:
ST. JOHN
LATERAN

FRANCISCAN PILGRIMAGE PROGRAMS

ROME: ST. JOHN LATERAN

EVENTS
San Giovanni in Laterano was more closely connected with the life of Francis and the whole Franciscan movement than any other building in Rome.

In 1209 Francis and his eleven companions came to Rome. They had a papal audience with the powerful Innocent III to seek approval of their way of life. Innocent had a dream that revealed to him the crumbling of the Lateran Basilica and Francis' role in supporting and rebuilding the church.

Innocent gave verbal approval to the brothers' way of life, commissioned them to preach penance, and tonsured the twelve at the Lateran.

Francis preached to Innocent III.

San Giovanni was also the scene of the Fourth Lateran Council held in 1215 at which Francis was probably present. Perhaps he also met Saint Dominic (2C 148, 150).

SPIRITUALITY
Francis presented himself as a God-inspired and utterly honest and self-confident person. The strength of his inner spirit (the result of time spent in the caves) moved Innocent to approve Francis' way of life.

Francis' message from the crucifix at San Damiano ("Go, rebuild my church") began to take on universal and global dimensions.

Francis' Rule was composed of Gospel texts. The event at St. John Lateran emphasized the prominence of the Word for Francis.

Francis promised obedience to the successors of Peter.

REFLECTION
Why did the pope listen to Francis?

Why is it important to have this "form of life" confirmed by the church?

How do I regard the papacy? Could I promise obedience the way Francis did? If I could speak with the pope, what would I like to say?

BASILICA OF ST. JOHN LATERAN

HISTORICAL NOTES

The story of St. John Lateran begins back in the year 312 A.D. when Constantine celebrated his victory over Maxentius, taking control of Rome. Upon crossing the Milvian Bridge to enter into the city, Constantine had a vision of a cross in the sky with the following inscription written on it: "In This Conquer." This message inspired Constantine to grant greater freedom to Christians whose religious practices were questioned by many Romans.

Needing a place from which to command his new empire, Constantine chose the Lateran Palace for his headquarters. This property had belonged to the patrician family named Laterani. They had been put to death and their property confiscated during the reign of the Emperor Nero. It now became the Emperor Constantine's property.

To strengthen bonds with the pope, Constantine had a basilica built on the Laterani grounds. Upon completion it was dedicated by Pope Sylvester on November 9, 324. It was named the Church of Christ the Savior. The Pope's residence and papal offices were established next to this basilica. In 904 the Church was renamed in honor of two Johns, St. John the Baptist and St. John the Apostle. Since that time it has been called St. John Lateran. Constantine had built another basilica over the tomb of St. Peter during his reign as Emperor. Though this basilica was magnificent in its own right, and pilgrims traveled to the tomb of Peter to venerate Peter's place in church history, the papal residence remained at St. John Lateran. In 1506 Pope Julius II commissioned a new basilica to be built over the tomb of St. Peter. Succeeding popes took up residence adjacent to this new basilica. However, St. John Lateran is still the "Mother Church" of Rome, and the Pope presides here as its Bishop.

Over the years this church endured destruction due to the invasion of vandals, due to earthquakes and fires, and due to the ravages of time. Many popes commissioned rebuilding projects and invited artists and architects to use their talents to restore it to a place of splendor. In the 13th century two Franciscan artists, Jacopo Torriti and Jacopo de Camerino, were commissioned by Pope Nicholas IV to restore the magnificent mosaic in the apse. These Franciscans were sure to incorporate St. Francis, St. Anthony, Pope Nicholas IV, and the artists themselves throughout the new mosaic design. Giotto was responsible for painting frescos on the walls of the church in the 14th century. Only a fragment remains today depicting Pope Boniface VIII proclaiming the first Jubilee Year. In the 17th century the church was "modernized" by the great architect Boromini. And in the 19th century Pope Leo XIII enlarged and restored the church. He was responsible for transferring the remains of Pope Innocent III here from Perugia, recalling Innocent's role in announcing one of the greatest church councils of the time in 1215, the Fourth Lateran Council. Pope Leo XIII himself chose to be buried here.

Elements of Franciscan history unfold here at St. John Lateran. Francis traveled here in 1209 to request the approval of his new way of life from Pope Innocent III. Eventually his Rule of 1223 was approved in these papal offices. It is here that Pope Innocent III had a dream of Francis holding up the Church of St. John Lateran, and Francis dreamed of his future brotherhood that would grow and be under his protection. In 1926 Mussolini commissioned a statue of Francis to celebrate the 700th anniversary of Francis' death, and to honor Francis as Patron of Italy. This statue stands across the street from St. John Lateran. Francis' hands are raised up high, and the view from behind this statue gives the impression that Francis is indeed fulfilling Innocent's dream of holding up the "Mother Church of Rome."

FRANCISCAN READINGS

THOMAS OF CELANO, FIRST LIFE 32–33

How Francis seeks approval for a rule of life

When blessed Francis saw that the Lord God was *daily increasing* their numbers, he wrote for himself and his brothers present and future, simply and in few words, a form of life and a rule. He used primarily words of the holy gospel, longing only for its perfection. He inserted a few other things necessary for the practice of a holy way of life. Then he went to Rome with all his brothers, since he greatly desired that the Lord Pope Innocent the Third confirm for him what he had written.

Presiding over *God's Church* at that time was the lord Pope Innocent the Third, a glorious man, prolific in learning, brilliant in speech, burning with zeal for justice in matters which the cause of the Christian faith demanded. When he recognized the wish of the men of God, he first considered the matter and then gave his assent to their request, something he completed by a subsequent action. Exhorting and then warning them about many things, he blessed Saint Francis and his brothers and said to them: "Go with the Lord, brothers, and as the Lord will see fit to inspire you, preach penance to all. When the almighty *Lord increases* you in numbers and grace, come back to me *with joy*, and I will grant you more things than these and, with greater confidence, I will entrust you with greater things."

THE LEGEND OF THREE COMPANIONS 46–53

Francis and Innocent III—confirmation of a way of life

Seeing that the Lord would increase his brothers in number and merit, since there were already twelve most perfect men expressing the same belief, blessed Francis said to the eleven, he being the twelfth, their leader and father: "Brothers, I see that the Lord mercifully wants to increase our congregation. Then, going to our mother, the holy Roman Church, let us inform the Supreme Pontiff what the Lord has begun to do through us, that, with his will and command, we may continue doing what we have undertaken."

And since the proposal of their father pleased the other brothers, and they had embarked together with him on the journey to the Curia. ...

When they arrived in Rome and found the bishop of the city of Assisi there, they were received with immense joy, for he honored blessed Francis and all the brothers with special affection. ... After he learned their purpose and understood their plan, however, he was overjoyed and promised them his counsel and help.

The bishop was known to the cardinal bishop of Sabina, named Lord John of Saint Paul, a man truly full of God's grace, who loved, in particular, servants of God. ... Then asking blessed Francis the reason why he came and hearing from him their entire proposal and intention, he offered to be their procurator at the Curia.

That cardinal then went to the Curia and told the Lord Pope Innocent III: "I found a most perfect man, who wishes to live according to the form of the holy Gospel, and to observe evangelical perfection in all things. I believe that the Lord wills, through him, to reform the faith of the holy Church throughout the world." Hearing this, the lord pope was greatly amazed and had the cardinal bring blessed Francis to him.

On the following day, therefore, the man of God was presented by that cardinal to the pope, to whom he revealed his entire holy proposal. The pope, a man of extraordinary discernment, in due fashion assented to Francis's request, and encouraged him and his brothers in many ways. He blessed them saying: "Go with the Lord, brothers, and as He will see fit to inspire you, preach penance to everyone. When almighty God increases you in number and grace, come back to us. We will grant you more, and entrust you with a greater charge."

Before the saint left his presence, the Lord Pope wanted to know whether what had been, and what would be conceded, was according to the Lord's will. And so, he said to him and his companions: "My dear young sons, your life seems to Us exceptionally hard and severe. While We believe there can be no question about your living it because of your great zeal, We must take into consideration those who will come after you lest this way of life seem too burdensome."

The pope saw that their constancy of faith and the anchor of their hope were so firmly grounded in Christ, that they did not want to be shaken from their enthusiasm. So he said to blessed Francis: "My son, go and pray that God will reveal to you whether what you ask proceeds from His will. In this way, knowing the Lord's will, We may accede to your desires."
Once God's saint had prayed, as the Lord Pope suggested, the Lord spoke figuratively to him in spirit: "There was a little, poor and beautiful woman in a desert, whose beauty fascinated

a great king. He wanted to take her as his wife, because he thought that, from her, he would have handsome sons. After the marriage was celebrated and consummated, there were many sons born and raised. Their mother spoke to them in this way: 'My sons, do not be ashamed, for you are sons of the king. Therefore, go to his court and he will provide for all your needs.' When they went to see the king, he was struck by their good looks, and noticing a resemblance to himself in them, he asked them: 'Whose sons are you?' When they answered that they were the sons of the little poor woman living in the desert, the king embraced them with great joy. 'Do not be afraid,' he said, 'for you are my sons. If strangers are fed at my table, how much more will you, who are my lawful sons.' He then ordered the woman to send to his court all of the children she had borne to be fed. ..."

After he completed his prayer, he presented himself to the Supreme Pontiff and narrated point-by-point the story that the Lord had revealed to him. "My lord," he said, "I am that little poor woman whom the loving Lord, in His mercy, has adorned, and through whom He has been pleased to give birth to legitimate sons. ...

On hearing this, the pope was greatly amazed, especially since, before blessed Francis's arrival, he had seen in a vision the church of Saint John Lateran threatening to collapse, and a religious, small and of shabby appearance, supporting it on his own shoulders. When he awoke, stunned and shaken, as a discerning and wise man, he pondered what this vision meant to tell him. A few days later, blessed Francis came to him, made known his proposal, as we have said, and asked him to confirm the rule he had written in simple words, using the words of the holy Gospel, for whose perfection he fully longed. As he was reflecting on how enthusiastic blessed Francis was in God's service, and comparing his vision with that shown to the man of God, he began to say to himself: "This is indeed that holy and religious man through whom the church of God will be sustained and supported."

So he embraced him and approved the rule he had written. ...

As he was leaving the City, the man of God, with his brothers, set out into the world, greatly surprised at how easily his desire had been granted. He was growing each day in the hope and trust of the Savior, who had earlier shown him by holy revelations what was to happen.

For before he had obtained these things, one night when he had gone to sleep, it seemed to him that he was making his way down a road beside which there was a lovely, strong and thick tree that was exceedingly high. As he approached and stood under it, marveling at its height and beauty, the holy man suddenly rose to so great a height, that he touched the top of the tree and very easily bent it even to the ground.

It really happened this way, when the Lord Innocent, a very high, lovely, and strong tree in the world, bent himself so kindly to his wish and request.

THOMAS OF CELANO, FIRST LIFE 73

How Francis preaches to Honorius III

Once he came to the city of Rome on a matter concerning the Order, and he greatly yearned to speak before the Lord Pope Honorius and the venerable cardinals. Lord Hugo, the renowned bishop of Ostia, venerated the holy man of God with special affection. When he learned of his arrival, Lord Hugo was filled with fear and joy, admiring the holy man's fervor yet aware of his simple purity. *Trusting* to the mercy *of the Almighty* that never fails the faithful *in time of need*, he led the holy man before the Lord Pope and the venerable cardinals.

As he stood in the presence of so many princes of the Church, blessed Francis, after receiving permission and a blessing, fearlessly *began to speak*.

He was speaking with such fire of spirit
that he could not contain himself for joy.
As he brought forth the word from his mouth,
he moved his feet as if dancing,
not playfully but burning with the fire of divine love,
not provoking laughter but moving them to tears of sorrow.
For many of them *were touched in their hearts*,
amazed at the grace of God
and the great *determination* of the man.

The venerable lord bishop of Ostia was waiting fearfully, praying to God that they would not despise the blessed man's simplicity; for both the glory and the disgrace of the holy man would reflect on himself, since he was the father set *over the* saint's *household*.

RITUAL PRAYER

FRANCIS AND INNOCENT III

CAST OF CHARACTERS

Narrator	John	Francis
Guido	Innocent	Christ

Narrator:
When blessed Francis saw that the Lord was daily adding to their number, he wrote for himself and his brothers present and to come, simply and with a few words a form of life and Rule, using for the most part the words of the holy Gospel. He then came to Rome with all the aforementioned brothers, desiring very much that what he had written should be confirmed by the Lord Pope Innocent III. At the time the venerable bishop of Assisi was at Rome, Guido by name, who honored Francis and all his brothers. When he saw them, he was annoyed.

Guido:

I wonder why they are here in Rome. Perhaps they are here because they wish to leave their native region.

Narrator:

But when he had heard the reason for their coming and understood their purpose, he rejoiced greatly in the Lord.

Guido:

I promise to give you my advice and help in these things.

Narrator:

St. Francis also approached the Lord Bishop of Sabina, John of St. Paul, who asked him:

John:

Would it not be better for you to turn to the life of a monk or hermit?

Narrator:

But Francis refused his counsel. In the end the Cardinal of Sabina acquiesced to his petitions and strove, from then on, to further Francis' endeavors before the Lord Pope. When they had arrived at the Papal Court, Francis was brought before the Pope. The Vicar of Christ was at the Lateran Palace, walking in a hall known as the Mirror Hall when Francis arrived and was announced. The Lord Pope was lost in deep thought when, upon seeing Francis, he said:

Innocent:

I know nothing about this man. Send him away!

Narrator:

Francis took his leave with all humility. (PAUSE)

The following night God showed the pope a vision.

Innocent:
I had a vision in which I saw a palm tree sprouting between my feet and growing until it was a fine tree. As I was wondering what the vision meant, the divine light made it clear to me that the palm tree was the beggar I had turned away the previous day.

Narrator:
The next morning he gave his servants the order:

Innocent:
Search the city for this man until you find him. Then bring him to me without delay.

Narrator:
And the servants searched the city of Rome and found Francis in St. Anthony's hospice. When he appeared before the Supreme Pontiff, Francis told him of his plans.

Francis:
I implore you, Holy Father, in all humility to approve the Rule, the way of life for the brothers and for me.

Narrator:
Innocent III was famous for his learning and had to be careful. He thought: "If we refuse this beggar's request because it is new or too difficult, we may be sinning against Christ's Gospel, because he is only asking us to approve a form of the Gospel life. Anyone who says that a vow to live according to the perfection of the Gospel contains something new or unreasonable or too difficult to be observed is guilty of blasphemy against Christ, the author of the Gospel."

Innocent:
My son, pray to Christ that he may show us his will through you. When We are sure of that, We can grant your request without fear.

Narrator:
The holy man agreed. (PAUSE)

He prayed earnestly and exhorted his companions to pray to God. His answer from the Lord was as follows:

Christ:
Francis, speak thus to the pope. A certain woman who was poor but very beautiful lived in a certain desert. A certain king loved her because of her very great beauty; he gladly married her and begot very handsome sons by her. When they had grown to adulthood and been brought up nobly, their mother said to them: "Do not be ashamed, my loved ones, in that you are poor, for you are all sons of that king. Go gladly to his court and ask him for whatever you need." Hearing this they were in admiration and rejoiced, and buoyed up by the assurance of their royal origin, they regarded want as riches, knowing that they would be heirs. They boldly presented themselves to the king and they did not fear the face of him whose likeness they bore. Recognizing his own likeness in them, the king wondered and asked whose sons they were. When they said they were the sons of that poor woman living in the desert, the king embraced them and said: "You are my sons and heirs; fear not. For if strangers are fed at my table, it is all the more just that I see to it that those be fed to whom my entire heritage is reserved by right." The king then ordered the woman to send all the sons he had begotten to the court to be provided for.

Narrator:
The saint was made happy and glad by the parable and reported the holy message to the pope. (PAUSE)
The woman was Francis, because he was fruitful in many sons. The desert was the world. The sons were the great multitude of brothers. The king was the Son of God, to whom they bore resemblance by their holy poverty. The Lord Pope wondered

at the parable proposed to him and recognized without doubting that Christ had spoken in the man.

Innocent:

I, too, recall a certain vision I had a few days before. I had seen in my sleep the Lateran Basilica about to fall to ruin, when a certain person, small and despised, propped it up by putting his own back under it lest it fall. Surely you are that man, who by your works and by the teaching of Christ will give support to the church. For this reason, I give assent to your request. Go with the Lord, brothers, and as the Lord will deign to inspire you, preach penance to all. Then, when the almighty Lord shall give you increase in number and in grace, return to me with joy, and I will add many more things to these and entrust greater things to you with greater confidence.

Narrator:

So the Pope approved the Rule and gave them a mission to preach repentance, conferring clerical tonsure on the laymen among Francis' companions so that they could preach the word of God without interference. The Lord was with Francis wherever he went, cheering him with revelations and encouraging him by his gifts. For one night after he had given himself to sleep, he dreamed:

Francis:
I had a dream. It seemed that I was walking along a certain road, at the side of which stood a tree of great height. The tree was beautiful and strong, thick and exceedingly high. It happened as I drew near to it, and was standing beneath it, admiring its beauty and its height that I touched the top of the tree, and taking hold of it with my hand, I bent it to the ground.

Narrator:
And so indeed it happened, for the Lord Innocent, the highest and loftiest tree in the world, graciously stooped to Francis' petition and desire.

Adapted from the following sources: 1C 32, 33; 2C 16, 17; LMj III:9–10.

CLOSING PRAYER—
ATTRIBUTED TO POPE INNOCENT III

All:
O Christ, the mighty Father's Son, remembering the Mother who bore you and nourished you, grant me salvation of body and soul. Wipe away my sins; create in me a pure heart. Grant me sure hope, right faith, perfect charity, and the grace beyond every other—a holy death. Death may take my body, but let no other death come near me. In my resurrection, my eyes shall then behold you, and I shall remain with you. Amen.

EUCHARIST

READING: 1 CORINTHIANS 3:9–13, 16–17

A reading from the first letter of Paul to the Corinthians
For we are God's servants, working together; you are God's field, God's building. According to the grace of God given to me, like a skilled master builder I laid a foundation, and

someone else is building on it. Each builder must choose with care how to build on it. For no one can lay any foundation other than the one that has been laid; that foundation is Jesus Christ. Now if anyone builds on the foundation with gold, silver, precious stones, wood, hay, straw—the work of each builder will become visible, for the Day will disclose it, because it will be revealed with fire, and the fire will test what sort of work each has done.

Do you not know that you are God's temple and that God's Spirit dwells in you? If anyone destroys God's temple, God will destroy that person. For God's temple is holy, and you are that temple. **The word of the Lord.**

RESPONSE: How lovely is your dwelling place, O Lord of hosts!

PSALM 84

How lovely is your dwelling place,
O LORD of hosts!
My soul longs, indeed it faints
for the courts of the LORD;
my heart and my flesh sing for joy
to the living God. **R.**

Even the sparrow finds a home,
and the swallow a nest for herself,
where she may lay her young,
at your altars, O LORD of hosts,
my King and my God.
Happy are those who live in your house,
ever singing your praise. **R.**

Happy are those whose strength is in you,
in whose heart are the highways to Zion.
As they go through the valley of Baca

they make it a place of springs;
the early rain also covers it with pools.
They go from strength to strength;
the God of gods will be seen in Zion. **R.**

O LORD God of hosts, hear my prayer;
give ear, O God of Jacob!
Behold our shield, O God;
look on the face of your anointed. **R.**

For a day in your courts is better
than a thousand elsewhere.
I would rather be a doorkeeper
in the house of my God
than live in the tents of wickedness. **R.**

ALLELUIA: I have chosen and sanctified this house, says the Lord, that my name may remain in it forever.

GOSPEL: LUKE 19:1–10

A reading from the holy Gospel according to Luke

[Jesus] entered Jericho and was passing through it. A man was there named Zacchaeus; he was a chief tax collector and was rich. He was trying to see who Jesus was, but on account of the crowd he could not, because he was short in stature. So he ran ahead and climbed a sycamore tree to see him, because he was going to pass that way. When Jesus came to the place, he looked up and said to him, "Zacchaeus, hurry and come down; for I must stay at your house today." So he hurried down and was happy to welcome him. All who saw it began to grumble and said, "He has gone to be the guest of one who is a sinner." Zacchaeus stood there and said to the Lord, "Look, half of my possessions, Lord, I will give to the poor; and if I have defrauded anyone of anything, I will pay back four times as much." Then Jesus said to him, "Today salvation has come to this house, because he too is a son of Abraham. For the Son of Man came to seek out and to save the lost." **The Gospel of the Lord.**

RITUAL PRAYER

TO BE LIVING STONES IN THE CHURCH

INTRODUCTION

Let us use our imagination to recall Francis coming here to St. John Lateran in 1209. He has been a penitent rebuilding churches. His hands are showing the work they have done. Symbolic of that work, and of our own call to rebuild the church, is the pile of stones here before us, stones taken from the quarry in Assisi collected by members of the staff. Francis' initial understanding of his call must have slowly changed and matured in his spirit as, surprisingly to him, a few brothers began to accompany and work with him. As Francis saw that the brothers were steadfast in their purpose for joining him, new questions and concerns surfaced in his consciousness. And so he said: "Brothers, I see that the Lord mercifully wants to increase our congregation. Then, going to our mother, the holy Roman Church, let us inform the Supreme Pontiff what the Lord has begun to do through us, that, with his will and command, we may continue doing what we have undertaken" (L3C 46). So the brothers set out for Rome.

RESPONSE: We shall go up with joy to the house of our God.

PSALM 122

I was glad when they said to me,
"Let us go to the house of the LORD!"
Our feet are standing within your gates, O Jerusalem.

Jerusalem—built as a city that is
bound firmly together. **R.**

To it the tribes go up,
the tribes of the LORD,
as was decreed for Israel,
to give thanks to the name of the LORD.
For there the thrones for judgment were
set up,
the thrones of the house of David. **R.**

Pray for the peace of Jerusalem:
"May they prosper who love you.
Peace be within your walls,
and security within your towers." **R.**

For the sake of my relatives and friends
I will say, "Peace be within you."
For the sake of the house of the LORD our God,
I will seek your good. **R.**

PRAYER

Loving God, today we struggle with the mystery of rebuilding
and renewing the church. We come here to St. John Lateran,
as Francis did with his first companions, to seek wisdom,
direction, and guidance. In our desire to rebuild we express
our fidelity and love for the church and our wish to work
together in harmony with all entrusted with the responsibility
of leadership. With confidence we open our hearts to your Spirit
who is ever present in our company, and who lives with you
and your Son, Jesus, forever and ever.

READING I: THOMAS OF CELANO, SECOND LIFE 10

With his heart already completely changed—soon his body was
also to be changed—he was walking one day by the church of

San Damiano, which was abandoned by everyone and almost in ruins. *Led by the Spirit* he went in to pray and knelt down devoutly before the crucifix. He was shaken by unusual experiences and discovered that he was different from when he had entered. As soon as he had this feeling, there occurred *something unheard of in previous ages:* with the lips of the painting, the image of Christ crucified spoke to him. "Francis," it said, *calling him by name,* "go rebuild My house; as you see, it is all being destroyed."

RESPONSE G 4 "City of God, " refrain

READING II: THE LEGEND OF THREE COMPANIONS 47–51

When they arrived in Rome and found the bishop of the city of Assisi there, they were received with immense joy, for he honored blessed Francis and all the brothers with special affection ... The bishop was known to the cardinal bishop of Sabina, named Lord John of Saint Paul, a man truly full of God's grace, who loved, in particular, servants of God. ... That cardinal then went to the Curia and told the Lord Pope Innocent III: "I found a most perfect man, who wishes to live according to the form of the holy Gospel, and to observe evangelical perfection in all things. I believe that the Lord wills, through him, to reform the faith of the holy Church throughout the world." Hearing this, the Lord Pope was greatly amazed and had the cardinal bring blessed Francis to him.

On the following day, therefore, the man of God was presented by that cardinal to the pope, to whom he revealed his entire holy proposal. ... On hearing this, the pope was greatly amazed, especially since, before blessed Francis's arrival, he had seen in a vision the church of Saint John Lateran threatening to collapse, and a religious, small and of shabby appearance, supporting it on is own shoulders. When he awoke, stunned and shaken, as a discerning and wise man, he pondered what this vision meant to tell him. A few days later, blessed Francis came to him, made known his proposal, as we have said, and asked him to confirm the rule he had written in simple words, using the words of the holy Gospel, for whose perfection he fully longed. As he was reflecting on how enthusiastic blessed Francis was in God's service, and comparing his vision with that shown to the man of God, he began to say to himself: "This is indeed that holy and religious man through whom the church of God will be sustained and supported."

So he embraced him and approved the rule he had written. He also gave him and his brothers permission to preach penance everywhere, with the stipulation that the brothers who preach obtain permission from blessed Francis.

RESPONSE: G 4, refrain

READING III: 1 PETER 2:4–5, 9; EPHESIANS 2:19–22

Come to him, a living stone, though rejected by mortals yet chosen and precious in God's sight, and like living stones, let yourselves be built into a spiritual house, to be a holy priesthood, to offer spiritual sacrifices acceptable to God through Jesus Christ.

But you are a chosen race, a royal priesthood, a holy nation, God's own people, in order that you may proclaim the mighty acts of him who called you out of darkness into his marvelous light.

So then you are no longer strangers and aliens, but you are citizens with the saints and also members of the household of God, built upon the foundation of the apostles and prophets, with Christ Jesus himself as the cornerstone. In him the whole structure is joined together and grows into a holy temple in the Lord; in whom you also are built together spiritually into a dwelling place for God. **The word of the Lord.**

REFLECTION

INVITATION TO TAKE ASSISI STONE (MUSIC)

OUR FATHER / BLESSING

ROME: SAN FRANCESCO A RIPA

FRANCISCAN PILGRIMAGE PROGRAMS

ROME: SAN FRANCESCO A RIPA

EVENTS

Francis visited Rome on a number of occasions, during which he needed a place to stay. He lodged generally where the poor were gathered. For this reason, tradition tells us, he would go to Trastevere where the Church of San Francesco a Ripa is now located.

Francis would have preached and ministered to the poor who lived in this area. Francis also stayed, in all likelihood, with the Antonines, who ran a type of hospital for the poor. This was situated near St. John Lateran, across the street from the current Antonianum.

SPIRITUALITY

Francis learned that the beggars and the poor confront him with the gospel. This challenged him to make a choice for or against the invitation of that gospel.

San Francesco a Ripa invites us to consider the role of the poor in our lives and the role the poor play in the work of evangelization.

Francis learned that there is no substitute for direct contact with the economically poor.

In the very early stages of the order, the brothers chose to live outside Assisi and to work among the lepers and the poor. This was directly related to their formation and conversion process.

REFLECTION

The poverty of the human person is discovered in embracing one's creatureliness in relationship to the Most High God. We are invited to find our freedom by accepting this stance in life.

The poor invite me to recognize a sacredness in every human person and circumstance. Contact with the poor therefore provides its own kind of enrichment to each person.

In reflecting on my attitude toward material goods, opinions, judgments, good works, and accomplishments, to what do I cling and what might God be calling me to let go of in order to be free to respond wholeheartedly?

San Francesco a Ripa introduces us to St. Charles of Sezze, Blessed Louise Albertoni, and St. Hyacinth Mariscotti, holy man and women of the Franciscan family who preceded us. How do I look at such people? At the lives of the saints?

SAN FRANCESCO A RIPA

HISTORICAL NOTES

San Francesco a Ripa is found in a section of Rome called Trastevere. In antiquity this was the area of the Jews, where, very likely, the apostles did their first preaching. The Vatican is part of Trastevere, wherein, according to tradition, Peter was martyred and buried. Pope Callistus had his difficulties with the Hebrews (*ebrei*) here, and it was here that he formed a Christian meeting place, a *titulus*, San Callisto in Trastevere.

Not far from San Francesco is the small church of San Benedetto in Piscinula, which has the oldest romantic campanile in Rome (1069). Next to the church is a small chapel believed to be near the actual cell of St. Benedict (9th century).

Brother Mariano of Florence in his *Itinerarium urbis Romae* (1518) tells us that San Francesco a Ripa was formerly the Hospital of St. Blase. Luke Wadding suggests that Francis obtained from the Abbot of Sts. Cosmas and Damian in 1212 a hospice in the Hospital of St. Blase, thanks to Jacoba dei Settesoli, a wealthy friend and benefactor of the friars.

By 1517 the Hospital of St. Blase was gone, and San Francesco became a convent of secondary importance. However, the convento took on importance during the spiritual renewal under the so-called *Riformati* (first half of the 16th century) when, around 1579, the convento passed over to the Riformati and became the provincialate and the studium for Postulator of the Reform until 1887, when it was transferred to Via Merulana, the Collegio Sant' Antonio.

In 1698 the cell of Francis was completed as it is today, and in 1701 the church's renovation was finished. The 1700s closed with the French Revolution, and after 1809 until the fall of Napoleon, the friars of San Francesco had no peace and were forced out of their convento. Similarly, in 1848, two hundred Garibaldians camped in their house.

With the law, enacted in Rome in 1873, suppressing religious corporations and provinces, the friars of San Francesco once again had to abandon their convento. On November 12, 1873, the convento became the barracks of the famous *bersaglieri* (a branch of the Italian military). It was also in this same year that hundreds of homeless families invaded the convento to find shelter. The friars were assigned a small section of the old building where the pastor and his assistants lived. In 1906 San Francesco became a parish, and in 1926, the 7th centenary of the death of St. Francis, a missionary college (presently a pensione) was built next to the parish offices.

The church of San Francesco a Ripa is the final resting place for a number of important persons, among them St. Charles of Sezze and Blessed Louise Albertoni (Secular Franciscan). These saints, as did many Franciscans after them, including those living today, found great inspiration at this place and carried out an effective and compassionate ministry to the poor, who still populate the surrounding area.

HOLY LIVES ASSOCIATED
WITH SAN FRANCESCO A RIPA

Servant of God Lady Jacoba di Settesoli (d. 1239)

Lady Jacoba was a noblewoman of Rome. Although her husband died when she was still very young, she chose to raise her children alone without the need for a second marriage. She had decided to dedicate her life to God by following in the penitential footsteps of St. Francis and became a member of the Brothers and Sisters of Penance, known as the Third Order. She spent her life devoted to prayer and good works among the poor. St. Francis had a special fondness for Lady Jacoba, even referring to her as "Brother Jacoba," meaning that she had the privilege of entering the friars' cloister to nurse Francis in his final hours. Jacoba is buried in the Tomb Chapel of St. Francis in Assisi.

Blessed Louise Albertoni (d. 1533)

Also a noblewoman of Rome, Louise, like Jacoba, married well but lived a life of austerity and charity. When her husband died, she entered the Third Order (now known as the Secular Franciscan Order) and spent her time practicing the most severe penances. She contemplated the sufferings of the Lord to such an extent that she could not keep herself from shedding constant tears. In order not to offend the dignity of the poor, Louise hid coins in the bread she baked for the needy.

St. Hyacinth Mariscotti (d. 1640)

Hyacinth, too, was born into a wealthy and noble family of Rome. Instead of marrying she sought to enter a convent in Viterbo as a secular tertiary. Hyacinth lived a luxurious life in the community; her furnishings, dress, and special foods were grave obstacles toward a true conversion of heart. When she was struck with a terrible illness, her confessor rebuked her obstinate attitudes. Upon regaining her health, she chose to lead a very penitential life, performing the lowliest tasks. She also fostered a devotion to the sufferings of Christ and had visions of the Virgin Mary as the Mother of Mercy who comforted her in her resolve.

St. Charles of Sezze (d. 1670)

Born of poor heritage, Charles made himself rich in his love for God and contemplative prayer. He was not clever enough to study for the priesthood, so his parents sent him into the fields. At seventeen, however, his love for the Virgin Mary led him to make a promise of chastity. After recovering from a terrible illness, he made another vow to try his vocation among the friars. He soon edified his confreres with his sincerity and simplicity of heart. However, another illness caused him to be sent to Rome to recuperate. While there he received the gift of enlightenment concerning the things of God and began writing many volumes on mystical theology. Theologians and cardinals consulted him for advice. Before he died, his left side was pierced with a ray of light like an arrow that emanated from the Sacred Host.

FRANCISCAN READINGS

THOMAS OF CELANO, FIRST LIFE 76

Francis' charity and compassion for the poor

> *The father of the poor,*
> the poor Francis,
> conforming himself to the poor in all things,
> was distressed to see anyone poorer than himself,
> not out of any desire *for empty glory,*
> but from a feeling of simple compassion.
> Though he was content with a ragged and rough tunic,
> he often wished to divide it with some poor person.

This richest poor man, moved by a great feeling of pity, in order to help the poor in some way, used to approach the rich people of this world during the coldest times of the year, asking them to loan him their cloaks or furs. As they responded even more gladly than the blessed father asked, he used to say to them, "I shall accept this from you only on the condition that you never expect to have it returned." The first poor man who happened to meet him, he would then clothe with whatever he had received, exulting and rejoicing.

He was deeply troubled whenever he saw one of the poor insulted or heard *a curse* hurled at any creature. It happened that a certain brother insulted a poor man begging alms, saying: "Are you sure that you are not really rich and just pretending to be poor?" When Saint Francis, *the father of the poor,* heard this, he was deeply hurt and he severely rebuked the brother who had said these things. Then he ordered the brother to strip naked in front of the poor man and to kiss his feet, to beg his forgiveness. He used to say: "Anyone who curses the poor insults Christ whose noble banner the poor carry, since Christ *made himself poor for us in this world.*" That is also why, when he met poor people burdened with wood or other heavy loads, he would offer his own weak shoulders to help them.

THOMAS OF CELANO, SECOND LIFE 85

Correcting a brother who judges the poor

Another day, when he was preaching, a sick poor man came to the place. Taking pity on the man's double misfortune—that is, his need and his illness—he began to speak about poverty with his companion. And since suffering with the suffering, he had moved beyond *to the depths of his heart,* when the saint's companion said to him: "My brother, it is true that he is poor, but it could be that in the whole province there is no one who desires riches more!" At once the saint rebuked him, and as the companion acknowledged his fault, said to him: *"Quickly now, strip off* your tunic; throw yourself down at the poor man's feet and confess your fault! And, don't just ask his pardon, but also beg for his prayers!" The brother obeyed, made his amends and returned. The saint said to him: "Brother, whenever you see a poor person, a mirror of the Lord and his poor Mother is placed before you. Likewise in the sick, look closely for the *infirmities* which He accepted *for our sake."*

THOMAS OF CELANO, FIRST LIFE 17

Francis' service of lepers and the poor

Then the holy lover of profound humility moved to the lepers and stayed with them. For God's sake he served all of them with great love. He washed all the filth from them, and even cleaned out the pus of their sores, just as he said in his *Testament:* "When I was in sin, it seemed too bitter for me to see lepers, and the Lord led me among them and I showed mercy to them." For he used to say that the sight of lepers was so bitter to him that in the days of his vanity when he saw their houses even two miles away, he would cover his nose with his hands.

When he started thinking of holy and useful matters with the grace and *strength of the Most High,* while still in the clothes of the world, he met a leper one day. Made stronger than himself, he came up *and kissed him.* He then began to consider himself less and less, until by the mercy of the Redeemer, he came to complete victory over himself.

While staying in the world and following its ways, he was also a helper of the poor. He extended a hand of mercy to those who had nothing and he poured out compassion for the afflicted. One day, contrary to his custom (since he was very polite), he rebuked a poor person seeking alms from him, and he was immediately *led to penance.* He began to say *to himself* that to refuse what was asked by someone begging in the name of such a great King would be both a shame and a disgrace. And so he fixed this *in his heart:* to the best of his ability, never to deny anything to anyone begging from him for God's sake. This he did and with such care that he offered himself completely, in every way, first practicing before teaching the gospel counsel: *"Give to the one who begs from you, and do not turn away from the one who wants to borrow from you."*

ST. BONAVENTURE, MAJOR LEGEND VII:1

Francis' love of poverty

Among the gifts of charisms
which Francis obtained from the generous Giver,
he merited,
as a special privilege,
to grow in the riches of simplicity
through his love of the highest poverty.
The holy man,
realizing that she was a close friend of the Son of God,
yet was nowadays an outcast throughout almost the whole world,
was eager to espouse her *in an everlasting love.* ...
No one coveted gold as he coveted poverty;
no one was as careful of guarding a treasure
as he was of this pearl of the Gospel.
In this especially would his sight be offended:
if he saw in the brothers
anything which did not accord completely with poverty.
Truly, from the beginning of his religious life until his death,

his wealth was
a tunic, a cord, and underwear,
with these he was content.

EUCHARIST

READING: 2 CORINTHIANS 4:5–7

A reading from the second letter of Paul to the Corinthians

For what we preach is not ourselves, but Jesus Christ as Lord, with ourselves as your servants for Jesus' sake. For it is the God who said, "Let light shine out of darkness," who has shone in our hearts to give the light of the knowledge of the glory of God in the face of Christ. But we have this treasure in earthen vessels, to show that the transcendent power belongs to God and not to us. **The word of the Lord.**

RESPONSE: The Lord hears the cry of the poor.

PSALM 34

I will bless the Lord at all times;
his praise shall continually be in my mouth.
My soul makes its boast in the Lord;
let the humble hear and be glad. **R.**

O magnify the Lord with me,
and let us exalt his name together.
I sought the Lord, and he answered me,
and delivered me from all my fears. **R.**

Look to him, and be radiant;
so your faces shall never be ashamed.
This poor soul cried, and was heard by the Lord,
and was saved from every trouble.

The angel of the LORD encamps around those who fear him, and delivers them. **R.**

ALLELUIA: Blessed are you who are poor, for the kingdom of God is yours.

GOSPEL: MATTHEW 6:19–23

A reading from the holy Gospel according to Matthew

"Do not store up for yourselves treasures on earth, where moth and rust consume and where thieves break in and steal; but store up for yourselves treasures in heaven, where neither moth nor rust consumes and where thieves do not break in and steal. For where your treasure is, there your heart will be also. The eye is the lamp of the body. So, if your eye is healthy, your whole body will be full of light; but if your eye is unhealthy, your whole body will be full of darkness. If then the light in you is darkness, how great is the darkness!" **The Gospel of the Lord.**

PRAYER SERVICE

FRANCIS AND THE BEGGARS

REFRAIN: G 35 "The Cry of the Poor," verse 1

READING I: THE LEGEND OF THREE COMPANIONS 3

One day when he was in the shop where he was selling cloth, totally absorbed in business of this sort, a poor man came in, begging alms for the love of God. Preoccupied with thoughts of wealth and the care of business, he did not give him alms. Touched by divine grace, he accused himself of great rudeness, saying: "If that poor man had asked something from you for a great count or baron, you would certainly have granted him his request. How much more should you have done this for the King of kings and the Lord of all!"

Because of this incident, he resolved in his heart, from then on, not to deny a request to anyone asking in the name of so great a Lord.

REFRAIN: G 35, verse 2

READING II: THOMAS OF CELANO, SECOND LIFE 8

Once on pilgrimage to Rome, out of love for poverty he took off his fine clothing and dressed himself in a poor man's clothes. He happily settled among the poor in the square in front of the church of Saint Peter, a place where the poor are abundant. Considering himself one of them, he eagerly ate with them. If his embarrassed friends had not restrained him, he would have done this many times.

REFRAIN: G 35, verse 3

READING III: THOMAS OF CELANO, SECOND LIFE 91

The mother of two of the brothers once came to the saint, confidently *asking for alms*. Sharing her pain the holy father said to Brother Peter of Catanio: "Can we give some alms to our mother?" He used to call the mother of any brother his mother and the mother of all the brothers. Brother Peter replied: "There is *nothing left* in the house which we could *give* her." Then he added: "We do have one New Testament, for reading the lessons at matins, since we don't have a breviary." Blessed Francis said to him: "Give our mother the New Testament so she can sell it to care for her needs, for through it we are reminded to help the poor. I believe that God will be pleased more by the giving than by the reading."

REFRAIN: G 35, verse 4

READING IV: ISAIAH 58:6–8

A reading from the book of the prophet Isaiah

Is not this the fast that I choose: to loose the bonds of injustice, to undo the thongs of the yoke, to let the oppressed go free, and to break every yoke? Is it not to share your bread with the hungry, and bring the homeless poor into your house; when you see the naked, to cover them, and not to hide yourself from your own kin? Then your light shall break forth like the dawn, and your healing shall spring up quickly; your vindicator shall go before you, the glory of the LORD shall be your rear guard. **The word of the Lord.**

QUIET REFLECTION

INTERCESSIONS

OUR FATHER / PRAYER

SONG

ROME: TAGLIACOZZO

FRANCISCAN PILGRIMAGE PROGRAMS

ROME: TAGLIACOZZO

EVENTS

Thomas of Celano documented that Francis came to the Marsica area in the Abruzzi region but there is no documentation that he visited Tagliacozzo.

It is clear that the brothers were present in this region, attracting the young Thomas from the small town of Celano to join the Order in 1216.

Ancient tradition holds that Thomas himself founded and dwelt in a hermitage near the town of Tagliacozzo. But his stay was short lived due to the summons by Pope Gregory IX to write the official biography of St. Francis in preparation for his canonization in 1228.

Thomas returned in his later years to serve as spiritual director for the Poor Clare Sisters of San Giovanni di Val dei Varri, located near Tagliacozzo. During this time he may have been working on his second biography of Francis entitled *The Remembrance of the Desire of the Soul*. He likely traveled between Assisi and the Monastery of San Giovanni while writing both *The Desire* and *The Treatise on the Miracles*.

Thomas is also considered by many to be the author of the *Legend of Saint Clare*. His experience among the Poor Clare Sisters would certainly qualify him to write this legend.

According to tradition Thomas died on October 4, 1260, and was buried in the chapel at the Poor Clare Monastery. When the monastery was closed in 1476, Thomas' remains were moved to the Church of St. Francis in Tagliacozzo. This church remains under the care of the Conventual friars.

SPIRITUALITY

Francis, Clare, and Thomas, along with many other Franciscan men and women, have shared their spiritual thoughts and experiences through the gift of writing.

Reading spiritual works of Franciscan authors, past and present, is a source of inspiration for those who ponder the meaning of their words.

Writing can be a window to the soul, allowing one to share in God's activities within.

When one journals, writes a letter, or jots down memories in a diary, the Spirit often guides this writing, making one aware of the deeper mysteries waiting to be told through the act of writing.

REFLECTION

What role does writing or keeping a journal play in your prayer?

As you read the written works of Franciscan brothers and sisters, in what ways do they invite you into a deeper understanding of God?

What do these authors reveal about themselves to you in their writings?

HISTORICAL NOTES

TAGLIACOZZO

A drive of about an hour and a half, east and a little north of
Rome, brings us to Tagliacozzo, the resting place of Francis'
first biographer, Thomas of Celano. The town lies in a
picturesque valley surrounded by the mountains of the Abruzzi
region. The visit here provides the setting for our initial
exploration into the sources of St. Francis, for Thomas of

Celano laid the foundation for so many others who would give us information, either vital or controversial, on the life of the saint. According to ancient tradition it was Thomas of Celano himself who founded this church and hermitage/friary. It is documented in the town archives that an altar was consecrated on this spot on November 20, 1233. The earliest chapel was called St. Mary's Outside the Walls (outside the walls of the castle). This original chapel was now where the uppermost part of the choir is located. Because the hermitage chapel was on a hill and in order to enlarge it, the friars had to level the hill to build the gothic church that we see today. However, they left the choir elevated so that the actual space where the first friars built their chapel could still be venerated.

The dwelling of the friars was a short distance from the hermitage chapel. That space is located where daily Mass is now celebrated. This chapel can be reached from the courtyard. You will notice that part of the mountain that formed the first cavelike shelter for the early friars is still part of the back wall of the chapel.

Celano was probably here for only a short time because his duties called him to be in Assisi writing the biography. He was requested to become spiritual director of the Clares of San Giovanni in Val dei Varri. It was with the Clares, according to tradition, that he died on October 4, 1260. He was buried in their monastery chapel.

Around 1476 the Clares who lived in the monastery of Val dei Varri (not far from Tagliacozzo) decided to leave their home because of constant danger from brigands in the area.

In 1506 the Franciscan pope, Julius II, placed the monastery and property of the Clares at the disposition of the Franciscans of Tagliacozzo, and thus, even if the nuns were no longer present, the friars (de familia of Tagliacozzo) would remain custodians of the remains of their confrere, Thomas.

In 1516 a new provincial, Friar Agapito, secretly transferred Thomas's body from San Giovanni in Val dei Varri to Tagliacozzo. The bishop asked for a papal inquiry into why the friars had taken Blessed Thomas out of his diocese. All was finally settled when the friars explained that they had the right because he was legally in their custody and because that area had been overrun with bandits for so long that Thomas' body would be safer elsewhere.

At first Thomas' body was placed beside the high altar, in an area to the right of a low arch. In 1960 his body was reexamined and placed in a glass urn. In 1983 it was placed within the wall in the nave, as we see today.

In 1809 the anticlerical laws of the French occupancy caused the friary to be suppressed. The townspeople petitioned the imperial courts against such an action stating that the friars of Tagliacozzo faithfully served the needs of all people. They not only established a school for children of both sexes, they also generously offered the food in their garden to the poor. Napoleon refused the petition, and the friary remained either abandoned or under diocesan control for many years. Finally in 1960, the 700th anniversary of the death of Thomas of Celano, Pope John XXIII restored the church, the friary and Thomas' tomb to the custody of his confreres.

From "Chiesa e Convento di S. Francesco dei Frati Minori Conventuali in Tagliacozzo," Nicola Petrone, O.F.M. Conv., in 1984.

THOMAS OF CELANO

Thomas of Celano came from the Abruzzi mountains and grew up in a town by the name of Celano. Most probably he was of noble birth and had already received a classical education before he entered the Order of Friars Minor. His first experience of the order was his reception into it by Francis himself at the Porziuncola sometime between 1213 and 1215.

In the Chapter of 1221, Thomas offered to be among the twenty-four friars sent to Germany under the leadership of Caesar of Speyer. When Caesar returned to Italy in 1223, he named Thomas as his vicar of the friars in Germany. Thomas had already served as custos of the friars in Mainz, Worms, and Cologne. The new minister of Germany, Albert of Pisa, reconfirmed Thomas as vicar.

We are not certain exactly when Thomas returned to Italy, but he was already in Assisi before Francis' canonization on July 16, 1228. (He may have returned by the time of Francis' death.) But it was at this time that his main contribution to the brotherhood was about to begin. He was commissioned by Gregory IX to write a life of Francis at the time of the canonization, or maybe even as much as a year earlier. The choice of Thomas could have been suggested by Elias, as Elias certainly would have known this man of learning. Thomas fulfilled his commission, and he was able to present Gregory IX his completed work on February 25, 1229.

During the next fifteen years drastic changes were taking place in the order. There was a rapid succession of ministers general. At the Chapter of Genoa in 1244, Crescentius of Jesi was elected minister general and ordered the Chapter to solicit from all the brothers of the order everything they knew or remembered about Francis. The material was to be sent to the minister general, who in turn handed it over to Thomas. Thus Thomas began his second work on Francis of Assisi. By 1247 he had completed his Second Life.

This was not sufficient in the minds of some of the friars. Because mention of many miracles they remembered was lacking, John of Parma, successor to Crescentius, requested that Thomas gather material that recorded the miracles attributed to Francis. Thomas did this sometime after 1250, and his third work was then confirmed by the General Chapter of 1254.

By this time Thomas sought a quieter life as chaplain to the Poor Ladies in the monastery of Tagliacozzo, located about sixteen miles from his native Celano. However, his work was not finished. After the death of Clare in 1253, Alexander IV requested a biography of St. Clare. Thomas is believed to be the author of *The Legend of Saint Clare*, which he completed in 1256. However, authorship of this work is still debated. This was his last major literary work. He died in 1260, or shortly thereafter, and was then buried in the monastery of the Clares in Tagliacozzo.

After the Poor Clare monastery was abandoned in 1476, it became annexed to the Friary of the Conventual Friars. In the church of that friary, named St. Francis, St. Thomas's body rests today. In 1327 his remains were placed in an urn with the following inscription: *Beatus Thomas de Celano, S(ancti) F(rancisci) D(Disciplus), scriptorcronicarum, et sequentia Mortuorum.*

The life of Thomas of Celano in the order spanned the developing and turbulent years of 1215–1260. He lived through the terms of all of the early ministers general up to and including St. Bonaventure. While leaders rose and fell, Thomas' presence was constant as he offered his literary gifts to help the friars in their remembrance of Francis. Thomas gives the order the beginnings of a literary tradition that is stamped with the presence of Francis. Thomas was repeatedly asked to write, and this must mean his words were accepted by the friars. His works are for us an indication of the thinking and memory of the friars.

THE WRITINGS OF THOMAS OF CELANO

The Life of Saint Francis was written by order of Pope Gregory IX and approved by him in Perugia on February 25, 1229.

The Remembrance of the Desire of a Soul was written as a result of the General Chapter of 1244 when Crescentius of Jesi, minister general, ordered all the friars to send him in writing "deeds and writings" of St. Francis. Many friars, including Leo, Rufino, and Angelo, responded. When the material had been collected, Thomas was commissioned to write the *Second Life*. He completed the task by July of 1247, the date of the opening of the General Chapter at Lyons. It was approved either by the General Chapter or shortly afterward by the new minister general, John of Parma.

The Treatise on the Miracles was written between 1250 and 1253. John of Parma, at the urging of the friars to record other reported miracles, asked Thomas to complete this project and thus include other incidents not recorded in the previous two lives.

That Alexander IV commissioned *The Legend of St. Clare* at the time of the canonization of St. Clare in 1255 is hardly doubted, but the authorship has not always been clear. Internal evidence could help substantiate the claim of Thomas as author. Although there are many of these indications, some uncertainty remains.

The Legend for Use in the Choir was written around 1230, a year or so after the approval of the *First Life*. This work is divided into nine lessons, and it was used by the friars in their Office of Readings.

Dies Irae, Dies Illa was one of the most famous Latin hymns of the Middle Ages. Recent scholarship indicates there is no reason now to doubt Thomas' authorship of this hymn, which could be one of the reasons Thomas was asked to do other writings. In this case the hymn would be dated prior to 1228. Thomas already must have had a literary reputation prior to 1228, and so there are undoubtedly other literary works flowing from his pen other than those related to Francis or Clare.

FRANCISCAN READINGS

THOMAS OF CELANO, FIRST LIFE 56–57

How Thomas of Celano joins the friars

Not *too long after* this, [Francis] began to travel towards Morocco to preach the gospel of Christ to the Miramamolin and his retinue. He was so carried away with desire that he would sometimes leave behind *his companion on the journey* and hurry ahead, intoxicated in spirit, in order to carry out his purpose. But the good God, out of pure kindness, was pleased to be mindful of me and many others. After he reached Spain God *withstood him to his face*, striking him with illness, and called him back from the journey he had begun.

Shortly afterwards when Francis returned to the Church of Saint Mary of the Portiuncula, some literate men and nobles gladly joined him. He received such men with honor and dignity, since he himself was very noble and distinguished in spirit, and respectfully gave to each his due. In fact, since he was endowed with outstanding discernment, he wisely considered in all matters the dignity of rank of each one.

THOMAS OF CELANO, FIRST LIFE 151

Thomas' request to be remembered in prayer by all who read his words

We have said a little about the miracles of our blessed father Francis, and have left out much, to inspire in those who wish *to follow his footsteps* an eagerness to seek the grace of new blessings. Thus he, who so magnificently renewed the whole world by word and example, life and teaching, might always graciously water the souls of those *who love the name of the Lord* with new showers of heavenly gifts.

For the love of the Poor Crucified, and by His sacred *stigmata* which the blessed Father Francis *bore in* his *body*, I ask all those who read, see or hear these words, to remember *me, a sinner, before God*. Amen.

THOMAS OF CELANO, SECOND LIFE 1–2

Thomas of Celano's reasons for this writing

The holy gathering of the last general chapter and you, most reverend father, chose to charge us, insignificant as we are, to write down the deeds as well as the words of our glorious father Francis, for the consolation of our contemporaries and the remembrance of future generations.

We, more than others, learned these things through constant living together and mutual intimacy with him over a long time. ... We simply want to benefit each and everyone. So we beg those who read this to interpret it kindly and to bear with or correct the simplicity of the narrator so that reverence for the person who is our subject may remain intact. ...

In the first place, this work contains some marvelous details about the conversion of Saint Francis not included in earlier legends written about him because they were never brought to the author's attention. Then we will attempt to express and carefully state the *good, pleasing and perfect will* of our most holy father. This concerns both himself and his followers, the exercise of heavenly discipline, and that striving for highest perfection which he always expressed in love for God and in living example for others. Here and there, according to the opportunity, we have included a number of his miracles. We describe in a plain and simple way things that occur to us, wishing to accommodate those who are slower and, if possible, also to please the learned.

THOMAS OF CELANO, SECOND LIFE 221, 223

Prayer of Francis' companions to him

Behold, our blessed father, the efforts of our simple capacities have attempted to praise your wondrous deeds to the best of our ability, and to tell at least a few of the countless virtues of your holiness for your glory. We know that our words have much diminished the splendor of your outstanding deeds, since they have been found unequal to expressing the great deeds of such perfection.

We ask you, and also those who read this, to keep in mind our affection and our effort, and to rejoice that the heights of your life are beyond the best efforts of human pens. For who, oh outstanding saint, could be able to bring into himself the burning *ardor of your spirit* or to impress it on others? Who would be able to conceive those inexpressible feelings which flowed uninterruptedly between you and God? But we wrote these things delighting in your sweet memory which, while we still live, we try to express to others even if it is by stammering. ...

Draw us, then, to *yourself,*
that we may run after the fragrance of your perfumes. ...
This *little flock* is stumbling
along in your footsteps;

the weakness of our eyes cannot bear
the shining rays of your perfection.
Give us such days as we had of old,
oh mirror and exemplar of the perfect! …

We also pray with all our heart's affection, oh kind father, for
that son of yours who now and earlier has devoutly written
your praises. He, together with us, offers and dedicates to you
this little work which he put together, not in a manner worthy
of your merit but at least devoutly, and as best he could.

From every *evil*
mercifully preserve
and *deliver* him.
Increase holy merit in him,
and, by your prayers,
join him forever to the company of the saints.

EUCHARIST
READING: 1 CORINTHIANS 1:18–25

A reading from the first letter of Paul to the Corinthians

For the message about the cross is foolishness to those who are perishing, but to us who are being saved it is the power of God. For it is written, "I will destroy the wisdom of the wise, and the discernment of the discerning I will thwart." Where is the one who is wise? Where is the scribe? Where is the debater of this age? Has not God made foolish the wisdom of the world? For since, in the wisdom of God, the world did not know God through wisdom, God decided, through the foolishness of our proclamation, to save those who believe. For Jews demand signs and Greeks desire wisdom, but we proclaim Christ crucified, a stumbling block to Jews and foolishness to Gentiles, but to those who are the called, both Jews and Greeks, Christ the power of God and the wisdom of God. For God's foolishness is wiser than human wisdom, and God's weakness is stronger than human strength. **The word of the Lord.**

RESPONSE: The judgments of God are true, and all of them are just.

PSALM 19

The law of the LORD is perfect,
reviving the soul;
the decrees of the LORD are sure,
making wise the simple; **R.**

The precepts of the LORD are right,
rejoicing the heart;
The commandment of the LORD is clear,
enlightening the eyes; **R.**

The fear of the LORD is pure,
enduring forever;
the ordinances of the LORD are true
and righteous altogether. **R.**

More to be desired are they than gold,
even much fine gold;
sweeter also than honey,
and drippings of the honeycomb. **R.**

ALLELUIA: We teach a secret and hidden wisdom of God, which God decreed for our glory before time began.

GOSPEL: MATTHEW 5:13–16

A reading from the holy Gospel according to Matthew

"You are the salt of the earth; but if salt has lost its taste, how can its saltiness be restored? It is no longer good for anything, but is thrown out and trampled under foot. You are the light of the world. A city built on a hill cannot be hid. No one after lighting a lamp puts it under the bushel basket, but on the lampstand, and it gives light to all in the house. In the same way, let your light shine before others, so that they may see your good works and give glory to your Father in heaven." **The Gospel of the Lord.**

RIETI VALLEY

RIETI VALLEY

EVENTS

This is a valley of healing ministry. Here Francis sought a cure for his eye disease. Francis loved mountains, where he could feel and sense his spirit stretching for God Most High. God comforts Francis with heavenly music and his love for music, is enriched here in this valley.

The Rieti Valley is outlined in the form of a cross by four Franciscan sanctuaries: Poggio Bustone, where Francis knew the experience of redemption (cf. 1C, 26); Greccio, where he reenacted Bethlehem and forever changed the way the world celebrates Christmas; Fonte Colombo, where Francis wrote the Franciscan Rule of Life; and La Foresta, where the friars in this region would like to claim that he composed *The Canticle of the Creatures*. With the exception of Assisi and La Verna, no other places in Italy are so full of memories of St. Francis.

SPIRITUALITY

The two valleys that Francis especially loved were the Valley of Spoleto and the Valley of Rieti. He was born and died in the Valley of Spoleto, and he made his first pilgrimage to the Valley of Rieti (his second homeland). There he spent the last troubled years of his life. The Valley of Rieti, perhaps more than any other place in Franciscan Italy, preserves the pristine spirit of Francis. One sees it in each convento and mountain setting, where a sense of simplicity, poverty, peace, and love for nature is evident.

The charm of these places is derived from the beauty of nature and the enviable richness of Lady Poverty. The riches of art and architecture are not to be found. Removed from the extensive wear and tear of tourism, these locales breathe a spirit of humility and silence. They are simple, poor, and lowly, as Francis wanted, and thus speak their Franciscan humility to pilgrims and tourists who climb up to experience them. In these regions the larger and more interesting part of Francis' life, and early Franciscan history, unfold.

REFLECTION

Allow yourself to have a spiritual experience of a mountain.
What connection is there between simplicity and peace of heart?

This valley witnessed some of Francis' first preaching efforts. We, too, are commissioned to proclaim the gospel's call to conversion, to repentance, to peace. Explore the power of witness as a means of evangelization.

Take notice of elements that speak of the Italian soul: wheat fields (bread), olive trees (oil), vineyards (wine), flowers (love for living things), the people.

RIETI VALLEY

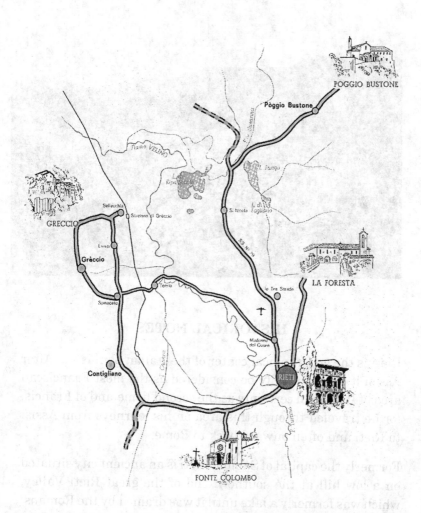

RIETI VALLEY

HISTORICAL NOTES

Rieti is the geographical center of the Italian peninsula. After
Assisi it can truthfully be considered as the most Franciscan
area of Italy, and certainly as the second homeland of Francis,
for he traveled through this area on his journeys from Assisi
to Rieti and often onward back to Rome.

Formerly the capital of Sabina, Rieti is an ancient city situated
on a low hill at the southern end of the great Rieti Valley,
which was formerly a lake until it was drained by the Romans.
The city now rises where three rivers, the Salto, the Velino,
and the Turano, intersect. The region came under the
domination of Rome in 290 B.C. With the fall of the empire
came many problems, and during the Middle Ages the valley
experienced discord and war. The town is still surrounded by

its old fortifications. As a Guelph city in support of the pope, Rieti offered shelter to six pontiffs for various lengths of stay.

Today the cathedral and the bishop's residence beside it are the most important monuments of the city. In 1927 a small statue of St. Francis, the town's most celebrated guest, was placed in the cathedral square.

This valley was the scene of some of Francis' first preaching efforts. It was probably from this valley that Francis sent out the brothers to preach for a first time—after returning from Rome with Innocent III's approval of their way of life.

FRANCISCAN READINGS

THOMAS OF CELANO, FIRST LIFE 99

Sojourn at Rieti

Many came with their medicines to help him but no remedy could be found. So he went to the city of Rieti where a man was staying who was said to be the greatest expert in curing that disease. When he arrived there he was received kindly and respectfully by the whole Roman Curia, which was then staying in that city. He was especially well received by Lord Hugolino, the bishop of Ostia, who was renowned for his upright conduct and holy life.

THOMAS OF CELANO, SECOND LIFE 126

Francis refreshed by heavenly music

In the days when he was staying at Rieti for the treatment of his eyes, he called one of the companions, who in the world had been a lute player, and said to him: "Brother, *the children of this world* do not understand *the divine* sacraments. Human lust has turned musical instruments, once assigned to the divine praises, into enjoyment for their ears. But I would like you, brother, to borrow a lute secretly and bring it here and to play some decent song to give some consolation to Brother Body, which is filled with pain." But the brother answered: "I would be quite embarrassed to do this, father, for I fear people will suspect me of being tempted to my old levity." And the saint said to him: "Then, brother, let's let it go! It is good to let go of many things to avoid offending people's opinion."

The following night, as the holy man was keeping vigil and meditating on God, suddenly a lute was playing with wonderful harmony an extraordinarily *sweet melody*. He could see no one, but the *changes in his hearing* suggested that the lute player was moving back and forth from one place to another. At last, with his *spirit turned to God*, he enjoyed such delight in that sweet-sounding song that he thought he had exchanged this world for the other.

When he *arose in the morning*, the saint called the brother in question and told him *everything from beginning to end*, adding: "The Lord, who *consoles* the afflicted, has never left me without *consolation*. See, since I could not hear the lutes of humans, I have heard a more delightful lute."

ASSISI COMPILATION 111

How Francis teaches by example

At one time blessed Francis was staying at the hermitage of Sant' Eleuterio, near the town of Condigliano in the district of Rieti. Since he was wearing only one tunic, one day because of the extreme cold, and out of great necessity, he patched his tunic and that of his companion with scraps of cloth on the inside, so that his body began to be comforted a little. A short while afterwards, when he was returning from prayer one day, he said with great joy to his companion: "I must be the form and example of all the brothers; so, although it is necessary for my body to have a tunic with patches, nevertheless I must take into consideration my brothers who have the same need, but perhaps do not and cannot have this. Therefore, I must stay down with them, and I must suffer those same necessities they suffer so that in seeing this, they may be able to bear them more patiently."

We who were with him could not say how many and how great were the necessities that he denied his body in food and clothing, to give good example to the brothers and so that they would endure their necessities in greater patience. At all times, especially after the brothers began to multiply and he resigned the office of prelate, blessed Francis had as his highest and principal goal to teach the brothers more by actions than by words what they ought to do and what they ought to avoid.

OTHER READINGS
AC 66—Refreshed by heavenly music
2C 41; LMj XI:5; AC 95—Francis' healing of Canon Gedeone
AC 89—Francis' gift of a mantle to a poor woman
1C 61—Story of the fish at the Lake of Rieti (Piediluco).

RIETI VALLEY: POGGIO BUSTONE

FRANCISCAN PILGRIMAGE PROGRAMS

RIETI VALLEY: POGGIO BUSTONE

EVENTS

Francis greeted the people: *"Buon giorno, buona gente."*

Francis had an experience of God on this mountain (cf. 1C 26).

Francis found restful solitude on the mountain.

Francis sent out the brothers, two by two, to preach.

Francis was assured of peace and forgiveness for all his sins.

God revealed the future of the Order to Francis.

Francis confessed human frailty in public (cf. 2C 131).

SPIRITUALITY

We can sum up Francis' experience at Poggio Bustone in four words: solitude, forgiveness, peace, preaching.

On this mountain Francis experienced the revelation of God. Climb the mountain and allow yourself to sense God's presence and healing spirit.

Francis recognized the good in others through his greeting: "Buon giorno, buona gente" (Good morning, good people). He praises the goodness of God in the goodness of the people.

REFLECTION

It is fair to say of Francis that there were two things in the world he loved more than anything else: mountains and music. What does this say about him and his spirituality?

Try to understand Francis' oft-repeated prayer: "O God, be merciful to me, a sinner." Why should he, or you or I, feel and pray this way?

Consider the meaning of Francis' confession in public in 2MP 62. What does it mean to confess to one another? Does it make sense to you? Why?

POGGIO BUSTONE

HISTORICAL NOTES

Poggio Bustone is the most northern of the four Franciscan sanctuaries in the Rieti Valley, some sixteen kilometers from Rieti itself. It is also perhaps the most impressive of the Franciscan places in this valley, set as it is in a high, rugged, and remote area. Francis came here in 1209. As he passed through the walls into the village, the people were curious to see who this was. And with a smile he gave them the greeting: "Good morning, good people," ("*Buon giorno, buona gente*").

It is said that Francis found a small deserted hermitage in existence on his first visit to Poggio Bustone and, delighted by the loneliness of the spot, took possession of it for himself and his brothers.

Because the first time Francis visited Poggio Bustone he met some inhabitants and greeted them with *"Buon Giorno, buona gente,"* every year on the morning of October 4, a man with a tambourine goes around the village, knocks at every door, and calls out the same greeting. At one time, in memory of Francis, near the center of this town you were able to see a white stone in a wall that said:

BUON GIORNO, BUONA GENTE
Saluto rivolto da S Francesco
entrando a Poggio Bustone nel 1209

The Convento di San Giacomo is currently occupied by a small number of friars and is available for individuals and groups to use for reflection and spiritual exercises. It is said to have been founded by Francis in 1217. Below the *convento*, down a flight of stairs, is a hermitage-like sanctuary where Francis planted a cross to remind him of the redemption. From San Giacomo a steep path leads up to the *santuario* of 1209, about a half hour walk. One passes six little chapels, each with a memory of the saint.

This little hermitage consists of a small chapel hewn out of the rock. An inscription reads: *"In questo sacro speco per molti anni abito il Padre San Francesco col Beato Egidio ed altri suoi compagni"* ("Our holy father Francis lived in this sacred place for many years with Blessed Giles and his other companions"). There is also a representation of Francis sleeping, supporting Giles asleep on his shoulder.

Here Francis experienced the spectacular greatness of God, begged mercy for his sins, and knew God's revelation of forgiveness and the future of the Order.

Another cave, even smaller than the former, contains a picture showing Francis receiving a book from an angel with the words:

"Francisce, hic remissa sunt peccata tua, sicut postulasti" ("Francis, here your sins are forgiven as you have asked").

The incident referred to in 1C 26–27 is to have taken place here. Thus we call this place a "Sanctuary of Light (enlightenment) and Peace (from forgiveness of sin)."

FRANCISCAN READINGS

ST. BONAVENTURE, MAJOR LEGEND I:5

Francis' search for solitary places fit for recollection, such as Poggio Bustone

He then began to seek out solitary places, favorable to grieving, where, with *unutterable groans*, he concentrated incessantly on meriting to be heard by the Lord after the long perseverance of his prayers.

One of those days, withdrawn in this way, while he was praying and all of his fervor was totally absorbed in God, Christ Jesus appeared to him as fastened to a cross. His *soul melted* at the sight, and the memory of Christ's passion was so impressed on the innermost recesses of his heart.

THOMAS OF CELANO, SECOND LIFE 131

Public confession of eating lard during a fast

Once at the hermitage of Poggio about the time of the Lord's nativity a large crowd assembled for the sermon, which he began with this opening: "You all believe me to be a holy man, and that is why you came to me with great devotion. But I declare to you that this whole Lent I have eaten food flavored with lard." In this way he often blamed pleasure for what was, in fact, a concession to illness.

SECOND MIRROR OF PERFECTION 62

Francis' public confession

Likewise, at another time, when he was staying in a certain hermitage for the Lent of Saint Martin, he ate some food cooked with lard, because oil did not agree with him during his illnesses. When the forty days had ended and he was preaching to a large crowd of people, in the opening words of his sermon he told them: "You came to me with great devotion, believing me to be a holy man. But I confess to God and to you that during this Lent, I have eaten food flavored with lard."

Indeed, it happened almost always that when he ate with seculars, or when the brothers prepared a special dish for him because of his illnesses, he immediately told this to the brothers or lay people who did not know about it, whether inside the house or outside. He would publicly say: "I ate such and such foods." He did not wish to conceal from people what was known to God.

In the same way, if his soul were tempted to vainglory, pride, or any vice, no matter where he was, or in whose presence, whether they be religious or lay, he would at once confess it to them openly, without concealing anything. That is why he told his companions one day: "I want to live in hermitages and other places where I stay, as if all the people see me. If they think I am a holy man and I were not to lead a life becoming a holy man, I would be a hypocrite."

When it was bitterly cold, one of the companions, who was his guardian, wanted to sew a small piece of fox fur underneath his tunic because of the illness of his spleen and stomach. Blessed Francis answered him: "If you want me to wear fur under the tunic, allow me to sew a piece of the fur on the outside of it that everyone may know that I have a piece of fox fur underneath." And this is what he had done; and, although it was very necessary, he wore it for only a short time.

THOMAS OF CELANO, FIRST LIFE 29

Missioning of the brothers

At that same time, another good man entered their religion, and they increased their number to eight. Then the blessed Francis called them all to himself and told them many things about *the kingdom of God*, contempt of the world, denial of their own will, and subjection of the body. He separated them into four groups of two each.

"Go, my dear brothers," he said to them, "*two by two* through different parts of the world, *announcing peace* to the people and *penance for the remission of sins*. Be *patient in trials*, confident that the Lord will fulfill His plan and promise. Respond humbly to those who question you. *Bless those who persecute you*. Give thanks to those who harm you and bring false charges against you, for because of these things an *eternal kingdom is prepared* for us."

Accepting the command of holy obedience *with* much *joy and gladness*, they humbly prostrated themselves on the ground before Saint Francis. Embracing them, he spoke sweetly and devotedly to each one: *"Cast your care upon the Lord, and he will sustain you."* He used to say this phrase whenever he transferred brothers by obedience.

PRAYER

SONG

RESPONSE: To you we owe our hymn of praise, O God, in Zion.

PSALM 65

Praise is due to you, O God, in Zion;
and to you shall vows be performed.
By your strength you established the mountains;
you are girded with might. **R.**

You silence the roaring of the seas,
the roaring of their waves, the tumult of the peoples.
Those who live at earth's farthest bounds
are awed by your signs;
you make the gateways of the morning and the evening
shout for joy. **R.**

You visit the earth and water it, you greatly enrich it;
the river of God is full of water;
you provide the people with grain,
for so you have prepared it.
You water its furrows abundantly, settling its ridges,
softening it with showers,
and blessing its growth. **R.**

You crown the year with your bounty;
your wagon tracks overflow with richness.
The pastures of the wilderness overflow,
the hills gird themselves with joy,
the meadows clothe themselves with flocks,
the valleys deck themselves with grain,
they shout and sing together for joy. **R.**

READING: THOMAS OF CELANO, FIRST LIFE 26–27

One day he was marveling at the Lord's mercy in the kindness shown to him. He wished that the Lord would show him the course of life for him and his brothers, and he went to a place of prayer, as he so often did. He remained there a long time *with fear and trembling* before *the Ruler of the whole earth*. He recalled *in the bitterness of* his *soul the years* he spent badly, frequently repeating this phrase: *"Lord, be merciful to me, a sinner."* Gradually, an indescribable joy and tremendous sweetness began to well up deep in his heart.

He began to lose himself;
his feelings were pressed together;
and that darkness disappeared
which fear of sin had gathered in his heart.
Certainty of the forgiveness of all his sins poured in,
and the assurance of being revived in grace was given to him.
Then he was caught up above himself and totally
engulfed in light,
and, with his inmost soul opened wide,
he clearly saw the future.
As that sweetness and light withdrew,
renewed in spirit,
he now seemed to be *changed into another man*.

He returned and said to the brothers with joy: *"Be strong,* dear brothers, and *rejoice in the Lord.* Do not be sad, because you seem so few, and do not let my simplicity or yours discourage you. The Lord has shown me that God will make us grow into a great multitude, and will spread us to the ends of the earth.
…"

REFLECTION

Allow yourself to have a spiritual experience of the mountain. Climbing a mountain makes us aware of burdens. We groan and sort out what is necessary for the journey. This can serve as a fine metaphor for our spiritual journey.

SILENT TIME ON THE MOUNTAIN

EUCHARIST

READING: ROMANS 8:31–39

A reading from the letter of Paul to the Romans

What then are we to say about these things? If God is for us, who is against us? He who did not withhold his own Son, but gave him up for all of us, will he not with him also give us everything else? Who will bring any charge against God's elect? It is God who justifies. Who is to condemn? It is Christ Jesus, who died, yes, who was raised, who is at the right hand of God, who indeed intercedes for us. Who will separate us from the love of Christ? Will hardship, or distress, or persecution, or famine, or nakedness, or peril, or sword? As it is written, "For your sake we are being killed all day long; we are accounted as sheep to be slaughtered."

No, in all these things we are more than conquerors through him who loved us. For I am convinced that neither death, nor life, nor angels, nor rulers, nor things present, nor things to come, nor powers, nor height, nor depth, nor anything else in all creation, will be able to separate us from the love of God in Christ Jesus our Lord. **The word of the Lord.**

RESPONSE: To you, O Lord, I lift up my soul.

PSALM 25

To you, O LORD, I lift up my soul. O my God, in you I trust;
do not let me be put to shame;
do not let my enemies exult over me. **R.**

Do not let those who wait for you be put to shame;
let them be ashamed who are wantonly treacherous. **R.**

Make me to know your ways, O LORD;
teach me your paths. Lead me in your truth,
and teach me, for you are the God of my salvation;
for you I wait all day long. **R.**

ALLELUIA: Go and teach all people my gospel. I am with you always, until the end of the world.

GOSPEL: LUKE 24:44–53

A reading from the holy Gospel according to Luke

Then he said to them, "These are my words that I spoke to you while I was still with you—that everything written about me in the law of Moses, the prophets, and the psalms must be fulfilled." Then he opened their minds to understand the scriptures, and he said to them, "Thus it is written, that the Messiah is to suffer and to rise from the dead on the third day, and that repentance and forgiveness of sins is to be proclaimed in his name to all nations, beginning from Jerusalem. You are witnesses of these things. And see, I am sending upon you what my Father promised; so stay here in the city until you have been clothed with power from on high." Then he led them out as far as Bethany, and, lifting up his hands, he blessed them. While he was blessing them, he withdrew from them and was carried up into heaven. And they worshiped him, and returned to Jerusalem with great joy; and they were continually in the temple blessing God. **The Gospel of the Lord.**

RIETI VALLEY: FONTE COLOMBO

FRANCISCAN PILGRIMAGE PROGRAMS

RIETI VALLEY: FONTE COLOMBO

EVENTS

Francis, with companions, put together the final version of the friars' Rule of Life. Rome approved it on November 29, 1223. Francis underwent the cauterization of his eyes.

Francis came to Fonte Colombo for solitude. One sees vestiges of *A Rule for Hermitages* concretized here: some caves or shelters along the side of the mountain, the little church bell atop the Chapel of Mary Magdalen, which Francis rang to call the brothers out of solitude to common prayer.

SPIRITUALITY

One position on the development of the Rule maintains that Francis and the brothers struggled together in a common venture to formulate a way of life. Another position maintains that Christ himself dictated the Rule to Francis. For this reason Fonte Colombo is sometimes called the Mt. Sinai of the Franciscan Order. As God appeared to Moses on Mt. Sinai and gave him The Law, so Christ appeared to Francis and gave him The Rule.

Whatever position one takes, it is important to remember that Francis and his way of life gave birth to a new movement in the church and society. He and the brothers dreamed a future they believed in, which became possible and viable with the grace of God.

Fonte Colombo invites us to reflect on our commitment to the gospel and Franciscan vision of life and offers the opportunity for recommitment.

REFLECTION

Note the importance of water (*fons columbarum*) and fire on this mountain. Here Francis sought out God's will for himself and his brothers. In collaboration with the brothers he was assured of God's direction. How do you discern?

Consider the role of "sickness" in the development of Francis' life and journey toward God—a movement toward "light."

As Franciscans we profess a Rule of Life. Just as the Rule of 1223 underwent a long process of development, we must remember that we make our profession not only to a Rule but to *life* and its ongoing development today. We search out God's will in it within the context of community for our times. What might this mean to you?

How would you respond to Francis' brothers attempt to persuade him to water down the Rule?

Many Franciscan chapels were either dedicated to St. Mary Magdalen or at least had her picture inside. She is the example of penitent living. The gospel's call to repentance is never ending.

FONTE COLOMBO

HISTORICAL NOTES

This densely wooded mountain (formerly called Monte Rainerio) was visited by Francis in 1217. The origin of the name Fonte Colombo is derived from *fons columbarum* ("fountain of the doves"), a name that tradition says Francis himself gave to the spring. The beautiful spring of fresh water, gushing out from beneath a high cliff, is located in the woods of the sanctuary. It probably had been the property of the Benedictines of Farfa, who then donated it to the Friars Minor.

Two important events took place here: (1) Francis, in consultation with his companions and fellow brothers, put together the final version of the Franciscan Rule of Life before taking it to Rome for approval (autumn 1223); (2) the eye operation or cauterization, very likely in January 1226, probably happened in this hermitage.

The church dates from the 15th century: It was consecrated on July 19, 1450, and is dedicated to St. Francis.

Down the hill sits the Chapel of Our Lady, Chapel of Mary Magdalen, which is the most perfect example of a primitive Franciscan church left to us. It was in existence at the time of Francis, having been built in the 12th century or earlier. Note the small bell rung by Francis to summon friars from solitude to common prayer. The small altar is thought to be original. On the window to the left there is the letter T (Tau), which authorities hold was drawn by St. Francis himself. It was discovered in the early 1920s when the window was opened after having been blocked for probably several hundred years.

Along the mountain lies the *Sacra Speco* ("Sacred Cave"). The cave of Brother Leo is at the bottom of a steep flight of stairs, a natural grotto where he devoted himself to prayer. There is also the stump of the oak tree, now protected by a stone hut, where Jesus is to have appeared when he confirmed the Rule. Then one comes to the Sacred Cave, where the last section of stairs leads to a crevice in the mountain, said to be caused by an earthquake. It is the most important place in the sanctuary. According to tradition Francis fasted and prayed for forty days and wrote the Rule in 1223. Just above the Sacred Cave is the Chapel of St. Michael the Archangel, sometimes called the "Rule Chapel."

The Hermitage of St. Francis was a small house in the time of Francis; it was donated to him in 1217 along with the Chapel of Our Lady and the surrounding forest. Here Francis underwent his eye operation, and here other events also took place. The brothers lived in this hermitage for two hundred years until the convent of St. Bernardine was built.

FRANCISCAN READINGS

ST. BONAVENTURE, MAJOR LEGEND IV:11

Francis and the Rule

When the Order was already widely spread and Francis was considering having the rule which had been approved by Innocent permanently confirmed by his successor Honorius, he was advised by the following revelation from God.

It seemed to him that he was gathering tiny bread crumbs from the ground, which he had to distribute to a crowd of hungry brothers who stood all around him. He was afraid to give out such little crumbs, fearing that such minute particles might slip between his fingers, when a voice said to him from above: "Francis, make one host out of all the crumbs, and give it to those who want to eat." He did it, whoever did not receive it devoutly, or showed contempt for the gift received, soon appeared obviously covered with leprosy.

In the morning the holy man told all this to his companions, regretting that he did not understand *the mystery of the vision.* On the following day, while *he kept vigil in prayer,* he heard this voice coming down from heaven: "Francis, the crumbs of last night are the words of the Gospel; the host is the rule and the leprosy is wickedness."

Since he therefore wanted the Rule that had been taken from a more widespread collection of Gospel passages to be confirmed, he went up to a certain mountain led by the Holy Spirit, with two of his companions, to condense it into a shorter form as the vision had dictated. There he fasted, content with only *bread* and *water*, and dictated the rule as the Holy Spirit suggested to him while he was praying. When he came down from the mountain, he gave the rule to his vicar to keep. After

a few days had elapsed, the vicar claimed that it had been lost
through carelessness. The holy man went off again to the place
of solitude and rewrote it *just as before,* as if he were taking
the words from the mouth of God. And he obtained confirmation
for it, as he had desired, from the lord Pope Honorius, in the
eighth year of his pontificate. Fervently exhorting the brothers
to observe this rule,

Francis used to say

that nothing of what he had placed there

came from his own efforts

but that he dictated everything

just as it had been revealed by God.

To confirm this with greater certainty by God's

own testimony,

when only a few days had passed,

the stigmata of Our Lord Jesus were imprinted upon him

by the finger *of the living God,*

as the seal of the Supreme Pontiff, Christ,

for the complete confirmation of the rule

and the commendation of its author,

as will be described below,

after our exposition of his virtues.

SECOND MIRROR OF PERFECTION 1

Francis and the Rule

After the second rule which blessed Francis wrote had been lost,
he went up a *mountain* with Brother Leo of Assisi and Brother
Bonizo of Bologna to make another rule, which he had written
at Christ's instruction.

A group of many ministers came to Brother Elias, who was the
vicar of the blessed Francis. "We heard that Brother Francis is
making a new rule," they told him, "and we fear that he will
make it so harsh that we will not be able to observe it. We
want you to go to him and tell him that we refuse to be bound

to that rule. Let him make it for himself and not for us."

Brother Elias replied to them that he did not want to go because he feared the rebuke of blessed Francis. When they insisted that he go, he said that he refused to go without them; so they all went together.

When Brother Elias and the ministers were near the place where blessed Francis was staying, Brother Elias called him. Blessed Francis responded, and seeing the ministers, he said: "What do these brothers want?" "These are ministers," Brother Elias answered, "who heard that you are making a new rule. They fear that you are making it very harsh, and they say and say publicly, they refuse to be bound by it. Make it for yourself and not for them."

Then blessed Francis turned his face toward heaven and spoke to Christ in this way: "Lord! Didn't I tell you, they wouldn't believe me?" The voice of Christ was then heard in the air, saying "Francis, nothing of yours is in the *Rule*: whatever is there is mine. And I want the *Rule* observed in this way: to the letter, to the letter, to the letter, and without a gloss, without a gloss, without a gloss." And He added: "I know how much human weakness is capable of, and how much I want to help them. therefore, those who refuse to observe it, should leave the Order." Then blessed Francis turned to the brothers and said: "Did you hear? Did you hear? Do you want me to have you told again?" Confused and terrified, the ministers departed blaming themselves.

ASSISI COMPILATION 17

Objection to Francis' Rule by Elias and ministers

When blessed Francis was on a mountain with Brother Leo of Assisi and Brother Bonizo of Bologna to make the *Rule*— because the first, which he had written at Christ's instruction, was lost—a great many ministers gathered around Brother Elias, who was the vicar of blessed Francis. "We heard that Brother Francis is making a new rule," they told him, "and we fear that he will make it so harsh that we will not be able to observe it. We want you to go to him and tell him that we refuse to be bound to that *Rule*. Let him make it for himself and not for us."

Brother Elias replied to them that he did not want to go because he feared the rebuke of Brother Francis. When they insisted that he go, he said that he refused to go without them; so they all went.

When Brother Elias, with those ministers, was near the place where blessed Francis was staying, he called him. Blessed Francis responded and, seeing those ministers, he said: "What do these brothers want?" "These are ministers," Brother Elias answered, "who heard that you are making a new rule. They fear that you are making it very harsh, and they say, and say publicly, that they refuse to be bound by it. Make it for yourself and not for them."

Then blessed Francis turned his face to heaven and spoke to Christ in this way: "Lord! Didn't I tell you they wouldn't believe you?" The voice of Christ was then heard in the air, saying "Francis, nothing of yours is in the *Rule*: whatever is there is all mine. And I want the *Rule* observed in this way: to the letter, to the letter, to the letter, and without a gloss, without a gloss, without a gloss." And He added: "I know how much human weakness is capable of, and how much I want to help them. Those who refuse to observe it should leave the Order." Then blessed Francis turned to the brothers and said: "Did you hear? Did you hear? Do you want me to have you told again?" Then the ministers, confused and blaming themselves, departed.

THOMAS OF CELANO, SECOND LIFE 166

Eye cauterization

At the time of an eye disease, he is forced to let himself be treated by a physician. A surgeon is called to the place, and when he comes he is carrying an iron instrument for cauteriz-

ing. He ordered it to be placed in the fire until it became red hot. But the blessed Father, to comfort the body, which was struck with panic, spoke to the fire: "My brother Fire, your beauty is the envy of all creatures, the *Most High created* you strong, beautiful and useful. *Be gracious to me* in this hour; be courteous! For a long time I have loved you in the Lord. I pray the *Great Lord* who created you to temper now your heat that I may bear your gentle burning."

When the prayer is finished, he makes the sign of the cross over the fire and then remains in the place unshaken. The surgeon takes in his hands the red-hot glowing iron. The brothers, overcome by human feeling, run away. The saint joyfully and eagerly offered himself to the iron. The hissing iron sinks into tender flesh, and the burn is extended slowly straight from the ear to the eyebrow. How much pain that burning caused can best be known by the witness of the saint's words, since it was he that felt it. For when the brothers who had fled return, the father says with a smile: "Oh you *weak souls of little* heart; why did you run away? *Truly I say to you,* I did not feel the fire's heat, nor any pain in my flesh." And turning to the doctor, he says: "If the flesh isn't well cooked, try again!" The doctor had experienced quite a different reaction in similar situations, exalts this as a divine miracle, saying: "I tell you, brothers: *today I have seen wonderful things!*" I believe he had returned to primeval innocence, for when he wished, the harshest things grew gentle.

OTHER READINGS

2C 44; 2MP 110; AC 68—Hospitality to a doctor friend
2MP 33—Francis' gift of a cloak to a poor woman
AC 83; LMj V:9; AC 86; 2MP 115—Eye cauterization

PRAYER

RITUAL READING OF THE RULE

OPENING PRAYER

Today, we your sons and daughters remember the call you have given us in our profession of the Rules of the First Order, the Second Order, and the Third Order Secular or Regular. We ask for your help to continue to live the life of the Gospel, according to our respective rules, that we might ever witness to your kingdom here on earth.

READING: MATTHEW 19:16-21

A reading from the holy Gospel according to Matthew

Then someone came to him and said, "Teacher, what good deed must I do to have eternal life?" And he said to him, "Why do you ask me about what is good? There is only one who is good. If you wish to enter into life, keep the commandments," He said to him, "Which ones?" And Jesus said, "You shall not murder; you shall not commit adultery; you shall not steal; you shall not bear false witness; honor your father and mother; also, you shall love your neighbor as yourself." The young man said to him, "I have kept all these; what do I still lack?" Jesus said to him, "If you wish to be perfect, go, sell your possessions, and give the money to the poor, and you will have treasure in heaven; then come, follow me." When the young man heard this word, he went away grieving, for he had many possessions.

REFRAIN: G 24 "Only This I Want," verse 1

PROCLAMATION OF THE RULES OF FRANCIS' FAMILY

PART I: A "FORM OF LIFE"

First Order:
LR I:1-3—The Rule and Life of the Lesser Brothers is this: to observe the Holy Gospel of Our Lord Jesus Christ by living in obedience, without anything of one's own, and in chastity.

Brother Francis promises obedience and reverence to our Lord Pope Honorius and his successors canonically elected and to the Roman Church. Let the other brothers be bound to obey Brother Francis and his successors.

Second Order:
RCl I:1-5—The form of life of the Order of the Poor Sisters that Blessed Francis established is this: to observe the Holy Gospel of our Lord Jesus Christ, by living in obedience, without anything of one's own, and in chastity.

Clare, the unworthy servant of Christ and the little plant of the most blessed Francis, promises obedience and reverence to the Lord Pope Innocent and his canonically elected successors, and to the Roman Church. And as, at the beginning of her conversion she, together with her sisters, promised obedience to Blessed Francis, so now she promises his successors to observe the same obedience inviolably. And the other sisters shall always be obliged to obey the successors of

Blessed Francis and Sister Clare and the other canonically elected Abbesses who succeed her.

Third Order Regular:
TOR Rule 1—The form of life of the Brothers and Sisters is this: to observe the holy Gospel of our Lord Jesus Christ, living in obedience, in poverty and in chastity. Following Jesus Christ after the example of St. Francis, let them recognize that they are called to make greater efforts in their observance of the precepts and counsels of our Lord Jesus Christ. Let them deny themselves (cf. Mt 16, 24) as they have promised the Lord.

Secular Franciscan Order:
TOS Rule 4—The rule and life of the Secular Franciscans is this: to observe the gospel of our Lord Jesus Christ by following the example of Saint Francis of Assisi, who made Christ the inspiration and the center of his life with God and people. Christ, the gift of the Father's love, is the way to him, the truth into which the Holy Spirit leads us, and the life which he has come to give abundantly.

Secular Franciscans should devote themselves especially to careful reading of the gospel, going from gospel to life and life to the gospel.

REFRAIN: G 24, verse 2

PART II: "POVERTY"

First Order:
LR VI:1–6—Let the brothers not make anything their own, neither house, nor place, nor anything at all. As pilgrims and strangers in this world, serving the Lord in poverty and humility, let them go seeking alms with confidence, and they should not be ashamed because, for our sakes, our Lord made Himself poor in this world. This is that sublime height of most exalted poverty which has made you, my most beloved brothers,

heirs and kings of the Kingdom of Heaven, poor in temporal things but exalted in virtue. Let this be your portion which leads into the land of the living. Giving yourselves totally to this, beloved brothers, never seek anything else under heaven for the name of our Lord Jesus Christ.

Second Order:

RCl VI:10–15—As I, together with my sisters, have ever been solicitous to safeguard the holy poverty which we have promised the Lord God and blessed Francis, so, too, the Abbesses who shall succeed me in office and all the sisters are bound to observe it inviolably to the end: that is, by not receiving or having possession or ownership either of themselves or through an intermediary, or even anything that might reasonably be called property, except as much land as necessity requires for the integrity and proper seclusion of the monastery, and this land may not be cultivated except as a garden for the needs of the sisters.

Third Order Regular:

TOR Rule 22—The truly poor in spirit, following the example of the Lord, live in this world as pilgrims and strangers (Mt 10:27-29). They neither appropriate nor defend anything as their own. So excellent is this most high poverty that it makes

us heirs and rulers of the Kingdom of Heaven. It makes us materially poor, but rich in virtue. Let this poverty alone be our portion because it leads to the land of the living. Clinging completely to it let us, for the sake of our Lord Jesus Christ, never want anything else under heaven.

Secular Franciscan Order:

TOS Rule 11—Trusting in the Father, Christ chose for himself and his mother a poor and humble life, even though he valued created things attentively and lovingly. Let the Secular Franciscans seek a proper spirit of detachment from temporal goods by simplifying their own material needs. Let them be mindful that according to the gospel they are stewards of the goods received for the benefit of God's children.

REFRAIN: G 24, verse 3

PART III: "VIRTUOUS LIVING IN THE COMMUNITY"

First Order:

LR X:7–12—Moreover, I admonish and exhort the brothers in the Lord Jesus Christ to beware of all pride, vainglory, envy and greed, of care and solicitude for the things of this world, of detraction and murmuring. Let those who are illiterate not be anxious to learn, but let them pay attention to what they must desire above all else: to have the Spirit of the Lord and Its holy activity, to pray always to Him with a pure heart, to have humility and patience in persecution and infirmity, and to love those who persecute, rebuke and find fault with us, because the Lord says: *Love your enemies and pray for those who persecute and calumniate you. Blessed are those who suffer persecution for the sake of justice, for theirs is the kingdom of heaven. But whoever perseveres to the end will be saved.*

Second Order:

RCl X:6–13—In fact, I admonish and exhort the sisters in the Lord Jesus Christ to beware of all pride, vainglory, envy, avarice, care and anxiety about this world, detraction and murmuring, dissension and division. Let them be always eager to preserve among themselves the unity of mutual love which is the bond of perfection. Let those who do not know how to read not be eager to learn. Let them direct their attention to what they should desire to have above all else: the Spirit of the Lord and Its holy activity, to pray always to Him with a pure heart, and to have humility, patience in difficulty and infirmity, and to love those who persecute, blame, and accuse us, for the Lord said: *Blessed are those who suffer persecution for the sake of justice, for theirs is the kingdom of heaven* (Mt. 5:10). But *whoever perseveres to the end will be saved.*

Third Order Regular:

TOR Rule 20—Let the sisters and brothers be gentle, peaceful and unassuming, mild and humble, speaking respectfully to all in accord with their vocation. Wherever they are, or wherever they go throughout the world, they should not be quarrelsome, contentious, or judgmental towards others. Rather, it should be obvious that they are joyful (cf. Phil 4,4), good-humored, and happy in the Lord as they ought to be. And in greeting others, let them say: "The Lord give you peace."

Secular Franciscan Order:

TOS Rule 17a, 19—In their family they cultivate the Franciscan spirit of peace, fidelity, and respect for life, striving to make of it a sign of a world already renewed in Christ. Mindful that they are bearers of peace which must be built up unceasingly, they should seek out ways of unity and fraternal harmony through dialogue, trusting in the presence of the divine seed in everyone and in the transforming power of love and pardon.

REFRAIN: G 24

REFLECTION

PRAYER: EARLIER RULE XXIII: 9–11

Therefore,
let us desire nothing else,
let us want nothing else,
let nothing else please us and cause us delight
except our Creator, Redeemer and Savior,
the only true God,
Who is the fullness of good,
all good, every good, the true and supreme good,
Who alone is good,
merciful, gentle, delightful, and sweet,
Who alone is holy,
just, true, holy, and upright,
Who alone is kind, innocent, clean,
from Whom, *through Whom* and in Whom
is all pardon, all grace, all glory. ...

Therefore,
let nothing hinder us,
nothing separate us,
nothing come between us.

Wherever we are,
in every place,
at every hour,
at every time of the day,
every day and continually,
let all of us truly and humbly believe,
hold in our heart and love,
honor, adore, serve,
praise and bless,
glorify and exalt,

magnify and give thanks
to the Most High and Supreme Eternal God. ...
Who,
without beginning and end,
is unchangeable, invisible,
indescribable, ineffable,
incomprehensible, unfathomable,
blessed, praiseworthy,
glorious, exalted,
sublime, most high,
gentle, lovable, delightful,
and totally desirable above all else
for ever.
Amen.

EUCHARIST

READING: EXODUS 19:16–19

A reading from the book of Exodus

On the morning of the third day there was thunder and lightning, as well as a thick cloud on the mountain, and a blast of a trumpet so loud that all the people who were in the camp trembled. Moses brought the people out of the camp to meet God. They took their stand at the foot of the mountain. Now Mount Sinai was wrapped in smoke, because the LORD had descended upon it in fire; the smoke went up like the smoke of a kiln, while the whole mountain shook violently. As the blast of the trumpet grew louder and louder, Moses would speak and God would answer him in thunder. **The word of the Lord.**

RESPONSE: Come let us sing joyfully to God.

PSALM 95

O come, let us sing to the LORD;
let us make a joyful noise to the rock of our salvation!
Let us come into his presence with thanksgiving;
let us make a joyful noise to him with songs of praise!
For the LORD is a great God,
and a great King above all gods. **R.**

In his hand are the depths of the earth;
the heights of the mountains are his also.
The sea is his, for he made it, and the dry land,
which his hands have formed. **R.**
O come, let us worship and bow down,
let us kneel before the LORD, our Maker!
For he is our God, and we are the people of his pasture,
and the sheep of his hand.
O that today you would listen to his voice! **R.**

ALLELUIA: Happy are the pure of heart, for they shall see God.

GOSPEL: MATTHEW 5:1-12

A reading from the holy Gospel according to Matthew

When Jesus saw the crowds,
he went up the mountain;
and after he sat down, his
disciples came to him. Then he began to speak, and taught
them, saying: "Blessed are the poor in spirit, for theirs is
the kingdom of heaven. Blessed are those who mourn, for
they will be comforted. Blessed are the meek, for they will

inherit the earth. Blessed are those who hunger and thirst for righteousness, for they will be filled. Blessed are the merciful, for they will receive mercy. Blessed are the pure in heart, for they will see God. Blessed are the peacemakers, for they will be called children of God. Blessed are those who are persecuted for righteousness' sake, for theirs is the kingdom of heaven. Blessed are you when people revile you and persecute you and utter all kinds of evil against you falsely on my account. Rejoice and be glad, for your reward is great in heaven, for in the same way they persecuted the prophets who were before you." **The Gospel of the Lord.**

RENEWAL OF COMMITMENT TO FRANCISCAN LIFE

INTRODUCTION

Today we find ourselves here at Fonte Colombo, the Sinai of our Franciscan Order. Here in a cave, Francis sought out in deep prayer our Lord Jesus Christ and his will for the Order. Here in a cave, Francis wept and anguished in the struggle to give birth to a Rule. Here in a cave, Francis composed a Rule that influences the entire Franciscan family. Here in this chapel cave, we gather to renew our commitment to our mission as Franciscans.

RESPONSE: I will fulfill my vows to the Lord in the presence of all the people.

PSALM 116

What shall I return to the LORD for all his bounty to me?
I will lift up the cup of salvation
and call on the name of the LORD,
I will pay my vows to the LORD
in the presence of all his people. **R.**

Precious in the sight of the LORD

is the death of his faithful ones.
O LORD, I am your servant; I am your servant,
the child of your serving girl.
You have loosed my bonds.
I will offer to you a thanksgiving sacrifice
and call on the name of the LORD. **R.**

I will pay my vows to the LORD
in the presence of all his people,
in the courts of the house of the LORD,
in your midst, O Jerusalem.
Praise the LORD! **R.**

READING: PHILIPPIANS 3:8–14
A reading from the letter of Paul to the Philippians

More than that, I regard everything as loss because of the surpassing value of knowing Christ Jesus my Lord. For his sake I have suffered the loss of all things, and I regard them as rubbish, in order that I may gain Christ and be found in him, not having a righteousness of my own that comes from the law, but one that comes through faith in Christ, the righteousness from God based on faith. I want to know Christ and the power of his resurrection and the sharing of his sufferings by becoming like him in his death, if somehow I may attain the resurrection from the dead. Not that I have already obtained this or have already reached the goal; but I press on to make it my own, because Christ Jesus has made me his own. Beloved, I do not consider that I have made it my own; but this one thing I do: forgetting what lies behind and straining forward to what lies ahead, I press on toward the goal for the prize of the heavenly call of God in Christ Jesus. **The word of the Lord.**

RENEWAL OF COMMITMENT

Leader:
Brothers and sisters,
In the presence of the Lord, our God,
and before the Blessed Virgin Mary,
our holy Father Francis, our holy Mother Clare,
and this gathering,
I invite you to renew your commitment
to the Franciscan vision of life.

All:
All praise be yours, O Lord,
for all creation gives you glory.
All praise be yours, O Lord,
for all good comes from you.
All praise be yours, O Lord,
for you call us to the life of your risen Son.

Today, we your sons and daughters
renew and rededicate ourselves
to the call you have given us.
We renew and profess our commitment
to a Gospel vision of life,
handed on to us by our father, Francis,
and our mother, Clare,
and we ask your help
to continue to live the life of the Gospel,
with obedience to your Spirit and your church,
with poverty that imitates the life of your Son
and his most holy mother
and with chastity that frees us to love you,
your people, and all creation with unmeasured love.
All praise be yours, O Lord!

BLESSING OF FRANCIS AND CLARE

Francis:
And whoever observes these things, let him be blessed *in*

heaven with the blessing of the Most High Father, and *on earth* with the blessing of His Beloved Son with the Most Holy Spirit, the Paraclete, and all the powers of heaven and with all the saints. And, as far as I can, I, little brother Francis, your servant, confirm for you, both within and without, this most holy blessing. (Test 40–41)

Clare:

I, Clare, a servant of Christ, a little plant of our most holy Father Francis, ... bless you during my life and after my death, as I am able, out of all the blessings with which *the Father of mercies has* and does *bless* His sons and daughters *in heaven* and on earth and a spiritual father and mother have blessed and bless their spiritual sons and daughters. Amen.

Always be lovers of your souls and those of all your sisters. And may you always be eager to observe what you have promised the Lord.

May the Lord always be *with you* and may you always be with Him. Amen.
(BCl 6, 11–16)

RIETI VALLEY: GRECCIO

FRANCISCAN PILGRIMAGE PROGRAMS

RIETI VALLEY: GRECCIO

EVENTS
Here we remember, above everything else, the Christmas celebration of 1223. This has, ever since, popularized the practice of displaying the Christmas crèche. Francis also celebrated Easter here and offered the brothers a lesson in poverty.

Greccio offers another mountain retreat where Francis experienced solitude.

SPIRITUALITY
Bonaventure says: The example (reenactment of the Bethlehem event) that Francis put before the world was calculated to rouse the hearts of those weak in the faith. Celano adds: Many saw a vision of a child come to life in Francis' arms. This vision was not unfitting, for the child had been forgotten in the hearts of many; but by the working of his grace, he was brought to life again through St. Francis and stamped upon their fervent memories. Francis used very concrete means to awaken faith in the lives of the people. This incarnational approach is central to our Franciscan heritage.

The mystery of the Incarnation was one of the pivotal elements of Francis' spirituality; the cross and the Eucharist were the other two.

REFLECTION
Francis concretized the mysteries of the faith. Explore the current significance of this for evangelization.

Greccio is the "Franciscan Bethlehem," which highlights the humanity of Christ. Examine other stories in Francis' life that emphasize the wonder and beauty of the human nature God has assumed and given to us. What do I think of my own human nature?

The condition of a child is the condition that each person is invited to return to in order to enter the kingdom of heaven. How and why?

Why should Francis have chosen Greccio to reenact the Bethlehem event? Examine the readings on Greccio for any clues.

GRECCIO

HISTORICAL NOTES

Francis' first visit to the Castello di Greccio, a village perched on a hilltop, is placed in 1217. His preaching converted the inhabitants, and consequently they begged Francis not to leave. Giovanni di Velita, realizing the effect of Francis' presence on the district, decided to build him and his followers more permanent quarters near to Greccio. The legend states that St. Francis was unwilling to accept the offer, fearing distractions and disturbances to his brothers. Finally he agreed to the suggestion that the hermitage be built at least a stone's throw away. A small boy was called up and given a burning torch to throw as far as he could. To everyone's astonishment, the torch landed not a few yards below in the valley, but on a rocky hill a mile or two away facing the town of Greccio. Thus St. Francis went with his brothers to the spot indicated by the torch, where some caves, hollowed out in the cliffs, provided all he needed in the way of dwelling.

Here at Greccio, in the Chapel of the Presepio (also called the Chapel of St. Luke), which is the focal point of the entire sanctuary, a most famous event took place on Christmas Eve.

This is a natural cave to which Francis returned after his long and wearisome business in Rome regarding the Rule. At Greccio Francis found peace. Celano's *First Life of Francis* 84–87 tells the rest.

Outside the cave chapel is an open-air balcony, where one can take in the wonders of nature and the green valley below.

One can visit the dormitory of St. Francis, a dark, narrow cave where Francis and some companions lived for several years. The space was so limited that each brother had an assigned place marked by a rough cross painted on the wall, traces of which still remain. One of Francis' cells was at the back of this dormitory so he could be alone. Celano tells us Francis was fond of staying here because it was rich in poverty and because in a secluded cell, hewn out of a projecting rock, he could more freely devote himself to heavenly discipline.

Very near the dormitory is the refectory. It was reconstructed in 1955 when the front of the chapel was enlarged. (See readings about events that happened here: 2MP 20; 2C 61; AC 74; LMj VII:9.)

A staircase leads to the floor above, where we find the dormitory of St. Bonaventure, so-called because it was built in 1260 when he was the Minister General. It consists of a short corridor with small wooden cells on either side.

Passing through this to the outdoors, we come to the grotto of John of Parma, entered by a rough stairway below a trap door. In this tiny cave Blessed John spent thirty-two years (1257-1289) after having been deposed from the generalship of the

Order for his supposed sympathy with the teachings of Joachim of Flora.

Returning through the dormitory of Bonaventure, a door leads into the present-day choir of St. Bonaventure, where stalls and a primitive form of lectern are original.

The New Chapel contains the oldest portrait of Francis and shows him as he was in his final years. This portrait (1225?) is supposed to have been painted to the order of Jacoba dei Settesoli. There is also the New Church with a year-round Presepio.

It is probable that the dormitory cave was occupied by Brothers Leo, Angelo, and Rufino when they were here in 1246; and there is a tradition that in this spot was written The Legend of Three Companions, or at least the original letters that they sent to tell the Minister General of some of the deeds of St. Francis of which they had personal knowledge, or of which they had learned from other friars.

FRANCISCAN READINGS

THOMAS OF CELANO, SECOND LIFE 35

Francis' love for Greccio

The saint used to enjoy staying in the brothers' place at Greccio. He found it rich in poverty and there, in a remote little cell on a cliff, he could give himself freely to heavenly things. This is the place where he had earlier recalled the birth of the *Child of Bethlehem*, becoming a child with the Child.

THOMAS OF CELANO, FIRST LIFE 84–86

Francis' inspiration to reenact the events of Bethlehem

We should note then, as matter worthy of memory and

something to be recalled with reverence, what he did, three years prior to his death, at the town of Greccio, on the birthday of our Lord Jesus Christ. *There was a certain man in that area* named John who *had a good reputation* but an even better manner of life. Blessed Francis loved him with special affection. ... Blessed Francis had John summoned to him some fifteen days prior to the birthday of the Lord. "If you desire to celebrate the coming feast of the Lord together at Greccio," he said to him, "hurry before me and *carefully make ready* the things I tell you. For I wish to enact the memory of that babe *who was born in Bethlehem*: to see as much as is possible with my own bodily eyes the discomfort of his infant needs, how he *lay in a manger*, and how, with an ox and an ass standing by, he rested on hay." Once the good and faithful man had heard Francis's words, *he ran quickly* and prepared in that place all the things that the holy man had requested.

Finally, *the day of joy* has drawn near,
the time of exultation *has come.*
From many different places the brethren have been called.
As they could,
the men and women of that land with exultant hearts
prepare candles and torches to light up that night
whose shining star has enlightened every day and year.
Finally, the holy man of God comes
and, finding all things prepared,
he saw them and was glad.
Indeed, the manger is prepared,
the hay is carried in,
and the ox and the ass are led to the spot.

There simplicity is given a place of honor,
poverty is exalted,
humility is commended,
and out of Greccio is made a new Bethlehem.

The night is lit up like day,
delighting both man and beast.
The people arrive, ecstatic at this new mystery of new joy.
The forest amplifies the cries
and the boulders echo back the joyful crowd.
The brothers sing, giving God due praise,
and the whole night abounds with jubilation.
The holy man of God stands before the manger,
filled with heartfelt sighs,
contrite in his piety,
and overcome with wondrous joy.
Over the manger the solemnities of the Mass are celebrated
and the priest enjoys a new consolation.

The holy man of God is dressed in the vestments of the Levites, since he was a Levite, and with full voice sings the holy gospel. Here is his voice: a powerful voice, *a pleasant voice,* a clear voice, a musical voice, inviting all to the highest of gifts. Then he preaches to the people standing around him and pours forth sweet honey about the birth of the poor King and the poor city of Bethlehem. … The gifts of the Almighty are multiplied there and a virtuous man sees a wondrous vision. For the man saw a little child lying lifeless in the manger and he saw the holy man of God approach the child and waken him from a deep sleep. Nor is this vision unfitting, since in the hearts of many the child Jesus has been *given over to oblivion.* Now he is awakened and impressed on their loving memory by His own grace through His holy servant Francis. At length, the night's solemnities draw to a close and everyone went home with joy.

ASSISI COMPILATION 74

Francis converting the people of Greccio

For blessed Francis found the hermitage of the brothers at Greccio to be becoming and poor and the inhabitants, although poor and simple, were more pleasing to him than those of the rest of the region. For this reason he rested and stayed there, especially because there was a poor cell, very isolated, in which the holy father would stay.

Many of these people, with the grace of God, entered religion because of his example and preaching and that of his brothers. Many women preserved their virginity and, remaining in their own homes, dressed in the clothing of religion. And although each remained in her own home, each of them lived the common life decently, afflicting her body with fasting and prayer. Thus it seemed to the people and to the brothers that their manner of living was not among seculars and their relatives, but among holy and religious people who had served the Lord a long time, despite their youthful age and simplicity. That is why, with joy, blessed Francis often said to the brothers about the men and women of this town: "Even in a large city not as many people have been converted to penance as in Greccio, which is only a small town."

For frequently, when the brothers of that place used to praise the Lord in the evening, as the brothers at that time were accustomed to do in many places, the people of that town, both the great and the small, would come outside. Standing on the road in front of the town, they would respond to the brothers in a loud voice: "Praised be the Lord God!" Even children, who could not yet speak, when they saw the brothers, would praise the Lord as best they could.

THOMAS OF CELANO, FIRST LIFE 83

Verbal portrait of Francis

How handsome,
how splendid!
How gloriously he appeared
in innocence of life,
in simplicity of words,
in purity of heart,
in love of God,
in fraternal charity,
in enthusiastic obedience,
in agreeable compliance,
in angelic appearance.

Friendly in behavior,
serene in nature,
affable in speech,
generous in encouragement,
faithful in commitment,
prudent in advice,
efficient in endeavor,
he was *gracious in everything!*

Tranquil in mind,
pleasant in disposition,
sober in spirit.
lifted in contemplation,
tireless in prayer,
he was fervent in everything!

Firm in intention,
consistent in virtue,
persevering in grace,
he was the same in everything!

Swift to forgive,
slow to grow angry,
free in nature,
remarkable in memory,
subtle in discussing,
careful in choices,
he was simple in everything!

Strict with himself,
kind with others,
he was discerning in everything!

THOMAS OF CELANO, SECOND LIFE 61

Easter at Greccio: a lesson in poverty

On a certain Easter Day the brothers in the hermitage of Greccio set the table more carefully than usual, with white clothes and glassware. The Father came down from his cell and went to the table. He saw that it was elevated and elaborately decorated, but he did not smile at all at that smiling table. He secretly tiptoed away, put on his head the hat of a poor man who was there at the time, and with a staff in hand, *went outside*. He waited *outside, at the door*, until the brothers had started eating. They were accustomed not to wait for him when he did not come at the usual signal.

As they began to eat, that true *poor man cried out* at the door: "For the love of the Lord God, *give alms* to this poor, sick pilgrim!" And the brothers replied: "Come in, man, for the love of Him you invoked." He quickly came in, and showed himself to those dining. You can imagine the surprise the pilgrim provoked in those homebodies! The beggar was given a bowl and, sitting on the ground by himself, placed his dish on the ashes. "Now," he said, "I am sitting like a Lesser Brother!" And he said to the brothers: *"The examples of the Son of God's* poverty should move us more than other religious. I saw here a table all prepared and decorated, and recognized it as not the table of poor men who go door to door."

THOMAS OF CELANO, SECOND LIFE 64

Francis and a feather pillow

Since we have mentioned beds, an incident comes to mind which may be useful to retell. From the time when this holy man *had turned to Christ* and *cast the things of this world into oblivion*, he never wanted to lie on a mattress or place his head on a feather pillow. He never broke this strict resolution, even when he was sick or receiving the hospitality of strangers. But it happened that while he was staying at the hermitage of Greccio his eye disease became worse than usual, and he was forced against his will to use a small pillow. The first night, during the morning vigil, the saint called his companion and said to him: "Brother, I couldn't sleep this whole night, or remain upright and pray. My head was spinning, my knees were giving way, and the whole framework of my body was shaking as if I had eaten bread made from ryegrass. I believe," he added, "there's a devil in this pillow I have for my head. Take it away, because I don't want the devil by my head any more."

The brother, sympathizing with the father's complaint, caught the pillow thrown at him to take away. But as he was leaving, he suddenly lost the power of speech. Struck by terror and paralyzed, he could not move his feet from where he stood nor could he move his arms. After a moment, the saint recognized this and called him. He was set free, came back in and told him what he *had suffered*. The saint said to him: "Last night as I was saying compline I knew for certain that the devil had come into my cell. Our enemy," he added, "is very cunning and subtle; when he can't harm you inside, in your soul, he at least gives you cause for complaint in your body."

JOHN DUNS SCOTUS ON THE INCARNATION

Blessed John Duns Scotus (1266-1308) teaches us that the Word Incarnate, the Son of God who became the Son of Mary, is the main reason why God created the universe. The Trinity first thought of the Word Incarnate, then of other human beings to be his companions and his social body, and then of the material universe as a home for this human family. So the rest of the universe is for the sake of human beings, and humankind is for the sake of Jesus Christ, in whom human nature is united to the divine Word. God could not have intended the glorified God-Man only for the sake of redeeming human beings who had sinned. This for two reasons:

—firstly, the more important thing [the glorified God-Man] could not depend for his existence on the less important [human beings who sinned] (Ordinatio 19,1,6;7,3);

—secondly, as human beings are free and might not have sinned, God could not make the most wonderful thing in creation, the glorified Christ, depend on the chance that Adam and Eve would sin (Reportata 3,7,4,4–5).

OTHER READINGS

AC 119; LMj V:2; 2MP 98—Francis' fight with the devil
2MP 20; LMj VII:9—Lesson on poverty
1C 60; LMj VIII:8—A rabbit

PRAYER SERVICE

PREPARATION FOR GRECCIO

READING I: ISAIAH 7:10–14

A reading from the book of the prophet Isaiah

Again the LORD spoke to Ahaz, saying, Ask a sign of the LORD your God; let it be deep as Sheol or high as heaven. But Ahaz said, I will not ask, and I will not put the LORD to the test. Then Isaiah said: "Hear then, O house of David! Is it too little for you to weary mortals, that you weary my God also? Therefore the Lord himself will give you a sign. Look, the young woman is with child and shall bear a son, and shall name him Immanuel. **The word of the Lord.**

RESPONSE: CM 1 "A Child Is Born"

READING II: LATER ADMONITION AND EXHORTATION TO THE BROTHERS AND SISTERS OF PENANCE 48–53

And *the Spirit of the Lord will rest* upon all those men and women who have done and persevered in these things and It will make a home and *dwelling place in them.* And they will be the children of the heavenly Father, Whose works they do. And they are spouses, brothers and mothers of our Lord Jesus Christ.

We are spouses when the faithful soul is united by the Holy Spirit to our Lord Jesus Christ. We are brothers, moreover, when we do *the will of* His *Father Who* is in heaven; mothers when we carry Him in our heart and body through love and a pure and sincere conscience; and give Him birth through a holy activity, which must shine before others by example.

REFRAIN: CM 1

READING III: ST. BONAVENTURE, MAJOR LEGEND X:7

It happened, three years prior to his death, that he decided to celebrate at the town of Greccio the memory of the birth of the Child Jesus with the greatest possible solemnity, in order to arouse devotion. So that this would not be considered a type of novelty, he petitioned for and obtained permission from the Supreme Pontiff.

He had a manger prepared,
hay carried in and an ox and an ass led to the spot.
The brethren are summoned,
the people arrive,
the forest amplifies with their cries,
and that venerable night is rendered
brilliant and solemn
by a multitide of bright lights
and by resonant and harmonious hymns of praise.
The man of God stands before the manger,
filled with piety,
bathed in tears, and overcome with joy.
A solemn Mass is celebrated over the manger,
with Francis, a levite of Christ, chanting the holy Gospel.
Then he preaches to the people standing around him
about the birth of the poor King,
whom, whenever he means to call him,
he called in his tender love,
the Babe from Bethlehem.
A certain virtuous and truthful knight,
Sir John of Greccio,
who had abandoned worldly military activity out of
love of Christ
and had become an intimate friend of the man of God,
claimed that he saw a beautiful little child asleep in that manger
whom the blessed father Francis embraced in both of his arms
and seemed to wake it from sleep.
Not only does the holiness of the witness
make credible
the vision of the devout knight,
but also the truth it expresses
proves its validity
and the subsequent miracles confirm it.
For Francis's example,
when considered by the world,

is capable of arousing
the hearts of those who are sluggish in the faith of Christ.
The hay from the crib
was kept by the people
and miraculously cured sick animals
and drove away different kinds of pestilence.
Thus God glorified his servant in every way
and demonstrated the efficacy of his holy prayer
by the evident signs of wonderful miracles.

REFRAIN: CM 1

INTERCESSIONS (Responses in bold type)

Jesus Christ is the joy and happiness of all who look forward
to his coming. Let us call upon him.
Come, Lord, and do not delay!

In joy, we wait for your coming.
Come, Lord Jesus.

Before time began, you shared life with God, Most High.
Come now and save us.

You created the world and all who live in it.
Come to redeem the work of your hands.

You did not hesitate to become a human being like us, subject
to death.
Come to free us from the power of death.

You came to give us life to the full.
Come and give us your unending life.

You desire all people to live in love in your kingdom.
**Come and bring together those who long to see you face
to face.**

EUCHARIST

OPENING PROCLAMATION

Woman:
Francis observed the birthday of the child Jesus with inexpressible eagerness over all other feasts, saying:

Man:
It is the feast of feasts, on which God, having become a tiny infant, clung to human breasts.

Woman:
He kissed pictures of those infant members with thoughts filled with yearning, and his compassion for the Child flooded his heart and made him stammer words of sweetness after the manner of infants.

His name was like honey and the honeycomb in Francis' mouth. When the question rose about eating meat that day, since that Christmas Day was a Friday, he replied, saying to Brother Morico:

Man:
You sin, Brother, calling the day on which the Child was born to us a day of fast. It is my wish that even the walls should eat meat on such a day, and if they cannot, they should be smeared with meat on the outside.

Woman:
On this day, Francis wanted the poor and the hungry to be filled by the rich, and more than the usual amount of grain and hay given to the oxen and asses.

Man:
If I could speak to the emperor, I would ask that a general law be made that all who can should scatter corn and grain along the roads so that the birds might have an abundance of food on the day of such great solemnity, especially our sisters the larks (2C 199–200).

READING I: CM 1 "A Child Is Born"

OR

FIRST READING: ISAIAH 9:2–7

A reading from the book of the prophet Isaiah

The people who walked in darkness have seen a great light; those who lived in a land of deep darkness—on them light has shined. You have multiplied the nation, you have increased its joy; they rejoice before you as with joy at the harvest, as people exult when dividing plunder. For the yoke of their burden, and the bar across their shoulders, the rod of their oppressor, you have broken as on the day of Midian. For all the boots of the tramping warriors and all the garments rolled in blood shall be burned as fuel for the fire. For a child has been born for us, a son given to us; authority rests upon his shoulders; and he is named Wonderful Counselor, Mighty God, Everlasting Father, Prince of Peace. His authority shall grow continually, and there shall be endless peace for the throne of David and his kingdom. He will establish and uphold it with justice and with righteousness from this time onward and forevermore. The zeal of the LORD of hosts will do this. **The word of the Lord.**

READING II: THOMAS OF CELANO, FIRST LIFE 84–86. OR: ST. BONAVENTURE, MAJOR LEGEND X:7

ALLELUIA: Good News and great joy to all the world; today is born our Savior, Christ the Lord.

GOSPEL: LUKE 2:1–14
A reading from the holy Gospel according to Luke

In those days a decree went out from Emperor Augustus that all the world should be registered. This was the first registration and was taken while Quirinius was governor of Syria. All went to their own towns to be registered. Joseph also went from the town of Nazareth in Galilee to Judea, to the city of David called Bethlehem, because he was descended from the house and family of David. He went to be registered with Mary, to whom he was engaged and who was expecting a child. While they were there, the time came for her to deliver her child. And she gave birth to her firstborn son and wrapped him in bands of cloth, and laid him in a manger, because there was no place for them in the inn. In that region there were shepherds living in the fields, keeping watch over their flock by night. Then an angel of the Lord stood before them, and the glory of the Lord shone around them, and they were terrified. But the angel said to them, "Do not be afraid; for see—I am bringing you good news of great joy for all the people: to you is born this day in the city of David a Savior, who is the Messiah, the Lord. This will be a sign for you: you will find a child wrapped in bands of cloth and lying in a manger." And suddenly there was with the angel a multitude of the heavenly host, praising God and saying, "Glory to God in the highest heaven, and on earth peace among those whom he favors!" **The Gospel of the Lord.**

THE CRADLE OF GRECCIO

We live in God

as in a house

with a roof of stars

and a bed of grass

and we

every

thing are

his dreams

and like God limited

only by our

dreams

but for our lust

to conjure

horror though

who has looked

upon helplessness

has looked upon God

imaged best

in a baby.

William Hart McNichols, S.J., S.F.O.
Used with permission.

RIETI
VALLEY:
LA FORESTA

FRANCISCAN PILGRIMAGE PROGRAMS

RIETI VALLEY: LA FORESTA

EVENTS

La Foresta was the scene of an event in Francis' latter days when he was already a sick man, half blind. Reluctantly, on the advice of Cardinal Hugolino, his friend and the protector of his Order, and of Brother Elias, then its General Minister, he set out from the Porziuncola for Rieti. The Papal Court was residing there and Francis sought counsel from Tebald the Saracen, the papal surgeon.

The priest of San Fabiano (La Foresta) offered Francis hospitality. The people discovered where Francis was staying, came out to visit with him, and helped themselves to the grapes of the priest's vineyard.

SPIRITUALITY

This sanctuary was a humble hermitage and one of the remote places sought out by Francis for solitude. Its remoteness seems to beckon the pilgrim to come apart from the frenetic and frenzied activities of life to sit at the feet of God in the silence of solitude.

In Luke 8:18 we read: "... for to those who have, more will be given; and from those who do not have, even what they seem to have will be taken away." Carroll Stuhlmueller wrote: "This intriguing remark can be paraphrased: the one who has time to pray and reflect will be given more; the one who has not taken the time to turn to God and friend for advice will lose even the little wisdom that he or she possesses." *(Biblical Meditations* [Ramsey, N.J.: Paulist Press, 1984], 51). Francis sought this time for himself.

This same quote from Luke could be applied to the episode of the pillaged grapes. The priest grumbled about the people eating up most of his harvest. Francis stretches the hospitality and the generosity of the priest by a trust in God that never fails.

REFLECTION

Do I have a hermitage or place of solitude to which I can withdraw to slow down and change the frenetic pace of my life for a while?

How do I use the gifts God has given me? Do I look at them as too meager and try to hoard? Do I trustingly step forth in a spirit of generosity, to share those gifts with others, watching them multiply?

LA FORESTA

HISTORICAL NOTES

The sanctuary of La Foresta—Santa Maria della Foresta, originally San Fabiano — is not more than three miles from the city of Rieti. To reach it one leaves Rieti by the Porta Conca, outside the railway station.

La Foresta itself is a very modest, charming building with a towered church. It is surrounded by hills in a delightful setting: woods (*bosco*), pastures and cypresses.

Francis had recently received the stigmata on Mount La Verna. At that time he was, as Thomas of Celano records, "oppressed with various sicknesses more grievous than before." In the summer of 1225, in obedience to Hugolino, he consented to set out for Rieti with Brother Masseo and the companions who were to be his nurses to the end. He traveled through Terni and along the road following the course of the Velino River, finally arriving in the Rieti Valley. News of the saint's arrival preceded him, and to escape the multitude, he detoured some three miles before reaching the city of Rieti and asked hospitality of the poor priest of San Fabiano at La Foresta. This would become the setting for the miracle of the grapes.

The friars eventually took possession of San Fabiano and rededicated it in honor of Our Lady, calling it Santa Maria della Foresta. It was so consecrated in 1231 by Pope Gregory IX, the former Cardinal Hugolino. The *cisterna*, or vat of the miracle, is still pointed out there.

FRANCISCAN READINGS

ASSISI COMPILATION 67

How Francis provides for an abundant harvest

Because of the disease of his eyes, blessed Francis at that time was staying in the church of San Fabiano near the same city, where there was a poor secular priest. At that time the Lord Pope Honorius and other cardinals were in the same city. Many of the cardinals and other great clerics, because of the reverence and devotion they had for the holy father, used to visit him almost every day.

That church had a small vineyard next to the house where blessed Francis was staying. There was one door to the house through which nearly all those who visited him passed into the vineyard, especially because the grapes were ripe at that time, and the place was pleasant for resting.

And it came about that for that reason almost the entire vineyard was ruined. For some picked the grapes and ate them there, while others picked them and carried them off, and still others trampled them underfoot.

The priest began to be offended and upset. "I lost my vintage for this year!" he said. "Even though it's small, I got enough wine from it to take care of my needs!"

When blessed Francis heard of this, he had him called and said to him: "Do not be disturbed or offended any longer. We can't do anything about it. But trust in the Lord, because for me, His little servant, He can restore your loss. But, tell me, how many measures of wine did you get when your vineyard was at its best?"

"Thirteen measures, father," the priest responded.

"Don't be sad over this any more," blessed Francis told him, "and don't say anything offensive to anyone because of it, or argue with anyone about it. Trust the Lord and my words, and if you get less than twenty measures of wine, I will make it up to you."

The priest calmed down and kept quiet. And it happened by divine dispensation that he obtained twenty measures and no less, just as blessed Francis had told him. Those who heard about it, as well as the priest himself, were amazed. They considered it a great miracle due to the merits of blessed Francis, especially because not only was it devastated, but even if it had been full of grapes and no one had taken any, it still seemed impossible to the priest and the others to get twenty measures of wine from it.

We who were with him bear witness that whenever he used to say: "This is the way it is ... or this is the way it will be ...", it always happened as he said. We have seen many of these fulfilled not only while he was alive but also after his death.

PRAYER SERVICE

READING: ASSISI COMPILATION 67

Leader:
Based on the story we have just heard, you are asked to think of a gift God has given you, something for which you can claim

ownership, and indicate how you are able to share your gift with others just as the priest shared his grapes.

SHARED REFLECTION

After someone shares this goodness of God, the grapes and/or wine is passed to that person who partakes of some.

EUCHARIST

READING: JOEL 2:21–24, 26–27

A reading from the prophet Joel

Do not fear, O soil; be glad and rejoice, for the LORD has done great things! Do not fear, you animals of the field, for the pastures of the wilderness are green; the tree bears its fruit, the fig tree and vine give their full yield. O children of Zion, be glad and rejoice in the LORD your God; for he has given the early rain for your vindication, he has poured down for you abundant rain, the early and the later rain, as before. The threshing floors shall be full of grain, the vats shall overflow with wine and oil.

You shall eat in plenty and be satisfied, and praise the name of the LORD your God, who has dealt wondrously with you. And my people shall never again be put to shame. You shall know that I am in the midst of Israel, and that I, the LORD, am your God and there is no other. And my people shall never again be put to shame. **The word of the Lord.**

RESPONSE: The earth has yielded its fruit, the Lord our God has blessed us.

PSALM 67

May God be gracious to us and bless us
and make his face to shine upon us,
that your way may be known upon earth,
your saving power among all nations. **R.**

Let the nations be glad and sing for joy,
for you judge the peoples with equity
and guide the nations upon earth. **R**.

The earth has yielded its increase;
God, our God, has blessed us.
May God continue to bless us;
let all the ends of the earth revere him. **R**.

ALLELUIA: Those who sow in tears shall reap with shouts of joy.

GOSPEL: LUKE 12:15–21

A reading from the holy Gospel according to Luke

And Jesus said to them, "Take care! Be on your guard against all kinds of greed; for one's life does not consist in the abundance of possessions." Then he told them a parable: "The land of a rich man produced abundantly. And he thought to himself, 'What should I do, for I have no place to store my crops?' Then he said, 'I will do this: I will pull down my barns and build larger ones, and there I will store all my grain and my goods. And I will say to my soul, 'Soul, you have ample goods laid up for many years; relax, eat, drink, be merry.' But God said to him, 'You fool! This very night your life is being demanded of you. And the things you have prepared, whose will they be?' So it is with those who store up treasures for themselves but are not rich toward God." **The Gospel of the Lord.**

ASSISI: HOMECOMING

FRANCISCAN PILGRIMAGE PROGRAMS

ASSISI: HOMECOMING

EVENTS
The births, lives, and deaths of Francis and Clare occurred in Assisi.

SPIRITUALITY
... Assisi is (in the words of about fifty writers):
a city on a hill that cannot be hidden ... a holy city ... the unique town ... the unchanged town ... one of the holy cities of our Western world ... one of the most sacred cities on earth ... the mystical city par excellence ... an enchanted city ... one of the sacred refuges where art and prayer unite ... the town at whose feet everything base dies ... a temple ... a house of prayer ... a house of God ... a holy reliquary ... a shrine ... a citadel of the spirit ... a beacon ... a lighthouse.

A city of light ... a city of silence and eternity ... a place of and at peace ... a town of peace and love ... a nest of peace ... a haven of peace suspended between heaven and earth ... a sabbath-day town ... an asylum of silence ... an oasis.

A vast convent ... a heavenly cloister ... a holy hive ... a kind of monastery ... a lost paradise ... a particle of paradise ... the gate to heaven ... the way that leads to heaven ... the entrance hall of eternity.

A garden land ... a garden of peace and bliss ... the most beautiful garden in all the world ... the chosen home of dreams and serenity.

A fountain of grace ... a cascade of blessings ... a fountain of life and compassion ... a center for inner renewal and healing ... a heavenly pharmacy ... a little city of the soul ... one of the most glorious cities of the world of the spirit ... a place on earth where the Kingdom of God has resided ... one of the capitals of the spiritual life ... the finest capital in the world—the capital of love.

Assisi is a heart ... an affair of the heart. ...

One speaks to the heart. In Assisi one feels close to the heart of Christ.

REFLECTION
Assisi has been called the New Jerusalem. What does this say?

Sit at a bar, a corner on a street, a little piazza, and let your spirit soar, your imagination run wild. Picture Francis and Clare. Look at the faces of Assisians to discover the faces of Francis and Clare.

WELCOME TO ASSISI

KEY CEREMONY

INTRODUCTION

As we await the distribution of keys, let us acknowledge God's special presence here through Francis and Clare.

READING: REVELATION 3:7-8, 10, 12

A reading from the book of Revelation

These are the words of the holy one, the true one, who has the key of David, who opens and no one will shut, who shuts and no one opens: "I know your works. Look, I have set before you an open door, which no one is able to shut. I know that you have but little power, and yet you have kept my word and have not denied my name.

Because you have kept my word of patient endurance, I will keep you from the hour of trial that is coming on the whole world to test the inhabitants of the earth.

If you conquer, I will make you a pillar in the temple of my God; you will never go out of it. I will write on you the name of my God, and the name of the city of my God, the new Jerusalem that comes down from my God out of heaven, and my own new name." **The word of the Lord.**

REFLECTION

Our prayer for you is that your pilgrimage stay in Assisi will set your hearts burning. To symbolize our wish for you, we give you the key to your room. Yes, it will be used for rest and refreshment, for personal prayer and riposo, but *"rest"* has been defined as *"purposeful contemplation."* And so we hope that each time you use this key to open your door, it may be a reminder of the contemplative stance to which we are called, a stance that invites us to reflect on each event of life and draw from it graces that the mystical experience of the place holds for us — this place—Assisi!

May your room provide *refreshment* then and *true rest* as you contemplate what God is doing in you.

ASSISI: BRIEF HISTORY

"The Assisium of the Romans, and Ascesi in the Middle Ages, is an ancient Umbrian city which, after the period of Etruscan domination, passed into the hands of the Romans about 339 B.C.E. Traces of the Roman occupation are everywhere apparent; there are remains of a theatre, baths, temple, etc. St. Rufino preached the Gospel here and was martyred in 238. In the early Middle Ages, it was captured by Totila, later on by Charlemagne, and was subjected thereafterwards to the dukes of Spoleto; it regained its independence in 1184 when it became a 'comune.' St. Francis was born here in 1181 and St. Clare in 1194. During the two following centuries it was constantly at war with Perugia until at length it became a part of the States of the Church. It was occupied by the French under Napoleon and on the fall of the Empire once again became subject to the Papal States until September 1860, when it was annexed with the rest of Umbria to the Kingdom of Italy."

Peter Frederick Anson, *The Pilgrim's Guide to Franciscan Italy* [London: Sands and Co., 1927], 6; cf. Michael Adams, *Umbria* [London: Faber and Faber, 1964].

ASSISI: ITS STREETS AND PIAZZAS

Historians and archaeologists believe that Assisi was always a sacred city. It was in fact a sanctuary town, meaning it had a complex of temples to various gods. The forum, or government center, was located near the present cathedral of San Rufino. The present main square was not the forum, but rather a market, a gathering place, and the center of worship and sacrifice.

The most prominent feature of the square was the Roman temple. But what has been called the temple of Minerva (goddess of wisdom) for several centuries is now being seriously questioned. Historians and archaeologists now believe that the temple was dedicated to the twin Roman gods Castor and Pollux. The claim of Assisi being dedicated to Minerva only came about in the sixteenth century when a broken statue (with the whole upper half missing) was unearthed under the piazza. There were really only three major goddesses that it could have been. The team settled on Minerva because she is shown seated (the symbol of her moral teaching authority).

Recent scholarship reasons that the abundance of water in such a small town as Assisi actually offers the primal suspicion that the temple and the town were dedicated more so to Castor and Pollux than Minerva. These twin Roman gods healed with the aid of water. Castor and Pollux were always honored with two temples (sometimes called "twin temples," although the word "twin" here only meant there were two temples that were associated with the same deity, not that they were exactly alike). In Assisi the large six-pillared temple was complemented by another small temple in front of it (indicated by markings in the piazza pavement). This small temple more than likely had statues of Castor and Pollux standing beside a horse, the symbol of their expertise as horse tamers and warriors. The horse was also the symbol of strength and courage, appropriate as a symbol for the bond of these brothers who became role models for the Roman army. Also, another confirming piece of evidence of Assisi being dedicated to Castor and Pollux was the "Assisi gate" of Perugia. It was the custom in ancient times to name a city gate for the city in whose direction it faced. Thus, the Assisi gate (also called the gate of the "Rising Sun," since it faced east, and which still exists), would always display the gods of the city it faced somewhere on its structure. The Perugian Assisi gate has Castor and Pollux carved onto it, not Minerva.

Lives of Castor and Pollux

In both Greek and Roman mythology, these were the twin sons of Leda, wife of the Spartan king Tyndareus. Their sister was the beautiful and fabled Helen of Troy. Their father was Zeus, father of the gods. Yet, although these boys were twins, only Pollux was immortal. Castor (from which we get *castrate,* meaning "to sever manhood") was somehow the mortal son of Tyndareus. Pollux was conceived when Zeus appeared to Leda in the form of a swan.

The brothers were inseparable in all things. They loved each other and fought valiantly in every great adventure in which they found themselves. One day Castor was slain by a farmer in a dispute about oxen. Pollux was inconsolable. He went to his father, Zeus, and asked for either death for himself or immortality for his brother. Zeus said that Pollux could share his own immortality with his brother Castor. Half of the twin's eternity would be spent in the underworld of death, and half would be spent alive with the gods on Mount Olympus. The twin gods are the patrons of sailors, soldiers, brotherly love, and sacrifice unto death. They are the constellation Gemini.

Early Christian Assisi

As the ancient Romans honored the idea of brotherhood and sacrifice unto death, so the early Christians began to replace the twin myths with the Christian physician twins of Cosmas and Damian. In Assisi this is how the church of San Damiano became linked with the idea of fraternity and healing. The original name of the church honored both brothers—Cosmas and Damian—but the name was later shortened.

Medieval Assisi and the Rise of the Comune

Feudalism really ended with the development of trade. The rise of a middle class came about because of the desire for the buying and selling of goods. A "middle class" demanded the right to improve their lives and the right to govern themselves. In 1198–1202 a great civil war broke out in Assisi with the middle class opposing the noble class. It was a period of great violence in which the nobles were murdered or exiled to Perugia. St. Clare's family was among these. The people began tearing apart the castle, which was the symbol of the dominance of the nobility, those with inherited landed power. It is important to see the symbolism in the nobles' castle being torn apart and transformed into stones that built up the curtain wall of the whole city. After the fighting, the whole city was a citadel of common people. It was at this time that the piazza became the center of government and social life. Before this, social life and government were centered in the castle and its great hall, far removed from the common folk. The piazza was called *comune* ("the square of the common people"). Soon a civic tower was built with a mechanical clock on its face. This was the *torre del popolo* ("tower of the people"). Before this time the nobles showed their power by building large towers. But all of those were torn down during the civil war, and then there was only one tower in the town. That tower of power and authority was the "people's tower." The clock at the top and the city's measurements at the bottom showed that even time and trade belonged to the common people and no longer to a few privileged nobles.

The architecture of the piazza itself bespeaks a sacred space for the common folk. The piazza is encircled like a cloister. There are many porticos also reminiscent of a cloister. The fountain is raised on three steps, which has always been the symbol of the fountain of life in the center of a monastery garden. The fountain is also typically eight-sided, representing baptism. Thus the whole vision of the piazza cries out that it is a democratic and sacred space. At the west end of the piazza we notice an outdoor portico known as the "temple of the people." This is where outdoor liturgy could be celebrated. This portico has the same dimensions as the earlier Roman temple dedicated to Castor and Pollux (originally located in the center of the piazza).

Brotherhood
It is important to understand the piazza as a sacred place, reclaiming a sense of brotherhood. Before the uprising of the common people, the Middle Ages were known as anything but fraternal. It was a time when brother fought against brother because of inheritance rights. Noble and royal brothers hated each other and caused great division in society because of their lust for titles, land, and power. Francis turned all of the fratricide around, for he and his *comune* believed that brother must love brother and work for the common good. The lives and examples of Castor and Pollux, and Cosmas and Damian, two sets of twins, lead the way to appreciating the right ordering of brotherhood. They were examples of those who were

willing to die for each other. This was the root and heart of Roman and Christian Assisi. As the noted author Arnaldo Fortini always claimed, Francis and Clare were formed by their town as much as they tried to reform it.

OTHER CHURCHES IN ASSISI

San Pietro: an ancient site connected with the Benedictines at the time of Francis and Clare. Some frescoes date to the 14th and 15th centuries. There are also numerous tombs of ancient Assisi families.

Santo Stefano: a parish church from as early as 1166. It is constructed of stone from Monte Subasio. The presbytery is still covered by the original stone vault. According to a local holy tradition, the bells of the small bell tower tolled spontaneously at the death of St. Francis.

San Giacomo Murorupto: located near the ruins of the city walls. It was built first in 1088 to satisfy a penance of three hundred years imposed upon a noble of Assisi. In 1256, three years after the death of St. Clare, it was donated to the Poor Ladies. The abbess at the time, Sister Benedetta, exchanged it with the canons of the cathedral of San Rufino for the church of San Giorgio, where the remains of Clare were entombed.

San Gregorio: across the street from the house of Bernard of Quintavalle. It dates from the late 13th century. This church was the home of the oldest confraternity in Assisi.

FRANCISCAN READINGS

THE LEGEND OF THREE COMPANIONS 7–8

Francis: king of youth; God's visit to Francis

A few days after he returned to Assisi, one evening his friends chose him to be in charge so that, according to his whim, he would pay their expenses. He made arrangements for a sumptuous banquet, as he had done so often in the past.

When they left the house bloated, his friends walked ahead of him, singing throughout the city. Holding in his hand the scepter of his office as their leader, he fell slightly behind them. He was not singing, but was deeply preoccupied. Suddenly he was visited by the Lord who filled his heart with so much tenderness that he was unable to speak or move. He could only feel and hear this marvelous tenderness; it left him so estranged from any sensation that, as he himself said later, even if he had been completely cut to pieces, he would not have been able to move.

When his companions glanced back and saw him so removed from them, they went back surprised at seeing him already *changed into another man*. They asked him: "What were you thinking about that you did not follow us? Were you perhaps thinking about taking a wife?"

He answered in an unequivocal voice: "You are right! I was thinking about taking a wife more noble, wealthier, and more beautiful than you have ever seen." *They laughed at him*. For he said this not of his own accord, but because he was inspired by God. In fact, the bride was the true religion that he later embraced, a bride more noble, richer and more beautiful because of her poverty.

From that very hour he began to consider himself of little value and to despise those things which he had previously held in love. Since he was not entirely detached from worldly vanities, this change was not yet perfect. He retired for a short time from the tumult and business of the world and was anxious to keep Jesus Christ in his inmost self, and, *after selling all he had*, he desired to buy *the pearl*, concealing it from the eyes of mockers.

THE LEGEND OF THREE COMPANIONS 21

Begging for stones on Assisi's streets

Therefore, Francis, the servant of God, stripped of all that is of the world, is free for divine justice and, despising his own life, he gives himself to divine service in every way he can.

Returning to the church of San Damiano, joyful and eager, he made a hermit's habit for himself, and comforted the priest of that church with the same words with which the bishop had comforted him.

Then, getting up and going back to the city, he began to praise the Lord throughout the piazzas and neighborhoods, like one inebriated with the Spirit. When he finished praising the Lord in this way, he turned to obtaining stones for the repair of the church.

... Many ridiculed him thinking he was mad, while others, prompted by piety, were moved to tears seeing how quickly he had come from such pleasure and worldy vanity to such an intoxication of divine love. Disregarding their scorn, he thanked God with burning enthusiasm.

OTHER READINGS

LMj I:1–2—Francis' life in the world
1C 1–2—Francis' wanton youth
L3C 24—Francis begging for oil on Assisi's streets
L3C 26—Francis: messenger of peace
2C 15; L3C 27–29—Bernard giving away his possessions
1C 3–22—Francis' early years
L3C 1–24—Francis' early years

PRAYER: COMING HOME

REFRAIN: G 4 "City of God", verse 1

READING I: FROM *THE LAND OF ST. FRANCIS OF ASSISI*

From the church of St. Mary-of-the-Angels a winding road leads up through olive trees to Assisi, which lies spread out before us in all its majestic glory. Seen thus from below, it looks a formidable place, a war-like town, an impregnable fortress, built on a buttress of Monte Subasio.

And is it not still a citadel, one of the most glorious of the spiritual world? Merely to look at Assisi is to be moved by one of those profound experiences which two or three times in life, shake us to the depths of our inmost being — when before some great picture we are suddenly confronted with Pure Beauty, when between the lines of some book we read the very laws of life, when from a height we suddenly look out ... on a panorama so marvellous and so compelling that we are forced to fall on our knees.

How can words express the wonderful impression felt by every Christian soul, however little religious, when first faced by this vision of the land of St. Francis [and St. Clare]. Places where great men [and women] lived always move us and serve, in some curious way, to mould our feelings. And landscape appeals most of all in this way, because it does not change and we can say to ourselves—"That is the horizon [they] looked out on, these are the hills and plains, unchanged through the centuries, in which [their] eyes delighted." And so at Assisi—Nature stirs us more than convent or churches. These trees, reddened by the summer sun, these golden elms, these ripening meadows—all will be clothed in fresh green again and again, long after these great walls have crumbled away.

Gabriel Faure, *The Land of St. Francis of Assisi,* [London: The Medici Society Limited, 1924], 71–72.

RESPONSE: G 4, verse 2

READING II: "ASSISI"

I know a city on a hill, a mountain's castled crown,
Where, like the stars the angels tread, the streets go up and down,
A city very small and kind and full of strange renown.

It stands upon an eastern height and looks towards the West.
Far off, it sees Perugia, its ancient foe, at rest;
And all the birds of Italy are gathered to its breast.

So small, so kind, but smaller far in the dim gulf below,
This world of [ours] and all the tides that toss [us] to and fro,
While on its crag that city stands, crowned with the sunset glow.

Still, like a lean dark cypress there, against the clouds on high,
Brother of sun and moon and star, he towers into the sky,
As long ago, with arms up-stretched, while all things else went by.

Stone of his own immortal hill has made those ramparts bright,
The warm white stone that glows at dusk with a soft unearthly light,
And delicate tones of heaven's own rose while the plains are
lost in night.

They told me of the lamp-lit tomb where dust in dust was laid,
Of painted wings from Paradise that on their walls decayed;
But not of this, this flower of light, that fades, and cannot fade.

They did not tell me how it chanced that the small bright streets
were bare,
And hushed for love, as love went up, by cloister and winding stair,
Till a little lamplit window shone like an altar lit for prayer.

Oh bravely, bravely flash the swords beneath St. Peter's dome.
Proudly the silver trumpets ring across the world from Rome;

But this was on a higher hill, and a little nearer home.

A little nearer home that night, when skies had ceased to glow;
And the great plain of Umbria was dark as death below,
Assisi grew into the light, as flowers and children grow.

Alfred Noyes, in *St. Francis and the Poet,* ed. Elizabeth Patterson [New York: The Devin-Adair Co., 1956], 47–49.

RESPONSE: G 4, verse 3

READING III: WELCOME TO ASSISI

It may be that this is your first visit to Assisi. Today may be a dream fulfilled, one you have been cherishing for many a long year. Now you want to see it, all of it, at last, and are expecting a lot from a visit to lovely Assisi. You may have known persons who have come back time after time, who want to be refreshed once more with that sweet comfort and consolation they were blessed with when they visited here the first time. The opportunity is now yours.

Assisi has its rare fascination. It is endowed with a world of artistic works. The picturesque old city is set in an enchanting landscape. It is a center of most unusual beauty of every sort, but that same beauty could be a distraction from an awareness of the mysterious secret lying behind so much splendor of color and golden sunlight. There are visitors who come and contemplate the sun setting gloriously over the Spoleto valley but miss the experience of something still more grandiose lying behind the magnificent spectacle. And there are others who arrived at Assisi armed with lists of famous artists' names, and walked through the galleries of a museum. They did not know how to stop being just tourists. It is not likely that they will listen to the voice of Assisi speaking to them.

Assisi is charged with the custody of St. Francis' and St. Clare's spirit which pervade the very air, and become almost tangible in its sanctuaries. To discover and make one's own that secret is certainly a worthy aspiration on the part of anyone coming to the Seraphic city.

Adapted from S. Majarelli, O.F.M., *Assisi: Franciscan Itinerary* [Assisi: Porziuncola Press, 1971], 5–6.

RESPONSE: G 4, verse 4

READING IV: "ASSISI DAWN"

> We awoke to a golden dawn.
> The quiet of beautiful Assisi lay around us,
> Transforming everything.
> We stood at the window and marveled
> At the light and shadows playing
> Across the Umbrian Plains below,
> With Perugia in the distance, high on its hill.
> A city of Ancient Days!
>
> Church bells tolled our spirits awake
> And birds carolled their songs to our ears.
> The city began to stir.
> Francis, of this Italian hillside village,
> Once strode through its streets,
> And sang his songs,
> Preached to the birds,
> Became its messenger of gladness!
>
> We felt his spirit filling us
> With the wonder of his life,
> And we stepped forth
> To the wonder of our own!
> The glorious golden glow of dawn
> Trims the whole world
> With halos!

Francis and Helen Line, *Man with a Song* [Garden City, NY: Image Books, 1979; reprint, Chicago: Franciscan Herald Press, 1979], 102.

CLOSING PRAYER

O holy city of Assisi, you are renowned throughout the world for the one fact of having been the birthplace of the "Poverello," of your Saint, all celestial in his ardor. May you comprehend this privilege and manifest to the people your faithfulness to the Christian tradition which for you, too, is a cause of true and everlasting honor. Amen.

Blessed Pope John XXIII, on pilgrimage to the Tomb of St. Francis. October 4, 1962.

EUCHARIST

HOMECOMING

READING: REVELATION 21: 9–14, 16, 18, 22–27

A reading from the book of Revelation

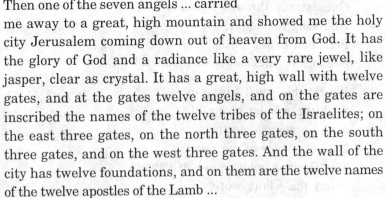

Then one of the seven angels ... carried me away to a great, high mountain and showed me the holy city Jerusalem coming down out of heaven from God. It has the glory of God and a radiance like a very rare jewel, like jasper, clear as crystal. It has a great, high wall with twelve gates, and at the gates twelve angels, and on the gates are inscribed the names of the twelve tribes of the Israelites; on the east three gates, on the north three gates, on the south three gates, and on the west three gates. And the wall of the city has twelve foundations, and on them are the twelve names of the twelve apostles of the Lamb ...

The city lies foursquare, its length the same as its width. ... The wall is built of jasper, while the city is pure gold, clear as glass ...

I saw no temple in the city, for its temple is the Lord God the Almighty and the Lamb. And the city has no need of sun or moon to shine on it, for the glory of God is its light, and its lamp is the Lamb. The nations will walk by its light, and the kings of the earth will bring their glory into it. Its gates will never be shut by day—there will be no night there. People will bring into it the glory and the honor of the nations. But nothing unclean will enter it, nor anyone who practices abomination or falsehood, but only those who are written in the Lamb's book of life. **The word of the Lord.**

RESPONSE: O God, you are my portion and my cup.

PSALM 16

Protect me, O God, for in you I take refuge.
I say to the LORD, "You are my Lord;
I have no good apart from you."
The LORD is my chosen portion and my cup;
you hold my lot. **R.**

The boundary lines have fallen for me in pleasant places;
I have a goodly heritage.
I bless the LORD who gives me counsel;
in the night also my heart instructs me. **R.**

I keep the LORD always before me;
because he is at my right hand,
I shall not be moved.
Therefore my heart is glad, and my soul rejoices;
my body also rests secure. **R.**

For you do not give me up to Sheol,
or let your faithful one see the Pit.
You show me the path of life.
In your presence there is fullness of joy;
in your right hand are pleasures forevermore. **R.**

ALLELUIA: I have yearned to gather you under my wings.

GOSPEL: LUKE 19:1–10

A reading from the holy Gospel according to Luke

[Jesus] entered Jericho and was passing through it. A man was there named Zacchaeus; he was a chief tax collector and was rich. He was trying to see who Jesus was, but on account of the crowd he could not, because he was short in stature. So he ran ahead and climbed a sycamore tree to see him, because he was going to pass that way. When Jesus came to the place, he looked up and said to him, "Zacchaeus, hurry and come down; for I must stay at your house today." So he hurried down and was happy to welcome him. All who saw it began to grumble and said, "He has gone to be the guest of one who is a sinner." Zacchaeus stood there and said to the Lord, "Look, half of my possessions, Lord, I will give to the poor; and if I have defrauded anyone of anything, I will pay back four times as much." Then Jesus said to him, "Today salvation has come to this house, because he too is a son of Abraham. For the Son of Man came to seek out and to save the lost." **The Gospel of the Lord.**

ASSISI: CHIESA NUOVA

FRANCISCAN PILGRIMAGE PROGRAMS

ASSISI: CHIESA NUOVA

EVENTS
This was Francis' family home, where Francis spent his first twenty-five years; in this place he developed a specific relationship with his father and mother.

Francis left home to go to war against Perugia. He dreamt of military victory and of becoming a magnificent knight.

In 1206 Pietro Bernardone imprisoned Francis for selling his father's goods. Lady Pica, his mother, set him free.

His father's shop (at street level) was where Francis encountered a beggar.

SPIRITUALITY
The merchant class was on the rise. In a real sense Francis' family background directed him to mercantile spirituality: *"Do ut des,"* that is, "I give so that you may give in return." Money was given to the poor so that God's favor may be given to the donor.

We understand more than ever the importance of family relationships in the development of one's person and life of faith. Francis was deeply influenced by his relationship with his father and mother.

Reconciliation was a critical element in Francis' spirituality. Although there is no proof of such an event, one wonders about the possibility of reconciliation between Francis and his father, Pietro.

REFLECTION
Some claim that Francis was an adult child of an abusive father. Are there elements in our family history that are in need of reconciliation? Can we be motivated to consider it, if possible?

How would you describe Francis' youth? Using your imagination, try to put Francis' youthful parties and antics in the Assisi setting (cf. 1C 1; 2C 3).

What kind of relationship existed between Francis and his father? His mother? Why did Francis hide from them?

Read carefully *The Legend of Three Companions* 4–6. Note the process of Francis' conversion: asleep—half asleep—awake.

CHIESA NUOVA

HISTORICAL NOTES

There are three sites in Assisi that claim to be the birthplace and/or family home of St. Francis.

Chiesa Nuova: In 1615, King Philip III of Spain offered the money necessary for the friars of the Observant tradition to purchase the property on which stands the present church. This site was believed to have been the family home and cloth shop. The church was completed in 1619. The floor plan is that of a Greek cross with an octagonal center.

Immediately to the left of the entrance is a small opening in the central pilaster. This niche is considered to be either an actual cellar where Francis' father may have imprisoned his son in a moment of anger or merely a later dramatic representation of that event. The main altar and sanctuary are said to have been constructed on the site of St. Francis' bedchamber.

Exiting by a door to the left of the sanctuary, you will descend a flight of steps. On your right you will see an old wooden door on the second story. This is said to have been the entrance to the family home. Continuing to descend, you will enter into a small room said to have been the family's fabric shop.

San Francesco Piccolino: The "little Francis" is the name given to a little stable *(stalletta)* a few steps away from Chiesa Nuova. This room is said to have been the place in which Lady Pica gave birth to her son.

The Assisi archives document that this room and the building surrounding it did in fact belong to St. Francis' nephew Piccardo. A Secular Franciscan who remained celibate his whole life, Piccardo was also the lay procurator of the Basilica of St. Francis for thirty years. In 1282, the first centenary of the birth of St. Francis (as the inscription reads over the doorway), this stable was dedicated as a chapel commemorating Francis' birth. This chapel has become a place where local people will pray for the needs of children and for a healthy pregnancy of a family member or friend. The Conventual Franciscans have charge of San Francesco Piccolino.

Bartholomew of Pisa, who wrote the *Liber Conformitatum* at the end of the 15th century, knew nothing of this story. On the other hand, Benozzo Gozzoli, in the year 1452, painted the birth in the stable upon the walls of the church of St. Francis in Montefalco; and Sedulius, whose *Historia Seraphica* appeared in Antwerp in the year 1613, says that he saw the stable in Assisi converted into a chapel.

Via San Paolo: The noted author Arnaldo Fortini documents that the Bernardone family home stood between the churches of San Nicolo and San Paolo. Among the witnesses attesting to this, there is a certain Friar Nicholas of Assisi. He was a prominent notary during Francis' day, who stated that his home joined that of Francis' family. His house was next to San Nicolo.

Two years after Francis' death, the central piazza was enlarged. Several houses were destroyed in the process. Houses that now faced the piazza were taxed to pay for the civic improvements. Francis' nephews are documented as having paid these taxes. It has therefore been presumed that the location of Francis' nephews' home was also his own home as a youth, especially since it was the custom that members of the same trade should live in the same quarter of any given city. Indeed, it was the same nephew, Piccardo, who preserved the above-mentioned stable as a chapel honoring his uncle's birth and went to great lengths to preserve this location for posterity through a legal contract of inheritance rights only through the direct family line.

All that remains of what is presumed to be Francis' home (or property definitely belonging to the family) is a small cellar now used as the Nativity Chapel. The friars of the Third Order Regular who minister at Santa Maria Sopra Minerva (the piazza temple) also minister at this small chapel.

FRANCISCAN READINGS

LEGEND OF THE THREE COMPANIONS 2

Francis' birth, family, and business

The father of the blessed and evangelical man Francis was named Peter, the son of the merchant Bernardone; and he was absorbed in making money. On the other hand, Francis' mother Pica was an excellent woman; and like another Elizabeth, she gave birth to her blessed son in the absence of his father who had gone to France on business.

She wished the child to be called John, and on the very day of his baptism a pilgrim stopped to beg at the door. Having received alms from the serving maid the stranger said to her: "I beg you to show me the child born today for I greatly wish to see him."

The maid answered that this was impossible, but the pilgrim insisted that he would never go away unless his wish were granted. The maid was annoyed and went back into the house leaving the pilgrim outside; but, when the Lady Pica heard what had happened, she was amazed and told the maid to show the child to the stranger. When this was done the pilgrim took the baby into his arms with great devotion and joy, as Simeon had once taken the infant Jesus, and he said: "Today two children have been born in this city; this one will be among the best of [humankind], and the other among the worst."

The whole world has seen what was verified in Francis. . . .

When Peter returned from France, he insisted that his son should be called Francis after the country he had recently left.

Francis grew up quick and clever, and he followed in his father's footsteps by becoming a merchant. In business, however, he was very different from Peter, being far more high-spirited and open-handed. He was also intent on games and songs; and day and night he roamed about the city of Assisi with companions of his own age. He was a spendthrift, and all that he earned went into eating and carousing with his friends. For this his parents often remonstrated with him, saying that in squandering such large sums on himself and others, his style of living made him appear not so much their son as the son of some great prince. However, being rich and loving him tenderly, they allowed him free rein in order to avoid displeasing him. When the Lady Pica heard the neighbors commenting on her son's extravagance, she answered: "What do you think my son will be? Through grace he will become a son of God."

In all things Francis was lavish, and he spent much more on his clothes than was warranted by his social position. He would use only the finest materials; but sometimes his vanity took an eccentric turn, and then he would insist on the richest cloth and the commonest being sewn together in the same garment.

Marion A. Habig, ed. *St. Francis of Assisi: Omnibus of Sources* [Chicago: Franciscan Herald Press, 1973], 890-891.

THE LEGEND OF THREE COMPANIONS 3

Francis' personality; his refusal of alms to a beggar in his shop

He was naturally courteous in manner and speech and, following his heart's intent, never uttered a rude or offensive word to anyone. Moreover, since he was such a light-hearted and undisciplined youth, he proposed to answer back those speaking to him rarely in a brusque manner. His reputation, because of this, became so widespread throughout almost the entire region, that many who knew him said that, in the future, he would be something great.

From these stepping stones of natural strengths, he was brought to that grace that prompted him to look within himself: "You are generous and courteous to those from whom you receive nothing except passing and worthless approval. Is it not right that, on account of God who repays most generously, you should be courteous and generous to the poor?" From that day he looked on poor people generously and provided them affluently with alms. Although a merchant, he was a very flamboyant squanderer of wealth.

One day when he was in the shop where he was selling cloth, totally absorbed in business of this sort, a poor man came in, begging alms for the love of God. Preoccupied with thoughts of wealth and the care of business, he did not give him alms. Touched by divine grace, he accused himself of great rudeness, saying: "If that poor man had asked something from you for a great count or baron, you would certainly have granted him his request. How much more should you have done this for the King of kings and the Lord of all!"

Because of this incident, he resolved in his heart, from then on, not to deny a request to anyone asking in the name of so great a Lord.

THE LEGEND OF THREE COMPANIONS 5

Francis' dream of honor and glory in a military expedition

A few years later, a nobleman from the city of Assisi was preparing himself with knightly arms to go to Apulia in order to increase his wealth and fame. When Francis learned of this, he yearned to go with him to that same place, and to be knighted by that count, Gentile by name. He prepared clothing as expensive as possible, since even though he was poorer in riches than his fellow citizen, he was far more extravagant.

He was completely preoccupied in carrying this out, and was burning with desire to set out, when, one night, the Lord visited him in a dream. Knowing his desire for honors, He enticed and lifted him to the pinnacle of glory by a vision. That night while he was sleeping, someone appeared to him, a man *calling* him *by name*. He led him into a beautiful bride's elegant palace filled with knightly arms and on its walls hung glittering shields and other armor of knightly splendor. Overjoyed, he wondered what all this meant and asked to whom these brightly shining arms and this beautiful palace belonged. He was told that all these, including the palace, belonged to him and his knights.

Awakening in the morning, he got up with great joy. Since he had not yet fully tasted the spirit of God, he thought in a worldly way that he must be singled out magnificently, and he considered the vision a portent of future good fortune. He resolved then to undertake the journey to Apulia to be knighted by the count. He was even more cheerful than usual, prompting many people to wonder. When they asked him the reason why he was beaming with joy, he answered: "I know that I will become a great prince."

THE LEGEND OF THREE COMPANIONS 18

Francis' mother's release of him

But, since he was neither moved by words, nor exhausted by chains or blows, he endured all these things patiently, more fit and eager to carry out his holy plan.

When his father had to leave home on a pressing need, his mother remained at home alone with him. Since she did not approve of her husband's action, she spoke to her son in gentle words. When she realized she could not dissuade him from his holy intention, moved by her deep feeling for him, she removed the chains, and let him go free.

Thanking Almighty God, he returned to the place where he had been before, now enjoying greater freedom, since he passed the devil's temptations and had been taught by the lessons of temptation. More self-confident because of the injuries he had received, he made his way more freely and with an even greater heart.

In the meantime his father returned, and not finding his son, he turned on his wife in abuse, heaping sin upon sin.

OTHER READINGS

2C 3—Francis' birth and name
1C 5—Vision of arms in Francis' house
L3C 4–6—Francis' dream of knighthood
1C 10–13; LMj II: 2–3—Dealings with father and mother

EUCHARIST

READING: SIRACH 3:2–6, 12–14, 18

A reading from the book of Sirach

For the Lord honors a father above his children, and he confirms a mother's right over her children. Those who honor their father atone for sins, and those who respect their mother are like those who lay up treasure. Those who honor their father will have joy in their own children, and when they pray they will be heard. Those who respect their father will have long life, and those who honor their mother obey the Lord.

My child, help your father in his old age, and do not grieve him as long as he lives; even if his mind fails, be patient with him; because you have all your faculties do not despise him. For kindness to a father will not be forgotten, and will be credited to you against your sins.

The greater you are, the more you must humble yourself; so you will find favor in the sight of the Lord. **The word of the Lord.**

RESPONSE: Your children will be like olive shoots around your table.

PSALM 128

Happy is everyone who fears the LORD,
who walks in his ways.
You shall eat the fruit of the labor of your hands;
you shall be happy, and it shall go well with you. **R.**

Your wife will be like a fruitful vine within your house;
your children will be like olive shoots around your table.
Thus shall the man be blessed who fears the LORD.
The LORD bless you from Zion. **R.**

May you see the prosperity of Jerusalem
all the days of your life.
May you see your children's children.
Peace be upon Israel! **R.**

**ALLELUIA: The child grew in size and strength ... and
the grace of God was with him.**

GOSPEL: LUKE 2: 22, 39–40

A reading from the holy Gospel according to Luke

When the time came for their purification according to the
law of Moses, they brought Jesus up to
Jerusalem to present him to the Lord.

When they had finished everything
required by the law of the Lord, they
returned to Galiee, to their own town
of Nazareth. The child grew and
became strong, filled with wisdom; and
the favor of God was upon him. **The
Gospel of the Lord.**

THE CLOTH MERCHANT'S TALE

I

Then laying his clothes at my feet
he walks away, just like that,
the sun dyeing the evening sky
as we lift eyes to watch Francesco
disappear from our sight.

He does not descend to the valley,
but stops half-way at San Damiano,
and that is the end of it.
My son, my pride, outside the walls,
trades between San Damiano
and the Portiuncula's lepers.
Threadbare, he rebuilds ruined churches,
shuns the cloth trade for stone.

II

"I will no longer say, 'Father,
Pietro Bernardone,' but
'Our Father Who are in Heaven.'"
A vicious slap in the face
which I will never forgive.

Not that Francesco would stoop
to beg my forgiveness. After all,
what has God's son to do with
a hard working cloth merchant who,
like St. Joseph, only tried
to teach his adopted son?

God's curse on such ingratitude.

And when my flesh has finally
putrefied, may my skull turn to

powder, lest Francesco fashion it
into a gargoyle's spout
to flush his guilt like rain
from the church's leaden gutters.

III

Lady Pica, my sometime wife,
goes out to the olive trees
now that her darling Francesco's
gone. She sits like stone,
except for her moving hands
sewing mad patterns into cloth.
Her flesh sags with fasting,
her mad son preaches love.

The house of Bernardone's undone—
frayed cloth, flawed stone.

Murray Bodo, O.F.M. *The Cord* 44, no. 10 [1994]: 280–281. Reprinted with permission.

ASSISI:
SAN RUFINO

FRANCISCAN PILGRIMAGE PROGRAMS

ASSISI: SAN RUFINO

EVENTS
Francis and Clare were baptized in this cathedral. Also baptized here were Leo, Bernardo, Giles, Elias, Peter Catanio, Sylvester, and Rufino, among the first companions, and the infant who became Frederick II, emperor. This was the only baptismal font in Assisi until 1924 or 1925, and it is still there.

Francis preached here on a number of occasions. Clare may have heard him, which would have influenced her conversion journey.

Francis confessed his failings in public.

Clare's family home was very near the cathedral. Clare worshipped here on Palm Sunday, 1212, and later that night she journeyed to the Porziuncola to join Francis.

SPIRITUALITY
Baptism is the central moment in our Christian journey through life. Francis' and Clare's baptisms in San Rufino remind us of our own immersion into the full paschal mystery of Christ our Lord.

One can never underestimate the power and importance of preaching. Good preaching is God-inspired and moves hearts.

Clare's spiritual life was nurtured at San Rufino. She came to be known as a woman of prayer, penance, fasting, and love for the poor even while she lived in her family home. Francis responded to this and saw in Clare the strength to be a new leader of women. She becomes the "New Woman of the Valley of Spoleto."

REFLECTION
Francis and Clare complemented each other. How do you see yourself in the paradigm of complementarity?

Francis undertook a definite mission to the people. What was the mission, and how did he prepare for it?

Reflect on Francis' integration of prayer, evangelization, and fraternity.

Francis openly preached about his faults and often used himself as an example to instruct the people. Does this fact say anything about our own particular style of Franciscan preaching? How do you relate preaching to your own personal religious experience?

SAN RUFINO

HISTORICAL NOTES

St. Rufino

St. Rufino was the first bishop of Assisi and was martyred by the pagan populace in A.D. 238. He was drowned in the Tescio River with a millstone tied around his neck. St. Rufino's body was found by the few Christian faithful and buried in a small chapel dedicated in his memory. Eventually a larger church, San Rufino, was built over his crypt. By the Middle Ages, the canons of this church and the local nobility had gained such prominence as to eclipse the influence of the cathedral church, Santa Maria Maggiore. They conspired together to transfer the bishop's throne and the title of the cathedral to San Rufino.

The Cathedral

It was Bishop Ugone who began the present building in 1134. St. Clare's grandfather Offreduccio donated part of the land in front of his manor house for the enlargement of the new cathedral.

The bell tower of the cathedral was built over an ancient Roman reservoir, a well of travertine marble, more than two thousand years old. Toward the end of the 16th century, the interior of the cathedral was entirely rebuilt into the baroque style that we see today. The vault was reconstructed at a much lower level than the original roof, hiding the two side rose windows.

The rose window was made in 1140; the altar was consecrated in 1228. The Madonna del Pianto was said to have cried in 1494 on the occasion of fratricidal feuds taking place in the town. The pact of peace between the *Minores* and *Maiores* ("merchants" and "nobles") was made here in 1210.

Both Francis and Clare were baptized in the font located here, as were some of their earliest companions. Francis later regularly preached in San Rufino (LMj IV:4). He would arrive on Saturday and stay in a small room off the sacristy where he would pray and prepare for the Sunday liturgy. Here he confessed in public that he had eaten meat during an illness (LMj:VI:2).

FRANCISCAN READINGS

ST. BONAVENTURE, MAJOR LEGEND IV: 4

How Francis prepares to preach and appears in a vision to his brothers

While the brothers were still staying in the place already mentioned, one Saturday the holy man entered the city of Assisi to preach in the cathedral on Sunday morning, as was his custom. In a hut situated in the garden of the canons, away from his sons in body, the man devoted to God spent the night in his customary way, in the prayer of God. About midnight, while some of the brothers were resting and others were persevering in prayer, behold, *a fiery chariot* of wonderful brilliance entering the door of the house moved *here and there* through the little house three times. On top of it sat a bright globe that looked like the sun, and it made the night bright as day. *Those who were awake* were dumbfounded, while those sleeping were disturbed and, at the same time, terrified; they sensed the brightness with their hearts as much as with their

bodies, while the conscience of each was laid bare to the others
by the power of that marvelous light.

As they looked into each other's hearts,
they all understood together that the holy father,
while away from them in body,
was present in spirit
transfigured in such an image
radiant with heavenly brilliance
and inflamed with burning ardor
in a glowing *chariot of fire,*
as the Lord had shown him to them
that they might follow him as *true Israelites.*
Like a second Elijah,
God had made him
a chariot and charioteer for spiritual men.
Certainly we can believe
that *He opened the eyes*
of these simple men at the prayers of Francis
that they might see the *wonders of God*
just as he had once opened the eyes of a child
to see the mountain full of horses and chariots of fire
round about Elisha.
When the holy man returned to the brothers,
he began to probe the secrets of their consciences,
to draw courage for them from this wonderful vision
and to make many predictions about the growth of the
Order.
When he disclosed many things
that transcended human understanding,
the brothers completely realized
the Spirit of the Lord had come to rest upon him in such
fullness
that it was absolutely safe for them
to follow his life and teaching.

THOMAS OF CELANO, FIRST LIFE 47

Vision of the fiery chariot

Walking before God with simplicity
and among people with confidence,
the brothers merited at that time to rejoice in a divine
revelation.
They were on fire with the Holy Spirit
and with prayerful voices sang the *"Our Father"*
in the melody of the Spirit.
They did this at all hours and not simply those assigned,
since earthly concerns and the nagging anxiety of cares
troubled them little.

One night the blessed father Francis was away from them in
body. About midnight, some of the brothers were sleeping and
others were praying in silence with deep feeling, when a
brilliant *fiery chariot* entered through the little door of the
house, and moved *here and there* through the little house two
or three times. On top of it sat a large ball that looked like the
sun, and it made the night bright as day. *Those who were awake*
were dumbfounded, while those sleeping woke up *in a fright*,
for they sensed the brightness with their hearts as much as
with their bodies. *They gathered together* and *began to ask each*
other what all this *meant*. From the strength and grace of such
great light, the conscience of each was revealed to the others.

At last they understood, realizing that the soul of the holy
father radiated with great brilliance. Thus, thanks to the gift
of his outstanding purity and his deep concern for his sons, he
merited the blessing of such a gift from the Lord.

ASSISI COMPILATION 80

Francis' public confession at San Rufino

One time when he had recovered somewhat from a very serious illness, after some consideration, it seemed to him that he had received some little delicacies during that illness, although he ate only a little, since with his many, diverse, and serious illnesses he was not able to eat.

One day, although still sick from a quartan fever, he had the people of Assisi called to the piazza for a sermon. When he had finished preaching, he requested that no one leave until he returned.

Together with Brother Peter of Catanio, whom he chose as the first general minister, and with a few other brothers, he entered the church of San Rufino, going into the *confessio*. He ordered Brother Peter to obey and not contradict whatever he wanted to say and do to himself. And Brother Peter said to him: "Brother, in what concerns you and me, I cannot, and should not want anything else except what pleases you."

Taking off his tunic, blessed Francis ordered Brother Peter to lead him naked with a rope tied around his neck in front of the people. He ordered another brother to take a bowl full of ashes and, mounting the place from where he had preached, to throw them and sprinkle them on his head. But moved by piety and compassion towards him, the brother did not obey him. Brother Peter got up and, weeping bitterly with the other brothers, led him out as he had been ordered to do.

In this way he came back in front of the people naked, to the place where he had preached, and said: "You believe me to be a holy man, as do others who, following my example, leave the world and enter the religion and life of the brothers. But I confess to God and to you that during my illness I ate meat and broth flavored with meat."

Almost all the people began to weep out of piety and compassion for him, especially since it was wintertime and was very cold and he had not yet recovered from the quartan fever. They struck their breasts, accusing themselves. "This holy man," they said, "whose life we know, accuses himself with such shame over a just and manifest necessity. Yet because of excessive abstinence and the severity with which he treats his body from the moment of his conversion to Christ, we see him living in flesh that is almost dead. What shall we do, wretches that we are, we who all our life have lived, and wish to live, according to the will and desires of the flesh?"

THE LEGEND OF SAINT CLARE 7

Palm Sunday event, 1212

Therefore, when Sunday came, the young girl, thoroughly radiant with festive splendor among the crowd of women, entered the Church with the others. Then something occurred that was a fitting omen: as the others were going [to receive] the palms, while Clare remained immobile in her place out of shyness, the Bishop, coming down the steps, came to her and placed a palm in her hands. On that night, preparing to obey the command of the saint, she embarked upon her long desired flight with a virtuous companion. Since she was not content to leave by way of the usual door, marveling at her strength, she broke open—with her own hands—that other door that is customarily blocked by wood and stone.

THE LITTLE FLOWERS OF
SAINT CLARE

Palm Sunday event, 1212

Palm Sunday, March 18th, in the year 1212

Clare, with the other young girls and the ladies of Assisi, was at the Cathedral, the old church of San Rufino, where the bishop officiated on these solemn occasions.

The vestments and the hangings were of violet, this being Palm Sunday, the first day of Holy Week, which for the Church is "The Great Week" of the year.

In good time the girls of the town left their homes and headed for the Cathedral for the blessing of the palms. The rocky sides of Mount Subasio reflected the brightness of a timid spring, and some black swifts already flew in and out of the little turrets of the old castle. Of the later castle, the ruins of which still stand, there was no sign, because it was founded only in the year after that of which we speak. The girls had put aside their heavier woolen clothing and dressed themselves in their embroidered and flowered dresses. As they went on their way, their footsteps re-echoed along the narrow flagged streets and stone steps.

Palm Sunday liturgy was long. First came the blessing of the palms, then their distribution; a procession followed, and finally the Mass with the reading of the Passion as written by St. Matthew, during which the people always remained standing.

The ceremony began, "Hosanna to the Son of David. Blessed is He who comes in the name of the Lord: Hosanna in the highest." It was the liturgical repetition of Our Lord's entry into Jerusalem, riding on an ass. This recalled the great occasion when [people] spread their coats and cloaks on the ground before him like a carpet, and the children broke off branches of palm and olive and, waving them, ran ahead of Him and followed behind shouting the great cry of triumph: "Hosanna!"

After the readings, the responsories, the prayers and the blessing, the bishop began the distribution of the palms: first to the clergy, then to the faithful who kneeling took the palm from the bishop, kissed it, and then kissed his hand. The girls were the last to come up, modest and recollected, their faces slightly hidden under the veils they wore, and under a sort of linen head-dress. They approached the celebrant, genuflected, kissed the palm and his hand, and returned quietly to their places.

When Clare's turn came, she did not move. She remained seated with her head bent. She could not quite understand whether she had a feeling of holiness, a sudden bashful impulse, whether she ought to pray or just sit and dream.

In the succession of girls the bishop had noted her absence. He looked towards Clare, but she was not looking at him. Following his gaze went also that of the congregation, somewhat surprised and scandalized.

The bishop's look, however, was not of reproof, rather a certain

fatherly understanding. This expressed itself in a rather unusual way for, as though inspired, he rose from his chair, came down the steps of the sanctuary and went up to Clare, who remained unmoved. He presented her with the palm and blessed her, while the whole church followed the incident with astonishment.

Having returned to the altar, the bishop continued with the ceremony. The people sang, "All glory, praise and honor to Thee, redeemer King," and the children lovingly joined in with the chorus of "Hosanna!"

Clare, in her seat with the palm branch pressed to her heart, stared ahead of her, still immersed in a sort of stupor.

Piero Bargellini, *The Little Flowers of Saint Clare*, trans. Edmund O'Gorman, O.F.M. Conv. [Padova: Edizione Messagero, 1988]. Used with permission.

EUCHARIST

READING: ISAIAH 50:4–7

A reading from the book of the prophet Isaiah

The Lord GOD has given me the tongue of a teacher, that I may know how to sustain the weary with a word. Morning by morning he wakens—wakens my ear to listen as those who are taught. The Lord GOD has opened my ear, and I was not rebellious, I did not turn backward. I gave my back to those who struck me, and my cheeks to those who pulled out the beard; I did not hide my face from insult and spitting. The Lord GOD helps me; therefore I have not been disgraced; therefore I have set my face like flint, and I know that I shall not be put to shame. **The word of the Lord.**

RESPONSE: We shall go up with joy to the house of our God!

PSALM 122

I was glad when they said to me,
"Let us go to the house of the LORD!"
Our feet are standing within your gates, O Jerusalem. **R.**

Jerusalem—built as a city that is bound firmly together.
To it the tribes go up, the tribes of the LORD,
as was decreed for Israel,
to give thanks to the name of the LORD. **R.**

For there the thrones for judgment were set up,
the thrones of the house of David.
Pray for the peace of Jerusalem:

"May they prosper who love you.
Peace be within your walls,
and security within your towers." **R.**

For the sake of my relatives and friends
I will say, "Peace be within you."
For the sake of the house of the LORD our God,
I will seek your good. **R.**

ALLELUIA: Blessed is the One Who comes in the name of the Most High. Hosanna in the highest!

GOSPEL: MATTHEW 21:1–11

A reading from the holy Gospel according to Matthew

When they had come near Jerusalem and had reached Bethphage, at the Mount of Olives, Jesus sent two disciples, saying to them, "Go into the village ahead of you, and immediately you will find a donkey tied, and a colt with her; untie them and bring them to me. If anyone says anything to you, just say this, 'The Lord needs them.' And he will send them immediately." This took place to fulfill what had been spoken through the prophet, saying, "Tell the daughter of Zion, Look, your king is coming to you, humble, and mounted on a donkey, and on a colt, the foal of a donkey." The disciples went and did as Jesus had directed them; they brought the donkey and the colt, and put their cloaks on them, and he sat on them. A very large crowd spread their cloaks on the road, and others cut branches from the trees and spread them on the road. The crowds that went ahead of him and that followed were shouting, "Hosanna to the Son of David! Blessed is the one who comes in the name of the Lord! Hosanna in the highest heaven!" When he entered Jerusalem, the whole city was in turmoil, asking, "Who is this?" The crowds were saying, "This is the prophet Jesus from Nazareth in Galilee." **The Gospel of the Lord.**

RENEWAL OF BAPTISMAL PROMISES

Song

READING: 1 PETER: 2:4-5, 9-11

Come to him, a living stone, though rejected by mortals yet chosen and precious in God's sight, and like living stones, let yourselves be built into a spiritual house, to be a holy priesthood, to offer spiritual sacrifices acceptable to God through Jesus Christ.

But you are a chosen race, a royal priesthood, a holy nation, God's own people, in order that you may proclaim the mighty acts of him who called you out of darkness into his marvelous light.

Once you were not a people, but now you are God's people; once you had not received mercy, but now you have received mercy.

LIGHTING OF CANDLES

Leader:
Sisters and brothers, behold the light of Christ. This light was given to you as children of the light. May you continue to keep the flame of faith alive in your heart. And when the Lord comes, may you go out to meet him with Francis and Clare and all the saints in the heavenly kingdom. We pray in Jesus' name. Amen.

BLESSING OF WATER

Leader:
Dear friends, God uses the sacrament of water to give divine life to those who believe in God. Let us turn to God and ask God to pour the gift of life and blessing into this water.

Father, you have called us to this cleansing water and to new birth by sharing the faith of your church. Bless (+) this water, which recalls our baptism and full life in your Son Jesus Christ, through the power of the Spirit. We ask this in the name of Christ our Lord. Amen.

RENEWAL OF BAPTISMAL PROMISES

Leader:

Sisters and brothers, by water and the Holy Spirit you have, many years ago, received the gift of new life from God, who is love. Here at this baptismal font of Francis and Clare, let us be strengthened in this gift of faith by renewing the promises that we made in baptism when we rejected Satan and his works and promised to serve God faithfully in the holy Catholic Church.

And so: Do you reject sin so as to live in the freedom of God's children?

All:
I do.

Leader:

Do you reject Satan, father of sin and prince of darkness?

All:
I do.

Leader:

Do you believe in God the Father Almighty, Creator of heaven and earth?

All:
I do.

Leader:

Do you believe in Jesus Christ, the only begotten Son, our Lord, who was born of the Virgin Mary; was crucified, died, and was buried; rose from the dead and is now seated at the right hand of the Father?

All:
I do.

Leader:

Do you believe in the Holy Spirit, the holy Catholic Church, the communion of saints, the forgiveness of sins, the resurrection of the body, and life everlasting?

All:
I do.

Leader:
This is our faith. This is the faith of the Church. We are proud to profess it in Jesus our Lord. May God also keep us faithful to our Lord Jesus Christ forever and ever. Amen.

SIGNING WITH BLESSED WATER

Leader:
Since it is your desire to renew your baptism in the faith we have all professed together, come then to the baptismal font and sign yourself with the Sign of the Cross, the sign of our salvation.

Song

CONCLUDING PRAYER/BLESSING

By God's gift, through water and the Holy Spirit, we are reborn to everlasting life. In God's goodness may God continue to pour out blessings upon us. May God make us always, wherever we may be, faithful members of God's holy people. May God send peace upon all who are gathered here, in Christ Jesus our Lord. May almighty God, the Father, and the Son, and the Holy Spirit, bless you. Amen.

CLARE'S RITUAL OF DEPARTURE

Place of Reflection	Theme from the Life of Clare
Stop 1 Piazza San Rufino	Early Life of Clare
Stop 2 San Rufino side stairs	Nobility and Family Status
Stop 3 Midway down steps across the street	Awakening to Francis
Stop 4 San Francesco Piccolino	Crossing the Borders. ... Among the Poor
Stop 5 Curve facing the valley near elementary school	Discernment, Choices, and Consequences
Stop 6 Porta Moiano	Commitment—the Future

RESPONSE: C 3 "Gaze Upon Christ"

Stop 1 Early Life of Clare

How many good-byes did Clare say? When did she say those good-byes?

Reluctantly, good-bye to Assisi when her family fled to Perugia.

Good-bye to toys, to other things in the abandoned house, to friends in Assisi.

On this Palm Sunday at midnight, good-bye to Papa and Mama Offreduccio.

Good-bye to her very own life, with all its security, and power, and status.

Good-bye to nobility, good-bye.

But for Clare there were hellos too.

Hello to Jesus, whom she met through Francis.
Hello to the penitents, right at this very spot.
Hello to the faces of the Perugians who distrusted her family
        but still allowed them to resettle for a time in Perugia.
Hello to Francis and his brothers, right here in Assisi.
And on Palm Sunday at the hour of midnight, hello to Christ
her beloved: "Draw me after you Oh Heavenly Spouse, and I
will run to the aroma of your perfume and I WILL NOT TIRE."

Good-bye, Hello ... Clare ran to her beloved spouse.

RESPONSE: C 3

Stop 2 Nobility and Family Status

Clare, like other noblewomen of Assisi, has defined herself in
terms of her own family.
The men of the family are knights, and so the women are the
very summit of the social scale.
The downside is that they live very restricted lives,
enclosed within the boundaries of their own homes
and the customs of the nobility, such as arranged marriages,
and no juridical guarantees once their spouses die. The women
are defined in terms of the feudal lords.

Now Clare is leaving that prestigious but confining world. What
are her thoughts?
How will she define herself now?
What boundaries and parameters will still confine her?
Will this new freedom still be circumscribed by the feudal
church of the Middle Ages?

How will she keep alive and continue to live out
the new gospel freedom she has found?

RESPONSE: C 3

Stop 3 Awakening to Francis

Francis' deeds are known to the entire city.
Word spreads quickly in this small town.
What do the neighbors know about what is going on?
What has Clare heard about Francis? Does she know of
- the sale of the cloth at Foligno?
- the encounter before the San Damiano crucifix (did she go down and gaze on this same face of Christ)?
- Francis begging for stones to rebuild San Damiano?
- the stripping before Bishop Guido?
- Pietro's wrath?

Do the mothers, Ortulana and Pica, speak to each other during these days, trying to understand what is happening to their children?

When and where does Clare first hear Francis preach? In this neighborhood somewhere?
When does the fire within her begin to grow?
Where in this city does she meet with Francis as she continues to discern God's call?

And what do the neighbors say about this? Do they even know?

RESPONSE: C 3

Stop 4 Crossing the Borders ... Among the Poor

Clare has now crossed the boundary between the Maiores and the Minores.
She stops near the shop of Pietro Bernardone. Here the poor work dyeing the cloth, far removed from the knightly pursuits of her father's house.
Near here Francis is said to have been born in a stable
like his Lord and Savior Jesus Christ.

What does it mean to cross those invisible borders between privilege and distinction, disenfranchisement, marginality, and anonymity?

What is implied when this noblewoman crosses over to the other side, where there is little or no education, no luxuries, only the boredom of repetitive, uninteresting, and demeaning work?

What Gospel passages come to her mind?
Is there a further identification with Christ in this small physical, large psychological and spiritual border crossing?

RESPONSE: C 3

Stop 5 Discernment, Choices, and Consequences

Did it ever occur to Clare before how many choices she had?
When life seemed to be a predetermined existence, didn't she still have choices?
Didn't she choose the life of penance as a virgin?
Didn't she choose not to *hate* the Assisani for driving the noble families away?
Didn't she choose to give food to the poor and distribute her patrimony?

Looking at the people who live here in this part of Assisi, how many choices did they ever have?
And seeing the lepers, Mother of God, what possible choices could they have? "Unclean," people cry, "Unclean, Unclean."

How many times did Clare come to this very place,
always accompanied by a maid and a knight?
How many times did Clare turn back and run home?
Choices, yes, Clare made many choices.
She could still turn around and run home,
but where would her home be now?
Would she even be able to get back inside? Would she be able

to return after all these choices?
At this place, did she wonder if she had made the best choice this Palm Sunday night?

RESPONSE: C 3

Stop 6 Commitment—the Future

Before the Gate

Having made up her mind, did she pause to consider her decision one more time?
From here, the valley must have looked very dark and foreboding.
Who was guarding the gate? Were they asleep?
The gate was close to Bishop Guido's house, the bishop who earlier that day gave her the palm at Mass. Did he help her get past Porta Moiano?

Clare decided to walk through this gate—no longer able to keep the fire that is blazing contained within.

RESPONSE: C 3

Ritual of Passing through the Gate

As you stand in the center of Porta Moiano, recall the many decisions you have made in your life. Ponder the consequences of these decisions. As you pass through this gate, pray for the grace to remain faithful to commitments you have made.

At the Opposite Side of the Gate

Gaze upon the vast expanse of the valley, open and free. There are no boundaries.
Could Clare see the Maddalena Chapel and the Porziuncola from here? Absolutely not. She went into the unknown.
But looking back, see how narrow and confining this gate looks, with its tiny slit windows?

It is meant to keep people out.

Clare can never return here as a woman of nobility.

Now look at Santa Chiara. Clare could never have imagined that this new place would represent nearly eight hundred years of loyal discipleship on the part of her sisters.

Santa Chiara today holds two most precious Franciscan symbols:

> the San Damiano crucifix and

> the body of Clare.

Haven't we also received the call to go and rebuild God's house, which we know is falling into ruin?

Aren't we all called to be part of one family making up the Body of Christ—who is the center of and soul of both Francis and Clare?

This is our call. This is our challenge.

Closing Song: C 6 "What You Hold"

ASSISI: ROCCA MAGGIORE

FRANCISCAN PILGRIMAGE PROGRAMS

ASSISI: ROCCA MAGGIORE

EVENTS
The Rocca Maggiore was reduced to ruins by the people of Assisi in 1198. Francis, very likely, was part of the assault. Afterward the citizens used the stones to build a wall around the city. Francis would have been about sixteen years old.

SPIRITUALITY
Rocca Maggiore reminds us of our call to be peacemakers and ambassadors of reconciliation. Francis at first pursued a life of war and violence, and together with the people he used the stones of the fortress to build walls to keep people out. Following his conversion, he would spend the rest of his life breaking down walls to bring people in.

REFLECTION
Consider Francis' ministry of peace and reconciliation and our own contemporary call to the same. We are to be women and men dedicated to the cause of justice and peace.

The castle symbolizes the rivalries between pope and emperor, Assisi and Perugia, Maiores and Minores. Visiting this place might give one pause to reflect on Francis' ministry of peace and our own call to be peacemakers.

ROCCA MAGGIORE

HISTORICAL NOTES

Towering over the city of Assisi stands the imperial fortress called the Rocca Maggiore. This majestic structure (built in its present form between the 14th and 16th centuries) was the seat of imperial power for the Holy Roman Empire in the vicinity during Francis' and Clare's early years.

As Italy gradually emerged from the anarchy of the Barbarian invasions, order and authority reestablished themselves. Yet, conflict gradually arose between the two powerful forces present in central Italy: the Papacy and the Holy Roman Empire (Germanic). Rome had claimed the right to govern central Italy (the Papal States) through the (doubtful) donation of Constantine (312–327) and the acknowledgment of that gift by the German King Pepin the Short in 751.

By 1198 the political situation in central Italy (the Umbrian Valley) was aligned in this way: Perugia, archenemy of Assisi, was allied with the Papacy. Assisi itself was allied with the empire. The untimely death of Emperor Henry VI in that year left his three-year-old son as claimant to the throne. With imperial power in collapse, civil war began in Germany. The Papacy immediately asserted its authority over Umbria. Conrad of Urslingen, count of Assisi, transferred the allegiance of Assisi to the pope and returned to Germany to fight for the three-year-old, Frederick II.

It is at that moment in time that the merchant class of Assisi chose to assert its independence. Unwilling to accept the domination of either power, the citizenry took advantage of the power vacuum created by the transfer. On a spring evening in 1198, they attacked the Rocca Maggiore, leveling its mighty walls. Arnaldo Fortini commented, "... under the eyes of imperial and pontifical legates, they took up an assault on the Rocca, and to the sound of bells, destroyed it. Thus fell the very symbol of feudalism" (*Francis of Assisi* [New York: The Crossroad Publishing Co., 1981], 120). Francis (sixteen years old) and his brother and father surely worked for the destruction of this hated place.

Those shrewd merchants quickly realized two things: They must protect their city against retribution, and they must deal with the local nobility. To protect themselves they salvaged the rubble and used it to fortify and enlarge their city walls. They gave the nobility two choices. Either they must join the *comune* as citizens or they must leave. Those who joined were welcomed; those who did not were driven from their castles, which were then destroyed. For the most part they went to live in exile in Perugia. Clare's family was among them. Peace gradually returned with the defeat of Assisi at the Battle of Collestrada, 1202. St. Francis was made a prisoner of war during this battle, and the citizens of Assisi were forced to accept a humiliating truce.

More than 150 years later, in 1367, the pope was again trying to consolidate his power in central Italy. In his sincere desire to maintain the peace of the region, he sent Cardinal Egidio

(Giles) Albornoz to Assisi to rebuild the castle. Albornoz was welcomed as the papal governor of the territory. He was regarded as a just man and quite efficient, a man who made many improvements in the town with the willing help of the people. He enlarged and strengthened the curtain walls of the town, and he rebuilt the castle as we see it today.

But it was Pope Paul III who was really credited with ending strife in Assisi. He rebuilt the castle in Perugia so large that no one dared rise up in opposition against his authority in the region. It was the time of the Protestant Reformation, and Pope Paul, who initiated the Council of Trent, refused to hear of dissent among Catholics when he was having so much trouble with half of Europe changing faiths. Finally, the same pope had the cannons of the Assisi Rocca removed to the Rocca in Perugia.

By 1726 the people of Assisi complained that no one had been sent to repair the decaying walls of the castle. And even though there had been many years of peace, the town believed it should always be ready for war. But no pope heeded the threat, so the castle stood abandoned. People went in and out as they pleased, and peasants chopped away at the walls and stole cartloads of stones to repair their own houses.

In 1883 the government of the new Kingdom of Italy gave ownership of the Rocca to the *comune* of Assisi. Minimal repairs began to preserve its heritage. It was in 1972, however, when the director Franco Zeffirelli, decided to shoot several scenes of his film *Brother Sun, Sister Moon* at the Rocca, that the old structure actually got its long-awaited face-lift.

The Rocca Maggiore dominates the town of Assisi. Tradition states that it was the site of a pagan temple. There is a magnificent view over the Umbrian plain as far as Mont'Amiata to the west, the Sibelline and Abruzzi mountains to the south, and the Casentino to the north. In the valley below the Rocca runs the Tescio River.

From the Rocca one can see Monte Subasio along whose side is the road that leads up to the Carceri and to the Abbey of St. Benedict, the monastery of the monks who gave the Porziuncola to Francis (AC 56). Far to the left, when looking down on Assisi, you can see Spello and Foligno (1C 8). In the plain, a bit to the right, a tower juts up, which is the sanctuary of Rivo Torto (L3C 55), opposite which are Bevagna and Cannara, where Francis preached to the birds (LFl 16). More to the right looms the dome of St. Mary of the Angels, the Porziuncola, where Clare and Francis ate together (LFl 15). Continuing to the right one sees Bastia, where Francis first led Clare, then Ponte San Giovanni, the place of Francis' defeat and capture. Finally, on a far hill, proud sprawling Perugia can be seen.

FRANCISCAN READINGS

IN THE STEPS OF ST. FRANCIS

You will see something of what I mean if we open our pilgrimage by sitting on the top of Assisi's hill, with the ruin of the old castle behind, the city shackled to the slope below, and the wide vale of Spoleto filling up the floor of the world.

Before us now is the theatre in which most of the drama was staged. It all looks extraordinarily peaceful today. We sit among tall grasses and wild flowers, in an air pungent with the smell of mint, while innumerable butterflies flit about us— which seems to fit somehow the opening of a Franciscan tale. Lizards dart across the stones, and a lark, descendent perhaps of one of Francis' larks, sings its office in the limpid Italian sky. The grey olive trees go shimmering down the slope, all round and below the city walls. They carry our eyes to the great flat plain which is a patch-work of maize-fields and clover-fields, with the vines festooned from maple to elm between them. In the farthest distance run fold after fold of mountains, each a lighter grey than the last. And the last has a mysterious light above it like the light of another world.

Looking down on the city we can see right into the streets along which Francis went rioting at midnight with his boon companions, his lute slung before him and his voice lifted in troubadour songs, to the disturbance of graver citizens in their sleep. That was before the sword pierced him deep enough. We can see into the open piazzas where in his lifetime excited and gesticulating crowds must have discussed one sensation after another. "What's happened to Francis? He's quite different from what he used to be." "Have you heard of that awful row that is developing between that young idiot, Francis, and his father?" "Listen, all of you: old Bernadone is hailing his son before the bishop for trial." "Have you heard the latest? Would you believe it? Bernard of Quintavalle—Bernard, of all people, that sober and substantial townsman!—has thrown up everything and is going to join young Bernadone in his mad game. And Dr. Peter Cataneo too, a lay canon of the cathedral, if you please—he's caught the disease. He and Bernard are giving all their goods away to the poor now in the Piazza San Giorgio." One shift of our eyes, and we can see the Piazza San Giorgio. Then: "Listen, everybody: young Clare, the lovely daughter of Count [Favarone] of the Scifi—and she only eighteen!—eloped from her home at midnight last night and ran to young Francis' crazy establishment in the forest. What are children coming to?" Eighteen days later: "Agnes, Clare's sister, and only fifteen years old, has run off to join her! Her father and uncle are going with a strong force to get her back. ...."

Far away to our right, down there in the plain, do you see a grey chapel against some cypresses? That is San Paolo in Bastia, where Clare clung to the altar when her family came to drag her home again. Look left: do you see those haystacks against a farmhouse high up on the steep slope? That farmhouse holds the remains of the Benedictine nunnery of Sant'Angelo in Panzo, where Francis put Clare till he could find a home for her. Can you distinguish the path winding up to it? Up that path ran little Agnes to join her beloved sister. Up that path galloped knights and men-at-arms, determined to recover her. Do you see that file of cypresses marching down the hill to the left of the Porta Nuova? They mark the road to the little convent of San Damiano. There Francis installed Clare with her clinging sister, Agnes. There she founded the order of the Poor Clares, and there she lived, perhaps the most complete of all the creations of Francis. To San Damiano they brought him dying, and there she looked after him, mending his habit and making sandals for his wounded feet. There in the garden one day—do you see the garden?—he burst into his Song of Brother Sun and All the Creatures, though the sun of the East had blinded him and he could hardly see the creatures any more. To San Damiano his brothers, knowing how Clare had loved him, brought his dead body that she might weep over it for a little and say Addio.

And now leave San Damiano and see, right in the center of the picture as it ought to be, the dome of the great basilica that enshrines the Porziuncola, the tiny chapel of the "Little Portion" by which Francis chose to live and to die, and in which he dreamed such dreams of us men [and women] as we have not yet been great enough to fulfill—but there is time. "Good morning, good people."

Sitting up here beneath the old ruined *Rocca*, are we not indeed gazing over a country where once upon a time (as Angela of

Foligno said of herself with the unblushing truth of the saints) some men and women of our race, like early envoys seeking an alliance, "walked with the Holy Spirit among the vines"?

E. Raymond, in *Prayer at the Rocca Maggiore* [New York: H. C. Kinsey Co., 1939], 8–11.

PRAYER FOR THE THIRD MILLENNIUM

NINE WAYS TO BE A HOLY PERSON

Leader:
I invite you to take turns reading aloud these nine statements:

1. **Make Time for Prayer**. Make prayer a regular part of your daily life. Use personal prayer, the Scriptures, meditation, and the Liturgy of the Hours. Make a pilgrimage or retreat. Pray the Our Father as a prayer for Christian Unity.

2. **Practice Forgiveness**. Learn to forgive and be forgiven. Regularly examine your conscience, practice fasting, and celebrate the sacrament of reconciliation.

3. **Celebrate the Eucharist**. Actively participate each Sunday, and on other occasions whenever possible, in the eucharistic liturgy.

4. **Live a Just Life**. Work against discrimination, racism, and oppression. Treat all people with the dignity they deserve as sons and daughters of God.

5. **Help the Poor**. Practice charity by assisting those living in poverty, and promote community-based solutions to the cause of injustice and poverty.

6. **Be a Domestic Church**. Family is the domestic church. No matter what type of "family" you belong to, support and nurture the love and care within the family.

7. **Share Faith**. Talk about God's presence in your life with other people. Be an evangelizer.

8. **Join a Small Christian Community**. Form a community if one is not available to strengthen your faith and to receive support to live your faith.

9. **Know Your Faith**. Learn more about the teachings and traditions of the Church. Read the Scriptures. Take advantage of adult education and formation opportunities.

"Nine Ways to Live Jubilee and Be a Holy Person." Copyright 1998, United States Catholic Conference, Inc., Washington, D.C. Adapted and reprinted with permission. All rights reserved.

Leader:
I now invite you to share ways in which you strive to live as people of justice.

OPEN SHARING

SONG OF AFFIRMATION

PRAYER

Reader 1:
Blessed are you, Creator God, Who in your infinite love, gave us your only begotten Son. By the power of the Holy Spirit He became incarnate in the spotless womb of the Virgin Mary and was born in Bethlehem over two thousand years ago. He became our companion on life's path and gave new meaning to our history, the journey we make together in toil and suffering, in faithfulness and love, towards the new heaven and the new earth where you, once death has been vanquished, will be all in all.

All:
Praise and glory to You, Most Holy Trinity, You alone are God
most high!

Reader 2:
By your grace, O God, may this millennium be a time of deep
conversion and of joyful return to you. May it be a time of
reconciliation between people, and of peace restored among
nations, a time when swords are beaten into ploughshares and
the clash of arms gives way to songs of peace. Grant that we
may live docile to the voice of your Spirit, faithful to the way of
Christ, diligent in listening to your Word and in approaching
the wellsprings of grace.

All:
Praise and glory to You, Most Holy Trinity, You alone are God
most high!

Reader 3:
Gracious God, by the power of the Spirit, strengthen the
Church's commitment to the new evangelization and guide our
steps along the pathways of the world, to proclaim Christ by
our lives, and to direct our earthly pilgrimage towards the City
of heavenly light. May Christ's followers show forth their love
for the poor and the oppressed; may they be one with those in
need and abound in works of mercy; may they be compassionate
towards all, that they themselves may obtain indulgence and
forgiveness from you.

All:
Praise and glory to You, Most Holy Trinity, You alone are God
most high!

Reader 4:
God of Compassion, grant that we Your disciples, purified in
memory and acknowledging our failings, may be one, that the
world may believe. May dialogue between the followers of the

great religions prosper, and may all people discover the joy of being your children. May the intercession of Mary, Mother of your faithful people, in union with the prayers of the Apostles, the Christian martyrs, and the righteous of all nations in every age, make this millennium a time of renewed hope and of joy in the Spirit for each of us and for the whole Church.

All:

Praise and glory to You, Most Holy Trinity, You alone are God most high! To You, Creator of the universe and of humankind, through Jesus Christ, the Living One, Lord of time and history, in the Spirit who makes all things holy, be praise and honor and glory now and forever. Amen!

From Pope John Paul II, in *"Prayer for the Jubilee Year 2000."*

MILLENNIUM PLEDGE

Leader:

We are called "to bring GOOD NEWS to the poor . . . to proclaim release to the captives and recovery of sight to the blind, to let the oppressed go free." (Luke 4:18).

All:

As disciples of Jesus in this third millennium, we pledge to:

Pray regularly for greater justice and peace.

Learn more about Catholic social teaching and its call to protect human life, stand with the poor, and care for creation.

Reach across boundaries of religion, race, ethnicity, gender, and disabling conditions.

Live justly in family life, school, work, the marketplace, and the political arena.

Serve those who are poor and vulnerable, sharing more time and talent.

Give more generously to those in need at home and abroad.

Advocate for public policies that protect human life, promote human dignity, preserve God's creation, and build peace.

Encourage others to work for greater charity, justice, and peace.

BLESSING

Leader:
During this third millennium may you be filled with God's abundant grace to:

Slow down, identifying time for prayer, reflection, and meditation.

Nourish your spiritual life and grow closer to God.

Create a positive and hopeful outlook on life based on the belief that God is present in the world today through the Holy Spirit.

Be mindful of all who are victims of injustice in this world, advocating for their human rights and dignity.

We ask all of this in the name of Jesus Christ and the Holy Spirit.

All:
Amen, Amen, Amen.

ASSISI:
SAN DAMIANO
AND
ST. FRANCIS

FRANCISCAN PILGRIMAGE PROGRAMS

ASSISI: SAN DAMIANO AND
ST. FRANCIS

EVENTS
In 1205 Francis prayed before the crucifix in this dilapidated wayside church. The sources (L3C 13 and 2C 10) described well the event of Christ speaking to him from the cross, saying: "Francis, go, rebuild My house."

Francis restored this church in 1206, begging stones on the streets of Assisi (L3C 21).

In 1212 Francis brought Clare to San Damiano.

Francis composed *The Canticle of the Creatures* here in 1225.

SPIRITUALITY
The role of the cross is central to Francis' conversion journey. His experience at San Damiano was critical in this development.

San Damiano is closely linked with the reality of rebuilding. A strong Franciscan charism is "Rebuilding the Church" with its focus on renewing the people of God.

Eric Doyle, O.F.M., claimed that the Franciscan family has a many-faceted charism: the First Order emphasizes minority, the Third Order (regular and secular) emphasizes conversion and penance, and the Second Order emphasizes contemplation. Each branch of the Franciscan family rebuilds the church from its emphasized focus, always aware of the influence the other dimensions of the charism exert on the rebuilding process.

REFLECTION
San Damiano marked the beginning of Francis' journey; La Verna, its culmination. Can you find seeds of Francis' development at San Damiano? How did Francis respond to the crucified Jesus? How did this influence his life? What does it mean to discover the crucified Christ?

Francis' stay at San Damiano was a period of trial and formation (L3C 16). What effect did this have on him? What struggles did Francis go through here?

Francis stayed at San Damiano in 1224 "for fifty days and more" (AC 83). He was wracked with pain while living in a cell made of mats and infested with mice, which annoyed him day and night. Nevertheless, his creativity burst through his pain and he composed his *Canticle of the Creatures*, the first recognized piece of Italian literature. What does this say to you about pain in your own life?

What are your rebuilding tools?

SAN DAMIANO AND ST. FRANCIS

HISTORICAL NOTES

On the outskirts of Assisi, halfway down the hillside to the plain, is the church of San Damiano. Francis prayed before the crucifix in this dilapidated church in 1205 when he received the message, "Go, repair my house." Around 1206 Francis and some others (L3C 24) did restore this rustic church dedicated to SS. Cosmas and Damian.

In 1212 Francis brought Clare and her companions to this place, and they made it their monastery. Francis composed *The Canticle of the Creatures* here in 1225 when he was ill.

We do not know the exact date the friars moved into San Damiano—probably about 1270. For a time this place was the provincialate of the Umbrian province of Santa Chiara. Presently it is the novitiate for a number of Italian provinces, so the spirit of decision and responding to the call of Jesus is still very much alive at San Damiano.

Lord Ripon bought San Damiano in 1878 after its confiscation under the laws of suppression in 1860. During the eighth centenary of Francis' birth and four days before the feast of SS. Cosmas and Damian, the latest owner, Lord Peter Lothian, returned San Damiano as a donation, signed and sealed in Milan, September 22, 1983, to John Vaughn, Minister General of the Order of Friars Minor at that time.

To the right as you enter the church is the little money niche mentioned in a number of the legends.

The choir stalls in the apse are from 1504. In the center of the apse wall is a replica of the grill through which Clare and her sisters venerated the body of St. Francis on its way from the Porziuncola to the church of St. George (1C 116; AC 13).

The plain below was woods and marsh in Francis' day. It has since been drained and cleared to provide farmland.

Look at the facade of the sanctuary and try to figure out what the structure was like in Francis' time. The demarcation in the bricks shows the original San Damiano church.

FRANCISCAN READINGS

THOMAS OF CELANO, FIRST LIFE 8–9

Francis' offer of money to the priest at San Damiano

Returning toward the city of Assisi, he came across a church on the side of the road. It had been built in ancient times in honor of Saint Damian and was threatening to collapse because of age.

Arriving at this church, the new *soldier of Christ*, aroused by piety at such a great need, entered it with awe and reverence. He found a poor priest there, kissed his holy hands with great devotion, offered him the money he was carrying and explained his purpose in great detail.

The priest was astounded and, surprised at this sudden

conversion in incredible circumstances, he refused to believe what he was hearing. Because he thought he was being mocked, he refused to keep the money offered to him. ... But Francis stubbornly persisted and endeavored to create confidence in his words. He pleaded, begging the priest with all his heart to allow him to stay with him for the sake of the Lord. Finally the priest agreed to let him stay, but out of fear of Francis's parents did not accept the money. The true scorner of wealth threw it onto a window opening, since he cared for it as much as he cared for dust.

THE LEGEND OF THREE COMPANIONS 13

Message from the San Damiano crucifix

One day, when he was more passionately begging for the Lord's mercy, the Lord showed him that he would be told in the near future what he must do. From that moment on, he was filled with such great joy, that, failing to restrain himself in the face of happiness, he carelessly mentioned some of his secrets to others. He nevertheless spoke cautiously and in riddles, saying that he did not want to go to Apulia, but that he would accomplish great and noble deeds at home.

His companions noticed the change in him, indeed he was already estranged from them in his thoughts, even though he sometimes joined their company. And so they asked him as a joke: "Francis, do you want to get married?" He replied to them in a riddle, as we mentioned above.

A few days had passed when, while he was walking by the church of San Damiano, he was told in the Spirit to go inside for a prayer. Once he entered, he began to pray intensely before an image of the Crucified, which spoke to him in a tender and kind voice: "Francis, don't you see that my house is being destroyed? Go, then, and rebuild it for me." Stunned and trembling, he said: "I will do so gladly, Lord." For he understood that it was speaking about that church, which was near collapse because of its age. He was filled with such joy and became so radiant with light over that message, that he knew in his soul that it was truly Christ crucified who spoke to him.

Upon leaving the church, he found a priest sitting nearby and, putting his hands into the pouch, he offered him a handful of coins. "My Lord," he said, "I beg you, buy some oil and keep the light before the Crucified burning continually. When this money runs out, I will again give you as much as you need."

THE LEGEND OF THREE COMPANIONS 16

How Francis escapes from his father and lives with the priest

Overjoyed by the vision and hearing the words of the Crucified Christ, he got up, fortifying himself with the sign of the cross. And mounting his horse and taking cloth of different colors, he arrived at a city named Foligno and, after selling there the horse and everything he was carrying, he returned immediately to the church of San Damiano.

After he found a poor priest there, he kissed his hands with great faith and devotion; he offered him the money he was carrying, and explained his purpose in great detail. The priest, astounded and surprised at his sudden conversion, refused to believe this, and, thinking he was being mocked, refused to keep his money. But stubbornly persisting, he endeavored to create confidence in his words, and he begged the priest more emphatically to allow him to stay with him.

Finally the priest agreed to let him stay but, out of fear of his parents, did not accept the money. And so the true scorner of money, throwing it on a windowsill, cared for it as much as he cared for dust.

While he was staying there, his father, like a diligent spy, went around seeking to learn what might have happened to his son. And when he heard that he was so changed and was living in that place in such a way, he was touched inwardly with sorrow of heart and deeply disturbed by the sudden turn of events. Calling together his friends and neighbors, he ran to him.

Because he was a new knight of Christ, as he heard the threats of his pursuers and knew beforehand of their coming, he left room for his father's anger; and, going to a secret cave which he had prepared for this, he hid there for a whole month. That cave was known to only one person in his father's house. He would eat the food that, from time to time, was secretly brought to him there, praying all the while with flowing tears *that the Lord would free* him from destructive persecution, and that he could favorably fulfill his fervent wishes.

THE LEGEND OF THREE COMPANIONS 24

Francis' restoration of San Damiano

While he was working steadily at restoring the church, he wanted to have a lamp burning continually in the church, so he went through the city begging for oil. But when he was approaching a certain house, he saw a group of men gathered for a game. Ashamed to beg in front of them, he backed away. Mulling it over, he accused himself of having sinned. Hurrying back to the place where they were playing, he told everyone standing around his fault, that he was ashamed to beg because of them. And, in fervor of spirit, he entered that house and, for the love of God, begged in French for oil for the lamps of that church.

While laboring with others in that work, he used to cry to passers-by in a loud voice, filled with joy, saying in French: "Come and help me in the work of the church of San Damiano which, in the future, will be a monastery of ladies through whose fame and life our heavenly Father will be glorified throughout the church."

See how, filled with the spirit of prophecy, he truly foretold the future! For this is that sacred place where the glorious religion and most excellent Order of Poor Ladies and sacred virgins had its happy beginning about six years after the conversion of blessed Francis and through the same blessed Francis. Their wondrous life and renowned practices were fully approved by the Lord Pope Gregory IX, of holy memory, at that time the Bishop of Ostia, and confirmed by the authority of the Apostolic See.

ASSISI COMPILATION 83

How Francis lies ill at San Damiano and composes The Canticle of the Creatures

The Bishop of Ostia, who later became the apostolic bishop, seeing how blessed Francis was always severe with his body, and especially because he was rapidly losing his eyesight because he refused to have himself treated, admonished him with great kindness and compassion. He told him: "Brother, you do not do well in not allowing yourself to be helped with your eye disease, for your health and your life are of great value not only to yourself but also to others. If you have compassion for your sick brothers, and have always been and still are merciful to them, you must not be cruel to yourself in such a serious and manifest need and illness. I therefore order you to allow yourself to be helped and treated."

Likewise, two years before his death, while he was already very sick, especially from the eye disease, he was staying at San Damiano in a little cell made of mats.

The general minister, seeing and considering how tormented he was with the eye disease, ordered him to let himself be treated and helped. He also told him that he wanted to be present when the doctor began the treatment, especially so that he could more effectively arrange for him to be cared for and comforted, since he was suffering a great deal from it. At that time it was very cold, and the weather was not conducive to treatment.

Blessed Francis lay there for more than fifty days, and was unable to bear the light of the sun during the day or the light of a fire at night. He stayed in the dark in the house, inside that little cell. In addition, day and night he had great pains in his eyes so that at night he could scarcely rest or sleep. This was very harmful and was a serious aggravation for his eye disease and his other illnesses.

Sometimes he did want to rest and sleep, but there were many mice in the house and in the little cell made of mats where he was lying, in one part of the house. They were running around him, and even over him, and would not let him sleep. They even disturbed him greatly at the time of prayer. They bothered him not only at night, but also during the day, even climbing up on his table when he was eating, so much so that his companions, and he himself, considered it a temptation of the devil, which it was.

One night as blessed Francis was reflecting on all the troubles he was enduring, he was moved by pity for himself. *"Lord,"* he said to himself, *"make haste to help me* in my illnesses, so that I may be able to bear them patiently." And suddenly he was told in spirit: "Tell me, brother, what if, in exchange for your illnesses and troubles, someone were to give you a treasure? And it would be so great and precious that, even if the whole earth were changed to pure gold, all stones to precious stones, and all water to balsam, you would still judge and hold all these things as nothing, as if they were earth, stones and water, in comparison to the great and precious treasure which was given you. Wouldn't you greatly rejoice?"

"Lord," blessed Francis answered, "this treasure would indeed be great, worth seeking, very precious, greatly lovable, and desirable."

"Then, brother," he was told, "be glad and rejoice in your illnesses and troubles, because as of now, you are as secure as if you were already in my kingdom."

The next morning on rising, he said to his companions: "If the emperor were to give a whole kingdom to one of his servants, shouldn't he greatly rejoice? But, what if it were the whole empire, wouldn't he rejoice even more?" And he said to them: "I must rejoice greatly in my illnesses and troubles and be consoled in the Lord, giving thanks always to God the Father, to His only Son, our Lord Jesus Christ, and to the Holy Spirit for such a great grace and blessing. In His mercy He has given me, His unworthy little servant still living in the flesh, the promise of His kingdom.

"Therefore for His praise, for our consolation and for the edification of our neighbor, I want to write a new *Praise of the Lord* for his creatures, which we use every day, and without which we cannot live. Through them the human race greatly offends the Creator, and every day we are ungrateful for such great graces, because we do not praise, as we should, our Creator and the Giver of all good."

Sitting down, he began to meditate and then said: "Most High, all-powerful, good Lord." He composed a melody for these words and taught it to his companions so they could repeat it. For his spirit was then in such sweetness and consolation, that he wanted to send for Brother Pacifico, who in the world was called "The King of Verses," and was a very courtly master of singers.

He wanted to give him a few good and spiritual brothers to go through the world preaching and praising God.

He said that he wanted one of them who knew how to preach, first to preach to the people. After the sermon, they were to sing the *Praises of the Lord* as minstrels of the Lord. After the praises, he wanted the preacher to tell the people: "We are minstrels of the Lord, and this is what we want as payment: that you live in true penance."

He used to say: "What are the servants of God if not His minstrels, who must move people's hearts and lift them up to spiritual joy?" And he said this especially to the Lesser Brothers, who had been given to the people for their salvation.

The *Praises of the Lord* that he composed, that is, "Most High, all-powerful, good Lord," he called *"The Canticle of Brother Sun,"* who is more beautiful than all other creatures and can be most closely compared to God.

He used to say: "At dawn, when the sun rises, everyone should praise God, who created it, because through it the eyes are lighted by day. And in the evening, when it becomes night, everyone should praise God for another creature, Brother Fire, because through it the eyes are lighted at night."

He said: "For we are all like blind people, and the Lord lights up our eyes through these two creatures. Because of this, we must always praise the glorious Creator for these and for His other creatures which we use every day."

He did this and continued to do this gladly, whether he was healthy or sick. And he encouraged others to praise the Lord. Indeed, when his illness grew more serious, he himself began to say the *Praises of the Lord*, and afterwards had his companions sing it, so that in reflecting on the praise of the Lord, he could forget the sharpness of his pains and illnesses. He did this until the day of his death.

ASSISI COMPILATION 84

Reconciliation of the bishop and mayor of Assisi

At that same time when he lay sick, the bishop of the city of Assisi at the time excommunicated the podestà. In return, the man who was then podestà was enraged, and had this proclamation announced, loud and clear, throughout the city of Assisi: no one was to sell or buy anything from the bishop, or to draw up any legal document with him. And so they thoroughly hated each other.

Although very ill, blessed Francis was moved by piety for them, especially since there was no one, religious or secular, who was intervening for peace and harmony between them. He said to his companions: "It is a great shame for you, servants of God, that the bishop and the podestà hate one another in this way, and that there is no one intervening for peace and harmony between them."

And so, for that reason, he composed one verse for the *Praises*:
Praised be by You, my Lord, through those who give pardon for Your love,
     and bear infirmity and tribulation.
       Blessed are those who endure in peace
         for by You, Most High, they shall be crowned.

Afterwards he called one of his companions and told him: "Go to the podestà and, on my behalf, tell him to go to the bishop's residence together with the city's magistrates and bring with him as many others as he can."

And when the brother had gone, he said to two of his other companions: "Go and sing the *Canticle of Brother Sun* before the bishop, the podestà, and the others who are with them. I trust in the Lord that He will humble their hearts and they will make peace with each other and return to their earlier friendship and love."

When they had all gathered in the piazza inside the cloister of the bishop's residence, the two brothers rose and one of them said: "In his illness, blessed Francis wrote the *Praises of the Lord* for His creatures, for His praise and the edification of his neighbor. He asks you, then, to listen to them with great devotion." And so, they began to sing and recite to them. And immediately the podestà stood up and, folding his arms and hands with great devotion, he listened intently, even with tears, as if to the Gospel of the Lord. For he had a great faith and devotion toward blessed Francis.

When the *Praises of the Lord* were ended, the podestà said to everyone: "I tell you the truth, not only do I forgive the lord bishop, whom I must have as my lord, but I would even forgive one who killed my brother or my son." And so he cast himself at the lord bishop's feet, telling him: "Look, I am ready to make amends to you for everything, as it pleases you, for the love of our Lord Jesus Christ and of his servant, blessed Francis."

Taking him by the hands, the bishop stood up and said to him: "Because of my office humility is expected of me, but because I am naturally prone to anger, you must forgive me." And so, with great kindness and love they embraced and kissed each other.

And the brothers marveled greatly, considering the holiness of blessed Francis, that what he had foretold about peace and harmony between them had been fulfilled, to the letter. All the others who were present and heard it took it for a great miracle, crediting it to the merits of blessed Francis, that the Lord had so quickly visited them, and that without recalling anything that had been said, they returned to such harmony from such scandal.

Therefore we who were with blessed Francis bear witness that always whenever he would predict "such-and-such a thing is or will be this way," it happened almost to the letter. We have seen with our own eyes what would be too long to write down or recount.

THE CANTICLE OF THE CREATURES

Most High, all-powerful, good Lord.

Yours are *the praises, the glory, and the honor*, and all *blessing*,
To You alone, Most High, do they belong,

and no human is worthy to mention your name.
Praised be You, my *Lord*, with all *your creatures*,

especially Sir Brother Sun,

Who is the day and through whom You give us light.
And he is beautiful and radiant with great splendor;

and bears a likeness of You, Most High One.
Praised be You, my Lord, through Sister *Moon* and *the stars*,

in heaven You formed them clear and precious and beautiful.
Praised be You, my Lord, through Brother Wind,

and through the air, cloudy and serene, and every kind of weather,

through whom You give sustenance to Your creatures.
Praised be You, my Lord, through Sister *Water*,

who is very useful and humble and precious and chaste.
Praised be You, my Lord, through Brother *Fire*,

through whom *You light the night*,
and he is beautiful and playful and robust and strong.
Praised be You, my Lord, through our Sister Mother *Earth*,
who sustains and governs us,
and who produces varied *fruits* with colored flowers and *herbs*.

Praised be You, my Lord, through those who give pardon for
Your love,
and bear infirmity and tribulation.
Blessed are those who endure in peace
for by You, Most High, they shall be crowned.

Praised be You, my Lord, through our Sister Bodily Death,
from whom no one living can escape.
Woe to those who die in mortal sin.
Blessed are those whom death will find in Your most holy will,
for *the second death* shall do them no harm.

Praise and *bless* my *Lord* and give Him thanks
and serve Him with great humility.

OTHER READINGS:
LMj II:1—How Francis hears Christ from the cross and sells
cloth
1C 18—Repair of San Damiano
L3C 21–24; LMj II:7—Francis begging for San Damiano
AC 13—Clare seeing Francis for a last time

EUCHARIST
CANTICLE OF CREATION

READING: WISDOM OF SOLOMON 13:1–9

A reading from the book of Wisdom

For all people who were ignorant of God were foolish by nature; and they were unable from the good things that are seen to know the one who exists, nor did they recognize the artisan while paying heed to his works; but they supposed that either fire or wind or swift air, or the circle of the stars, or turbulent water, or the luminaries of heaven were the gods that rule the world. If through delight in the beauty of these things people assumed them to be gods, let them know how much better than these is their Lord, for the author of beauty created them. And if people were amazed at their power and working, let them perceive from them how much more powerful is the one who formed them. For from the greatness and beauty of created things comes a corresponding perception of their Creator. Yet these people are little to be blamed, for perhaps they go astray while seeking God and desiring to find him. For while they live among his works, they keep searching, and they trust in what they see, because the things that are seen are beautiful. Yet again, not even they are to be excused; for if they had the power to know so much that they could investigate the world, how did they fail to find sooner the Lord of these things? **The word of the Lord.**

RESPONSE:
A sung version of The Canticle of the Creatures

ALLELUIA: God was in Christ, to reconcile the world; and the Good News of reconciliation God has entrusted to us.
GOSPEL: JOHN 3:16–17

A reading from the holy Gospel according to John

[Jesus said to them:] "For God so loved the world that he gave his only Son, so that everyone who believes in him may not perish but may have eternal life. Indeed, God did not send the Son into the world to condemn the world, but in order that the world might be saved through him." **The Gospel of the Lord.**

EUCHARIST
REBUILD MY CHURCH

READING: 1 SAMUEL 3:1–10, 19–20

A reading from the first book of Samuel

Now the boy Samuel was ministering to the LORD under Eli. The word of the LORD was rare in those days; visions were not widespread. At that time Eli, whose eyesight had begun to grow dim so that he could not see, was lying down in his room; the lamp of God had not yet gone out, and Samuel was lying down in the temple of the LORD, where the ark of God was. Then the LORD called, "Samuel! Samuel!" and he said, "Here I am!" and ran to Eli, and said, "Here I am, for you called me." But he said, "I did not call; lie down again." So he went and lay down. The LORD called again, "Samuel!" Samuel got up and went to Eli, and said, "Here I am, for you called me." But he said, "I did not call, my son; lie down again." Now Samuel did not yet know the LORD, and the word of the LORD had not yet been revealed to him. The LORD called Samuel again, a third time. And he got up and went to Eli, and said, "Here I am, for you called me." Then Eli perceived that the LORD was calling the boy. Therefore Eli said to Samuel, "Go, lie down; and if he calls you, you shall say, 'Speak, LORD, for your servant is listening.'" So Samuel went and lay down in his place. Now the LORD came and stood there, calling as before, "Samuel! Samuel!" And Samuel said, "Speak, for your servant is listening."

As Samuel grew up, the LORD was with him and let none of his words fall to the ground. And all Israel from Dan to Beersheba knew that Samuel was a trustworthy prophet of the LORD. **The word of the Lord.**

RESPONSE: Here I am Lord, I come to do your will unreservedly.

PSALM 127

Unless the LORD builds the house,
those who build it labor in vain.
Unless the LORD guards the city,
the guard keeps watch in vain. **R.**

It is in vain that you rise up early
and go late to rest,
eating the bread of anxious toil;
for he gives sleep to his beloved. **R.**

Sons are indeed a heritage from the LORD,
the fruit of the womb a reward.
Like arrows in the hand of a warrior
are the sons of one's youth. **R.**

Happy is the man who has his quiver full of them.
He shall not be put to shame
when he speaks with his
enemies in the gate. **R.**

ALLELUIA: Blessed are you, Father, Lord of heaven and earth; you have revealed to little ones the mysteries of the kingdom.

GOSPEL: JOHN 2:13–22

A reading from the holy Gospel according to John

The Passover of the Jews was near, and Jesus went up to Jerusalem. In the temple he found people selling cattle, sheep, and doves, and the money changers seated at their tables. Making a whip of cords, he drove all of them out of the temple, both the sheep and the cattle. He also poured out the coins of the money changers and overturned their tables. He told those who were selling the doves, "Take these things out of here! Stop making my Father's house a marketplace!" His disciples remembered that it was written, "Zeal for your house will consume me." The Jews then said to him, "What sign can you show us for doing this?" Jesus answered them, "Destroy this temple, and in three days I will raise it up." The Jews then said, "This temple has been under construction for forty-six years, and will you raise it up in three days?" But he was speaking of the temple of his body. After he was raised from the dead, his disciples remembered that he had said this; and they believed the scripture and the word that Jesus had spoken. **The Gospel of the Lord.**

MORNING PRAYER
ENCIRCLED BY CREATION

Leader:
We pray today, hoping to become more aware of the wholeness and holiness that are ours by our very identity as human persons and followers of St. Francis, by virtue of our creation at the hand of a loving God, and by the power of the dream that lives within us.

We celebrate this unity with our past and our future, within ourselves and with each other, with the larger Franciscan family, with our church, and with our world.
We believe with Francis that because of creation, and still more powerfully because of the Incarnation, nothing is profane,

nothing is unholy for those who know how to see. Everything is charged with the presence of God.

We invoke the Spirit and her life-giving presence inherent in creation to inspire and sustain our reflection and sharing today, to weave connections between us, linking us to each other, strengthening us from within and without.

We are invited to relax for a few minutes and allow the ancient elements of creation, fire, air, water, and the earth, to encircle us, to ring round us, gracing us with their wisdom and joining us to each other.

FIRE

Leader:
We celebrate the gift of fire.

(A person takes the symbol of fire, circles the group during the reading, then returns the symbol to its place.)

Reader:
We recognize the sun, creation's source of energy and life, and are in awe of its power to warm the death of winter into spring's green life. We close our eyes before its brilliance and still can feel its warmth and see its light against the shadow. Its radiance speaks of the divine power that has brought us into being that today sustains and enlightens our life. Let the sun's rays bathe each of us, the fire's heat warm us, and its radiance penetrate deep within our spirit.

Fire has held mystery since the beginning of time. Francis had always been fascinated by fire. Staring at it had always been a great joy, as it rose and blazed and flickered and roared, changeable and audacious, vivid and beautiful, revealing a thousand glowing and immaterial shapes like blazing spirits.

All:
Fire communicates the presence of God and a passionate love

of life and people. May the power, the warmth, the passion, and the mystery of fire be given us.

AIR

Leader:
We celebrate the gift of air.

(A person takes the symbol of air, circles the group during the reading, then returns the symbol to its place.)

Reader:
Air is invisible and all pervasive, the force with which our Creator God breathed life into us. Without air we die. It sustains every living plant and creature, and sculpts even rock into strange and beautiful shapes. Air is the breath of life. We breathe deeply and know our breathing to be a prayer, a communion with the source of life. The air that we breathe today is the same air breathed by great women and men who have gone before us, our ancestors and friends.

All:
The air that now fills our lungs was breathed by Francis and Clare, by brothers and sisters, friends and family members who have gone before us, and by Jesus himself.

Great Spirit, whose voice we hear in the winds, whose power we feel in the raging storm, let your breath give life to our world.

WATER

Leader:
The Spirit of Yahweh hovered over the water. It is the gift of water we celebrate today.

(A person takes the symbol of water, circles the group during the reading, then returns the symbol to its place.)

Reader:
We claim the water of life, whose rush announces the birth of

a baby, nourishes seeds, and plants roots deep in the earth. We celebrate water without which all that lives would shrivel and wither away, water of our life.

"Come to me and I will give you living water, and you will never be thirsty again." John 4:13–14

All:
Today we pray that our thirst be kept alive until the justice that we thirst for is realized. Today we celebrate our common thirst and the God who gifts us with water.

EARTH

Leader:
We claim the gift of earth.

(A person takes the pot of earth, circles the group during the reading, then returns the pot to its place.)

Reader:
From ancient times, the earth has been portrayed as feminine. Humankind has experienced the earth as life-giving and nourishing, rhythmic and fertile. We are radically joined with the earth, a mothering earth from whose womb all life comes, and to whose breast all life returns. It is by the fruits of the earth we live. On her lands we walk and play and love.

We pray that we might walk gently on this earth, that we might read her wisdom in every leaf and rock and field and care for her with tender respect.

All:
Today we celebrate the earth, our own physical selves, and all that enables us to find our creator in the rich and varied gift of the universe.

Adapted from *More Than Words: Prayer and Ritual for Inclusive Communities*, Janet Schaffran and Pat Kozak [Oak Park, Ill: Meyer Stone Books, 1988].

RITUAL PRAYER

SAN DAMIANO CRUCIFIX

Leader:
We adore you, Lord Jesus Christ, here and in all your churches in the whole world,

All:
Because by your holy Cross you have redeemed the world.

CANTICLE: PHILIPPIANS 2:6–11

Leader:
Let everything in heaven and on earth bend the knee at the name of Jesus.

[1]   Though he was in the form of God,
            Jesus did not deem equality with God
            something to be grasped at.

[2]   Rather, he emptied himself
            and took the form of a slave
            being born in the likeness of us all.

[1]   He was known to be of human estate,
            and it was thus that he humbled himself,
            obediently accepting even death,
            death on a cross!

[2]   Because of this,
            God highly exalted him
            and bestowed on him the name
            above every other name.

All: So that at Jesus' name

every knee must bend
in the heavens, on the earth,
and under the earth,
and every tongue proclaim
to the glory of God the Father:
Jesus Christ is Lord!

READING: THOMAS OF CELANO, SECOND LIFE 10

With his heart already completely changed—soon his body was also to be changed—he was walking one day by the church of San Damiano, which was abandoned by everyone and almost in ruins. *Led by the Spirit* he went in to pray and knelt down devoutly before the crucifix. He was shaken by unusual experiences and discovered that he was different from when he had entered. As soon as he had this feeling, there occurred *something unheard of in previous ages*: with the lips of the painting, the image of Christ crucified spoke to him. "Francis," it said, *calling him by name*, "go rebuild My house; as you see, it is all being destroyed." Francis was more than a little stunned, trembling, and stuttering like a man out of his senses. He prepared himself to obey and pulled himself together to carry out the command. He felt this mysterious change in himself, but he could not describe it. So it is better for us to remain silent about it too. From that time on, compassion for the Crucified was impressed into his holy soul. And we honestly believe the wounds of the sacred Passion were impressed deep in his heart, though not yet on his flesh.

Silent reflection

Distribution of San Damiano Crucifix

Song

FIRE ABOVE /WATER BELOW

The least little brothers
had this tale to tell,
how once he had
accepted the offer
of a prostitute,
if she would obey
the nature of brother fire
and lay down
with him
in the womb of the earth
where all our desires
are purified.
And they recalled
this wonder too,
how one night
out of the heart
of the earth he flew,
all engaged
in dazzling flames
driven like Elijah
enroute home.
He spun round and
round their waking dreams,
touching their hopes
and prayers
with tongues of fire.
And this
most amazing miracle,
which made them weep
and run like rain
to remember:
how mercy had
always poured out
through him
because he used

> all authority given
> to him
> to serve.

William Hart McNichols, S.J., S.F.O., November 1988
Used with permission.

Il Signore ti benedica e
ti custodisca +
Ti mostri la Sua Faccia
ed abbia misericordia
di te +
Volga a te il Suo sguardo
e ti dia pace +
Il Signore ti benedica +

ASSISI: SANTA MARIA MAGGIORE

FRANCISCAN PILGRIMAGE PROGRAMS

ASSISI:
SANTA MARIA MAGGIORE

EVENTS
Francis perhaps helped to restore this cathedral in 1216.

Francis was brought here before Bishop Guido to settle a dispute with his father. He stripped naked and renounced his father.

Here Francis had the brothers sing the second last strophe of *The Canticle of the Creatures* about pardon, thus reconciling the mayor and bishop.

Francis resided here for a time in 1226, shortly before he died.

SPIRITUALITY
Nudus nudum Christum sequi– ("Naked to follow the naked Christ") is a teaching of St. Jerome that was picked up in the Middle Ages to designate a higher and more rigorous ascent to God. Nudity was also a form of humiliation canonically expected of the public penitent. Francis stripped himself naked; he stripped himself of the clothing in which he sang, danced, joked, and participated with friends in the world. In so doing he said no to one life and took up a life of penance. In stripping and handing over everything to his father, Francis renounced his inheritance. He began a life totally dependent on God.

REFLECTION
What is it like to stand naked before another? What feelings emerge? What in the inner spirit is awakened?

Francis stripped himself naked before his father, the bishop, and the townspeople and then renounced his father and claimed only God the Most High as father. Try to reconstruct the scene. What is the significance of nakedness for Francis—here and elsewhere?

Francis and his father had a strained relationship. How would you describe it? What was Pietro Bernardone's response to his son's actions?

Francis and his father are both from another culture and background. They expressed their emotions openly and readily. What difference does their temperament make?
What was the relationship between Francis and Bishop Guido? How does this relationship extend to all the clergy?

How do you understand Francis' break with his father and what significance does this action have in your own life?

SANTA MARIA MAGGIORE

HISTORICAL NOTES

This church served as the Cathedral of Assisi until the 11th century. St. Francis is supposed to have helped restore the building with his own hands in the year 1216. Behind the high altar on the exterior of the apse can be seen this inscription: "*MCCXVI indictione quarta et anni decimi tempore episcopi Guidi et fratris Francisci*" ("In the year 1216, in the fourth year of indiction and the tenth year in the episcopacy of Bishop Guido, and brother Francis"). The interior was formerly covered with frescoes, which were almost entirely destroyed by an earthquake in 1832.

Next to Santa Maria Maggiore is the bishop's palace, which has been completely redone. Many important events took place here—most notably Francis' renunciation of his father. Francis resided here for a few days prior to his death, before he was removed to the Porziuncola. It was here then that he composed the second last strophe of *The Canticle of the Creatures* on "pardon" to patch up the conflict between the civil and ecclesiastical rulers of Assisi.

It has been a long-standing belief that the church of St. Mary Major was built over the home of the notable Roman poet Sextus Propertius (ca. 50–15 B.C.E). We know that he was born of a wealthy family in Assisi and that when he was ten his father died and his mother took him to Rome. Although well educated and encouraged to practice law, he chose to indulge in poetry instead. He became a friend to other great Roman poets, such as Ovid, Virgil, and Horace. The young Propertius wrote romances that immortalized a woman named Cynthia, the unattainable love of his life, an older, more sophisticated and yet passionate woman. Later he turned his attention to the art of honoring patriotism, although he tried to remain aloof from the intrigue of politics.

FRANCISCAN READINGS

ST. BONAVENTURE, MAJOR LEGEND II:4

How Francis strips himself in public, renouncing his father

Thereupon the father of the flesh worked on leading the child of grace, now stripped of his money, before the bishop of the city that he might renounce his family possessions into his hands and return everything he had. The true lover of poverty showed himself eager to comply and went before the bishop without delaying or hesitating. He did not wait for any words nor did he speak any, but immediately took off his clothes and gave them back to his father. Then it was discovered that the man of God had a hair shirt next to his skin under his fine clothes. Moreover, drunk with remarkable fervor, he even took off his trousers, and was completely stripped naked before everyone. He said to his father: "Until now I have called you father here on earth, but now I can say without reservation, *'Our Father who art in heaven,'* since I have placed all my treasure and all my hope in him." The bishop, recognizing and admiring such intense fervor in the man of God, immediately stood up and in tears drew him into his arms, covering him with the mantle that he was wearing. Like the pious and good man that he was, he bade his servants give him something to cover his body. They brought him a poor, cheap cloak of a farmer who worked for the bishop, which he accepted gratefully and, with his own hand, marked a cross on it with a piece of chalk, thus designating it as the covering of a crucified and half-naked poor man.

> Thus the servant of the Most High King
> was left naked
> that he might follow
> his naked crucified Lord, whom he loved.
> Thus the cross strengthened him
> to entrust his soul
> to the wood of salvation
> that would save him from the shipwreck of the world.

THOMAS OF CELANO, FIRST LIFE 13–15

Francis: his mother, his father, and his stripping before the bishop

When his father had left home for a little while on pressing family business, the man of God remained bound in the prison of his home. His mother, who had remained at home alone with him, did not approve of her husband's action and spoke to her son in gentle words. After she saw that she could not dissuade her son from his intention, *she was moved by* maternal *instinct*. She broke his chains and let him go free. Thanking Almighty God, he quickly returned to the place he had been before. Since he had passed the test of temptations, he now enjoyed greater freedom. Throughout these many struggles, he began to exhibit a more joyful appearance. From the injuries inflicted he received a more confident spirit and, now free to go anywhere, he moved about with even greater heart.

Meanwhile, the father returned and, not finding him and heaping sin upon sin, he turned to reviling his wife. He raced to the place, shaking and screaming, so that if he could not call his son back, he might at least drive him from the area. But since *the fear of the Lord is the assurance of fortitude*, when the child of grace heard that his father in the flesh was coming to him, he went out on his own to meet his father crying out loudly that binding and beating lead to nothing. In addition, he declared he would gladly suffer anything for the name of Christ.

When the father saw that he could not recall him from the journey he had begun, he became obsessed with recovering the money. The man of God had desired to spend it on feeding the poor and on the buildings of that place. But the one who did not love money could not be deceived even by this appearance of good, and the one who was not bound by any affection for it was not disturbed in any way by its loss. The greatest scorner of the things of earth and the outstanding seeker of heavenly riches had thrown it into the dust on the windowsill. When the money was found, the rage of his angry father was dampened a little and his thirsty greed was quenched a bit by its discovery. Then he led the son to the bishop of the city to make him renounce into the bishop's hands all rights of inheritance and return everything that he had. Not only did he not refuse this, but he hastened joyfully and eagerly to do what was demanded.

When he was in front of the bishop, he neither delayed nor hesitated, but immediately took off and threw down all his clothes and returned them to his father. He did not even keep his trousers on, and he was completely stripped bare before everyone. The bishop, observing his frame of mind and admiring his fervor and determination, got up and, gathering him in his own arms, covered him with the mantle he was

wearing. He clearly understood that this was prompted by God and he knew that the action of the man of God, which he had personally observed, contained a mystery. After this *he became* his *helper.* Cherishing and comforting him, he embraced him in the depths of charity.

Look!
Now he wrestles naked with the naked.
After putting aside all that is *of the world,*
he is mindful only of divine justice.
Now he is eager to despise his own life,
by setting aside all concern for it.
Thus
there might be peace for him,
a poor man on a hemmed-in path,
and only the wall of the flesh would separate him
from the vision of God.

A PRAYER INSPIRED BY THE OUR FATHER

O *Our Father* most holy:
Our Creator, Redeemer, Consoler, and Savior:

Who are in heaven:
In the angels and the saints,
enlightening them to know, for *You, Lord, are light;*
inflaming them to love, for You, Lord are love;
dwelling in them and filling them with happiness,
for You, Lord, are Supreme Good, the Eternal Good,

from Whom all good comes
without Whom there is no good.

Holy be Your Name:
May knowledge of You become clearer in us
that we may know
the breadth of Your blessings,
the length of Your promises,
the height of Your majesty,
the depth of Your judgments.

Your kingdom come:
That You may rule in us through Your grace
and enable us *to come* to *Your Kingdom*
where there is clear vision of You,
perfect love of You,
blessed companionship with You,
eternal enjoyment of You.

Your will be done on earth as in heaven:
That we may love You
with our whole heart by always thinking of You,
with our whole soul by always desiring You,
with our whole mind by always directing all our intentions to You,
and by seeking Your glory in everything,
with all our whole strength by exerting
all our energies and affections of body and soul
in the service of Your love and of nothing else;
and we may love our neighbor as ourselves
by drawing them all to Your love with our whole strength,
by rejoicing in the good of others as in our own,
by suffering with others at their misfortunes,
and by giving offense to no one.

Give us this day:
in remembrance, understanding, and reverence
of that love which [our Lord Jesus Christ] had for us

and of those things that He said and did and suffered for us.

our daily Bread:
Your own beloved Son, our Lord Jesus Christ.

Forgive us our trespasses:
through Your ineffable mercy
through the power of the passion of Your beloved Son
and through the merits and intercession
of the ever blessed Virgin and all Your elect.

As we forgive those who trespass against us:
And what we do not completely forgive,
make us, Lord, forgive completely
that we may truly love our enemies because of You
and we may fervently intercede for them before You,
returning no one evil for evil
and we may strive to help everyone in You.

And *lead us not into* temptation:
hidden or obvious,
sudden or persistent.

But *deliver us from evil:*
past,
present,
and to come.

Glory to the Father, and to the Son, and to the Holy Spirit.
As it was in the beginning, is now, and will be forever.
Amen.

OTHER READINGS
2MP 10; AC 58—Francis and Bishop Guido
AC 84; 2MP 101—Reconciliation of the bishop and mayor
AC 99–100—Francis at the bishop's palace before Francis' death
LMj XIV:6; 2C 220—Francis' appearance to the bishop of Assisi
in a vision

EUCHARIST

READING: JOB 1:8–15, 18–22

A reading from the book of Job

The LORD said to Satan, "Have you considered my servant Job? There is no one like him on the earth, a blameless and upright man who fears God and turns away from evil." Then Satan answered the LORD, "Does Job fear God for nothing? Have you not put a fence around him and his house and all that he has, on every side? You have blessed the work of his hands, and his possessions have increased in the land. But stretch out your hand now, and touch all that he has, and he will curse you to your face." The LORD said to Satan, "Very well, all that he has is in your power; only do not stretch out your hand against him!" So Satan went out from the presence of the LORD. One day when his sons and daughters were eating and drinking wine in the eldest brother's house, a messenger came to Job and said, "The oxen were plowing and the donkeys were feeding beside them, and the Sabeans fell on them and carried them off, and killed the servants with the edge of the sword; I alone have escaped to tell you."

While he was still speaking, another came and said, "Your sons and daughters were eating and drinking wine in their eldest brother's house, and suddenly a great wind came across the desert, struck the four corners of the house, and it fell on the young people, and they are dead; I alone have escaped to tell you." Then Job arose, tore his robe, shaved his head, and fell on the ground and worshiped. He said, "Naked I came from my mother's womb, and naked shall I return there; the LORD gave, and the LORD has taken away; blessed be the name of the LORD." In all this Job did not sin or charge God with wrongdoing. **The word of the Lord.**

RESPONSE: Lord, bend your ear and hear my prayer.

PSALM 143

Hear my prayer, O LORD;
give ear to my supplications in your faithfulness;
answer me in your righteousness. **R.**

Do not enter into judgment with your servant,
for no one living is righteous before you.
For the enemy has pursued me, crushing my life to the ground,
making me sit in darkness like those long dead. **R.**

Therefore my spirit faints within me;
my heart within me is appalled.
I remember the days of old, I think about all your deeds,
I meditate on the works of your hands. **R.**

I stretch out my hands to you;
my soul thirsts for you like a parched land.
Answer me quickly, O LORD; my spirit fails.
Do not hide your face from me,
or I shall be like those who go down to the Pit. **R.**

**ALLELUIA: They divided my garments among them and
for my clothing they cast lots.**

GOSPEL: MATTHEW 27: 27–31; JOHN 19:23–25

**A reading from the holy Gospel according to Matthew
and John**

Then the soldiers of the governor took Jesus into the governor's
headquarters, and they gathered the whole cohort around him.
They stripped him and put a scarlet robe on him, and after
twisting some thorns into a crown, they put it on his head.
They put a reed in his right hand and knelt before him and
mocked him, saying, "Hail, King of the Jews!" They spat on

him, and took the reed and struck him on the head. After mocking him, they stripped him of the robe and put his own clothes on him. Then they led him away to crucify him.

When the soldiers had crucified Jesus, they took his clothes and divided them into four parts, one for each soldier. They also took his tunic; now the tunic was seamless, woven in one piece from the top. So they said to one another, "Let us not tear it, but cast lots for it to see who will get it." This was to fulfill what the scripture says, "They divided my clothes among themselves, and for my clothing they cast lots." And that is what the soldiers did. Meanwhile, standing near the cross of Jesus were his mother, and his mother's sister, Mary the wife of Clopas, and Mary Magdalene. **The Gospel of the Lord.**

RITUAL SERVICE

RESPONSE: F 9 "I Am a Poor One"

THE LEGEND OF THREE COMPANIONS 19–20

Then the father [Peter Bernardone] hurried to the palace of the commune complaining to the city magistrates about his son and asking them to make him return the money he had taken from the house. When the magistrates saw how distraught he was, they sent a messenger to summon Francis to appear before them. He told the messenger that he had been made free by God's grace and, since he was a servant of almighty God alone, was no longer bound by the magistrates. The magistrates, unwilling to force the issue, told his father: "Because he is in the service of God, he no longer falls within our power."

RESPONSE: F 9

Realizing that he could accomplish nothing with the magistrates, he made the same complaint before the bishop of the city. The bishop, a discerning and understanding man, duly called him to appear in order to respond to his father's complaint. [Francis] answered the messenger: "I will appear before the lord bishop, because he is the father and lord of souls."

Then he came before the bishop and was received by him with great joy. "Your father," the bishop said to him, "is infuriated and extremely scandalized. If you wish to serve God, return to him the money you have, because God does not want you to spend money unjustly acquired on the work of the church. [Your father's] anger will abate when he gets the money back. My son, have confidence in the Lord and act courageously. Do not be afraid, for He will be your help and will abundantly provide you with whatever is necessary for the work of his church."

RESPONSE: F 9

Then the man of God got up, joyful and comforted by the bishop's words, and, as he brought the money to him, he said: "My Lord, I will gladly give back not only the money acquired from his things, but even all my clothes." And going into one of the bishop's rooms, he took off all his clothes, and, putting the money on top of them, came out naked before the bishop, his father, and all the bystanders, and said: "Listen to me, all of you, and understand. Until now I have called Pietro di Bernardone my father. But, because I have proposed to serve God, I return to him the money on account of which he was so upset, and also all the clothing which is his, wanting to say from now on: '*Our Father who are in heaven*,' and not 'My father, Pietro di Bernardone.'"

Exchange between Bishop, Francis and people

Silent reflection

REPONSE F 9

Then his father, overcome with unbearable pain and anger, took the money and all the clothing. While he was carrying these home, those who were present at this spectacle were indignant at him, for he left nothing for his son to wear. Moved by piety, they began to weep over him.

The bishop, focusing his attention on the man of God's frame of mind and enthusiastically admiring his fervor and determination, gathered him into his arms, covering him with his mantle. For he clearly understood his deeds were prompted by divine counsel, and realized that what he had seen contained no small mystery. And so, from that moment, *he became* his *helper*, exhorting, encouraging, loving, and embracing him with the depths of his charity.

PSALM 23

The LORD is my shepherd, I shall not want.
He makes me lie down in green pastures;
he leads me beside still waters;
he restores my soul. **R**.

He leads me in right paths for his name's sake.
Even though I walk through the darkest valley,
I fear no evil; for you are with me;
your rod and your staff—they comfort me. **R**.

You prepare a table before me in the presence of my enemies;
you anoint my head with oil; my cup overflows.
Surely goodness and mercy shall follow me all the days of my life,
and I shall dwell in the house of the LORD my whole life long.
R.

ASSISI:
HOUSE OF
BERNARD OF
QUINTAVALLE

FRANCISCAN PILGRIMAGE PROGRAMS

ASSISI: HOUSE OF BERNARD OF QUINTAVALLE

EVENTS
Bernard was perplexed by the behavior and stories of Francis. So he
invited Francis to share a meal and spend the night in his house. It was
from here that they went, with Peter Catanio, to the Church of San Nicolo,
to consult the Scriptures about their way of life.

SPIRITUALITY
Bernard, together with Francis, discerned a vocation. It was done in
consultation with the Scriptures.

REFLECTION
What does it mean to test and be tested by another? What importance
does that have in building a relationship?

Bernard found credibility in Francis. What makes for credibility in our
lives? What makes religious life credible in the church?

Consider well the responsibility we have when preaching to others.

HOUSE OF BERNARD OF QUINTAVALLE

HISTORICAL NOTES

The only thing we know about this house is taken from *The Legend of Three Companions* 27–28 and parallels. The house is below the Piazza del Comune, on Via Bernardo da Quintavalle. Across the street is the church of San Gregorio, now used as a recital and lecture hall. The Quintavalle family remained prominent in Assisi for many centuries, although this particular residence came into the possession of another prominent Assisi family six hundred years ago, the Pennacchi.

Arnaldo Fortini writes:

Bernardo's house stood within the bishop's citadel. A portion of it can still be seen, its windows now walled up, standing among other centuries-old houses, its arches of rose-coloured stone (of recent construction) like reminders of ancient gaiety in their contrast to the dark colour of the façade. There used to be a piazza in front of the house called the piazza of San Gregorio.

Across from Bernardo's house is the church of San Gregorio. ... It is reached from the Piazza del Commune by an alleyway that goes down

among ancient houses that are warmed by the
flames of carnations. Clumps of wild flowers
climb all the way up the rough wood canopy of
the majesty on the side of the church. ... We
are in the heart of the old Roman city....
Dreams and memories flutter through the peace
of the narrow and torturous street, which is
lined by walled-up doors of ancient shops that
one time rang with the work of artisans.

Francis of Assisi [New York: The Crossroad Publishing Co., 1981], 267.

FRANCISCAN READINGS

ST. BONAVENTURE, MAJOR LEGEND III:3

The life of the first brothers

Therefore
as the truth of the man of God's simple teaching and life
became known to many,
some men began to be moved to penance
and, abandoning all things,
joined him in habit and life.
The first among these was
Bernard, a venerable man,
who was made a *sharer* in the divine *vocation*
and merited to be the firstborn son of the blessed Father,
both in priority of time and in the gift of holiness.

For this man, as he was planning to reject the world perfectly
after his example, once he had ascertained for himself the
holiness of Christ's servant, sought his advice on how to carry
this out. On hearing this, God's servant was filled with the
consolation of the Holy Spirit over the conception of his first
child. "This requires counsel that is from God," he said.

When morning had broken they went into the church of Saint Nicholas, and, after they had prepared with a prayer, Francis, a worshiper of the Trinity, opened the book of the Gospels three times asking God to confirm Bernard's plan with a threefold testimony. At the first opening of the book this text appeared: *If you will be perfect, go, sell all that you have, and give to the poor.* At the second: *Take nothing on your journey.* And at the third: *If anyone wishes to come after me, let him deny himself and take up his cross and follow me.* "This is our life and rule," the holy man said, "and that of all who wish to join our company. Go, then, if you wish to be perfect, and carry out what you have heard."

ASSISI COMPILATION 12

Francis speaking of Brother Bernard

The day Lady Jacoba prepared that confection for blessed Francis, the father remembered Bernard. "Brother Bernard likes this confection," he said to his companions. Calling one of his companions, he told him: "Go, tell Brother Bernard to come to me immediately." The brother went at once and brought him to blessed Francis. Sitting next to the bed where blessed Francis was lying, Brother Bernard said: "Father! I beg you, bless me and show me your love. I believe that, if you show me your love with fatherly affection, God Himself and the other brothers of the religion will love me more."

Blessed Francis was not able to see him, since many days earlier he had lost his sight. Extending his right hand, he placed it on the head of Brother Giles, the third of the first brothers, who at that moment was sitting next to Brother Bernard. He thought he was placing it on the head of Brother Bernard. Feeling the head of Brother Giles, like a person going blind, he immediately recognized him by the Holy Spirit, and said, "This is not the head of my Brother Bernard."

Brother Bernard immediately drew closer to him. Blessed Francis, placing his hand on his head, blessed him. "Write what I tell you," he then said to one of his companions. "Brother Bernard was the first brother the Lord gave me. He began first and most perfectly fulfilled the perfection of the holy Gospel, distributing all his goods to the poor. Because of this and his many other prerogatives, I am bound to love him more than any other brother in the whole religion. As much as I am able, it is my will and command that whoever becomes general minister should love and honor him as he would me. Let the other provincial ministers and the brothers of the whole religion hold him in my place." Because of this, Brother Bernard was greatly consoled as were the other brothers who saw this.

THE LEGEND OF THREE COMPANIONS 27–29

The vocation of Brother Bernard

As both the truth of blessed Francis's simple teaching as well as that of his life became known to many, two years after his conversion, some men began to be moved to do penance by his example and, leaving all things, they joined him in life and habit. The first of these was Brother Bernard of holy memory.

He knew well how luxuriously blessed Francis had lived in the world; now he observed his constancy and zeal in the divine service, how, in particular, he was restoring dilapidated churches with a great deal of work, and what an austere life he was leading. He planned wholeheartedly to give everything he possessed to the poor, and, with determination, to join him in life and garb.

Therefore, one day approaching the man of God in secret, he disclosed his plan to him, and arranged to have him come that evening to his home. Thanking God, for he did not then have a companion, blessed Francis was overjoyed, especially since Lord Bernard was a person of great stature.

On the appointed evening, blessed Francis came to his house, his heart filled with great joy, and spent that whole night with him. Among many things, Lord Bernard said to him: "If, for

many years, someone holds on to the possessions, many or few, he has acquired from his lord, and no longer wishes to keep them, what is the better thing for him to do with them?" Blessed Francis answered that he must give back to the lord what was received from him. And Lord Bernard said: "Then, brother, I want to give away all my worldly goods for the love of my Lord who gave them to me, as it seems best to you." The saint told him: "We will go to the church early in the morning and, through the book of the Gospels, we will learn how the Lord instructed his disciples."

Rising at daybreak, then, together with another man named Peter, who also wanted to become a brother, they went to the church of San Nicolò next to the piazza of the city of Assisi. They entered for prayer, but, because they were simple, they did not know how to find the passage in the Gospel about renunciation. They prayed devoutly that the Lord would show them his will on opening the book the first time.

Once they had finished prayer, blessed Francis took the closed book and, kneeling before the altar, opened it. At its first opening, the Lord's counsel confronted them: *If you wish to be perfect, go, sell everything you possess and give to the poor, and you will have a treasure in heaven.*

Blessed Francis was overjoyed when he read this passage and thanked God. But since he was a true worshiper of the Trinity, he desired it to be confirmed by a threefold affirmation. He opened the book a second and a third time. When he opened it up the second time he saw: *Take nothing for your journey*, etc., and at the third opening: *If any man wishes to come after me, he must deny himself*, etc.

Each time he opened the book, blessed Francis thanked God for confirming his plan and the desire he had conceived earlier. After the third divine confirmation was pointed out and explained, he said to those men, Bernard and Peter: "Brothers, this is our life and rule and that of all who will want to join our company. Go, therefore, and fulfill what you have heard."

Then Lord Bernard, who was very rich, after selling all he had and acquiring a large sum of money, went and distributed it all to the city's poor. Peter likewise followed the divine counsel according to his means.

After getting rid of everything, they both received the habit which the saint had adopted after he put aside the habit of a hermit; and, from that hour, they lived with him according to the form of the holy Gospel as the Lord had shown them. This is why blessed Francis said in his *Testament*: "The Lord Himself revealed to me that I should live according to the form of the holy Gospel."

OTHER READINGS

LFl 2—Conversion of Brother Bernard
Fortini, 266–70—Bernard as first companion

ASSISI:
RIVO
TORTO

FRANCISCAN PILGRIMAGE PROGRAMS

ASSISI: RIVO TORTO

EVENTS

After Francis and the brothers returned from Rome, having had their way of life approved by Innocent III (1209), they set up their initial fraternal life at Rivo Torto, outside Assisi.

Francis woke up in the middle of the night to eat with a hungry friar, to help him avoid embarrassment. Brother Giles joined Francis at Rivo Torto. Here "Brother Fly" was asked to leave the fraternity.

A farmer and his donkey evicted the brothers who then moved on to the Porziuncola.

SPIRITUALITY

This is part of the honeymoon period during the early years of the Franciscan fraternity. One's vision is clear and the way of simplicity is unencumbered.

Murray Bodo wrote: "[Rivo Torto] was the honeymoon of [the brothers'] marriage to Lady Poverty, and the brotherhood never again captured the rapture of those days."

The Journey and the Dream, [Cincinnati: St. Anthony Messenger Press, 1988], 35.

REFLECTION

Rivo Torto invites us to an uncluttered and simple heart.

Consider the wisdom of "letting go" of a cherished practice in order to stand in support of and solidarity with another.

Wholesome fraternal life is worth every effort it takes.

RIVO TORTO

HISTORICAL NOTES

After St. Francis received approval of his Rule and Life from Pope Innocent III in the spring of 1209, he and his eleven companions returned to their native territory, the Spoleto Valley, where they discovered an abandoned shed near a crooked stream (*rivus tortus*). Certain documents, especially the last will and testament of Francis' nephew Piccardo di Angelo di Pica (d. 1253), attest that Francis' family had sizable land holdings in the area of Rivo Torto. Therefore, he was familiar with the area and its people.

The stream of Rivo Torto, like so many in the area, was nothing more than a drainage ditch collecting water from the surrounding mountains, much as it still does today. The trickle of a stream eventually flowed into the Topino River and then to the great Tiber, joining it in its long journey toward Rome and the Mediterranean. The shed, which the Italians call a *tugurio*, was considered by the peasants to be the poorest possible farmhouse. Several memorable events took place at this *protoconvento*, but after a short while, a farmer walked his donkey back into the shed and reclaimed it for himself. Since the friars had been attending services at St. Mary of the Angels (Porziuncola) while living at Rivo Torto, they asked the Benedictines if they could live there instead.

Although during Francis' lifetime the friars were not to live at Rivo Torto again, the fame of the saint and his followers would not allow any place where they preached or lived to be forgotten. Shortly after Francis' death his memory was venerated at the shed of Rivo Torto to such an extent that around 1250 an altar was built in the *turgurio* establishing it as a place of public prayer.

After some neglect through the years, by 1455 the bishop of Assisi authorized the friars to build a chapel where Mass could be celebrated. The chapel then became known as Our Lady of Rivo Torto. The General Chapter of 1491 declared its desire to maintain devotion to the ancient site of Rivo Torto. In 1586 the Franciscan Pope, Sixtus V, restructured the entire chapel and friary. In 1671 the bishop of Assisi consecrated a renovated chapel in honor of Our Lady of Consolation. Rivo Torto became a parish church in 1847. By 1926, the seventh hundredth anniversary of the death of St. Francis, the Italian Ministry of Public Monuments decided to dismantle all of the ornate additions that had literally made the *tugurio* unrecognizable as a peasant's donkey shed.

The tedious excavation discovered an encircling foundation wall of a three-sectioned building. Geologists determined that because of the arrangement, the type of mortar, and the level of the water table, this foundation was at least seven hundred years old. Building on this foundation, the *tugurio* was scrupulously reconstructed in the style of other such existing medieval dwellings.

In 1935 Rivo Torto became a seminary for aspirants and a novitiate. It now serves as a parish and retreat facility. An earthquake in 1984 caused sufficient damage for the sanctuary to be closed for ten years. When it was rededicated in 1994, Rivo Torto was graced with new stained glass windows created by Alberto Farina, O.F.M., of Florence, and a statue of Francis in the courtyard designed by Felice Rossetti, O.F.M. Conv., of Siena.

From *La Voce*, Diocesan Newspaper of Assisi. 30 December 1994, no. 48.

RIVO TORTO

REFLECTIVE PRAYER SERVICE
BASED IN FRANCISCAN SOURCES

ASSISI COMPILATION 50

One time in the very beginning, that is, at the time when blessed Francis began to have brothers, he was staying with them at Rivo Torto. One night, around midnight, when they were all asleep in their beds, one of the brothers cried out, saying: "I'm dying! I'm dying!" Startled and frightened all the brothers woke up.

Getting up, blessed Francis said: "Brothers, get up and light a lamp." After the lamp was lit, blessed Francis said: "Who was it who said, 'I'm dying?'"

"I'm the one," the brother answered.

"What's the matter, brother?" blessed Francis said to him. "Why are you dying?"

"I'm dying of hunger," he answered.

So that that brother would not be ashamed to eat alone, blessed Francis, a man of great charity and discernment, immediately had the table set and they all ate together with him. This brother, as well as the others, were newly converted to the Lord and afflicted their bodies excessively.

After the meal, blessed Francis said to the other brothers: "My brothers, I say that each of you must consider his own constitution, because, although one of you may be sustained with less food than another, I still do not want one who needs more food to try imitating him in this. Rather, considering his constitution, he should provide his body with what it needs. Just as we must beware of overindulgence in eating, which harms body and soul, so we must beware of excessive abstinence even more, because the Lord desires mercy and not sacrifice."

And he said: "Dearest brothers, great necessity and charity compelled me to do what I did, namely, that out of love for our brother we ate together with him, so he wouldn't be embarrassed to eat alone. But I tell you, in the future I do not wish to act this way because it wouldn't be religious or decent. Let each one provide his body with what it needs as our poverty will allow. This is what I wish and command you."

FOR REFLECTION: What holds me back from taking care of myself physically, spiritually? How do I seek balance for wholeness?

SECOND MIRROR OF PERFECTION 36

At the beginning of the religion, when he was staying at Rivo Torto with only two brothers whom he had at that time, the third brother, a man named Giles, came to him from the world to receive his life. When he had stayed there for a few days, still wearing his secular clothes, a poor man happened to come to the place asking alms of blessed Francis. Turning to Giles, blessed Francis said to him: "Give the poor brother your mantle." Immediately, with great joy, he took it off his back and gave it to the poor man. It then seemed to him that, at that moment, the Lord immediately had infused new grace into his heart because he had given the poor man his mantle with joy. So he was received by blessed Francis and constantly progressed in virtue to a very great state of perfection.

FOR REFLECTION: What holds me back from giving freely?

ASSISI COMPILATION 97

For the will of blessed Francis, as he often said, was that no brother should procrastinate in going for alms, so that he not be ashamed to go later on. Indeed, the greater and nobler a brother had been in the world, so much the more pleased and happy was he when he went for alms and did servile work of this sort because of good example. Thus it was in the early days. At the religion's beginning, when the brothers were staying at Rivo Torto, there was a brother among them who prayed little, did not work, and did not want to go for alms because he was ashamed; but he would eat heartily. Giving the matter some thought, blessed Francis knew through the Holy Spirit that the man was carnal. He therefore told him: "Go on your way, Brother Fly, because you want to feed on the labor of your brothers, but wish to be idle in the work of God, like Brother Drone that does not want to gather or work, yet eats the work and gain of the good bees."

So he went his way. And because he lived according to the flesh, he did not ask for mercy.

FOR REFLECTION: How am I sensual? Cluttered? Anaesthetized? How do I move to get uncluttered?

THOMAS OF CELANO, FIRST LIFE 43

(One day Otto IV passed by Assisi, probably traveling along the Via Antica, about one quarter mile from Rivo Torto. Traces of the road can be seen among the paths that cut across the fields.)

He taught them to mortify not only vices and to check the promptings of the flesh, but also to check the external senses, through which death enters the soul. At that time the emperor Otto passed through that area, traveling in great pomp and circumstance to receive the crown of an earthly empire. The most holy father and his followers were staying in that small hut next to the very parade route. He did not go outside to look and did not allow the others to do so, except for one who, without wavering, proclaimed to the emperor that his glory would be short-lived. The glorious holy one, living within himself and walking in the *breadth of his heart*, prepared in himself a worthy *dwelling place of God*. That is why the uproar outside did not seize his ears, nor could any cry intrude, interrupting the great enterprise he had in hand. Apostolic authority resided in him; so he altogether refused to flatter kings and princes.

FOR REFLECTION: In what ways do I glorify self? How do I need to switch to give God glory?

THE LEGEND OF THREE COMPANIONS 55

The blessed father with his sons were staying in a place near Assisi called Rivo Torto where there was a hut abandoned by all. The place was so cramped that they could barely sit or rest. Very often for lack of bread, their only food was the turnips that they begged in their need, here and there.

The man of God would write the names of the brothers on the beams of that hut, so that anyone wishing to rest or pray would know his place, and so that any unusual noise would not disturb the mind's silence in such small and close quarters.

One day while the brothers were staying in that place, a peasant came with his donkey, wanting to stay in that hut with it. And so that he would not be driven away by the brothers, on walking into the hut, he said to his donkey: "Go in, go in, because we will do well in this place."

When the holy father heard the peasant's words and realized his intention, he was annoyed at him, most of all because he made quite an uproar with his donkey, disturbing all the brothers who were then immersed in silence and prayer. Then the man of God said to his brothers: "I know, brothers, that God did not call us to prepare a lodging for a donkey, nor to have dealings with men. While we are preaching the way of salvation to people and are giving them wise counsel, we should dedicate ourselves most of all to prayer and thanksgiving."

They left that hut for the use of poor lepers, moving to a small dwelling near Saint Mary of the Portiuncula where they stayed from time to time before acquiring that church.

FOR REFLECTION: How do I discern what it means to stand firm, how to give in?

OTHER READING
Fortini, 291–293—"Winter at Rivo Torto"

ASSISI: LA MADDALENA & SAN RUFINO D'ARCE

FRANCISCAN PILGRIMAGE PROGRAMS

ASSISI: LA MADDALENA AND SAN RUFINO D'ARCE

EVENTS

The chapels of San Rufino d'Arce and La Maddalena are all that remain of six leprosaria that existed outside of Assisi providing care for lepers isolated from the city centers.

Both Francis and Clare ministered to the leper outcasts at this site, located at an intersecting point between Rivo Torto, the Porziuncola and San Damiano.

New candidates to the Franciscan way of life began their formation process by living with and ministering to the lepers.

La Maddalena, formerly called San Lazzaro d'Arce, remains a place of prayer and devotion for the local residents of the area. San Rufino d'Arce is now cared for by Franciscan sisters who live in a convent connected with this chapel.

SPIRITUALITY

Throughout many centuries men and women saw in the faces of lepers the face of Jesus Christ and were moved to care for them despite the risks to their own personal health.

Countless men and women were a different kind of penitent, marked not with edifying sackcloth and crosses, but with *gattinelli* ("tunics"), gloves, personal water flasks and *tentenelle* ("wooden clappers") that announced their presence and alienated them from unsuspecting passersby.

Francis, Clare, and the early companions reshaped their understanding of penitential life, of poverty, and of fraternity by living and working with the lepers. They followed Jesus literally by "washing their feet" and "doing this in memory of Me."

Fears that seem most bitter become sweet when embraced and recognized as the presence of God.

Conversion begins when we take ourselves where we do not want to go— with the despised and the outcast. It is lived out in our compassionate and merciful presence among them.

REFLECTION

Who are the lepers in your personal life, your living situation, your neighborhood, the world?

Have you experienced a moment when that which was most bitter to you became sweetness, joy, and peace?

How have you been "initiated" on your spiritual journey by contact with those who are poor or alienated?

What opportunities do you take to serve others by "washing their feet," doing all in memory of Jesus?

LA MADDALENA
AND SAN RUFINO D'ARCE

HISTORICAL NOTES

Two chapels, Santa Maria Maddalena and San Rufino d'Arce, are located in the Umbrian Valley, about halfway between the Porziuncola and Rivotorto. San Damiano is visible from this location as well. In this intersection of Franciscan presence, these chapels are all that remain of what was originally a leper colony, one of several existing in the area at the time of Francis and Clare. Records and communal statutes verify this as the place to which Francis was drawn in the early days of his leper ministry. It is clear that after Clare joined Francis and his companions, she and her sisters also came to this site to minister to the lepers.

Lepers have been the objects of pious care for centuries. Many men and women were inspired by the passage from Isaiah 53:2–3: "For he grew up before him like a young plant, and like a root out of dry ground; he had no form or majesty that we should look at him, nothing in his appearance that we should desire him. He was despised and rejected by others; a man of suffering and acquainted with infirmity; and as one from whom others hide their faces he was despised, and we held him of no account." This same passage was used to describe Jesus, who was despised, rejected, and crucified on Good Friday. Care for the lepers became synonymous with embracing Christ. As early as the time of Gregory the Great, there was a story of the monk Martyrius who found a leper fallen by the wayside. He wrapped him in a cloak and took him to his monastery. When he went to lay him on a bed, the leper in his arms had changed into Jesus Christ.

Several religious orders were founded specifically to care for lepers: the Knights of St. Lazarus and the Crucigers, or Crosiers. The Order of Crucigers was founded during the papacy of Alexander III in 1173. Alexander had special compassion for the lepers. During the Third Lateran Council, he directed laws to deal with social concerns, especially the lepers. Clergy were not to prevent lepers from having churches of their own and cemeteries, and their own priest. No tithes were to be asked of lepers.

One of the houses that the Crucigers established is called Casa Gualdi. It is located on the road leading from Assisi down to the Porziuncola. Brother Moricus was a member of the Crucigers and became critically ill. He begged Francis to come and pray for him. Francis responded, healing Moricus, who left the Crucigers and joined the Friars Minor. A bronze plaque remains on the outside wall of Casa Gualdi depicting Francis giving his final blessing to the city of Assisi as he is taken to the Porziuncola to die.

The original name for Santa Maria Maddalena was San Lazzaro d'Arce. Most leper hospices were named after the leper Lazarus and later after another despised person from the gospels, Mary Magdalen. On this site a hospital once existed for the care of the lepers. The chapel is all that remains today.

Nearby is another small chapel called San Rufino d'Arce. It is named after the young martyr Rufino, an altar server who refused to lie on behalf of one of the local priests. He was drowned in a cistern located near the present chapel dedicated in his honor. He is buried in the Cathedral of San Rufino where the bishop martyr Rufino is also buried. His coffin is located at the side altar, to the left of the main altar.

Some suggest that San Rufino d'Arce served the needs of the male lepers while Maria Maddalena cared for the spiritual needs of the women. Most believe that because of their proximity, both chapels were part of the original leper hospital. However, some scholars suggest that San Rufino d'Arce was not related to the leper colony at all, but rather was one of several churches that served the rural people in the area.

It is clear that Francis worked in this area. Not only that, some suggest that Clare and her sisters joined the brothers in ministering to the needs of the lepers here. There are numerous accounts of how Francis embraced the leper early in his conversion process, leading Francis to recognize the face of Christ in these poorest of the poor. Lepers will appear time and again in the stories that recount the life of St. Francis.

Lepers were more than objects of pity for Francis. The early principles of fraternal life developed by living in the midst of the lepers. The focus of life was not just on ministry but on mercy and compassion in the presence of these poor. Francis was formed by his experience among them. In turn he expected the early recruits in his order, whether nobles or commoners, to spend time in formation among the lepers. The memory of lepers never left his mind and heart. It explains why in his Testament he wrote this final recollection before he died: "The Lord gave me, Brother Francis, thus to begin doing penance in this way: for when I was in sin, it seemed too bitter for me to see lepers. And the Lord Himself led me among them and *I showed mercy* to them. And when I left them, what had seemed bitter to me was turned into sweetness of soul and body. And afterwards I delayed a little and left the world." *The Testament 1–3.*

FRANCISCAN READINGS

THE LEGEND OF THREE COMPANIONS 11

Embracing a leper

One day, while he was praying enthusiastically to the Lord, he received this response: "Francis, everything you loved carnally and desired to have, you must despise and hate, if you wish to know my will. Because once you begin doing this, what before seemed delightful and sweet will be unbearable and bitter; and what before made you shudder will offer you great sweetness and enormous delight."

He was overjoyed at this and was comforted by the Lord. One day he was riding his horse near Assisi, when he met a leper. And, even though he usually shuddered at lepers, he made himself dismount, and gave him a coin, kissing his hand as he did so. After he accepted a kiss of peace from him, Francis remounted and continued on his way. He then began to consider himself less and less, until, by God's grace, he came to complete victory over himself.

After a few days he moved to a hospice of lepers, taking with him a large sum of money. Calling them all together, as he kissed the hand of each, he gave them alms. When he left there, what before had been bitter, that is, to see and touch lepers, was turned into sweetness. For, as he said, the sight of lepers was so bitter to him, that he refused not only to look at them, but even to approach their dwellings. If he happened to come near their houses or to see them, even though he was moved by pity to give them alms through an intermediary, he always turned away his face and held his nose. With the help of God's grace, he became such a servant and friend of the lepers, that, as he testified in his *Testament,* he stayed among them and served them with humility.

ASSISI COMPILATION 9

Serving the lepers

From the beginning of his conversion blessed Francis, with God's help, like a wise man, established himself and his house, that is, the religion, upon a firm rock, the greatest humility and poverty of the Son of God, calling it the religion of "Lesser Brothers."

On the greatest humility: thus at the beginning of the religion, after the brothers grew in number, he wanted the brothers to stay in hospitals of lepers to serve them. At that time whenever nobles and commoners came to the religion, they were told, among other things, that they had to serve the lepers and stay in their houses.

On the greatest poverty: as stated in the *Rule*, let the brothers remain as strangers and pilgrims in the houses in which they stay. Let them not seek to have anything under heaven, except holy poverty, by which, in this world, they are nourished by the Lord with bodily food and virtue, and, in the next, will attain a heavenly inheritance.

He established himself on the greatest poverty and humility, because, although he was a great prelate in the church of God, he wanted and chose to be lowly not only in the church of God, but also among his brothers.

ST. BONAVENTURE, MAJOR LEGEND I:5

Embracing a leper

One day, therefore, while he was riding his horse through the plain that lies below the city of Assisi, he met a leper. This un- foreseen encounter struck him with not a little horror. Recall- ing the plan of perfection he had already conceived in his mind, and remembering that he must first conquer himself if he wanted to become a knight of Christ, he dismounted from his horse and ran to kiss him. As the leper stretched out his hand as if to receive something, he gave him money with a kiss. Immedi- ately mounting his horse, how- ever, and turning all around,

even though the open plain stretched clear in all directions, he could not see the leper anywhere. He began, therefore, filled with wonder and joy, to sing praises to the Lord, while propos- ing, because of this, to embark always on the greater.

THE LITTLE FLOWERS OF SAINT FRANCIS 25

Francis' loving care for the lepers

Sir Saint Francis, the true disciple of Christ, while living in this miserable life, always strove with all his strength to follow Christ, the perfect teacher. Therefore, it often happened by divine action, that those whose bodies he healed were healed in soul by God at the same time, as we read of Christ. Not only did he willingly serve the lepers himself, but besides this he set down that the brothers of his Order, while staying or travelling through the world, should serve the lepers for love of Christ, who wished for our sake to be *considered a leper*.

EUCHARIST

READING: LEVITICUS 13:1–2, 44–46

A reading from the book of Leviticus

The LORD spoke to Moses and Aaron, saying: When a person has on the skin of his body a swelling or an eruption or a spot, and it turns into a leprous disease on the skin of his body, he shall be brought to Aaron the priest or to one of his sons the priests.

The priest shall pronounce him unclean; the disease is on his head. The person who has the leprous disease shall wear torn clothes and let the hair of his head be disheveled; and he shall cover his upper lip and cry out, "Unclean, unclean." He shall remain unclean as long as he has the disease; he is unclean. He shall live alone; his dwelling shall be outside the camp. **The word of the Lord.**

RESPONSE: The Lord surrounds us with love and compassion.

PSALM 103

Bless the LORD, O my soul, and all that is within me,
bless his holy name.
Bless the LORD, O my soul, and do not forget all his benefits—
R.

who forgives all your iniquity,
who heals all your diseases,
who redeems your life from the pit,
who crowns you with steadfast love and mercy,

who satisfies you with good as long as you live
so that your youth is renewed like the eagle's. **R.**

The LORD works vindication and justice
for all who are oppressed.
He made known his ways to Moses,
his acts to the people of Israel. **R.**

The LORD is merciful and gracious,
slow to anger and abounding in steadfast love.
He will not always accuse,
nor will he keep his anger forever.
He does not deal with us according to our sins,
nor repay us according to our iniquities. **R.**

ALLELUIA: If you wish, Lord, you can make me clean.

GOSPEL: MARK 1:40–45

A reading from the holy Gospel according to Mark

A leper came to [Jesus] begging him, and kneeling he said to him,
"If you choose, you can make me clean." Moved with pity, Jesus
stretched out his hand and touched him, and said to him, "I do
choose. Be made clean!" Immediately the leprosy left him, and he
was made clean. After sternly warning him he sent him away at
once, saying to him, "See that you say nothing to anyone; but go,
show yourself to the priest, and offer for your cleansing what Moses
commanded, as a testimony to them." But he went out and began
to proclaim it freely, and to spread the word, so that Jesus could no
longer go into a town openly, but stayed out in the country; and
people came to him from every quarter. **The Gospel of the Lord.**

ASSISI:
PORZIUNCOLA

FRANCISCAN PILGRIMAGE PROGRAMS

ASSISI: THE PORZIUNCOLA

EVENTS

Francis rebuilt this tiny chapel, the PORZIUNCOLA, which became the center of Francis' movement. Francis lived with his brothers in small huts around the chapel. Francis sent out brothers two by two to all parts of the world.

Francis loved this chapel because of its dedication to Mary, Mother of the Word.

Here, in 1212, Francis received Clare, then took her to Bastia.

In 1216 Francis had a vision and obtained *Il Perdono di Assisi*, approved by Honorius III.

General Chapters took place, perhaps twice a year, around this chapel. Thus it was the scene of important decision-making.

Francis and Clare shared a meal here (LFl 15).

After returning from the Holy Land (1220), Francis attempted to tear down a house built here for the brothers by the people of Assisi (2C 57).

Francis died here, October 3, 1226.

SPIRITUALITY

The Porziuncola conjures up sentiments and thoughts linked with having a center, a heart. This place symbolizes Francis' heart. It invites us to ponder who or what is at the center of life for us.

The Porziuncola invites us to consider our call to preach penance and peace to all. Formation into a missionary spirit is central to the spirituality of this place.

The Porziuncola calls us to a spirit of reconciliation and forgiveness: toward ourselves, others, and creation and in our relationship to God. There is perhaps no more powerful theme in all of Scripture.

REFLECTION

Francis' hearing the Gospel, February 23, 1208, gave him a lifelong direction. We listen to the Scriptures to guide our lives.

A definite lifestyle developed around the Porziuncola. Try to picture what it was like from reading the sources. How is the brothers' lifestyle meaningful for us?

The Chapter of Mats, 1221, and other chapters, make the Porziuncola a "place of decisions." In this setting we find inspiration for our General/ Provincial chapters.

The Porziuncola is also called the "Sanctuary of Mission." The Franciscan Order is founded on the idea of mission.

THE PORZIUNCOLA

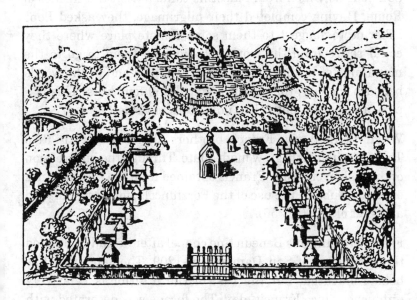

HISTORICAL NOTES

Francis was especially fond of St. Mary of the Angels, the "Little Portion"—a tiny chapel hidden away in the woods and marshes near Assisi. "This place the holy man loved more than other places in the world; for here he began humbly, here he progressed virtuously, here he ended happily" (LMj II:8).

Although blessed Francis was aware that the kingdom of heaven was established everywhere on earth, and believed that the grace of God could be given to the faithful everywhere, he learned from experience that St. Mary of the Angels was filled with a richer grace and often visited by celestial spirits. So he often said to the friars, "See to it my sons, that you never abandon this place. If you are thrown out of one door, go back through another, for *this* is truly a *holy place*, and the dwelling place of Christ and His Virgin Mother" (2MP 83).

The chapel's history is lost in legend. It is said that in the year 352, four holy men from Palestine came to visit the shrines of Rome. Having completed their pilgrimage, they asked Pope Liberius to suggest to them some remote place where they could retire from the world. He advised them to go to the mountains of Umbria. They came to Assisi; and in the woods beneath the city, they built a chapel and four huts. This is a pleasant legend, but it has no historical value.

When the Lord gave Francis brothers, they went first to Rivo Torto, but it quickly grew inadequate. Through the intercession of the bishop of Assisi, Francis obtained from the Benedictines of Monte Subasio the use of the Porziuncola, for which he paid a basket of fish (AC 56).

Francis rebuilt this Benedictine chapel after he had completed the rebuilding of San Damiano in 1209. The sanctuary has been renovated, but the rest of the interior is relatively untouched since Francis' day. The facade was decorated with mosaics later, but the side and back probably give a pretty good idea of what the Porziuncola Chapel was like.

The basilica that covers the chapel was begun in 1569 by decree of Pius V, on the site of a 13th century gothic church. It was meant to accommodate the huge crowds of pilgrims who came on August 2 for *Il Perdono*. The earthquake of 1832 did great damage to the church but spared the Porziuncola. From 1966 to 1970, in the course of making excavations, a foundation, perhaps of the building Francis attempted to tear down in 1220, was discovered. Also discovered were some other buildings from the time of Francis till the 15th century, and some rooms for prayer.

FRANCISCAN READINGS

THOMAS OF CELANO, FIRST LIFE 21–22

How Francis hears the Gospel and receives a life direction

Meanwhile, the holy man of God, having changed his habit and rebuilt that church, moved to another place near the city of Assisi, where he began to rebuild a certain church that had fallen into ruin and was almost destroyed. After a good beginning he did not stop until he had brought all to completion.

From there he moved to another place, which is called the *"Portiuncula,"* where there stood a church of the Blessed Virgin Mother of God built in ancient times. At that time it was deserted and no one was taking care of it. When the holy man of God saw it so ruined, he was moved by piety because he had a warm devotion to the Mother of all good and he began to stay there continually. The restoration of that church took place in the third year of his conversion. At this time he wore a sort of hermit's habit with a leather belt. He carried a staff in his hand and wore shoes.

One day the Gospel was being read in that church about how the Lord sent out his disciples to preach. The holy man of God, who was attending there, in order to understand better the words of the Gospel, humbly begged the priest after celebrating the solemnities of the Mass to explain the Gospel to him. The priest explained it all to him thoroughly line by line. When he heard that Christ's disciples should not *possess gold* or *silver* or *money*, or *carry on their journey a wallet or a sack, nor bread nor a staff,* nor *to have shoes* nor *two tunics,* but that they should preach the *kingdom of God* and *penance,* the holy man, Francis, immediately *exulted* in the *spirit of God.* "This is what I want," he said, "this is what I seek, this is what I desire with all my heart."

SECOND MIRROR OF PERFECTION 55

How Francis obtained the church of St. Mary of the Angels

Seeing that the Lord willed *to increase the number* of brothers, blessed Francis told them: "My dearest brothers and sons, I see that the Lord wants us to increase. Therefore, it seems good and religious to me to obtain from the bishop, or the canons of San Rufino, or from the abbot of the monastery of Saint Benedict, some church where the brothers can say their hours and only have next to it a small and poor little house built of mud and branches where they can sleep and work. This place is not suitable and not adequate for the brothers, since the Lord wants to increase them, and especially because here we do not have a church where the brothers can say their hours. And, should any brother die, it would not be proper to bury him here or in a church of the secular clergy." This *speech pleased all the* brothers.

So he went to the bishop of Assisi. He made the same speech to him. "Brother," the bishop answered him, "I do not have any church that I can give you." The canons said the same thing. Then he went to the abbey of Saint Benedict on Mount Subasio, and placed the same words before them. The abbot, guided by grace and the divine will, took counsel with his monks about this. They granted blessed Francis and his brothers the church of Saint Mary of the *Portiuncula*, as it was favorable for a lesser one and the poorest little church they had.

"Brother, we have granted your request," the abbot told blessed Francis. "But, if the Lord increases your congregation, we want this place to be the head of all your places." And this speech pleased blessed Francis and his brothers.

Blessed Francis was especially overjoyed at the place granted to the brothers, especially because of the name of this church of the Mother of Christ, and because it was such a small and poor little church, and because it was surnamed: "of the *Portiuncula*." This name foreshadowed that it was to be the mother and head of the poor Lesser Brothers. It was called "*Portiuncula*" after the neighborhood which from earliest times was called "*Portiuncula*."

Blessed Francis used to say: "This is why the Lord willed that no other church be granted to the brothers, and why the first brothers would not build any completely new church, and would not have any other but this one. For this church was a prophecy that has been fulfilled in the coming of the Lesser Brothers." And although it was already poor and almost in ruins, nevertheless, for a long time, the people of the city of Assisi and its entire neighborhood had held the church in the greatest devotion even till today, and it increases even daily.

ST. BONAVENTURE, MAJOR LEGEND II: 8

The formation of Francis' life journey by the Porziuncola

When he finally completed this church, he came to a place called the *Portiuncula* where there stood a church of the most Blessed Virgin Mother of God, built in ancient times but now deserted and no one was taking care of it. When the man of God saw it so abandoned, he began to stay there regularly in order to repair it, moved by the warm devotion he had toward the Lady of the world. Sensing that angels often visited there, according to the name of that church, which from ancient times was called Saint Mary of the Angels, he stayed there out of his reverence for the angels and his special love for the mother of Christ.

This place
the holy man loved more than other places in the world;
for here he began humbly,
here he progressed virtuously,

here he ended happily.
This place
he entrusted to his brothers at his death
as the the most beloved of the Virgin. ...

This is the place
where the Order of Lesser Brothers
was begun by Saint Francis
under the prompting of divine revelation.
For at the bidding of divine providence
which guided Christ's servant in everything,
he built up three material churches
before he preached the Gospel
and began the Order not only
to ascend in an orderly progression
from the sensible to the intelligible,
from the lesser to the greater,
but also
to symbolize mystically
in external actions perceived by the senses
what he would do in the future.
For like the three buildings he built up,
so the Church
—where there is victory
for the triple army of those being saved—
was to be renewed in three ways
under his leadership:
by the form, rule, and teaching of Christ
which he would provide.
And now we see
that this prophecy has been fulfilled.

THOMAS OF CELANO, FIRST LIFE 29

Francis' brothers departing two by two; the sanctuary of mission

At that same time, another good man entered their religion, and they increased their number to eight. Then the blessed Francis called them all to himself and told them many things about *the kingdom of God*, contempt of the world, denial of their own will, and subjection of the body. He separated them into four groups of two each.

"Go, my dear brothers," he said to them, "*two by two* through different parts of the world, *announcing peace* to the people and *penance for the remission of sins*. Be *patient in trials*, confident that the Lord will fulfill His plan and promise. Respond humbly to those who question you. *Bless those who persecute you*. Give thanks to those who harm you and bring false charges against you, for because of these things an *eternal kingdom is prepared* for us."

Accepting the command of holy obedience *with* much *joy and gladness*, they humbly prostrated themselves on the ground before Saint Francis. Embracing them, he spoke sweetly and devotedly to each one: "*Cast your care upon the Lord, and he will sustain you.*"

THE LEGEND OF THREE COMPANIONS 57

Chapters of the brothers

After blessed Francis had obtained that place of Saint Mary from the abbot of Saint Benedict, he ordered that a chapter be held there twice a year, that is, on Pentecost and on the Dedication of Saint Michael.

At Pentecost, all the brothers used to gather at the church of Saint Mary and discuss how they could better observe the *Rule*. They appointed brothers throughout the various provinces who would preach to the people, and assigned other brothers in their provinces. Saint Francis, however, used to give admonitions, corrections, and directives as it seemed to him to be according to the Lord's counsel.

ASSISI COMPILATION 56

The citizens of Assisi—building a house at the Porziuncola

One time, close to a chapter that was to be held—which in those days was held annually at Saint Mary of the *Portiuncula*—the people of Assisi considered that, by the Lord's grace, the brothers had already increased and were increasing daily. Yet, especially when they all assembled there for a chapter, they had nothing but a poor, small hut covered with straw, and its walls were built with branches and mud, as the brothers had built when they first came to stay there. After a general meeting, within a few days, with haste and great devotion, they built there a large house with stone-and-mortar walls without the consent of blessed Francis while he was away.

When blessed Francis returned from another region and came to the chapter, and saw that house built there, he was amazed. He considered that, seeing this house, the brothers would build or have built large houses in the places where they now stayed or where they would stay in the future. And especially because he wanted this place always to be a model and example for all the places of the brothers, before the chapter ended he got up one day, climbed onto the roof of that house, and ordered the brothers to climb up. And, intending to destroy the house, he, along with the brothers, began to throw the tiles covering it to the ground.

The knights of Assisi saw this, as well as others who were there on behalf of the city's Commune to protect that place from secular people and outsiders who were outside the place, arriving from all over to see the brothers' chapter. They saw that blessed Francis and the other brothers wanted to destroy that house. They immediately approached them and said to blessed Francis: "Brother, this house belongs to the Commune of Assisi and we are here on behalf of the same Commune, and we're telling you not to destroy our house." "If the house belongs to you," answered blessed Francis, "I don't want to touch it." He and the brothers who were with him immediately came down.

SECOND MIRROR OF PERFECTION 68

Chapter of Mats: Francis standing firm in his way of life

When blessed Francis was at Saint Mary of the Portiuncula for the general chapter known as the Chapter of Mats because the only dwellings there were made of rush-mats, there were five thousand brothers present. Many wise and learned brothers went to the Lord of Ostia, who was there and told him: "Lord, we want you to persuade Brother Francis to follow the advice of the wise brothers and allow himself to be guided by them." They cited the *Rule* of blessed Benedict, blessed Augustine, and blessed Bernard, which teach how to live in such order in such a way.

The cardinal related everything to blessed Francis, giving him some advice as well. Then blessed Francis took him by the hand, saying nothing, and led him to the brothers assembled in chapter, and spoke to the brothers in the fervor and power of the Holy Spirit: "My brothers! My brothers! God has called me by the way of simplicity and humility, and has truly shown me this way for me for those who want to trust and imitate me. Therefore I do not want you to mention to me any *Rule*, whether of Saint Augustine, or of Saint Bernard, or of Saint Benedict, or any other way or form of life except the one that the Lord in His mercy has shown and given to me. And the Lord told me what He wanted: He wanted me to be a new fool in this world.

God did not wish to lead us by any way other than this knowledge, but God will confound you by your knowledge and wisdom. But I trust in the Lord's police that through them God will punish you, and you will return to your *status*, with your blame, like it or not."

The cardinal was greatly shocked, and said nothing, and all the brothers were greatly afraid.

ASSISI COMPILATION 56

Lifestyle of the brothers during the early years at the Porziuncola

When he was near death, [Francis] said before the minister general and the other brothers: "I wish to make arrangements regarding the friary of the Portiuncula and leave them as a testament to my brothers so that this place will always be treated by them with great reverence and devotion.

"Let them do as the old brothers did. This was already a holy place; they preserved its holiness by praying there continually night and day and by observing silence there constantly. And if they sometimes spoke after the time determined for the beginning of silence it was always to converse about the glory of God and the salvation of souls with much uplifting fervor. ..."

They afflicted their bodies not only by fasting but also by frequent vigils, cold, insufficient clothing, and manual work. Very often, in fact, not to remain idle, they went and helped the poor in their fields; and these latter sometimes

gave them bread in return for the love of God. By these virtues and others as well, they sanctified themselves and sanctified this place. Those who succeeded them did likewise for a long time thereafter, but never with equal intensity.

SECOND MIRROR OF PERFECTION 83

How Francis admonished the friars never to leave St. Mary of the Angels

"See to it my sons, that you never abandon this place.
If you are thrown out of one door,
go back through another,
for *this* is truly a *holy place*,
and the dwelling place of Christ and His Virgin Mother.
Here
the Most High increased our numbers,
when we were only a few;
here
He *enlightened the* souls of His poor ones
with the light of His wisdom;
here
He kindled our wills with the fire of his love;
here
all who pray wholeheartedly will receive what they ask
while offenders will be severely punished.
Therefore, my sons, hold this place,
truly *the dwelling place of God*.
with all reverence
and as most worthy of all honor,
particularly dear to Him and to His mother.
In this place
in cries of joy and praise
with your whole heart
here praise God the Father
and His Son, the Lord Jesus Christ,
in the unity of the Holy Spirit."

THOMAS OF CELANO, SECOND LIFE 171

Story of the tree cricket

A cricket lived in a fig tree by the cell of *the holy one of God* at the Portiuncula, and it would sing frequently with its usual sweetness. Once the blessed father stretched out his hand to it and gently called it to him: "My Sister Cricket, come to me!" And the cricket, as if it had reason, immediately climbed onto his hand. He said to it: "Sing, my sister cricket, and with joyful song praise the Lord your Creator!" The cricket, obeying without delay, began to chirp, and did not stop singing until the *man of God*, mixing his own songs with its praise, told it to return to its usual place. Whenever the saint would come down from the cell he would always touch it with his hands and command it to sing, and it was always eager to obey his commands. And the saint said to his companions: "Let us give permission to our sister cricket to leave, who has up to now made us so happy with her praises, so that our *flesh may not boast* vainly *in any way.*" And as soon as it had received permission, the cricket went away and never appeared there again. On seeing all this, the brothers were quite amazed.

THOMAS OF CELANO, FIRST LIFE 108–110

The death of Francis

He was staying then in the palace of the bishop of Assisi, and he asked the brothers to carry him quickly to the place of Saint Mary of the Portiuncula. For he wanted to give back his soul to God in that place where, as noted above, he first came to know perfectly *the way of truth.*

Twenty years had now passed since his conversion, and his time was ending just as it had been shown to him by God's will. ...

After he had rested a few days in that place he so longed for, knowing *the time* of his death *was close at hand*, he called to

him two brothers, his special sons, and told them to sing *The Praises of the Lord* with a loud voice and joyful spirit, rejoicing at his approaching death, or rather at the life that was so near. ...

Then he ordered the book of the Gospels to be brought in. He asked that the Gospel according to John be read to him, starting with the passage that begins: *Six days before the Passover,* Jesus, knowing that the hour had come for him to pass from this world to the Father. ...

Many brothers *gathered* there, for whom *he was* both father and *leader*. They stood there reverently, all awaiting his blessed *departure* and happy *end*. And then that most holy soul was released from the flesh, and as it was absorbed into the abyss of light, his body *fell asleep in the Lord*.

ACTS OF THE PROCESS OF CANONIZATION OF ST. CLARE, WITNESS XII: 2–4; WITNESS XVII: 1, 5

On Clare being received by Francis at the Porziuncola

[Sister Beatrice, twelfth witness,] said, After Saint Francis heard of the fame of her [Clare's] holiness, he went many times to preach to her, so that the virgin Clare acquiesced to his preaching, renounced the world and all earthly things, and went to serve God as soon as she was able.

After that she sold her entire inheritance and part of that of the witness and gave it to the poor.

Then Saint Francis gave her the tonsure before the altar in the church of the Virgin Mary, called the Portiuncula. ...

Lady Bona, daughter of Guelfuccio of Assisi, said under oath she knew Saint Clare from the time she was in her father's house and had conversed and stayed with her in the house. She firmly believed, because of the great holiness of her life which she had before and after she entered Religion, that she had been sanctified in her mother's womb. ... Asked how Lady Clare was converted, she replied Saint Francis had cut off her hair in the church of St. Mary of the *Portiuncula*, as she had heard, because she, the witness, was not present since she had already gone to Rome to observe Lent.

THE LITTLE FLOWERS OF SAINT CLARE

Clare's reception and cutting of her hair at the Porziuncola

During the day when the friars were out working or preaching, St. Mary of the Angels was deserted, but at night it was all lit up with pine-torches and resounded with the praises of Our Lady.

And indeed, brighter than ever it was on that Sunday night when Clare, accompanied by Pacifica di Guelfuccio, came down towards it from Assisi. Waiting for her at the edge of the woods were Philip and Bernard with lighted torches. Still clad in their feast-day dresses, the girls followed the silent friars along the woodland path. The briars pulled and caught at their dresses, and it seemed as if invisible hands were trying to impede their progress through the woods. A few night birds, frightened by the torches, flitted across in front of the two fugitives.

At the door of the tiny chapel Francis waited, his facial lines furrowed by the shade and his eyes smarting from the smoke of burning pine-wood and lack of sleep: he looked out at Clare, who came forward and knelt before him. On each side of him were other bearded friars in their habits.

A passing stranger might have fled from this sight as a scene of brigandage; he might have thought the two girls had fallen into a den of robbers. Apparently eager hands took jewels and precious ornaments from Clare; they divested her of her wonderfully embroidered dress and took off her feet the little shoes of satin. They then put a coarse habit over her and fastened it round her waist with a rope.

Dressed in this way in her bare feet, they then led her into the gothic chapel. St. Mary of the Angels was splendid with sprays and branches of broom, but much of this woodland beauty was lost in the red light of the torches and in the smoke that came from them.

Like one condemned to death they led her on her knees to the foot of the altar. Francis took a razor and approached Clare. He knew what was customary to do. The young girl's tresses, fresher and yellower than the broom [ginestra], fell to the steps of the altar, and Francis placed on her shorn head a rough piece of woolen cloth.

And while she was thus being divested of all her worldly beauty, the friars in their rough habits and unshorn heads chanted forth, as was the custom, the Office of the Dead for a young lady stolen from the world and made a hostage of heaven.

Piero Bargellini, trans. Edmund O'Gorman, O.F.M. Conv. *Edizione Messaggero di Padova.* Used with permission.

MORNING/EVENING PRAYER

THE PORZIUNCOLA THE LITTLE PORTION

ANTIPHON: FROM FRANCIS' *OFFICE OF THE PASSION*

Holy Virgin Mary,
among the women born into the world,
there is no one like you.
Daughter and servant
of the most high and supreme King
and of the Father in heaven,
Mother of our most holy Lord Jesus Christ,
Spouse of the Holy Spirit,
pray for us
with Saint Michael the Archangel,
all the powers of heaven
and all the saints,
at the side of your most holy beloved Son,
our Lord and Teacher.
Glory to the Father, and to the Son, and to the Holy Spirit.
As it was in the beginning, is now, and will be forever.
Amen.

FOR EVENING PRAYER ONLY

Holy of Holies is this Place of Places,
Meetly held worthy of surpassing honor!
Happy thereof the surname of the Angels.
Happier yet the name, Blessed Mary,
Now a true omen the third name conferreth,
The Little Portion on the Little Brethren:
Here where by night a presence oft of Angels
Singing sweet hymns illumineth the watches.
Here was the old world's broad highway made narrow,
Here the way made broader for the Chosen People;

Here grew the Rule, here Poverty, here Our Lady,
Smiting back pride, called back the Cross amongst us.

Peter Frederick Anson, *The Pilgrim's Guide to Franciscan Italy*, "Second
Mirror of Perfection" trans by S. Evan. [Sands and Co.: London, 1927], 61.

Leader:

> Once upon a time
> there were some woods,
> a footpath,
> and a little chapel
> almost completely in ruins.

P. Théophile Desbonnets, *Assisi in the Footsteps of St. Francis* [Santa Maria
degli Angeli: Tipolitografia *Portiuncula*, 1993], 34.

Leader:
Francis repaired this chapel, brought it to birth, like a mother.
It became a symbol of a more prolific birth, the birth of a
movement.

Please Read Silently:
Then he went to another place which is called the *Portiuncula*
where there stood a church of the Blessed Virgin Mother of
God that had been built in ancient times but was now deserted
and cared for by no one. When the holy man of God saw how it
was thus in ruins, he was moved to pity, because he burned
with devotion toward the mother of all good; and he began to
live there in great zeal. It was the third year of his conversion
when he had finished repairing the church. (1C 21—adapted)

While her servant Francis was living in the church of the Virgin
Mother of God, he prayed to her who had conceived the Word
full of grace and truth, imploring her with continuous sighs to
become his advocate. Through the merits of the Mother of
Mercy, he conceived and brought to birth the spirit of the truth
of the Gospel. (LMj III: 1—adapted)

REFLECTION DURING THE DAY: I too conceived and gave birth to ...

RESPONSE: G 22 "Magnificat"

Leader:
His symbolic "child chapel" now belonged to him and the brothers, his "companion children." The chapel became their cradle. As more children were "born," additional repairs were needed for expansion.

Please Read Silently:
Seeing that God wanted to multiply the number of the brothers, one day blessed Francis said to them: "My dear brothers and sons, I see that the Lord wishes us to increase in number. In my opinion, it would be well and in conformity with religion to ask our bishop or the canons of San Rufino, or the abbot of the monastery of St. Benedict, for a small and poor church where the brothers may recite their Hours and, next to it, a small and poor house built of earth and wood where the brothers can sleep and go about their work." He went to the monastery of St. Benedict of Mount Subasio. The abbot, moved with pity, took counsel with his brothers. God having so decided, they gave blessed Francis and his brothers the church of St. Mary of the *Portiuncula*, the poorest church they owned. No poorer church could be found in the whole territory of the city of Assisi. This was what brother Francis had long desired. The abbot said to blessed Francis: "Brother, we have granted your request. But it is our wish that, if the Lord multiplies your Order, this friary will be the head of all those you will found." These words were approved by blessed Francis and by all the brothers. (AC 56—adapted)

REFLECTION DURING THE DAY: My child is ...(Children are) ...

RESPONSE: G 22

Leader:
Francis rented his "child chapel." So too did he realize that the "companion children" assembling there were on loan to him. Soon they would leave their home, as children should, to journey to other cities and towns.

Please Read Silently:
The abbot and his monks had given the church to blessed Francis and his brothers without any restriction: they had demanded no payment or yearly rent. Nevertheless, blessed Francis, as a good and prudent master, wanted to build his house on solid rock and his Order on true poverty. And so every year he sent a basket full of small fish, called *lasche*, to the monks. He did this as a sign of very great humility and poverty so that the brothers would not own any place as their own, or dwell in any place that was not the property of someone else, and so that they would not have the right either to sell or to alienate a property in any way whatsoever. And so each year the brothers brought their small fishes to the monks. Because of the humility of blessed Francis who did this because he wished them well, the monks in return offered him and his brothers the gift of a vessel of oil. (AC 56—adapted)

REFLECTION DURING THE DAY: My ties to my child(ren) have ...

RESPONSE: G 22

Leader:
Wonderful experiences surrounded the "child chapel."

Please Read Silently:
In ancient times it had been called St. Mary of the Angels, because it was said that the songs of angels were often heard there. (2MP 55—adapted)

REFLECTION DURING THE DAY: The wonderful experiences I remember are ...

RESPONSE: G 22

Leader:
Wonderful experiences surrounded the "companion children." The child chapel, their cradle home, became the place of their annual "Homecoming." One year about five thousand companion children returned to Francis, their mother.

Please Read Silently:
Once the most faithful servant of Christ, St. Francis, held a General Chapter on the plain of St. Mary of the Angels, where more than five thousand friars gathered together, all occupied only in talking about God or in praying, weeping, or doing deeds of charity. And they were so quiet and meek that there was no sound or noise. They prayed or recited the Office, or they talked about the salvation of souls. And in that camp each group made tents covered on top and round about with rushes and mats; accordingly this Chapter was called the Chapter of Rushes or Mats. They slept on the bare ground or on some straw, and their pillows were stones or pieces of wood. Francis preached to them. He said: "In order that you may better observe this, by merit of holy obedience I command all you friars who are gathered here that none of you is to have any care or anxiety concerning anything to eat or drink or the other things necessary for the body, but to concentrate only on praying and praising God." But the Lord Jesus Christ wanted to show that He takes special care of His sheep and His poor, for by God's providence it soon happened that he inspired the people of Perugia, Spoleto, Foligno, Spello, Assisi, and all the surrounding country to bring food and drink to that holy assembly. And all of a sudden people came from these places with many donkeys, mules, and wagons loaded with bread and wine, beans and cheese, and all other good things to eat that they thought these blessed poor men of Christ would need and could use. (LFl 18—adapted)

**REFLECTION DUR-
ING THE DAY: I re-
member one home-
coming when ...**

RESPONSE: G 22

Leader:
Just as any mother would
pardon her child, Francis
wanted this same pardon
for anyone who came to
this chapel. He asked the
pope to grant *Il Perdono*—
the pardon!

Please Read Silently:
"Most Holy Father," he said, "I recently repaired a church in
honor of the Blessed Virgin, Mother of Christ. I ask your
Holiness to grant pardon, without requiring any offering, in
that church on that anniversary of its consecration. If it please
your Holiness, because of the favors God has granted this place,
I ask that, whoever enters the place, having confessed their
sins and, if necessary, being absolved by a priest, be freed from
the guilt and punishment of all their sins that they have
committed from the day of their baptism until the time they
entered the church." And the pope responded: "I will grant your
request."

(F. Bartholi, Tract. de Ind. Porz., chapter 6, private translation)

**REFLECTION DURING THE DAY: I recall the freedom
of "Il Perdono" in my life when ...**

RESPONSE: G 22

Leader:
The area surrounding this chapel became a model village, a foreshadowing of the reign of God, for all times a pattern for a Christian way of life lived in fraternity.

Please Read Silently:
The holy man loved this place above all others; this place he willed to be preserved as a model of humility and highest poverty for their Order, reserving the ownership of it to others, and keeping only the use of it for himself and his brothers. The most rigid discipline was observed there in all things, both as to silence and work and as to the other ordinances of the *Rule*. To no one was admittance there granted except to specially appointed brothers who, coming from all parts of the world, the holy man wanted to be devoted to God and perfect in every way. So, too, admittance was prohibited to every secular person. He did not want the brothers dwelling there, who were restricted severely as to number, to have "itching ears" for news of worldly things, lest, with their meditation on heavenly things interrupted, they should be drawn to the business of interior things through those who spread rumors. It was not permitted to anyone there to utter idle words or repeat those uttered by others. If anyone at any time did this, he was taught through punishment to be careful not to let it happen again. Those who dwelt in this place were occupied with the divine praises without interruption day and night, and fragrant with a wonderful odor, they led an angelic life. (2C 18–19—adapted)

REFLECTION DURING THE DAY: One fraternity/ community experience I cherish ...

RESPONSE: G 22

Leader:
Here in the "child chapel" the Mother Francis died. It had been his *Portiuncula*—his "little portion of paradise."

Please Read Silently:
At last, when all God's mysteries had been accomplished in him, his holy soul was freed from his body and assumed into the abyss of God's glory, and Francis fell asleep in God. One of the friars, a disciple of his, saw his soul being borne on a white cloud over many waters to heaven, under the appearance of a radiant star. It shone with the brightness of sublime sanctity, full of the abundance of divine wisdom and grace that had earned for him the right to enter the home of light and peace, where he rests with Christ forever. At the time of St. Francis' death, when it was already dusk, a great flock of larks gathered over the building, although they normally prefer the light of day and avoid the shades of night. There they remained, flying about and singing with unusual joy, clearly testifying by the sweetness of their song to the glory of the saint who had so often called upon them to praise God. (LMj XIV:6—adapted)

REFLECTION DURING THE DAY: When Sister Death dances me into her embrace, I hope ...

RESPONSE: G 22

Leader:
Like the Mother whom we honor by this chapel, ponder these things in your heart. (Luke 2: 19—adapted)

FOR EVENING PRAYER ONLY

A SALUTATION OF THE BLESSED VIRGIN MARY

Hail, O Lady,
Holy Queen,
Mary, holy Mother of God,
Who are the Virgin made Church,
chosen by the most Holy Father in heaven
whom he consecrated with His most holy beloved Son
and with the Holy Spirit the Paraclete,

in whom there was and is
all fullness of grace and every good.

Hail His Palace!
Hail His Tabernacle!
Hail His Dwelling!
Hail His Robe!
Hail His Servant!
Hail His Mother!

And hail all You holy virtues
which are poured into the hearts of the faithful
through the grace and enlightenment of the Holy Spirit,
that from being unbelievers,
You may make them faithful to God.

RESPONSE: G 27 "Salve Regina"

EUCHARIST

READING I: PHILIPPIANS 3:8–14

A reading from the letter of Paul to the Philippians

More than that, I regard everything as loss because of the surpassing value of knowing Christ Jesus my Lord. For his sake I have suffered the loss of all things, and I regard them as rubbish, in order that I may gain Christ and be found in him, not having a righteousness of my own that comes from the law, but one that comes through faith in Christ, the righteousness from God based on faith. I want to know Christ and the power of his resurrection and the sharing of his sufferings by becoming like him in his death, if somehow I may attain the resurrection from the dead.

Not that I have already obtained this or have already reached the goal; but I press on to make it my own, because Christ Jesus has made me his own. Beloved, I do not consider that I have made it my own; but this one thing I do: forgetting what lies behind and straining forward to what lies ahead, I press on toward the goal for the prize of the heavenly call of God in Christ Jesus. **The word of the Lord.**

OR: SIRACH 24:1–4, 16–22

A reading from the book of Sirach

Wisdom praises herself, and tells of her glory in the midst of her people. In the assembly of the Most High she opens her mouth, and in the presence of his hosts she tells of her glory: "I came forth from the mouth of the Most High, and covered the earth like a mist. I dwelt in the highest heavens, and my throne was in a pillar of cloud.

Like a terebinth I spread out my branches, and my branches are glorious and graceful. Like the vine I bud forth delights and my blossoms become glorious and abundant fruits. Come to me, you who desire me, and eat your fill of my fruits. For the memory of me is sweeter than honey, and the possession of me sweeter than the honeycomb. Those who eat of me will hunger for more, and those who drink of me will thirst for more. Whoever obeys me will not be put to shame, and those who work with me will not sin." **The word of the Lord**.

RESPONSE: Taste and see the goodness of our God.

PSALM 34

I will bless the LORD at all times;
his praise shall continually be in my mouth.
My soul makes its boast in the LORD;
let the humble hear and be glad.
O magnify the LORD with me,
and let us exalt his name together. **R.**

I sought the LORD, and he answered me,
and delivered me from all my fears.

Look to him, and be radiant;
so your faces shall never be ashamed. **R.**

This poor soul cried, and was heard by the LORD,
and was saved from every trouble.
The angel of the LORD encamps
around those who fear him, and delivers them. **R.**

O taste and see that the LORD is good;
happy are those who take refuge in him.
O fear the LORD, you his holy ones,
for those who fear him have no want. **R.**

**READING II: THOMAS OF CELANO, FIRST LIFE 21–22
(Optional)**

**ALLELUIA: Go forth and preach the Good News to all
people, saying: "The reign of God is at hand."**

GOSPEL: LUKE 10:1–9

A reading from the holy Gospel according to Luke

After this the Lord appointed seventy others and sent them on
ahead of him in pairs to every town and place where he himself
intended to go. He said to them, "The harvest is plentiful, but
the laborers are few; therefore ask the Lord of the harvest to
send out laborers into his harvest. Go on your way. See, I am
sending you out like lambs into the midst of wolves. Carry no
purse, no bag, no sandals; and greet no one on the road.
Whatever house you enter, first say, 'Peace to this house!' And
if anyone is there who shares in peace, your peace will rest on
that person; but if not, it will return to you. Remain in the
same house, eating and drinking whatever they provide, for
the laborer deserves to be paid. Do not move about from house
to house. Whenever you enter a town and its people welcome
you, eat what is set before you; cure the sick who are there,
and say to them, 'The kingdom of God has come near to you.'"
The Gospel of the Lord.

OR: LUKE 1:26–33

A reading from the holy Gospel according to Luke

In the sixth month the angel Gabriel was sent by God to a town in Galilee called Nazareth, to a virgin engaged to a man whose name was Joseph, of the house of David. The virgin's name was Mary. And he came to her and said, "Greetings, favored one! The Lord is with you." But she was much perplexed by his words and pondered what sort of greeting this might be. The angel said to her, "Do not be afraid, Mary, for you have found favor with God. And now, you will conceive in your womb and bear a son, and you will name him Jesus. He will be great, and will be called the Son of the Most High, and the Lord God will give to him the throne of his ancestor David. He will reign over the house of Jacob forever, and of his kingdom there will be no end." **The Gospel of the Lord.**

PICNIC RITUAL

HOW ST. CLARE ATE A MEAL WITH ST. FRANCIS

Narrator 1:
When St. Francis was staying in Assisi, he often visited St. Clare and consoled her with holy advice. And as she had a very great desire to eat a meal with him once, she asked him several times to give her that consolation. But St. Francis always refused to grant her that favor. So it happened that his companions, perceiving St. Clare's desire, said to St. Francis:

Friars:
Father, it seems to us that this strictness is not according to divine charity—that you do not grant the request of Sister Clare, a virgin so holy and dear to God, in such a little thing as eating with you, especially considering that she gave up the riches and pomp of the world as a result of your preaching. So you

should not only let her eat a meal with you once, but if she were to ask an even greater favor of you, you should grant it to your little spiritual plant.

Francis:
So you think I should grant this wish of hers?

Friars:
Yes, Father, for she deserves this favor and consolation.

Francis:
Since it seems so to you, I agree. But in order to give her greater pleasure, I want this meal to be at St. Mary of the Angels, for she has been cloistered at San Damiano for a long time and she will enjoy seeing once more for a while the Place of St. Mary where she was shorn and made a spouse of the Lord Jesus Christ. So we will eat there together, in the name of the Lord.

Narrator 2:
He therefore set a day when St. Clare would go out of the monastery with one sister companion, escorted also by his companions. And she came to St. Mary of the Angels. And first she reverently and humbly greeted the Blessed Virgin Mary before her altar, where she had been shorn and received the veil. And then they devoutly showed her around the Place until it was mealtime. Meanwhile St. Francis had the table prepared on the bare ground, as was his custom.

Narrator 1:
And when it was time to eat, St. Francis and St. Clare sat down together, and one of his companions with St. Clare's companion, and all his other companions were grouped around that humble table. But at the first course St. Francis began to speak about God in such a sweet and holy and profound and divine and marvelous way that he himself and St. Clare and her companion and all the others who were at that poor little table were rapt in God by the overabundance of divine grace that

descended upon them.

Narrator 2:

And while they were sitting there, in a rapture, with their eyes and hands raised to heaven, it seemed to the [people] of Assisi and Bettona and the entire district that the Church of St. Mary of the Angels and the whole Place and the forest which was at that time around the Place were all aflame and that an immense fire was burning over all of them. Consequently the [people] of Assisi ran down there in great haste to save the Place and put out the fire, as they firmly believed that everything was burning up.

Narrator 1:

But when they reached the Place, they saw that nothing was on fire. Entering the Place, they found St. Francis with St. Clare and all the companions sitting around that very humble table, rapt in God by contemplation and invested with power from on high. Then they knew for sure that it had been a heavenly and not a material fire that God had miraculously shown them to symbolize the fire of divine love which was burning in the souls of those holy friars and nuns. So they withdrew, with great consolation in their hearts and with holy edification.

Narrator 2:

Later, after a long while, when St. Francis and St. Clare and the others came back to themselves, they felt so refreshed by spiritual food that they paid little or no attention to the material food. And when that blessed meal was over, St. Clare, well accompanied, returned to San Damiano. . . .To the glory of Christ. Amen!

Adapted from *The Little Flowers of St. Francis,* Raphael Brown, [New York: Image Books, 1958], 72–73.

ASSISI:
BASTIA

FRANCISCAN PILGRIMAGE PROGRAMS

ASSISI: BASTIA

EVENTS

The Benedictine monastery for women, San Paolo delle Abbadesse in Bastia, was granted the privilege of offering sanctuary by Pope Innocent III in 1201.

Clare walked three kilometers to this monastery seeking sanctuary after leaving her family home on Palm Sunday, March 18, 1212, and was received by Francis and the brothers at the Porziuncola.

Clare's Uncle Monaldo and seven knights from the Offreduccio family came not once but several times to storm the monastery church of San Paolo, defying the protection of sanctuary and demanding that Clare return to her senses and come home.

Clare confirmed her decision to enter Franciscan religious life by clinging to the altar in this church and revealing her tonsured head. Her family gave up and departed.

Clare left this place after seven to ten days, and accompanied by Francis, Bernard, and Philip, she went to Sant' Angelo in Panzo.

SPIRITUALITY

Clare was formed into the plan of God by being received at the Porziuncola, experiencing an intense novitiate at San Paolo delle Abbadesse, and professing her commitment to religious life at the altar there.

Here Clare lived her first twenty-four hours in absolute poverty, having no home among the brothers, no possessions that would allow her to stay to give as dowry to the Benedictine sisters, and no companions with whom to share her dreams.

Clare learned many things about living a religious life:
- Dowries provided security; she chose poverty.
- Authority resided in the role of the abbess; she led her future sisters as servant and handmaid.
- She learned the formal Liturgy of the Hours; she prayed a simpler prayer that included those who could not read.
- She lived the Benedictine Rule; she fulfilled her dream of following Francis by composing her own Rule.

Clare understood the meaning of being a "pilgrim and stranger." Within the first month of leaving her family home, she journeyed to three places and found her "home" in none of them.

REFLECTION

When did you receive the call from God to live the way of life you have chosen? What difficulties did you encounter in answering this call?

Where is your place of "sanctuary" where you can review choices, make decisions, and renew your conviction to live your vocation?

How free are you to move on to another place if you are not "at home" where you currently live?

BASTIA

HISTORICAL NOTES

The town of Bastia is located about four kilometers from Assisi and three kilometers from the Porziuncola. It is located near the banks of the Chiascio River. This area was a lake in prehistoric times. A city called Isola Romano was built on a rise as the lake receded; the name was later changed to Bastia.

San Paolo delle Abbadesse, a Benedictine monastery for women, was located just outside Bastia, but no one knows the date of its foundation. There were other Benedictine monasteries in the area, one being Sant' Appolinare, located near the bishop's residence in Assisi. These two monasteries were at odds for many years, but at the end of the 13th century, San Paolo eventually merged with Sant' Appolinare.

There are documents that tell something of the history of San Paolo delle Abbadesse. Numerous papal bulls name the vast property holdings: lands all around Isola Romano; houses and gardens in the region of Santo Stefano, Sant' Andrea, and San Pietro; olive orchards below the city wall of Assisi; vineyards in outlying regions; and even a church called Sant' Andrea della Valle located outside of Spoleto and all its holdings. All of these properties came from dowries.

In 1198 Pope Innocent III placed the monastery under the authority of Bishop Guido of Assisi. On May 5, 1201, a papal bull of Innocent III addressed Abbess Sibilia of San Paolo and confirmed that her monastery was under the Benedictine Rule. This same papal bull declared that her monastery could not be tithed and no interdict could be leveled against them. It granted them the privilege of offering sanctuary. Both Francis and Clare would have known of this privilege. Clare would also have been aware that, in order to stay for a longer period of time as a member of this monastery, she needed a dowry.

Clare was escorted to San Paolo delle Abbadesse after being received on Palm Sunday at the Porziuncola by Francis and his brothers. She was seeking sanctuary, knowing that her family would likely come to convince her to return home. In fact, shortly after her arrival, her Uncle Monaldo and seven knights from the Offreduccio family stormed the church of San Paolo, not once but several times, demanding that Clare return home. Clinging to the altar cloth, Clare finally revealed her shorn hair, a symbol of tonsure and commitment to religious life. The family gave up and returned home. In addition to recognizing the significance of tonsure, the family was also likely aware that they could be excommunicated for violating sanctuary and inflicting violence on a monastery that was under the protection of Bishop Guido. Also, monasteries with vast holdings, such as San Paolo, had armies at their disposal to defend and protect them. The Offreduccio knights realized that their obstacles to success were too great.

After these family interventions, the nuns at San Paolo met in Chapter and decided that keeping Clare was too risky, for these family skirmishes put them in a very difficult position. Clare agreed to leave San Paolo. Francis, accompanied by Bernard and Phillip, led Clare across the valley to Sant' Angelo in Panzo.

Today the only structure remaining of the Benedictine monastery is the Church of San Paolo. This romanesque structure now serves as a mortuary chapel for a large cemetery. Outside, the bell tower is striking in its simplicity and beauty. The simple interior of this church testifies to its antiquity, with narrow windows in the apse, a simple altar standing on a marble stone pedestal, and the plain, unadorned walls. This structure was badly damaged during the 1997 earthquake that caused destruction in the entire Umbrian Valley.

Two plaques on the side walls testify to the memory of Clare's presence here. One plaque was dedicated in 1862 to remember the events in Clare's life that happened in this church. It reads:

> This building had been a monastery of Benedictines from the 12th century, where Clare of Assisi was brought to be espoused to Christ. This took place during the difficulties between the Guelphs and the Ghibellines which involved use of armaments.
>
> After five centuries of ungrateful abandonment, on the advice of the people of Bastia this place was given as a cemetery for the deceased, the Mayor of the land being Giuseppi Angelini. MDCCCLXII (1862)

The second plaque commemorates the 7th anniversary of Clare of Assisi:

> Here is where Clare of the Scifi family fled from

her paternal home, and was found near the altar as a new spouse of Christ. The refuge was honored by this designation by the people of Bastia on the 18th of September, 1927, where they wanted to be worthily remembered on the 7th anniversary of the Saint of Assisi, who came here as a noble citizen in evangelical virtue and with true riches to the glory of God. PAX ET BONUM.

Translated from the Latin by Aaron Pembleton, O.F.M., 1993.

FRANCISCAN READINGS

THE LEGEND OF SAINT CLARE 9

The Offreduccio's attempts to take her home

But after the news reached her relatives, they condemned with a broken heart the deed and proposal of the virgin and, banding together as one, they ran to the place, attempting to obtain what they could not. They employed violent force, poisonous advice, and flattering promises, persuading her to give up such a worthless deed that was unbecoming to her class and without precedence in her family. But, taking hold of the altar cloths, she bared her tonsured head, maintaining that she would in no way be torn away from the service of Christ. With the increasing violence of her relatives, her spirit grew and her love—provoked by injuries—provided strength. So, for many days, even though she endured an obstacle

in the way of the Lord and her own [relatives] opposed her proposal of holiness, her spirit did not crumble and her fervor did not diminish. Instead, amid words and deeds of hatred, she molded her spirit anew in hope until her relatives, turning back, were quiet.

ACTS OF THE PROCESS OF CANONIZATION OF ST. CLARE, WITNESS XII: 4–5 (SR. BEATRICE, CLARE'S SISTER)

Clare's Conversion

Then Saint Francis gave her the tonsure before the altar in the church of the Virgin Mary, called the Portiuncula, and then sent her to the church of San Paolo delle Abbadesse. When her relatives wanted to drag her out, Lady Clare grabbed the altar cloths and uncovered her head, showing them she was tonsured. In no way did she acquiesce, neither letting them take her from the place nor remaining with them.

Then Saint Francis, Brother Philip and Brother Bernard took her to the church of Sant' Angelo in Panzo, where she stayed for a little time, and then to the church of San Damiano where the Lord gave her more sisters for her direction.

Asked how she [Beatrice] knew all these things, she replied since she was her sister, she saw some things and heard some from Lady Clare and others. Asked how long ago this was, she replied: about forty-two years ago.

ACTS OF THE PROCESS OF CANONIZATION OF ST. CLARE, WITNESS XVIII: 3 (LORD RANIERI DE BERNARDO OF ASSISI)

Clare's Commitment

Asked what good deeds she did, he replied she fasted, prayed, and willingly gave as many alms as she could. When she was sitting with those in the house, she always spoke of the things of God. As quickly as possible, she had her hair cut by Saint Francis. When her relatives wanted to take her from San Paolo and bring her back to Assisi, they could in no way persuade her, because she did not want to go. She showed them her tonsured head and so they let her stay.

EUCHARIST

READING: 1 CORINTHIANS 3:10–16

A reading from the first letter of Paul to the Corinthians

According to the grace of God given to me, like a skilled master builder I laid a foundation, and someone else is building on it. Each builder must choose with care how to build on it. For no one can lay any foundation other than the one that has been laid; that foundation is Jesus Christ. Now if anyone builds on the foundation with gold, silver, precious stones, wood, hay, straw—the work of each builder will become visible, for the Day will disclose it, because it will be revealed with fire, and the fire will test what sort of work each has done. If what has been built on the foundation survives, the builder will receive a reward. If the work is burned up, the builder will suffer loss; the builder will be saved, but only as through fire. Do you not know that you are God's temple and that God's Spirit dwells in you? **The word of the Lord**.

RESPONSE: Shepherd me, O God, beyond my wants, beyond my fears, from death into life.

PSALM 23

The LORD is my shepherd,
I shall not want.

He makes me lie down in green pastures;
he leads me beside still waters;
he restores my soul.
He leads me in right paths
for his name's sake. **R.**

Even though I walk through
the darkest valley,
I fear no evil;
for you are with me;
your rod and your staff
they comfort me. **R.**

You prepare a table before me
in the presence of my enemies;
you anoint my head with oil;
my cup overflows.
Surely goodness and mercy
shall follow me
all the days of my life,
and I shall dwell in the house of the LORD
my whole life long. **R.**

ALLELUIA: I am going to prepare a place for you, that where I am you also may be.

GOSPEL: JOHN 14:1–6

A reading from the holy Gospel according to John

"Do not let your hearts be troubled. Believe in God, believe also in me. In my Father's house there are many dwelling places. If it were not so, would I have told you that I go to prepare a place for you? And if I go and prepare a place for you, I will come again and will take you to myself, so that where I am, there you may be also. And you know the way to the place where I am going." Thomas said to him, "Lord, we do not know where you are going. How can we know the way?" Jesus said to him, "I am the way, and the truth, and the life. No one comes to the Father except through me." **The Gospel of the Lord.**

RITUAL FOR RENEWAL
OF VOWS BY POOR CLARES AT BASTIA

INTRODUCTION

GOSPEL: JOHN 14:1 6 (taken from the Eucharist Gospel above)

RESPONSE: Ps 23 "My Shepherd Is the Lord"

RENEWAL OF VOWS
We now invite our Poor Clare Sisters to come to the altar, place their hands on its stone surface, and renew their vows.

BLESSING: C 6 "What You Hold"

GREETING OF PEACE

ASSISI:
SAN DAMIANO
AND
ST. CLARE

FRANCISCAN PILGRIMAGE PROGRAMS

ASSISI: SAN DAMIANO AND ST. CLARE

EVENTS

While rebuilding this rundown church, Francis foretold (L3C 24) that Clare and the Poor Ladies would live here.

After living at San Paolo in Bastia and Sant' Angelo in Panzo, Clare moved into San Damiano. Here she venerated the San Damiano cross for nearly forty years. Approximately fifty women of diverse backgrounds joined Clare at San Damiano, forming the first community of Poor Ladies. These first members included her mother, Ortolana, her two sisters, Catherine (who became known as Agnes) and Beatrice, and her first cousin Balvina.

Clare turned the Saracens away by holding the little box of the Eucharist in full sight of the invading troops.

Francis visited Clare here one last time, allowing her to minister to him in his illness.

Clare wrote her *Rule* in consultation with her sisters. She was the first woman to have a rule approved by the Church.

Clare died here in 1253 surrounded by her sisters.

SPIRITUALITY

Clare lived absolute poverty at San Damiano, accepting no dowries.

Though enclosed, the influence of Clare and her sisters reached beyond the walls of San Damiano and refreshed the entire Umbrian Valley as well as the Catholic Church.

Love was a primary virtue embraced by this group of women. Jesus Christ became the center of their spirituality.

Believing in the redemptive power of our God, Clare healed many people by signing them with the Sign of the Cross; many miracles are still attributed to her healing power.

Clare saw her role of abbess as one of being both servant and handmaid to her sisters. She called forth the gifts and talents of all her sisters and included them in key decisions affecting their lives.

REFLECTION

What is contemplation? How does the contemplative dimension affect your life? Can you find a place of solitude where you can encounter God without distraction?

How is the virtue of loving charity practiced in your local communities and/or among your family and friends?

How do you view authority and leadership today? Is your leadership one of loving service to those who live or work with you?

What role does the Eucharist play in your spiritual growth?

How can you bring the healing power of Jesus to those in need?

SAN DAMIANO AND ST. CLARE

HISTORICAL NOTES

Francis prophesied that San Damiano would become a monastery for women. This Monastery of San Damiano was the protomonastery for the followers of the Lady Clare.

When facing the facade of this little church, to the right of the circular window, one can discern in the stones a vertical line rising up and then, more faintly, a diagonal line bearing left toward the roof. This was the original San Damiano. The front portico and all other surrounding structures are later additions of the 16th century. The door on the upper left side enters the dormitory of the sisters. A wooden stairway that led up to the door collapsed from the weight of people coming to mourn the death of Agnes, Clare's sister (The Chronicle of the 24 Generals).

A visit to this protomonastery begins in the main chapel. Behind the main altar and partly hidden by the choir stalls (1504) is a replica of a grill where the sisters received Communion and through which they viewed the body of St. Francis on October 3, 1226. The brothers held up his body for about one hour.

Pass through the doorway on the right to enter a little room. This was the original *sepolcreto* or "burial place" for the sisters. Agnes, Ortolana, Amata, Andrea, Illuminata, and Filippa were first buried here and later transferred to the Basilica of Santa Chiara. See also an ancient choir stall where the sisters prayed.

Proceed up the steps to the next level. On the way up look through the small window at St. Clare's garden, where Francis spent many weeks before his death.

Enter the room at the top of the stairs into the place the infirm sisters "heard Mass" from a small opening in the floor.

Proceed up the stairs to the next room—the dormitory of the sisters. Here they slept on poor mats. A cross and fresh flowers mark the spot where Clare, an invalid for several years before death, slept and died.

Leaving the dormitory by the far door, proceed down the stairs to the cloister garden below. Walk to the opposite side to view the sisters' refectory. Here the sisters took their daily meals. Here Clare welcomed Gregory IX for a meal and blessing of the bread. Clare's seat to the right is marked by fresh flowers.

For a detailed description of Clare's San Damiano, consult Ramona Miller, O.S.F., *In the Footsteps of St. Clare* [St. Bonaventure, N.Y.: Franciscan Institute Publications, 1993].

FRANCISCAN READINGS

THE LEGEND OF THREE COMPANIONS 24

Francis' prediction of the eventual arrival of the women at San Damiano

While he was working steadily at restoring the church, he wanted to have a lamp burning continually in the church, so he went through the city begging for oil. But when he was approaching a certain house, he saw a group of men gathered for a game. Ashamed to beg in front of them, he backed away. Mulling it over, he accused himself of having sinned. Hurrying back to the place where they were playing, he told everyone standing around his fault, that he was ashamed to beg because of them. And, in fervor of spirit, he entered that house and, for the love of God, begged in French for oil for the lamps of that church.

While laboring with others in that work, he used to cry to passers-by in a loud voice, filled with joy, saying in French: "Come and help me in the work of the church of San Damiano which, in the future, will be a monastery of ladies through whose fame and life our heavenly Father will be glorified throughout the church."

See how, filled with the spirit of prophecy, he truly foretold the future! For this is that sacred place where the glorious religion and most excellent Order of Poor Ladies and sacred virgins had its happy beginning about six years after the conversion of blessed Francis and through the same blessed Francis. Their wondrous life and renowned practices were fully approved by the Lord Pope Gregory IX, of holy memory, at that time the Bishop of Ostia, and confirmed by the authority of the Apostolic See.

THOMAS OF CELANO, SECOND LIFE 204–205

In praise of the virtues of Clare and the Poor Ladies

It would not be right to pass over in silence
the memory of a spiritual building,
much nobler than that earthly one,
that the blessed father established in that place
with the Holy *Spirit leading*
for the increase of the heavenly city,

after he had repaired the material church.
We should not believe
that for the sake of repairing a crumbling and perishable building,
that Christ spoke to him from the wood of the Cross
and in such an amazing way
that it *strikes fear* and inflicts pain
upon anyone who hears of it.
But, as earlier foretold by the Holy Spirit,
an Order of holy virgins was to be established there
to be brought one day
as a polished collection of *living stones*
for the restoration of the heavenly house.
The virgins of Christ
had begun to gather in that place,
assembled from diverse regions of the world,
professing the greatest perfection
in the observance of the *highest poverty*
and *the beauty of every virtue.*
Though the father gradually withdrew
his *bodily presence* from them,
he still offered *in the Holy Spirit*,
his affection to care for them.
The saint recognized that they were marked
with many signs of the highest perfection,
and that they were ready to bear any loss
and undergo any labor *for Christ*
and did not ever want to *turn aside*
from the holy *commandments.*
Therefore, he firmly promised them,
and others who professed poverty
in a similar way of life,
that he and his brothers
would perpetually offer them help and advice.
And he carried this out carefully
as long as he lived,

and when he was close to death
he commanded it to be carried out without fail always,
saying that
one and the same Spirit
had led the brothers and those little poor ladies
out of this world.

The brothers were sometimes surprised that he did not often visit such holy handmaids of Christ in his *bodily presence*, but he would say: "Don't imagine, dear brothers, that I don't love them fully. For if it were a crime to cherish them in Christ, wouldn't it be even worse to have joined them to Christ? Not calling them would not have been harmful, but not to care for them after calling them would be the height of cruelty. But *I am giving you an example, that as I do, so should you also do.* I don't want one volunteering to visit them, but rather command that those who are unwilling and very reluctant should be assigned to their service, as long as they are *spiritual men* tested by a longstanding, worthy way of life."

THE ASSISI COMPILATION 13

How, before dying, Francis sends a letter to Lady Clare promising that she will see him again

During the week in which blessed Francis died, Lady Clare was seriously ill. She was the first plant of the Order of Sisters, the abbess of the Poor Sisters of the monastery of San Damiano in Assisi, who emulated Saint Francis in observing always the poverty of the Son of God. She feared that she would die before blessed Francis. She wept in bitterness of spirit and could not be comforted, because she would not be able before her death to see her only father after God, that is, blessed Francis, her comforter both internally and externally, and her first founder in God's grace.

She sent word of this to blessed Francis through one of the brothers. Blessed Francis heard this and was moved to piety, since he loved her and her sisters with fatherly affection because of their holy manner of living, and especially because, a few years after he began to have brothers, she was converted to the Lord through his advice, working with the Lord. Her conversion not only greatly edified the religion of the brothers, but also the entire Church of God. Blessed Francis considered that what she desired, that is, to see him, could not be done then since they were both seriously ill. To console her, he wrote his blessing in a letter and also absolved her from any failings, if she had any, regarding his commands and wishes or the commands and wishes of the Son of God. Moreover, so that she would put aside all her grief and be consoled in the Lord, he, or rather the Spirit of God speaking through him, spoke to the brother she had sent. "Go and take this letter to Lady Clare, and tell her to put aside all her grief and sorrow over not being able to see me now. Let her be assured that before her death, both she and her sisters will see me and will receive the greatest consolation from me."

Soon afterwards blessed Francis passed away during the night. In the morning, all the people of the city of Assisi, men and women, with all the clergy, took the holy body from the place where he had died. With hymns and praises, all carrying tree branches, they carried him to San Damiano at the Lord's will, in order to fulfill that word which the Lord had spoken through His saint to console His daughters and servants.

The iron grille was removed from the window through which the servants of Christ usually receive communion and sometimes hear the word of God. The brothers lifted his holy body from the stretcher and, raising him in their arms, they held him in front of the window for over an hour. By then Lady Clare and her sisters had received the greatest consolation from him, although they wept profusely and were afflicted with great grief, because, after God, he was their one consolation in this world.

LETTERS OF SAINT CLARE
TO SAINT AGNES OF PRAGUE

For St. Clare's letters to St. Agnes of Prague, the editors of Pilgrim's Companion *selected the translation of Sr. Frances Teresa Downing, O.S.C.,* The Four Letters of Saint Clare to Saint Agnes of Prague*, because it is the work of a woman who has lived the Poor Clare life for some years.*

THE FIRST LETTER OF SAINT CLARE TO SAINT AGNES OF PRAGUE

1. To the honoured and most holy virgin, the Lady Agnes, daughter of the Most Excellent and Most Illustrious King of Bohemia: 2. Clare, the unworthy family servant of Jesus Christ and the unprofitable handmaid (cf. Lk 17:10) of the enclosed ladies of the monastery of San Damiano, is everywhere subject to her and her handmaid, and she recommends herself to her in every way with particular respect, that she may obtain the glory of eternal happiness (cf. Sir 50:5). 3. I greatly rejoice in the Lord and I exult on hearing the very reliable reports of Your holy conduct and life, which is common knowledge, not just to me but to almost the whole world. 4. As a result, it is not only I personally who am full of rejoicing but all those who do and wish to do the service of Jesus Christ. 5. In fact, while You, more than many, could have thoroughly enjoyed the pomps and honours and the grandeur of the world and could

quite legitimately and with outstanding glory, have been married to the illustrious Caesar—as would have been fitting to your and his excellence, 6. instead, You have rejected all that. With Your whole being and with all Your heart, You have preferred the most holy poverty and physical hardship. 7. You have taken to Yourself a Bridegroom of a far more noble kind, the Lord Jesus Christ, who will keep Your virginity unmarked and unimpaired forever.

8. Loving Him, You are chaste;
touching Him, You become more pure;
taking Him to Yourself, You are a virgin.
9. His resources are stronger,
his generosity of a higher kind,
his look more beautiful,
his love more tender
and every grace more attractive.
10. Now You are held close in the embrace of him
who has adorned Your breast with precious stones
and given pearls of great price for Your ears,
11. and completely surrounded You with springlike
and shining jewels
and crowned You with a coronet of gold,
as a particular token of holiness. (Sir 45:12)

12. Therefore, my dearest sister—or I should rather say, Lady greatly respected, because You are the bride, the mother and the sister of my Lord Jesus Christ (cf. 2 Cor 11:2; Mt 12:50) 13. You are most splendidly distinguished by the banner of inviolable virginity and most holy poverty, so be strengthened in the holy service which has been begun by the burning longing of the poor Crucified One. 14. He took up the cross of his passion for all our sakes, (cf. Heb 12:2;) snatching us from the power of the prince of darkness (cf. Col 1:13; Jn 12:31) in whose bondage we were held bound by the sin of our first parent, and reconciling us with God the Father (cf. Rom 5:10; 2 Cor 5:19).

15. O blessed poverty,
who guarantees eternal riches
to those who love and embrace her.
16. O holy poverty,
to those who hold and long for her
the Kingdom of heaven is promised by God (cf. Mt 5:3)
and eternal glory and blessed life is certainly shown forth.

17. O faithful poverty,
whom the Lord Jesus Christ held worthy to be embraced
before all else,
he who, because he spoke and they were made,
(Ps 33:9; 148:5)
ruled and still rules heaven and earth!

18. The foxes have holes, he said, and the birds of the air have nests, but the Son of Man, that is Christ, has nowhere to lay his head (Mt 8:20; Lk 9:58) but bowing his head, he gave up the Spirit. (Jn 19:30) 19. If, then, such and so great a Lord, coming to the virginal womb, wanted to be seen in the world as a despised, needy and poor man, (cf. 2 Cor 8:9) 20. it was so that those who were most poor and needy, starving to death for lack of this heavenly food, it was so that, in him, such people may be enriched by possessing the Kingdom of heaven. (cf. 2 Cor 8:9) 21. Exult all the more and rejoice, be filled with tremendous joy and spiritual happiness. 22. For, just as You were more pleased by the world's scorn than by its honours, by poverty than by temporal riches, so You have hidden your treasure in heaven, rather than on earth.

23. There neither rust consumes nor moth devours nor thieves break in and steal; (Mt 6:20) in heaven Your reward is very abundantly overflowing. (Mt 5:12) 24. Also You have quite rightly merited to be named the sister, the bride and the mother (cf. 2 Cor 11:2; Mt 12:50) of the Son of the Most High Father and the glorious Virgin. 25. For I firmly believe You to know

that the Kingdom of heaven is promised and given by the Lord to none but the poor, (cf. Mt 5:3) for while we are giving our affections to the transient we are losing the fruit of love. 26. We cannot be devoted to God and Mammon, for either one will be loved and the other hated, or one will be served and the other despised. (cf. Mt 6:24) 27. Somebody who is clothed cannot fight someone who is stripped, because the one who gives more purchase is the more quickly thrown to the ground. 28. Nor can we know glory in this world and also reign in it with Christ, because a camel will be able to go through the eye of a needle before a rich man can clamber up to the kingdom of heaven. (cf. Mt 19:24)

29. This is why You have thrown aside clothes, in other words temporal riches, so as to avoid surrendering to the one who wrestles with You, so that You can enter the heavenly Kingdom by the straight road and the narrow gate. (cf. Mt 7:13–14)

30. Indeed, what a great and praiseworthy piece of
commerce it is:
to leave the temporal for the eternal,
to be promised the heavenly in exchange for the earthly,
to receive a hundred-fold for one,
and to possess the blessed, eternal life. (cf. Mt 19:29)

31. This is why I have drawn Your Excellency and Your Holiness by such humble prayers as I am capable of in the bowels of Christ, (cf. Phil 1:8) in order that You may be strengthened in his holy service, 32. growing from good to better, from strength to strength, (cf. Ps 84:8) so that he to whom You are devoted with all the desire of Your mind may deign to pour out on You the reward You long for. 33. I also beg You, as much I possibly can in the Lord, that You remember in Your most holy prayers (cf. Rom 15:30) both me Your family servant although an unprofitable one (cf. Lk 17:10)—and the other sisters in the monastery with me, who are as devoted to

You as I am. 34. Helped in this way, we may be able to merit the mercy of Jesus Christ so that we, together with You, may likewise merit to come to the enjoyment of the eternal vision. 35. Farewell in the Lord and pray for me.

THE SECOND LETTER OF SAINT CLARE TO SAINT AGNES OF PRAGUE

1. To the daughter of the King of kings, the handmaid of the Lord of lords, (Rev 19:16; 1 Tm 6:15) most deservedly the bride of Jesus Christ, and for that reason the most noble queen, to the Lady Agnes; 2. from Clare, an unprofitable (Lk 17:10) and unworthy handmaid of the Poor Ladies: greetings and may you always live in the most high poverty. 3. I give thanks to the generous Giver of grace from whom we believe every good and perfect gift to come, (Jas 1:17) in that he has adorned you with the honour of such virtues and made you illustrous with insignia of such perfection, 4. so that, by being made a loving imitator of the Father of perfections, (cf. Eph 5:1) you might merit to be made perfect, lest his eyes should see anything imperfect in you. (cf. Mt 5:48; Ps 139:16) 5. This is that perfection which the King himself will share with you in the heavenly bridal chamber, where he is gloriously seated on a throne of stars, 6. for you have scorned, as insufficient, the pinnacle of an earthly kingdom, the offer of marriage to the Emperor, 7. being made, in the Spirit of great humility and most burning love, one who strives after the most holy poverty, cleaving to the footprints (1 Pt 2:21) of the one to whom you have merited to be united as in marriage. 8. Since I know that

you are adorned with virtues, however, I will spare you an exuberance of words, not wanting to burden you with superfluous ones, 9. even though I know that nothing seems superfluous to you if it can bring you some consolation. 10. Yet because one thing is necessary, (Lk 10:42) I bear witness to this one thing, and admonish you, for love of him to whom you have offered yourself as a holy and acceptable sacrifice. (Rom 12:1) 11. Then, like another Rachel (cf. Gen 29:16), remembering your purpose and always looking to the Beginning,

hold what you now hold,
do what you are now doing and do not cease.
12. Instead, run even more swiftly, light-footed,
without tripping,
so that your stepping raises no dust.
13. Confidently rejoicing, and lightheartedly,
tread carefully along the path of blessedness,
14. believing nothing, agreeing to nothing
which would make you want to call back this purpose
or which would place a stumbling-block on your way.
In that case you would not be giving back your vows
to the Most High (Rom 14:13; Ps 50:14)
in that perfection to which the Spirit of the Lord has called you.

15. In all this then, so that you may walk more surely along the way of the Lord's commands, (Ps 118:32) follow the advice of our venerable father, our Brother Elias, the Minister General. 16. Prefer this advice to that of others and hold it dearer than any gift. 17. If anyone says something else to you, or suggests anything else to you which would hinder your perfection, or which seems contrary to the divine call, although you must respect him, do not follow his advice;

18. instead, a poor virgin,
embrace the poor Christ.
19. See him, made contemptible for you,
and follow him, being made contemptible for him in this world.

20. Your Bridegroom, more beautiful than the children of mankind, (cf. Ps 45:3) was made the least of men for your salvation, despised, beaten and many times scourged all over his body, dying on the cross in the midst of anguish itself;

O most noble queen,
gaze, consider, contemplate,
longing to imitate.

21. If you suffer with him, you will reign with him,
grieving with him, you will rejoice with him,
dying with him on the cross of torments,
you will possess heavenly mansions with him
in the splendour of the saints,
(cf. Rom 8:17; 2 Tm 2:11–12)
22. and your name will be noted in the Book of Life,
and among men will have glory in the future.
(cf. Phil 4:3; Rv 3:5)

23. Therefore, in eternity and forever and ever, you will share in the glory of the heavenly Kingdom instead of an earthly and transient one, and you will live forever and ever, in everlasting good instead of a good which is to perish. 24. Farewell, most beloved sister and Lady, on account of the Lord, your Bridegroom. 25. And work hard at commending me, with my sisters, in your devout prayers to the Lord, that we may rejoice in the good things of the Lord which he is working in you through his grace. 26. We also strongly recommend ourselves to your sisters.

THE THIRD LETTER OF SAINT CLARE TO SAINT AGNES OF PRAGUE

1. To the Lady whom she most greatly respects in Christ; to the sister Agnes, whom she loves more than any Other mortal; to the blood-sister of the illustrious King of Bohemia but now the sister and bride of the most high King of heavens: (cf. Mt 12:50; 2 Cor 11:2) 2. from Clare, the most lowly and unworthy

handmaid of Christ and the slave of the Poor Ladies: the joy of salvation in the author of salvation (Heb 2:10) and whatever better thing can be desired. 3. The more I am filled with delight because you are safe and sound, happy, and achieving a good outcome to the race which you began so vigorously in order to gain the heavenly prize, (cf. Phil 3:14; 1 Cor 9:24) 4. the greater the exultation I breathe in the Lord, the more I know and am convinced that in following the footprints of the poor and humble Jesus Christ, you are wonderfully making up what is wanting, in me as much as in the other sisters. 5. Truly I can rejoice, nor can anyone make me a stranger to such joy, 6. since that which, under heaven, I had desired, I already hold. For I see that you, sustained by the wonderful privilege of wisdom from the mouth of God himself; have overthrown in a terrible and unexpected way the shrewdness of the astute enemy, and the pride that destroys human nature, and the vanity which infatuates the human heart.

7. A treasure beyond compare is hidden in the field of the world and in human hearts. With it, that by which everything was made from nothing (cf. Jn 1:3) has been bought. (cf. Mt 13:44; Lk 1:51) You have embraced it by humility, by the power of faith and the arms of poverty. 8. And, to use the very words of the Apostle himself, I judge you a co-worker of God himself (1 Cor 3:9; Rom 16:3) and one who holds up the members of his ineffable Body who are giving way. 9. Who could tell me not to rejoice at such wonderful joys? 10. Therefore, you too, my dearest, rejoice in the Lord always, (cf. Phil 4:4) 11. and, O Lady most beloved in Christ, joy of the angels and crown of the sisters, (cf. Phil 4:1) may neither bitterness nor clouds overwhelm you.

12. Place your mind in the mirror of eternity;
place your soul in the splendour of glory. (cf. Heb 1:3)
13. Place your heart in the icon of the divine substance (cf. Heb 1:3)

and transform your whole self through contemplation
into an image of his Godhead. (cf. 2 Cor 3:18)
14. Do this in order that you yourself may feel
what his friends feel
on tasting the hidden sweetness,
which God himself has kept from the beginning
for those who love Him. (cf. 1 Cor 2:9)
15. And completely passing over all those things
with which an untrustworthy and perturbed world
entangles its blinded lovers,
love totally the One who gave his whole self for your love,
16. the One at whose beauty the sun and moon wonder,
the One whose rewards, with their value and greatness,
have no end;
17. I am speaking of the One who is Son of the Most High,
whom the Virgin brought to birth
and after whose birth remained a virgin.

18. Cleave to his most sweet Mother who begot such a Son as the
heavens could not contain, (cf. 1 Kgs 8:27; 2 Chr 2:5) 19. and yet
received him within the small confines of her holy womb and held
him on her young girl's lap. 20. Who would not shrink from the ambush
of humanity's enemy, which schemes, through the pride of a fleeting
and deceptive glory, to reduce to nothing that which is greater than the
heavens? 21. See how obvious it already is, that through the grace of
God the faithful human soul, that most worthy creation, is far greater
than the heavens, 22. while the heavens, with other creatures, cannot
contain the Creator, and only the faithful soul itself is his mansion and
throne, and this only through love—which the ungodly lack 23. Truth
itself having said: anyone who loves me will be loved by my Father,
and I shall love him, and we shall come to him and make our home
with him. (Jn 14:21; 14:23)

24. As the glorious Virgin of virgins, materially,

25. so will you, spiritually,

certainly be able always to carry him in your chaste and

virginal body;

by following in her footprints,

particularly the prints of humility and poverty,

(cf. 1 Pt 2:21)

26. containing him by whom you and everything are contained,

(Wis 1:7)

possessing that which,

in comparison with the other transitory possessions

of this world;

you will possess more completely.

27. In this indeed, certain kings and certain queens of the world are mistaken. 28. Even though their pride may have been allowed to climb right to the sky and their heads have touched the clouds, in the end they will be thrown out like manure. (Jb 20:6–7) 29. Now about those things you asked me to open up for you: 30. namely, which would be those feasts that our most glorious Father Saint Francis urged us particularly to celebrate by having some variation in the food. Although I would think you already know this, I am prompted to respond because of your love. 31. Apart from the weak and infirm (for whom he counseled us, and commanded us, that in the matter of food we use our judgment as far as possible), in your prudence you should know that 32. we who are healthy and strong

enough should only eat Lenten fare, whether on ferial or feast days, thus fasting every day 33. except Sundays and the Birth of the Lord. Then we should eat twice in the day. 34. On the Thursdays of ordinary time, each one may choose, so that she who clearly does not want to, is not obliged to fast. 35. However, we who are healthy fast every day except Sundays and Christmas. 36. For the whole of Easter, as the writing of Blessed Francis says; and on the feasts of holy Mary and of the holy Apostles, we are not obliged to fast unless these feasts should fall on a Friday. 37. And, as has already been said, we who are healthy and strong enough shall always eat Lenten fare.

38. It is true that our flesh is not a flesh of bronze nor is our strength the strength of stone. (Jb 6:12) 39. On the contrary, we are fragile and prone to every bodily weakness, 40. and for that reason, retreat wisely and discretely, I beg you, my dearest, from that indiscreet and impossible austerity of abstinence which I know you have undertaken with ferocity. And in the Lord, I ask 41. that you praise the Lord living, that you give back to the Lord your reasonable homage and that your sacrifice (Rom 12:1) always be seasoned with salt. (Jb 6:6; Lv 2:13; Col 4:6) 42. May you always have strength in the Lord, as I very much hope I shall have strength, and recommend both me and my sisters in your holy prayers.

THE FOURTH LETTER OF SAINT CLARE TO SAINT AGNES OF PRAGUE

1. To the half of her soul and the special shrine of her heart's special love; to the illustrious queen, the bride of the Lamb of the eternal King; to the Lady Agnes, her dearest mother and the daughter who is special among all the others. 2. Clare, the unworthy family servant of Christ and unprofitable handmaid (cf. Lk 17:10) of his handmaids who abide in the monastery of

San Damiano of Assisi, 3. greetings; and with the rest of the
most holy virgins, may she sing the new song (Rv 14:3) before
the throne of God and of the Lamb, and may she follow the
Lamb wheresoever he goes. (Rev 14:4) 4. O mother and
daughter, (Mt 12:50) bride of the King of all ages, although I
have not written to you very often, in the measure that your
soul and mine equally desire—and very much wish for, as
well—do not be surprised, 5. nor believe that therefore the
fire of love for you burns any the less sweetly in the bowels of
your mother. 6. This is the hindrance, the lack of messengers
and the obvious danger of the roads. 7. However, now that I
am writing to you, dearest, I rejoice and exult with you in the
joy of the Spirit, (1 Thess 1:6) O bride of Christ, 8. because
you, like that other most holy virgin, Saint Agnes, are
wonderfully wedded to the spotless Lamb, (1 Pt 1:19) who takes
away the sins of the world, (Jn 1:29) having laid aside all the
vanities of this world.

9. Certainly, she is happy
who has been given to drink deeply at this sacred banquet
so that she might cleave with all her heart to him
(cf. Lk 14:15; Rv 19:9)
10. whose beauty all the blessed hosts of heaven wonder
unceasingly at, (cf. 1 Pt 1:12)
11. whose love stirs to love;
whose contemplation remakes;
whose kindliness floods;
12. whose sweetness fills;
whose memory glows gently;
13. whose fragrance brings the dead to life again;
of whom the glorious vision
will make all the citizens of the Jerusalem above
most blessed, (cf. Rv 21:2–10; Gal 4:26)
14. since she is the splendour of eternal glory,
the brightness of everlasting light

and an unspotted mirror.
(cf. Heb 1:3; Rv 21:11—23; Wis 7:26)
15. Gaze into this mirror daily,
a queen, bride of Jesus Christ,
and continually reflect your face in it, (cf. 2 Cor 11:2)
16. so that you may adorn your whole being,
within and without,
in robes set about with variety, (Ps 45:10)
17. adorned, as is only fitting, with virtues like flowers
and with garments every bit as ornate
as those of the daughter and dearly beloved bride
of the Most High King. (cf. Ps 45:11–12)
18. In that mirror, then, shine
blessed poverty, holy humility, and love beyond words,
as, by the grace of God, you can contemplate in the whole mirror.
19. Turn your mind, I say, to the border of this mirror,
to the poverty of him who was placed in a manger
(cf. Lk 2:12)
and wrapped in tiny garments.
20. O wonderful humility!
O astounding poverty!
21. The King of Angels,
the Lord of heaven and earth, (cf. Mt 11:25)
lays in a manger! (Lk 2:7)

22. Then, in the centre of the mirror, consider the humility, or at least the blessed poverty, the infinite and costly troubles which he took upon himself to redeem the human race. 23. At the edges of that same mirror, contemplate the love beyond words through which he chose to suffer on the Tree of the cross and, on that same Tree, to die the most disgraceful death of any.

24. Therefore, when it was placed on the wood of the cross,
that same mirror taught the one who passed by
to consider all this, saying:

25. "All you who pass by the way,
look and see if there is any sorrow like my sorrow!" (Lam 1:12)
26. It says, let us respond to him with one voice, one spirit,
crying out and grieving: "I hold this memory in my mind and
my spirit faints within me!" (Lam 3:20)

27. So may you always more and more strongly catch fire from
this burning love, O queen of the heavenly King! 28. Over and
above this, contemplating his inexpressible delights, riches and
everlasting honours, 29. and sighing with the immense longing
and love of your heart, may you cry out:

30. O heavenly Bridegroom, draw me after You,
we run in the fragrance of Your perfumes! (Sg 1:3)
31. I shall run and I shall never give up,
until You lead me into the wine-cellar, (cf. Sg 2:4)
32. until Your left arm is under my head
and Your right will happily embrace me,
then You will kiss me
with the most happy kiss of Your mouth.
(cf. Sg 1:1; 2:6; 8:3)

33. Placed in this contemplation, keep the memory of your little,
poor mother, 34. knowing that I have inscribed the happy
memory of you inseparably on the tablets of my heart, holding
you dearer than all others. (cf. 2 Cor 3:3) 35. What else? Let
the tongue of flesh be silent in loving you, let that be said and
spoken by the tongue of the Spirit. 36. O blessed daughter,
because love such as I have for you can never be expressed in
its fulness by the tongue of flesh, 37. I have written the half of
what it has said. I beg you, receive it generously and lovingly.
Hear in it, at least, the motherly affection through which I
daily feel a flame of love for you and your daughters, and to
which, over and over again, I commend myself and my
daughters in Christ. 38. In fact, these same daughters of mine,
but especially the most prudent virgin Agnes, our sister,

recommend themselves in the Lord to you and to your daughters as much as they can. 39. Farewell, dearest daughter, together with your daughters right up to the throne of the glory of the great God, (Ti 2:13) and pray for us. 40. By this letter, I recommend to your love as much as I can, the bearers of this letter, our dearest brothers Amatus, beloved by God and men, (Sir 45:1) and brother Bonagura. Amen.

ACTS OF THE PROCESS OF CANONIZATION OF ST. CLARE, WITNESS III:10–11 (SISTER PHILIPPA)

A sister who was cured of a fistula

When this witness was asked what sisters were cured by the blessed Clare with the sign of the cross, she said Sister Benvenuta di Lady Diambra was one. After twelve years of having a serious infection, called a fistula, under her arm, the sign of the cross was made by the Lady with the Lord's Prayer, and she was cured of her infection.

She also said Sister Amata, a nun of the monastery, was seriously ill with dropsy and fever and had a very swollen stomach. She had received the sign of the cross from the holy mother and had been touched with her hand. On the following morning she was cured so that her little body was restored to good health.

Asked how she knew it, she replied she saw when the holy mother made the sign of the cross and touched her, had seen that she had been sick for a long period of time; on the following day and thereafter, she saw her healthy.

CLARE: A LIGHT IN THE GARDEN

The Privilege of Poverty

Unbarring the locked door and sneaking out at night and stealing down to the Portiuncula in the moonlight, the wind nervously shaking the tiny olive leaves. The brothers waiting on the road with torches in their hands, their faces flushed by the flames, and Francis clipping her hair and the yellow locks falling lifeless onto the dirt floor. The disappointment and pain of having no home and then Francis bringing her to San Damiano and the joy of the Poor Ladies there in that precious little church that Francis himself had restored and their happy life there where everything was poor. Her battle with the Pope for the privilege of living in complete poverty and now his giving in and the announcement that he was this day to secure for her and the Poor Ladies the privilege of poverty forever. ...

Toward the end it all got mixed up in her mind.

It had taken over forty years for that to happen. But now as she lay in bed with the scent of death in the air, it all danced at once in her mind and her whole life was like a day, a moment of celebration.

Clare looked at the bare ceiling of the dormitory. Her eyes wandered wearily over the plain stone walls, and it all became a palace of poverty, a rich simplicity that she had spent her whole life preserving. She tried not to be possessive even of this impoverished place, for it was a place, after all, and her Lord and Savior Jesus Christ had no place to lay his head. Even from San Damiano she must be as detached as Francis was, for even the poorest place can become a rich possession for one who has nothing. Clinging to San Damiano was especially dangerous because of its association with Francis.

And then the little swallows who nested in the rafters of the ceiling began to fly in and out singing their excitement in the morning sun, and she remembered how Francis had always returned to the Portiuncula. It wasn't so much a place as a nest, a womb, a center where God had spoken, a source of renewal for the spirit. San Damiano was a sacred space where Lady Poverty lived. There she moved in her presence easily, warmed at the hearth of silence and renunciation, if God so willed. Clare would go wherever the Pope sent her, but wherever she went she would take Lady Poverty with her, and around her and the Poor Ladies would grow another holy space where the poor Christ would dwell.

She closed her eyes with effort, even that simple movement taxing her waning strength. She slept and the dreams kept rushing in. The dreams of memory.

Mercenary soldiers were in the courtyard again and she was shakily holding the ciborium in the open door. The quizzical looks on their faces and horses pawing the ground, their nervous neighs charging the tense atmosphere, and her prayers to the Eucharistic Christ and their panic and retreat as if from some invisible army. And fire filled the sky over the Portiuncula and she saw herself and Francis and the brothers eating a meal in the open. She was listening to Francis and speaking with him and the word Jesus *flew back and forth. It increased in speed and it caught fire and she and Francis were all light and the Seraphim beat the air with hot wings and the breath of God warmed the whole valley. ...*

She felt something at her wrist. She painfully lifted her eyelids and the room was on fire. At the foot of her straw mat stood one of the brothers, and in his hand he held the confirmation of her Rule of Life and the Privilege of Poverty from Innocent, the Vicar of Christ. She took it weakly in her open palm and its strength drove her hand to her heart and she slept.

Sister Death

Clare knew she was dying, and she couldn't believe how much like life it was. She had known physical and mental suffering for so many years that this new experience seemed like meeting an old, familiar friend. She welcomed Sister Death because she had no fear of her, because it was death who would bring her into life. It was Sister Death who would return Francis to her at last and bring before her eyes the Lord Jesus whom she had loved with all her heart and soul. This was not death, as other people knew death: an impersonal "it" bringing separation and pain. This was life; all those years of separation from Francis and her Lord were that impersonal death which others feared so much and tried so hard to postpone.

Her sisters were gathered around her now. And what was this? Here were Brothers Angelo, Leo and Juniper, her faithful friends. They had become even more dear to her after Francis' death, and she remembered now that she had sent for them to read the Passion of Jesus to her on her bed of pain. They had come to watch one hour with her.

Leo knelt and kissed the straw of her mat; Angelo consoled everyone, as usual; and Juniper began reading the Passion of the Lord in his inimitable, enthusiastic manner. Clare listened with great peace and joy, and then she said to all in the room: "Do you not see the King of Glory? Here he is before me."

She never knew if they saw the Lord or not, for she was caught up in the vision before her. Then the mother of Jesus entered the room and took Clare into her arms and carried her into heaven. And the light in the garden flamed high, the fire of its passing warming Assisi forever.

Murray Bodo, O.F.M. *Clare: A Light in the Garden* [Cincinnati: St. Anthony Messenger Press, 1992], 106–108. Used with permission.

THE SECRET OF THE GOLDEN FLOWER

Chiara,
a play of light
golden as the
rising sun
over Assisi,
played out
over fifty years
of agonizing sickness
after sickness
and vicious onslaughts
of the evil one.

She taught
her dearly loved sisters,
in O, a thousand ways,
in adoration and praises
of the Most High,
the passionate cultivation
of the enclosed garden. . . .
Jesus,
and a swift attention

to the tremulous stirring
of the Spirit's wings.

Once while listening
to a sermon
of Brother Philip,
she was seen
clear and bright
as day,
holding the Holy Child—
enfolded in the
secret of the golden flower.

William Hart McNichols, S.J., S.F.O., January 1989. Used with permission.

EUCHARIST

SAINT CLARE

READING I: HOSEA 2:14–16, 19–20

A reading from the book of the prophet Hosea

Therefore, I will now allure her, and bring her into the wilderness, and speak tenderly to her. From there I will give her her vineyards, and make the Valley of Achor a door of hope. There she shall respond as in the days of her youth, as at the time when she came out of the land of Egypt. On that day, says the LORD, you will call me, "My husband," and no longer will you call me, "My Baal."

And I will take you for my wife forever; I will take you for my wife in righteousness and in justice, in steadfast love, and in mercy. I will take you for my wife in faithfulness; and you shall know the LORD. **The word of the Lord.**

RESPONSE: They are borne in with gladness and joy to the house of God.

PSALM 45

Hear, O daughter, consider and incline your ear;
forget your people and your father's house,
and the king will desire your beauty. **R.**

Since he is your lord, bow to him;
the people of Tyre will seek your favor with gifts,
the richest of the people with all kinds of wealth. **R.**

The princess is decked in her chamber with gold-woven robes;
in many-colored robes she is led to the king;
behind her the virgins, her companions, follow.
With joy and gladness they are led along
as they enter the palace of the king. **R.**

READING II: 2 CORINTHIANS 4:6–10, 16–18

A reading from the second letter of Paul to the Corinthians

For it is the God who said, "Let light shine out of darkness," who has shone in our hearts to give the light of the knowledge of the glory of God in the face of Jesus Christ. But we have this treasure in clay jars, so that it may be made clear that this extraordinary power belongs to God and does not come from us. We are afflicted in every way, but not crushed; perplexed, but not driven to despair; persecuted, but not forsaken; struck down, but not destroyed; always carrying in the body the death of Jesus, so that the life of Jesus may also be made visible in our bodies.

So we do not lose heart. Even though our outer nature is wasting away, our inner nature is being renewed day by day. For this slight momentary affliction is preparing us for an eternal weight of glory beyond all measure, because we look not at what can be seen but at what cannot be seen; for what can be seen is temporary, but what cannot be seen is eternal. **The word of the Lord.**

ALLELUIA: Come, bride of Christ, receive the crown which Our God prepared for you for ever.

GOSPEL: JOHN 15:4–10

A reading from the holy Gospel according to John

Abide in me as I abide in you. Just as the branch cannot bear fruit by itself unless it abides in the vine, neither can you unless you abide in me. I am the vine, you are the branches. Those who abide in me and I in them bear much fruit, because apart from me you can do nothing. Whoever does not abide in me is thrown away like a branch and withers; such branches are gathered, thrown into the fire, and burned. If you abide in me, and my words abide in you, ask for whatever you wish, and it will be done for you. My Father is glorified by this, that you bear much fruit and become my disciples. As the Father has loved me, so I have loved you; abide in my love. If you keep my commandments, you will abide in my love, just as I have kept my Father's commandments and abide in his love. **The Gospel of the Lord.**

EUCHARIST

HEALING AT SAN DAMIANO

READING I: ISAIAH 61:1–3

A reading from the book of the prophet Isaiah

The spirit of the Lord GOD is upon me, because the LORD has anointed me; he has sent me to bring good news to the oppressed, to bind up the brokenhearted, to proclaim liberty

to the captives, and release to the prisoners; to proclaim the year of the LORD's favor, and the day of vengeance of our God; to comfort all who mourn; to provide for those who mourn in Zion—to give them a garland instead of ashes, the oil of gladness instead of mourning, the mantle of praise instead of a faint spirit. **The word of the Lord.**

RESPONSE: O Lord be gracious to me and heal me.

PSALM 41

Happy are those who consider the poor;
the LORD delivers them in the day of trouble.
The LORD protects them and keeps them alive;
they are called happy in the land. **R.**

You do not give them up to the will of their enemies.
The LORD sustains them on their sickbed;
in their illness you heal all their infirmities. **R.**

As for me, I said, "O LORD, be gracious to me;
heal me, for I have sinned against you."
Blessed be the LORD, the God of Israel,
from everlasting to everlasting.
Amen and Amen. **R.**

READING II: ROMANS 8:31–39

A reading from the letter of Paul to the Romans

What then are we to say about these things? If God is for us, who is against us? He who did not withhold his own Son, but gave him up for all of us, will he not with him also give us everything else? Who will bring any charge against God's elect?

It is God who justifies. Who is to condemn? It is Christ Jesus, who died, yes, who was raised, who is at the right hand of God, who indeed intercedes for us. Who will separate us from the love of Christ? Will hardship, or distress, or persecution, or famine, or nakedness, or peril, or sword? As it is written, "For your sake we are being killed all day long; we are accounted as sheep to be slaughtered." No, in all these things we are more than conquerors through him who loved us. For I am convinced that neither death, nor life, nor angels, nor rulers, nor things present, nor things to come, nor powers, nor height, nor depth, nor anything else in all creation, will be able to separate us from the love of God in Christ Jesus our Lord. **The word of the Lord.**

ALLELUIA: The crowd was amazed when they saw the healing power of Jesus.

GOSPEL: MATTHEW 15:29–31

A reading from the holy Gospel according to Matthew

After Jesus had left that place, he passed along the Sea of Galilee, and he went up the mountain, where he sat down. Great crowds came to him, bringing with them the lame, the maimed, the blind, the mute, and many others. They put them at his feet, and he cured them, so that the crowd was amazed when they saw the mute speaking, the maimed whole, the lame walking, and the blind seeing. And they praised the God of Israel. **The Gospel of the Lord.**

HEALING RITUAL AT SAN DAMIANO

OPENING REFLECTION

"... it is the steep ascent from choir through the narrow passageway opening into their Bridal Chamber that lifts Clare and the Poor Ladies above routine. For there is the room of redemptive suffering where Clare ministers to her sick sisters. ..."

From the poem "The Rooms of St. Clare," by Murray Bodo, O.F.M. Used with permission.

READING I: ACTS OF THE PROCESS OF CANONIZATION OF ST. CLARE, WITNESS I: 16–19 (SISTER PACIFICA)

This witness also said one time when five sisters were sick in the monastery, Saint Clare made the sign of the cross with her own hand over them and all of them were immediately cured.

Frequently when one of the sisters had some pain in either the head or another part of the body, the blessed mother cured her with the sign of the cross. Asked how she knew the things mentioned, she replied she was present. Asked who the five sisters were, she replied that she, the witness, was one, some of the others had died, others were living, but she did not remember whom. Asked the length of time she, the witness, was sick, she replied it was a long time.

Asked what the sickness was, she replied it was one that made her shriek, have a great fever and shake.

Asked about the others who had been cured, the length of time they had been sick, she replied she did not remember about the others as about herself. Asked when those sisters were cured, she replied: before the Lady was sick.

Asked about the time Saint Clare began that long illness, she replied she believed it was twenty-nine years.

She also said the medicine of that witness and of the other sisters when they were sick was that their mother made the sign of the cross over them.

Asked what words the Lady Clare used to speak when she made the sign of the cross, she replied they did not understand her because she spoke very softly.

Asked about the month and the day she, the witness, and the other sisters were cured, she replied she did not remember. Asked who was present when they were cured, she replied more sisters were present, but she did not remember how many nor who.

READING II: ACTS OF THE PROCESS OF CANONIZATION OF ST. CLARE, WITNESS II: 15 (SISTER BENVENUTA)

The said witness also said that a certain brother of the Order of Friars Minor, Stephen by name, was mentally ill. Saint Francis sent him to the monastery of San Damiano, so Saint Clare would make the sign of the cross over him. After she had done this, the brother went to sleep a little bit in the place where the holy mother usually prayed. Upon waking, he ate a little and then departed cured.

Asked who was present at this event, she replied the sisters of the monastery were, some [still] living, others dead.

Asked if she had known that brother beforehand, how many days she had seen him ill, and how much time well, she replied she did not know all these things, because she was enclosed. Brother Stephen, once cured, went on his way.

READING III: ACTS OF THE PROCESS OF CANONIZATION OF ST. CLARE, WITNESS II: 18 (SISTER BENVENUTA)

[Sr. Benvenuta] also said a young boy of the city of Spoleto, Mattiolo, three or four years old, had put a small pebble up one of the nostrils of his nose, so it could in no way be extricated. The young boy seemed to be in danger. After he was brought to Saint Clare and she made the sign of the cross over him, that pebble immediately fell from his nose. The young boy was cured.

REFLECTION

ANOINTING WITH OIL

Here in this most sacred space may you know the healing power of the crucified Jesus through the intercession of the Lady Clare.

OUR FATHER

CLOSING BLESSING

[Gaze] upon [Christ],
consider [Christ]
contemplate [Christ],
as you desire to imitate [Him].
If you suffer with Him, *you will reign with Him.*
[If you] weep [with Him], you shall rejoice with [Him];
[If you] die with Him on the cross of tribulation,
you shall possess heavenly mansions *in the splendor of the saints*
and, *in the Book of Life,* your *name* shall be called glorious among [all people]. (2LAg 20–22)

DISMISSAL

Go now in peace, knowing you are loved and healed.

CLARE, THE LIGHT

REFRAIN
O come with us and sing
To honor Christ our Light
Who robed the Lady Clare
With radiant glory bright.

Christ became the Way for us
Which Francis showed to Clare,
And she has taught us how to find
His footprints everywhere. (Ref.)

Clare was called when she heard the Word
Which Francis preached abroad,
She left her home, her wealth, her all
To follow Christ her Lord. (Ref.)

Christ revealed himself to Clare,
The poorest man of all,
He wooed her by humility
And won her by his call. (Ref.)

Clare saw Christ as a man of pain,
Most powerful when most weak,
The God who took our human flesh
Our wand'ring hearts to seek. (Ref.)

Christ called Clare to gaze on him
As in a pool of light,
Wherein she saw the Lord of love
The source of beauty bright. (Ref.)

Clare drank deep from the heart of God
The Spirit's liquid fire,
And now she calls across the years
To challenge and inspire. (Ref.)

Clare, all we who love your name
Cry out in joy and prayer:
Teach us your love of Christ, that we
May praise God everywhere. (Ref.)

Sr. Frances Teresa, O.S.C. Used with permission.

THE ROOMS OF SAINT CLARE

One has only to go into any room in any street for the whole of
that extremely complex force of femininity to fly in one's face.
(Virginia Woolf)

Hers is the mystery of rooms.
The room from whose window she watches
Francis walk across the Piazza San Rufino
and into whose tapestried forest

                she withdraws

to seek the unicorn's white horn
that brings her to that other room
where bishop Guido places
the palm into her open soul.

Rooms open on rooms.
St. Mary of the Angels, the room of vows
that opens onto the nuns of Bastia,
the monastery on Mt. Subasio, and
San Damiano with its rooms God has prepared for her,
each room conforming to the contours of her soul
like a fitted wedding dress.
There at San Damiano
she crosses the threshold

                into the royal chamber.
Above the marble altar-bed
she sees herself in the mirror that spoke to Francis.
She's radiant, calm, pure with desire.

She kneels and the room
opens upon mansions of possibility:
other brides cross the threshold with her,
fill the rooms of their own espousals.
Rooms spill out into streets of their village,
a courtyard around whose well they gather
to draw water, talk their own domesticity.
They gather for church
                      like women inside Assisi's
walls. They sing psalms, share the Bread of Life,
after which they pass
                  a further threshold
into Lady poverty's dining room where Clare
blesses another bread
                  crossed with want and penance.

But it is the steep ascent from choir
through the narrow passageway
                opening
into their Bridal Chamber
That lifts Clare and the Poor Ladies above routine.
For there is the room of redemptive suffering where
Clare ministers to her sick sisters,
lies bedridden sewing albs and altar linens.
There she opens the door, kneels
before her Eucharistic Lord, and
prays away the threatening advances
of the Emperor's mercenary soldiers.

There in the room of consummations
she holds her Rule that holds
all the rooms of the Poor Ladies' lives.
She presses the Book of Rooms to her heart and
crosses the final threshold into all the rooms
of her life

now graced with Him
who is the mirror she enters without effort,
without shattering the glass that
holds her image inside His.

Murray Bodo, O.F.M. in *Clare Centenary Series, Volume 8: Clare of Assisi*, ed. Ingrid Peterson, O.S.F. [St. Bonaventure, N. Y.: Franciscan Institute, 1996]. Reprinted with permission.

ASSISI: THE CARCERI

FRANCISCAN PILGRIMAGE PROGRAMS

ASSISI: THE CARCERI

EVENTS
Francis spent time in the caves on Monte Subasio. This time spent in prayer and solitude was critical in his initial and ongoing conversion process.

Francis appealed to Sylvester, living at the Carceri (and Clare at the Monastery of San Damiano), to help resolve his dilemma on whether to preach or give himself to a contemplative life.

SPIRITUALITY
The Carceri brings us face-to-face with solitude. Dacian Bluma, O.F.M., maintains that Francis spent about one-half of his converted life in hermitages.

It is in the experience and practice of solitude that Francis' life and the Franciscan movement sank its roots for all time.

The development of a regular rhythm of solitude gives birth to a sense of listening and depth in one's life.

REFLECTION
If Francis spent one-half of his converted life in hermitages, what does this say to those of us involved in very active ministry?

The Carceri is a place where Francis and the brothers went to pray. What is the contemplative aspect of Franciscan life for your expression of the Franciscan charism?

Francis was torn between a life of preaching and a life of contemplation. How does his solution serve as a guide for us?

The relationship between the "mothers" and the "sons" as expressed in Francis' teaching about a life of solitude suggests a degree of tenderness and intimacy among the early brothers. How does this find expression in our life as Franciscans today?

THE CARCERI

HISTORICAL NOTES

Until the 13th century, there was merely a small chapel here on the top of Monte Subasio; it belonged to the *comune*. St. Francis often retired to this area for solitude, and he renamed the chapel in honor of Mary. Not long after the death of Francis, the town granted his followers the use of the chapel and the woods, where there were various caves that served as shelters for the brothers. The *comune* decreed that no one should interfere with the reclusive life of the brothers living there, and even ordained that no one cut down or burn the trees of the forest at the Carceri. The town retains ownership of the land, and much of the forest is under the supervision of the national forest service.

Early in the 15th century, a small hermitage was added to the original chapel. In 1415 the Carceri passed into the hands of the Observants. Under St. Bernardine of Siena, who was novice master and provincial here (ca. 1420), the water from a small spring was channeled into a well and the hermitage was enlarged in order to give accommodations to more brothers, but the number never seems to have been more than ten or twelve. The Carceri is one of a number of remote places, all important in Franciscan life: Le Celle (near Cortona), Monte Casale (near Borgo San Sepolcro), Poggio Bustone, Greccio, Fonte Colombo, Lo Speco di Narni, and Cetona.

WHAT TO SEE

The entrance to the hermitage (Carceri) leads into the little courtyard (A) perched high atop the ravine. The little church (B) leads to the ancient chapel (C), which dates back to the time of Francis. On the back wall, beneath a fresco of Mary, there is an older fresco of the Crucifixion. At the left of the chapel is the tiny choir (D) where the Office is prayed. To the right there is a narrow passage and a stairway; take this path to the grotto of St. Francis (E). There, in a deep depression in the rock, Francis both prayed and slept. On leaving the grotto (F) you will notice two primitive frescoes. The bridge (G) that crosses the ravine leads to the grotto of Brother Leo. Going off along the various paths, you will find the caves of Bernard, Sylvester, Rufino, and Masseo. However, the friars really did not have their own grottoes; anyone who stayed at the Carceri chose any available cave or hut.

Return to the main area to visit the chapel (H) that contains the tomb of Blessed Barnabas Manassei of Terni (d. 1474), founder of Mons Pietatis. In the old cloister (if open) you can see the large mission cross (I) of St. Bernardine of Siena. Also, if it is open, you can visit the small refectory (J) that dates from the time of St. Bernardine.

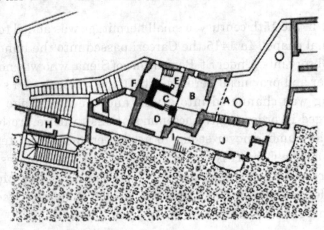

FRANCISCAN READINGS

THOMAS OF CELANO, FIRST LIFE 71

Francis' search for solitary places

With blessed devotion he visited the heavenly mansions;
and, totally *emptied of himself*,
he rested for a long time in the wounds of the Savior.
That is why he often chose solitary places
to focus his heart entirely on God.

But he was not reluctant,
when he discerned the time was right,
to involve himself in the affairs of his neighbors,
and attend to their salvation.
For his safest haven was prayer;
not prayer of a fleeting moment, empty and proud,
but prayer that was prolonged,
full of devotion, peaceful in humility.
If he began at night,
he was barely finished at morning.
Walking, sitting, eating, drinking,
he was focused on prayer.
He would spend the night alone praying
in abandoned churches and in deserted places
where,
with the protection of divine grace,
he overcame his soul's many fears and anxieties.

THOMAS OF CELANO, FIRST LIFE 91

Francis' search for solitary places

At one time the blessed and venerable father Francis, with
worldly crowds gathering eagerly every day to hear and see
him, sought out a place of rest and secret solitude. He desired

to free himself for God and *shake off any dust that clung to him* from the time spent with the crowds. It was his custom to divide the time given him to merit grace and, as seemed best, to spend some of it to benefit his neighbors and use the rest in the blessed solitude of contemplation. *He took with him* only a few companions—who knew his holy way of living better than others—so that they could shield him *from the interruption and disturbance of people*, respecting and protecting his silence in every way.

ST. BONAVENTURE, MAJOR LEGEND X:3

Francis' search for solitary places

And because he had learned in prayer
that the presence of the Holy Spirit for which he longed
was offered more intimately to those who invoke him,
the more It found them
far from the noise of worldly affairs.

Therefore seeking out solitary places, he used to go to deserted and abandoned churches to pray at night.

THOMAS OF CELANO, SECOND LIFE 94–95

Francis' prayer life

A *pilgrim* while *in the body, away from the Lord*,
Francis, the *man of God*,
strove to keep himself *present in spirit* to heaven,
and, being already made a fellow-citizen of the angels,
he was separated from them
only by the wall of the flesh.
With all his *soul* he *thirsted for* his Christ:
to him he dedicated not only his whole heart
but also his whole body.
We will tell only a few things, to be imitated by posterity

—to the extent that they can be told *to human ears*—
about the *wonders* of his prayer,
things we have *seen* with our own eyes.

He turned all his time into a holy leisure
in which to engrave *wisdom on his heart*,
so that, if he did not always advance,
he would not seem to give up.
If visits from people of the world
or any kind of business intruded,
he would cut them short
rather than finish them,
and hurry back to the things that are within.
The world had no flavor to him,
fed on the sweetness of heaven,
and divine delicacies had spoiled him
for crude human fare.
He always sought out a *hidden place*
where he could join to God
not only his spirit
but every member of his body.
When it happened that he was suddenly overcome in public
by a *visitation of the Lord*
so as not to be without a cell,
he would make a little cell out of his mantle.
Sometimes, when he had no mantle,
he would cover his face with his sleeve
to avoid revealing the *hidden manna*.
He would always place something between himself and
bystanders
so they would not notice *the Bridegroom's touch*.
Even when crowded in the confines of a ship,
he could pray unseen.
Finally, when none of these things was possible,
he made a temple out of his breast.

Forgetful of himself
he did not cough or groan;
and being absorbed in God took away any hard breathing or
external movement.

Thus it was at home.
But when praying in the woods or solitary places
he would fill the forest with groans,
water the places with tears,
strike his breast with his hand,
and, as if finding a more secret hiding place,
he often conversed out loud with his Lord.
There he replied to the Judge,
there he entreated the Father;
there he conversed with the Friend,
there he played with the Bridegroom.
Indeed, in order to make
all the marrow of his heart a holocaust in manifold ways,
he would place *before his eyes*
the One who is manifold and supremely simple.
He would often *ruminate* inwardly with unmoving *lips*,
and, drawing outward things inward,
he raised his spirit to the heights.
Thus he would direct all his attention and affection
toward the *one thing* he *asked of the Lord*,
not so much praying as becoming totally prayer.

THOMAS OF CELANO, FIRST LIFE 115

How Francis bears the characteristics of Jesus in his body

The brothers who lived with him know
that daily, constantly, talk of Jesus was always on his lips,
sweet and pleasant conversations about Him,
kind words full of love.
Out of the fullness of the heart his mouth spoke.

So the spring of radiant love
that filled his heart within
gushed forth.
He was always with Jesus:
Jesus in his heart,
Jesus in his mouth,
Jesus in his ears,
Jesus in his eyes,
Jesus in his hands,
he bore Jesus always in his whole body. ...
Often as he walked along a road,
thinking and singing of Jesus,
he would forget his destination
and start inviting all the elements
to praise Jesus.
With amazing love he bore
in his heart and always held onto
Christ Jesus and Him crucified.

DOCUMENT ON SOLITUDE OF ST. FRANCIS

1. Those who wish to be in a religious manner in solitude should be three or four brothers at most; two of them should be mothers and have two sons or at least one.

2. Those two, who are the mothers, should maintain the life of Martha and the two sons maintain the life of Mary and have one enclosure in which each one would have his cell, in which he could pray and sleep.

3. And they should always say Compline of the day immediately after sunset; and they should be zealous to preserve silence; and say their Hours; and they should get up for Matins and they should first seek the reign of God and [God's] justice [Mt 6:33].

4. And they should say Prime at the appropriate hour and after Terce they could be free from silence; and they could speak and go to their mothers.

5. And when they like, for the love of the Lord God, they could beg alms from them as destitute little ones.

6. And afterwards they should say Sext and None; and they should say Vespers at the appropriate hour.

7. And in the enclosure, where they stay, they should not allow any person to gain entry and they should not eat there.

8. Those brothers, who are the mothers, should be zealous to remain apart from every person; and through obedience to their ministers they should guard their sons from every person, so that no one would be able to speak with them.

9. And these sons should not speak with any person except with their mothers and with their minister and custodian, when it suits him to visit them with the blessing of the Lord God.

10. But the sons at some time should take on the duty of the mothers, alternating as it seems proper to them to arrange for an appointed time; they should be zealous to observe diligently and carefully everything said above.

André Cirino, O.F.M., trans. Unpublished text. Used with permission.

TRUE JOY FROM ASSISI

This cluster of tiny chapels, cells, and grottoes, hidden in an ilex grove halfway up Mount Subasio, was probably Francis' favorite hermitage—the one to which he withdrew most frequently for prayer, penance, and contemplation of God amid the beauty and rigors of His creation.

My reaction to its truly extraordinary radiation condenses the unanimous accounts of over a dozen writers: "There is an indescribable yet almost palpable atmosphere of peace and prayer and recollection. It is here, even more than at San Damiano, that one feels the living spirit and presence of St. Francis. Like all mystical graces, this is an experience which cannot be adequately expressed in words. ... It seemed so natural to pray in that green paradise-on-earth."

Marcel Brion probably strikes the keynote most perfectly: "It is here that one feels the heart of St. Francis beat most clearly, most strongly." Or as Father Desbonnets noted: "The Carceri above all will make us discover how much Francis was inclined by nature to contemplation and prayer."

Raphael Brown, *True Joy from Assisi* [Chicago: Franciscan Press, 1978]. Used with permission.

FRANCIS: THE JOURNEY AND THE DREAM
Of Mountain Hideaways
and
A RULE FOR HERMITAGES 1–10

Mount Subasio! Always there towering above Assisi, dominating the whole of the valley below, making the hill of the Rocca Maggiore seem a mere bump on the horizon. It was to Mount Subasio and the little hermitage, actually a simple cave, that Francis had returned again and again when the Dream began to fade. The sheer physical hardship of the long hike to the top and the cold hard rocks he slept on shook him again into the Romance of the Quest, the adventure of the knight of Christ. On the plain below, even in the Church of the Portiuncula, the dullness of life set in, and there was no glory of combat, no test of battle.

Francis feared that some day the brothers would lose the Vision and would settle down into routine and boredom. They had to be continually renewed, as he was, by places like the hermitage on Mount Subasio. There at that high altitude, in those stark caves, it was possible to return to the primitive, the elemental, in nature and in oneself.

Let those who wish to stay in hermitages in a religious way be three brothers or, at the most, four; let two of these be "the mother" and have two "sons" or at least one. Let the two who are "mothers" keep the life of Martha and the two "sons" the life of Mary. ...

There, too, decisions were simpler. The distractions of the daily preoccupations of living with others were stripped away, and you lived alone with Jesus in the purity and rigor of the mountain. The stone Francis slept on in the hermitage seemed softer by far than the bed he had slept upon in his father's house. The hermitage was a challenge, a sacrifice, something physical to lift his spirit and make it bellow with determination to win the race that St. Paul wrote about so beautifully.

And let one have one enclosure in which each one may have his cell in which he may pray and sleep.

Even in his weakest and most pain-filled moments at the hermitage, when Brother Body was filled with disease and infection, he could feel his spirit standing up and shouting, beating its chest and proclaiming victory of the inner man for all the world to hear.

And let them always recite Compline of the day immediately after sunset and strive to maintain silence, recite their Hours, rise for Matins, and seek first the kingdom of God and His justice. And let them recite Prime at the proper hour and, after Terce, they may end their silence, speak with and go to their mothers.

Oh, how sweet were the ways of penance and sacrifice! They filled the heart with new strength and the spirit with a determination that transcended every bodily weakness and cowardice. From the top of Mount Subasio you shouted, "Here I am, world! God is love! God is joy! God lifts up the valley and the plain! God forgets not the meek and humble of the earth below."

And when it pleases them, they can beg alms from them as poor little ones out of love of the Lord God.

And the rarer the atmosphere became, the more filled was Francis' spirit with the breath of God. Everyone, every brother for sure, should have a hermitage to run to when the heart fails, when the courage to go on flees.

And they may not permit anyone to enter or eat in the enclosure where they dwell. Let those brothers who are the "mothers" strive to stay far from everyone and, because of obedience to their minister, protect their "sons" from everyone so that no one can speak with them. And those "sons" may not talk with anyone except with their "mothers" and with the minister and his custodian when it pleases them to visit with the Lord's blessing.

From the mountaintop everything below was simplified and brought into perspective. Francis remembered, especially, the days of trouble in the Order, when the bad times descended upon St. Mary of the Angels as the rumors of troubles rushed down into the valley like a flash flood from the top of Mount Subasio. Then, when he had returned to the mountain retreat and looked back at St. Mary of the Angels, he couldn't even see the little church. There was only a vast plain, covered with mist, and Francis thought the mist must have come from his own brain sizzling out as it tried to come to grips with the confusion brought into the Dream by the increasing number of brothers.

Even the meeting [Chapter] of 1221, when over 5,000 brothers from far and wide had gathered at St. Mary of the Angels, would have been invisible from the hermitage. There one could only look up: "I have lifted my eyes to the hills." To look down was to gaze on mist and shadows and vague outlines of things that were of phantom importance. Only light and crisp air and the steep ascent and the heightened and purified senses mattered on Mount Subasio.

The hermitage was balance, was peace.

The "sons," however, may periodically assume the role of the "mothers," taking turns for a time as they have mutually decided.

He was always aware that he would have to return to the workaday world below, but it was possible to do so with joy, knowing that the mountain would not move, that the mountain would be there waiting, drawing him back. Mount Subasio was his magnetic mountain, pulling his spirit up, beckoning him to lift his eyes to the skies whenever the plain began to fix his stare in a horizontal orbit of despair.

Francis prayed, "Lord, for each of us a mountain, to rescue us from the plain!"

Let them strive to observe conscientiously and eagerly everything mentioned above.

Murray Bodo, O.F.M., *Francis: The Journey and the Dream* [Cincinnati: St. Anthony Messenger Press, 1988], 80–81.

BLESSING PRAYER TO BEGIN A DAY OF SOLITUDE

My Lord and my God,
You did call from their daily lives,
Your servants Moses, Elijah, John the Baptist,
Mary of Nazareth, and Your Son, Jesus,
[and Francis and Clare of Assisi]
to come apart and to spend time in solitude.
Some You have called to the desert,
some to mountain peaks,
others to the hidden hermitage within their own homes.
I have heard the ancient call [to solitude]
and seek to be alone with You.

[Being here in the land of Francis and Clare,]
I will use the space that I have.
My Lord, You who are the creator of all space,
You who make lonely desert places holy,
come and consecrate this place
as a temporary hermitage for me.
Cleanse it of noise
and anything that might call me out of its stillness.

May this space, sacred by Your blessing,
become for me a waiting room

where I shall wait upon You
my Lord, my Beloved, my Friend.

May prayerful peace 'flow outward from here,
touching with grace all those whom I love
and all the earth as well.
May all dark powers be impotent,
unable to cross the sacred circle
that surrounds this holy hermitage.
Help me, my Lord, to leave outside this hermitage
my plans for tomorrow, my memories of yesterday,
as I live fully and completely
in the wonder of Your present moment.

Lord, may my prayer be one with that of all persons,
[and all creation,]
who throughout this earth are in solitude and stillness,
forming a luminous and silent hymn of glory to You.

May Your blessing, Almighty God,
Father, Son, and Holy Spirit,
be upon this hermitage and this solitary time. Amen.

Fr. Edward Hayes, *Prayers for the Domestic Church* [Easton KS: Forest
of Peace Books, Inc., 1979], 146. Reprinted with permission.

PRAYER FOR ENDING A TIME OF SOLITUDE

My Lord, it is time for me to return.
I thank You for this quiet time apart,
unburdened by my normal duties of life.

This time alone has been renewing and re-creating for me
as body and spirit have been healed.
Its rest has given a boost to my body.
Its silence has been as a salve to my spirit.
This time apart from others

has renewed within me a desire to be in communion
with all those whom I love.
Fire within me the desire
to join them and all others
on the crowded journey of life.

I thank You, O Secret One,
for the graces of this time in solitude.
Each time I withdraw to be alone,
I learn more not to fear being alone.
I thus prepare myself for that final moment
when I shall pass through the desert of death,
with its absolute aloneness,
and come to absolute communion of life eternal
with You.

My Lord, I treasure this time now ending.
Help me, as I return to the flow of daily life.
Prepare me for what I shall find,
the good and the bad,
mistakes and successes,
whatever You have laid out for me.

May this holy time of prayerful solitude
fill me with the necessary energy
to once again take up the challenge
of finding holiness in the midst of my work,
in the center of my home.

Come, my Beloved,
and accompany me as I return
to the crowded and noisy crossroads of
life.
Amen.

Fr. Edward Hayes, *Prayers for the Domestic Church*
[Easton KS: Forest of Peace Books, Inc., 1979], 147.
Reprinted with permission.

EUCHARIST

READING: EPHESIANS 3:14–19

A reading from the letter of Paul to the Ephesians

For this reason I bow my knees before the Father, from whom every family in heaven and on earth takes its name. I pray that, according to the riches of his glory, he may grant that you may be strengthened in your inner being with power through his Spirit, and that Christ may dwell in your hearts through faith, as you are being rooted and grounded in love. I pray that you may have the power to comprehend, with all the saints, what is the breadth and length and height and depth, and to know the love of Christ that surpasses knowledge, so that you may be filled with all the fullness of God. **The word of the Lord.**

OR: JAMES 3:13–18

A reading from the letter of James

Who is wise and understanding among you? Show by your good life that your works are done with gentleness born of wisdom. But if you have bitter envy and selfish ambition in your hearts, do not be boastful and false to the truth. Such wisdom does not come down from above, but is earthly, unspiritual, devilish. For where there is envy and selfish ambition, there will also be disorder and wickedness of every kind. But the wisdom from above is first pure, then peaceable, gentle, willing to yield, full of mercy and good fruits, without a trace of partiality or hypocrisy. And a harvest of righteousness is sown in peace for those who make peace. **The word of the Lord.**

RESPONSE: My soul is longing for your peace, my God.

PSALM 131

O LORD, my heart is not lifted up,
my eyes are not raised too high;
I do not occupy myself with things
too great and too marvelous for me. **R.**

But I have calmed and quieted my soul,
like a weaned child with its mother;
my soul is like the weaned child that is with me.
O Israel, hope in the LORD
from this time on and forevermore. **R.**

**ALLELUIA: Seek first God's reign and God's justice ...
whatever you ask in my name, I will do.**

GOSPEL: JOHN 14:1–14

A reading from the holy Gospel according to John

"Do not let your hearts be troubled. Believe in God, believe
also in me. In my Father's house there are many dwelling
places. If it were not so, would I have told you that I go to
prepare a place for you? And if I go and prepare a place for
you, I will come again and will take you to myself, so that
where I am, there you may be also. And you know the way to
the place where I am going." Thomas said to him, "Lord, we do
not know where you are going. How can we know the way?"
Jesus said to him, "I am the way, and the truth, and the life.
No one comes to the Father except through me. If you know
me, you will know my Father also. From now on you do know
him and have seen him." Philip said to him, "Lord, show us
the Father, and we will be satisfied." Jesus said to him, "Have
I been with you all this time, Philip, and you still do not know
me? Whoever has seen me has seen the Father. How can you
say, 'Show us the Father'? Do you not believe that I am in the

Father and the Father is in me? The words that I say to you I
do not speak on my own; but the Father who dwells in me does
his works. Believe me that I am in the Father and the Father
is in me; but if you do not, then believe me because of the
works themselves. Very truly, I tell you, the one who believes
in me will also do the works that I do and, in fact, will do
greater works than these, because I am going to the Father. I
will do whatever you ask in my name, so that the Father may
be glorified in the Son. If in my name you ask me for anything,
I will do it." **The Gospel of the Lord.**

OR: MATTHEW 6:31-34

A reading from the holy Gospel according to Matthew

"Therefore do not worry, saying, 'what will we eat?' or 'What
will we drink?' or "What will we wear?' For it is the Gentiles
who strive for all these things; and indeed your heavenly Father
knows that you need all these things. But strive first for the
kingdom of God and his righteousness, and all these things
will be given to you as well.

So do not worry about tomorrow, for tomorrow will bring
worries of its own. Today's trouble is enough for today." **The
Gospel of the Lord.**

EUCHARIST

FOCUS ON PRAYER

READING: I Kings 19:9–12

A reading from the first book of Kings.

At that place he came to a cave, and spent the night there. Then the word of the LORD came to him, saying, "What are you doing here, Elijah?" He answered, "I have been very zealous for the LORD, the God of hosts; for the Israelites have forsaken your covenant, thrown down your altars, and killed your prophets with the sword. I alone am left, and they are seeking my life, to take it away." He said, "Go out and stand on the mountain before the LORD, for the LORD is about to pass by." Now there was a great wind, so strong that it was splitting mountains and breaking rocks in pieces before the LORD, but the LORD was not in the wind; and after the wind an earthquake, but the LORD was not in the earthquake; and after the earthquake a fire, but the LORD was not in the fire; and after the fire a sound of sheer silence. **The word of the Lord.**

RESPONSE: I will rest under the shelter of God's wings.

PSALM 63

O God, you are my God, I seek you,
my soul thirsts for you;
my flesh faints for you,
as in a dry and weary land where there is no water. **R.**

So I have looked upon you in the sanctuary,
beholding your power and glory.
Because your steadfast love is better than life,
my lips will praise you. **R.**

My soul is satisfied as with a rich feast,

and my mouth praises you with joyful lips
when I think of you on my bed,
and meditate on you in the watches of the night;
for you have been my help,
and in the shadow of your wings I sing for joy. **R.**

My soul clings to you;
your right hand upholds me.
But those who seek to destroy my life
shall go down into the depths of the earth. **R.**

ALLELUIA: Rising very early before dawn, Jesus went off to a deserted place, where he prayed.

GOSPEL: MARK 1:32–38

A reading from the holy Gospel according to Mark

That evening, at sundown, they brought to him all who were sick or possessed with demons. And the whole city was gathered around the door. And he cured many who were sick with various diseases, and cast out many demons; and he would not permit the demons to speak, because they knew him. In the morning, while it was still very dark, he got up and went out to a deserted place, and there he prayed. And Simon and his companions hunted for him. When they found him, they said to him, "Everyone is searching for you." He answered, "Let us go on to the neighboring towns, so that I may proclaim the message there also; for that is what I came out to do." **The Gospel of the Lord.**

ASSISI:
LE CELLE
DI CORTONA

FRANCISCAN PILGRIMAGE PROGRAMS

ASSISI: LE CELLE DI CORTONA

EVENTS
In 1211, Francis arrives for the first time at Le Celle seeking a place of solitude and there is evidence for an extended stay here a few months before his death.

Brother Elias, who worked on the Basilica of San Francesco in Assisi and is responsible for an addition to the original structure of Le Celle, likewise spent time here.

SPIRITUALITY
St. Anthony of Lisbon/Padua as well as St. Lawrence of Brindisi came to Le Celle. Both of these men had a strong propensity for solitude to seek a more intense union with God. Both men, as well as Francis and Elias, were leaders in their provinces, yet made time for coming apart to commune with God.

REFLECTION
What part does silence, solitude and contemplation play in the daily rhythm of your life? As a leader in fraternity or ministry, what is the role of solitude in your life? Is frequenting a solitary place to rest a while in God part of the rhythm of your life?

LE CELLE DI CORTONA

HISTORICAL NOTES

St. Francis was in Cortona as early as 1211. Desiring a place of solitude, a local citizen spoke to him about this solitary place and then gave it to him.

The name "Le Celle" seems to have already existed before St. Francis' arrival, perhaps derived from some small mills by the stream that made use of its water power. The place appeared remote and pristine enough for Francis to experience solitude.

When St. Francis came to Cortona, Brother Sylvester accompanied him (2C 108). Tradition claims that Francis met a local man, Guido, who offered him hospitality and ultimately joined the brotherhood.

On his arrival at Le Celle, Francis found solitude in a cave-like structure adjacent to a room which served as the dormitory for the brothers.

A small chapel was erected on a higher level at which altar St. Anthony of Lisbon/Padua celebrated Eucharist, dating the chapel prior to 1231, the year of his death.

The first biographers mention the presence of St. Francis at Le Celle (2C 38) and there is evidence for an extended stay here a few months before his death (1C 105) when he wrote his *Testament*.

In 1232 Brother Elias renovated and strengthened the existing structures adding a third level with five more rooms. He was living at Le Celle in 1247 and during his final illness in 1253.

At the beginning of the 14th century the Fraticelli, a branch of the Spirituals, had established themselves at Le Celle, but were driven out in 1318. Two centuries of neglect followed until the "Friars Minor of the Eremitical Life," today known as Capuchins, moved there in 1537. When they arrived, they extended the building further. They opened a novitiate there where Antonio Barberini, brother of Urban VIII, was a novice in 1594.

In 1590 St. Lawrence of Brindisi was elected provincial of the Capuchins of Tuscany. Staying frequently at Le Celle in solitude, tradition states that his private celebration of Eucharist there was prolonged through tears and ecstasies up to twelve hours.

The friary was closed by Napoleon in 1807 and four years later put up for sale. The Capuchins were able to return in 1824, were driven out again, and returned permanently in 1871.

The buildings, which cling to the side of the mountain, tended to pull away from it. This problem was remedied only in the 20th century.

FRANCISCAN READINGS

THOMAS OF CELANO, FIRST LIFE 105

How Elias accompanies the seriously ill Francis from Siena to Le Celle

Six months before the day of his death, he was staying in Siena for treatment of his eye disease. But then all the rest of his body started to show signs of serious illness. His stomach had been destroyed, and his liver was failing. He was vomiting a lot of blood, so much that he seemed close to death. On hearing of this in a place far away, brother Elias rushed to his side. At his arrival the holy father had recovered so much that they left that area and went together to Le Celle near Cortona. After reaching the place he *stayed for a while,* but then the swelling began in his abdomen, his legs, and his feet. His stomach became so weak that he could hardly eat any food at all. At that point, he asked brother Elias to have him carried to Assisi. The good son did what the kind father commanded and, when everything was ready, led him to the place he longed for. *The city rejoiced at the arrival* of the blessed father and all the people with one voice *praised God,* since *the whole multitude of the people* hoped that *the holy one of God* would die close to them, and this was the reason for so much rejoicing.

THOMAS OF CELANO, SECOND LIFE 38

How Francis consoles a woman trapped in an unhappy marriage

In those days, *the man of God* was traveling to "Le Celle" of Cortona. A noble woman from a village called Volusiano heard of this and hurried to see him. Exhausted from the long journey since *she was very refined and delicate,* she finally reached the saint. Our holy father was moved with compassion on seeing her exhausted and gasping for breath. "What pleases you, my lady?" he asked. "Father, please bless me," she said. The saint asked: "Are you married or single?" She replied: "Father, I have a husband, a very cruel man, an antagonist to my service of Jesus Christ. He stops me from putting into action the good will the Lord has inspired in me; and this is my greatest sorrow. So I beg you, holy man, pray for him, that divine mercy will *humble his heart*." The father was amazed at virility in a female, an aging spirit in a child. Moved by pity, he said to her: "Go, *blessed daughter*, and, regarding your husband, know that you will soon have consolation." And he added: "You may tell him for God and for me, that *now is the time of salvation*, and later it will be the time for justice."

After receiving his blessing, the lady returned home, found her husband and relayed the message. Suddenly *the Holy Spirit came upon him,* and he was changed from the old to the new man, prompting him to reply *very meekly*: "My lady, *let us serve the Lord* and *save our souls* in our own house." And his wife replied: "It seems to me that continence should be placed in the soul as its *foundation*, and the other virtues *built upon it*." "This," he said, "pleases me as it pleases you." They lived a celibate life for many years until, on the same day, both departed happily—one as a *morning holocaust*, and the other as an *evening sacrifice*.

What a fortunate woman!
She softened her lord for the sake of life!
In her was fulfilled that text from the Apostle:
The unbelieving husband will be saved by his believing wife.
But today
—to use a common saying—
you can count people like that on your fingers.

EUCHARIST

REFRAIN: HOLY GROUND

READER 1:   *The man of God,* the blessed Francis ... often chose solitary places to focus his heart entirely on God. ... He would spend the night alone praying in abandoned churches and in deserted places where, with the protection of divine grace, he overcame his soul's many fears and anxieties (1C 71).

REFRAIN

READER 2:   At one time the blessed and venerable father Francis, with worldly crowds gathering eagerly every day to hear and see him, sought out a place of rest and secret solitude. He desired to free himself for God. ...(1C 91).

REFRAIN

READER 3:   *In the clefts of the rock* he would build his nest and *in the hollow of the wall* his dwelling. With blessed devotion he visited the heavenly mansions; and, totally *emptied of himself,* he rested for a long time in the wounds of the Savior (1C 71).

REFRAIN

READING: 1 KINGS 19:9b–12

A reading from the first book of Kings.

The word of the LORD came to him, saying, "What are you doing here, Elijah?" He answered: "I have been very zealous for the LORD, the God of hosts; for the Israelites have forsaken your covenant, torn down your altars, and killed your prophets with the sword. I alone am left, and they are seeking my life, to take it away." He said, "Go and stand on the mountain before the LORD, for the LORD is about to pass by." Now there was a great wind, so strong that it was splitting mountains and breaking rocks in pieces before the Lord, but the Lord was not in the wind; and after the wind an earthquake, but the Lord was not in the earthquake; and after the earthquake a fire, but the Lord was not in the fire; and after the fire a sound of sheer silence. When Elijah heard it, he wrapped his face in his mantle and went out and stood at the entrance of the cave. **The word of the Lord.**

RESPONSE: Rest in God alone, my soul.

PSALM 62

For God alone my soul waits in silence;
from him comes my salvation.
He alone is my rock and my salvation, my fortress;
I shall never be shaken. **R**.

He alone is my rock and my salvation, my fortress;
I shall not be shaken.
On God rests my deliverance and my honor,
my mighty rock, my refuge is in God;
I shall not be disturbed. **R**.

Trust in him at all times, O people,
pour out your heart before him;
God is a refuge for us. **R**.

ALLELUIA: Come away to a deserted place all by yourselves and rest for a while.

GOSPEL: LUKE 10:38–42

A reading from the holy Gospel according to Luke.

Now as they went on their way, he entered a certain village, where a woman named Martha welcomed him into her home. She had a sister named Mary, who sat at the Lord's feet and listened to what he was saying. But Martha was distracted by her many tasks; so she came to him and asked, "Lord, do you not care that my sister has left me to do all the work by myself? Tell her then to help me."

But the Lord answered her: "Martha, Martha, you are worried and distracted by many things; there is need of only one thing. Mary has chosen the better part, which will not be taken away from her." **The Gospel of the Lord.**

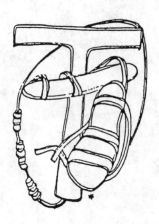

ASSISI: LAGO TRASIMENO

FRANCISCAN PILGRIMAGE PROGRAMS

ASSISI: LAGO TRASIMENO

EVENTS
Lago Trasimeno (Lake Trasimene) is the largest lake of peninsular Italy. It reminds us of one of the most famous battles of antiquity, the Battle of Trasimeno (217 B.C.), in which the Carthaginians of Hannibal defeated the Romans of Gaius Flaminius, thus opening the road to Rome.

Francis spent the Lent of 1211 or 1213 on Isola Maggiore, one of the islands in the lake. The island was unpopulated at that time. There were no buildings, so Francis lived in an improvised hut. Cappella dello Sbarco, the chapel of the hut, was built on the hill of the island. The Friars lived there in a large friary from 1328 till 1883.

SPIRITUALITY
Lago Trasimeno reminds us of one of the main tenets of Francis' spirituality: the call to a life of penance. Penance for Francis meant total absorption in God, a fascination with God. His experience on the island concretizes this focus for us.

Here we can also challenge ourselves to the mystery of fasting. What fills us up? What fills our hearts? What kind of fasting is necessary in our lives so that God is more and other "idols" become less?

REFLECTION
Examine Francis' observance of the liturgical seasons for the year, and reflect on how our spiritual life is bound up with the liturgical year.

LAGO TRASIMENO

HISTORICAL NOTES

Lago Trasimeno is the largest lake in the Italian Peninsula, more or less circular in shape and stretching as far as the eye can see. Three small islands are located in this lake. Isola Polvese is the largest and lies at the southern most edge of the lake; Isola Minore is the smallest and is on the northern end, close to Isola Maggiore, the island that Francis visited on retreat. Isola Maggiore is the only island populated by a small group of people.

On June 23, 217 B.C. a famous battle was fought between the Carthaginian army under the command of Hannibal, and the Roman army led by the Consul Gaius Flaminius. The odds were in Hannibal's favor, for his troops numbered around 40,000, while the Roman army numbered 25,000. Hannibal positioned his army in such a way as to trap the Romans who were in pursuit. The battle took place at dawn that caught the Romans by surprise. Blinded by a thick fog that had risen over Lago Trasimeno, and attacked on every side, many Roman soldiers threw themselves into the lake in an attempt to flee. Weighed down by their heavy armor, many drowned. On that fateful day in Roman history, 15,000 Roman soldiers perished and 6,000 were taken prisoner. The Carthaginians, on the other hand, only lost 2,000 soldiers.

The people who live on Isola Maggiore today continue the tradition of fishing, making Irish lace, and providing hospitality and food for tourists who flock the island during the summer months for holiday recreation. Today the number living on the island is between 30-50 people. Most workers come to the island by boat during the day.

Francis came to make his 40-day retreat in 1211 according to the tradition of the island. Records show that St. Salvatore was built as a parochial church as early as 1155, indicating the presence of some people prior to the time of Francis' visit. The Church of St. Michael was built around 1282 and in 1328 a church and a Franciscan monastery were erected to commemorate Francis' presence on the island. The façade of this great monastery is still readily visible when taking the boat to Isola Maggiore. One can appreciate its former splendor and its magnificent view of the lake. In 1883 the friars abandoned the monastery, and discussion is still under way about selling this property if it is in the public interest.

Information found in *Isola Maggiore: Tuoro on Trasimene Tourist Guide*. Published by the Cura della Scuola di Tipolitografia Montebluono in 1991 in Perugia.

FRANCISCAN READINGS

THE LITTLE FLOWERS OF SAINT FRANCIS 7

The wonderful forty days' fast of Francis

The true servant of Christ, Saint Francis, was in certain things like another Christ given to the world for the people's salvation.

So God the Father willed to make him in many of his actions conformed and similar to His Son, Jesus Christ. This is shown to us in the venerable company of the twelve companions and in the wondrous mystery of the sacred Stigmata and in the unbroken fast of the holy Lent which he made in the following way.

Once Saint Francis was alongside the Lake of Perugia on the day of Carnival, at the house of a man devoted to him, where he was lodged for the night. He was inspired by God to go to make that Lent on an island in the lake. So Saint Francis asked this devout man that, for love of Christ, he carry him with his little boat to an island of the lake where no one lived, and that he do this on the night of the Day of the Ashes, so that no one would notice. And this man, out of love—from the great devotion he had for Saint Francis—promptly fulfilled his request and carried him to that island. And Saint Francis took nothing with him except two small loaves of bread. Arriving at the island, as his friend was departing to return home, Saint Francis asked him kindly not to reveal to anyone that he was there, and that he should not come for him until Holy Thursday. And so that man departed, and Saint Francis remained alone.

Since there was no dwelling in which he could take shelter, he went into some very thick brush that was formed like a little den or a little hut by many bushes and saplings. And in this place he put himself in prayer and contemplation of heavenly things. And there he stayed the whole of Lent without eating or drinking, except for half of one of those little loaves, as his devoted friend found on Holy Thursday when he returned for him; for of the two loaves he found one whole one and a half; the other half, it is supposed, Saint Francis ate, out of reverence for the fast of the blessed Christ, who fasted for *forty days and forty nights* without taking any material food. And thus, with that half of a loaf he drove away from himself vainglory, and after the example of Christ he fasted forty days and forty nights.

Later in that place where Saint Francis had done such marvelous abstinence, God did many miracles through his merits. For this reason the people began to build houses and live there, and in a short time a good, large village was built there, and there was a place of the brothers there, called the Place of the Island, and the men and women of that village still have great reverence and devotion for that place where Saint Francis made that Lent.

ST. BONAVENTURE, MAJOR LEGEND VIII: 8

Francis and a rabbit

Another time at Greccio a small live hare was given to the man of God, which he put down on the ground free to run away where it pleased. At the call of the kind father, it leapt quickly into his lap. He fondled it with the pious affection of his heart and seemed to pity it like a mother. After warning it with gentle talk not to let itself be caught again, he let it go free. But as often as he placed it on the ground to run away, it always came back to the father's bosom, as if it perceived with some hidden sense of its heart the piety he had for it. Finally, at the father's command, the brothers carried it away to a safer place of solitude.

In the same way, on the island in the Lake of Perugia [also known as Lago Trasimeno], a little rabbit was caught and offered to the man of God. Although it fled from everyone else, it entrusted itself to his hands and his heart as if to natural security.

EUCHARIST

READING: DANIEL 1:3–17

A reading from the book of the prophet Daniel

Then [Nebuchadnezzar] commanded his palace master Ashpenaz to bring some of the Israelites of the royal family and of the nobility, young men without physical defect and handsome, versed in every branch of wisdom, endowed with knowledge and insight, and competent to serve in the king's palace; they were to be taught the literature and language of the Chaldeans. The king assigned them a daily portion of the royal rations of food and wine. They were to be educated for three years, so that at the end of that time they could be stationed in the king's court. Among them were Daniel, Hananiah, Mishael, and Azariah, from the tribe of Judah. The palace master gave them other names: Daniel he called Belteshazzar, Hananiah he called Shadrach, Mishael he called Meshach, and Azariah he called Abednego. But Daniel resolved that he would not defile himself with the royal rations of food and wine; so he asked the palace master to allow him not to defile himself. Now God allowed Daniel to receive favor and compassion from the palace master. The palace master said to Daniel, "I am afraid of my lord the king; he has appointed your food and your drink. If he should see you in poorer condition than the other young men of your own age, you would endanger my head with the king." Then Daniel asked the guard whom the palace master had appointed over Daniel, Hananiah, Mishael, and Azariah: "Please test your servants for ten days. Let us be given vegetables to eat and water to drink. You can then compare our appearance with the appearance of the young men who eat the royal rations, and deal with your servants according to what you observe." So he agreed to this proposal and tested them for ten days. At the end of ten days it was observed that they appeared better and fatter than all the young men who had been eating the royal rations. So the guard continued to withdraw their royal rations and the wine they were to drink, and gave them vegetables. To these four young men God gave knowledge and skill in every aspect of literature and wisdom; Daniel also had insight into all visions and dreams. **The word of the Lord.**

RESPONSE: Glory and praise forever!

PRAYER OF AZARIAH 1:29–34

Blessed are you, O Lord, God of our ancestors,
and to be praised and highly exalted forever;
and blessed is your glorious, holy name,
and to be highly praised and highly exalted forever. **R.**

Blessed are you in the temple of your holy glory,
and to be extolled and highly glorified forever.
Blessed are you who look into the depths from your throne on
the cherubim, and to be praised and highly exalted forever. **R.**

Blessed are you on the throne of your kingdom,
and to be extolled and highly exalted forever.
Blessed are you in the firmament of heaven,
and to be sung and glorified forever. **R.**

ALLELUIA: Blessed are the pure of heart, says the Lord; they shall see the glory of God.

GOSPEL: MATTHEW 15:10–20

A reading from the holy Gospel according to Matthew

Then he called the crowd to him and said to them, "Listen and understand: it is not what goes into the mouth that defiles a person, but it is what comes out of the mouth that defiles." Then the disciples approached and said to him, "Do you know that the Pharisees took offense when they heard what you said?" He answered, "Every plant that my heavenly Father has not planted will be uprooted. Let them alone; they are blind guides of the blind. And if one blind person guides another, both will fall into a pit." But Peter said to him, "Explain this parable to us." Then he said, "Are you also still without understanding? Do you not see that whatever goes into the mouth enters the stomach, and goes out into the sewer? But what comes out of the mouth proceeds from the heart, and this is what defiles. For out of the heart come evil intentions, murder, adultery, fornication, theft, false witness, slander. These are what defile a person, but to eat with unwashed hands does not defile." **The Gospel of the Lord.**

RITUAL SERVICE

THE LITTLE FLOWERS OF SAINT FRANCIS

Reader 1:

Once Saint Francis was alongside the Lake of Perugia on the day of Carnival, at the house of a man devoted to him, where he was lodged for the night. He was inspired by God to go to make that Lent on an island in the lake. So Saint Francis asked this devout man that, for love of Christ, he carry him with his little boat to an island of the lake where no one lived, and that he do this on the night of the Day of the Ashes, so that no one would notice. And this man, out of love—from the great devotion he had for Saint Francis—promptly fulfilled his request and carried him to that island.

Reader 2:

And Saint Francis took nothing with him except two small loaves of bread. Arriving at the island, as his friend was departing to return home, Saint Francis asked him kindly not to reveal to anyone that he was there, and that he should not come for him until Holy Thursday. And so that man departed, and Saint Francis remained alone.

Since there was no dwelling in which he could take shelter, he went into some very thick brush that was formed like a little den or a little hut by many bushes and saplings. And in this place he put himself in prayer and contemplation of heavenly things.

REFLECTION/HOMILY (only if the ritual is celebrated)

DISTRIBUTION OF LOAVES OF BREAD

Leader:
May our Lord Jesus Christ, symbolized by this bread, be your food for the journey of life.

Reader 3:
And there he stayed the whole of Lent without eating or drinking, except for half of one of those little loaves, as his devoted friend found on Holy Thursday when he returned for him; for of the two loaves he found one whole one and a half; the other half, it is supposed, Saint Francis ate, out of reverence for the fast of the blessed Christ, who fasted for *forty days and forty nights* without taking any material food. And thus, with that half of a loaf he drove away from himself vainglory, and after the example of Christ he fasted forty days and forty nights.

Reader 4:
Later in that place where Saint Francis had done such marvelous abstinence, God did many miracles through his merits. For this reason the people began to build houses and live there, and in a short time a good, large village was built there, and there was a place of the brothers there, called the Place of the Island, and the men and women of that village still have great reverence and devotion for that place where Saint Francis made that Lent.

To the praise of Jesus Christ
and the little poor man Francis.
Amen.

TIME FOR PRAYER AND FASTING

All are invited to go off into prayer on the island with an invitation to sustain oneself for the mid-day meal only on the loaves of bread, with some water.

FRANCIS: THE JOURNEY AND THE DREAM

An Apologia for Penance

What brings one to penance and mortification? Is there any sense or reason behind renunciation and austerity? Why would anyone embrace the pain of separation as a way of life? Francis knew that people had these questions on their minds when they met the brothers. And especially did people wonder when men like Bernard of Quintavalle, the merchant, and Peter Catani, the lawyer, left their professions and belongings behind and attached themselves to Francis.

To explain it was perhaps impossible, but it had something to do with restoring harmony within themselves and between themselves and their Creator. It was like a search for the Garden of Eden before the Fall. That Garden was the end of the Journey, and they of course knew it was not an attainable goal. Or was it? That was the question. In each of them there was the Dream of discovering within themselves a secret source of energy, a Presence that would transform their lives and restore the harmony of the Garden of Paradise.

They would still be human, subject to temptation and sickness, sin and death, but in listening to the One who stood at the door within and knocked, they would open the doors of their own hearts and experience the Divine Presence that stood at the center of their real selves. And there they would walk again with God in the cool of the evening. They would be united with God on a new level of consciousness and understanding.

So the pain of detachment was only a means of union. It was a way of stilling, of quieting everything that would prevent them from hearing that hushed knock of God within. That is why Francis had left his father. Pietro's world, his values and what he lived for, clamored so loud in Francis' ears, he could not hear the Voice in the heart of his real self. That is why he was willing and able to bear the insults and hooting of the citizens of Assisi; he heard a Voice within him that was even louder and more real than all the citizenry of the world. That is why he mortified his body when it clamored so loudly for attention that it threatened to drown out the peace of his Voice inside.

Everything then that he and the brothers had done and suffered was for union with God, who dwelt inside them. They had sacrificed everything that their love might be consummated there in that Garden of delights. And it had! The Journey had not been in vain, nor had the Dream deceived them.

Ah, my lover, my Lord, my God and my All! How terrible and dark were the alleys to You. What mazes, inside and out, have we run! But we found You, or rather, You found us. We were waiting at the door when You knocked and You entered into us and the Garden sprang to Life.

The walls of the Garden crumbled and fell, for we were no longer to be imprisoned by our false needs, our selfish walling in of things we thought were necessary to hoard and protect. Then the fragrance that burst forth from that new Garden surrounded us and drew more and more people to that Journey within, confident that they, too, would find the door where You were knocking, seeking to enter and walk with them that cool Journey through the Garden.

Murray Bodo, O.F.M., *Francis: The Journey and the Dream* [Cincinnati: St. Anthony Messenger Press, 1988], 74–75. Used with permission.

ASSISI: LA VERNA

FRANCISCAN PILGRIMAGE PROGRAMS

ASSISI: LA VERNA

EVENTS
Francis came to this mountain six times for solitude: 1213, 1216, 1218, 1220, 1223, 1224 (Arnaldo Fortini, *Francis of Assisi*, 547 ff.).

In September 1224, on his last visit, Francis received the grace of the Stigmata.

Francis composed here, in 1224, *The Praises of God* (2C 49). On the opposite side of the parchment, he wrote his *Blessing for Brother Leo.*

SPIRITUALITY
Francis' experience at San Damiano (2C 10) imprinted the image of the crucified Christ upon his heart. His experience at La Verna imprinted the Passion of Christ upon his flesh. Francis carried a lifelong, burning love for Jesus crucified.

Francis, as his prayer on La Verna indicates, wanted to know (biblical sense) and experience Christ completely. In order to do this he realized that somehow he would also have to share in his Passion. This is the basis behind his prayer where he asks for two graces: to know the love Christ had in his heart and to experience the depth of his suffering. (*Omnibus, Third Consideration of the Stigmata*, 1448.)

Mystical experience and suffering give birth to compassion. This is wonderfully exemplified here on La Verna between Leo and Francis (*Omnibus, Second Consideration of the Stigmata*, IX, 1438.)

Bonaventure began his great work, *The Soul's Journey Into God,* here at La Verna. He says: "There is no other path but through the burning love of the crucified" (prologue in that volume).

Francis would never isolate the Passion from the entire paschal mystery. An example of this connection is found in his *Office of the Passion,* where Psalm VII for Good Friday vespers celebrates the victory of resurrection. Francis joins victory with the very moment of death.

REFLECTION
Read Fioretti, *The Five Considerations on the Holy Stigmata* (Habig's *Omnibus*, 1429–1474). Read and pray the *Office of the Passion* (André Cirino, O.F.M. and Laurent Gallant, *Geste of the Great King*, Franciscan Institute, 2001.)

LA VERNA

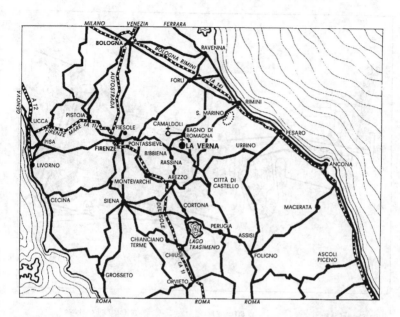

APPROACHES BY ROAD TO THE SHRINE

from Bibbiena . . . . . . 16 miles
» Pieve S. Stefano   13 miles
» Rassina . . . . . . 13½ miles

DISTANCES IN MILES FROM THE SHRINE

To Arezzo 31
» Assisi 71
» Camaldoli 28
» Cesena 68
» Florence 53

To Loreto 155
» Montecasale . . . 24
» Perugia 68
» Ravenna 84
» Rimini 84
» Rome 165
» S. Marino 62

THE SANCTUARY OF LA VERNA

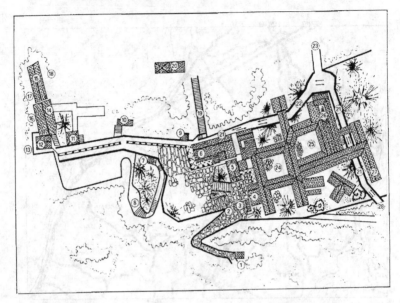

1 Chapel of the Birds	10 St Francis' Bed	20 Chapel of Blessed John
2 Old Entrance	11 Loddi Chapel	21 Entrance and exit passage
3 Toilets	12 Chapel of St Sebastian	22 Souvenirs
4 Guest-house	13 The Precipice	23 To De Gasperi memorial and Abetone
5 Chapel of Santa Maria degli Angeli	14 Chapel of the Cross	24 The Museum and fifteenth
6 Basilica	15 The Stigmata	century Cloister
7 St Francis' First Cell	16 Oratory of St Anthony	25 Cloister of the Guest-house
8 The Projecting Rock	17 Oratory of St Bonaventura	26 Cloister and Hall of St Clare
9 Chapel of the Pietà and Corridor	18 Brother Leo's Cell	27 The Pilgrims' Refectory
of the Stigmata	19 Steps to the Forest and La Penna	28 Toward La Melosa

LA VERNA

HISTORICAL NOTES

This sanctuary is called Franciscan Calvary, for it was here that Francis received the stigmata. In 1213 Francis set out for Morocco. On the way he and Brother Leo arrived at Montefeltro in Romagna and stopped at the nearby castle of San Leo. A great feast was going on in honor of a new knight. Taking advantage of the situation, Francis began to address the guests, and the count was so impressed that he decided to seek guidance in private from the saint. He was so pleased with Francis that the count, Orlando, said: "Brother Francis, I have a mountain in Tuscany which is very solitary and wild and perfectly suited for someone who wants to do penance in a remote place or who seeks to live a solitary life. It is called Mount La Verna. If that mountain should please you and your companions, I would gladly give it to you for the salvation of my soul."

When he heard this generous offer of something he had long set his heart upon, St. Francis expressed a great joy, and praising and giving thanks first to God and then to Count Orlando, Francis replied to him: "Sir, when you have returned to your home I will send some of my companions to you so that you may show them this mountain. If it appears to them well suited to prayer and doing penance, I here and now accept your most charitable offer."

A few months later, two companions of St. Francis presented themselves at the entrance to the castle of Count Orlando Cattani of Chiusi. They were given a warm and joyous welcome and lodged for the night. In the morning, provided with a strong escort of fifty armed men to protect them from the robbers and the wild beasts that infested the forest, they climbed the mountain and soon found a suitable place for a dwelling. There they built some small cells and, in the name of St. Francis, took possession of the mountain so generously donated by Count Orlando.

FRANCISCAN READINGS

FIORETTI, SECOND CONSIDERATION OF THE STIGMATA

The donation of the mountain to Francis and the brothers

In this connection you should know that when Count Orlando

heard that St. Francis had come with three companions to live on Mount La Verna, he was very happy. And the next day he left his castle with many men and came to visit him, bringing bread and other necessities for him and for his companions.

... St. Francis stood up and welcomed Count Orlando and his men with great affection and joy. And afterward they began to talk together. And after they had talked and St. Francis had thanked him for the holy mountain which he had given them and for his coming, he asked Count Orlando to have a poor little cell made for him at the foot of a very beautiful beech tree that was about a stone's throw from the friars' place, because that spot seemed to him very suitable for devout prayer. And Count Orlando had it made without delay.

Afterward, because evening was drawing near and it was time to leave, St. Francis preached a short sermon to them before they left.

... After he had preached and given them his blessing, since Count Orlando had to leave, he called St. Francis and his companions aside and said to them: "My dear friars, I do not want you to lack anything which you may need on this wild mountain, because of which you might have to give less attention to spiritual things. So I want you—and I say this once for all—just to send to my house for anything you need. And if you do not do so, I will really be offended. ..."

Then St. Francis had his companions sit down, and he gave them instructions regarding the way of life which they and whoever wished to live as religious in hermitages should lead. And among other things he especially stressed to them the observance of holy poverty, saying: "Don't pay so much attention to the charitable offer of Count Orlando that you should in any way offend our Lady Poverty. You can be sure that the more we despise poverty, the more will the world despise us and the greater need will we suffer. But if we embrace holy poverty very closely, the world will come to us and will feed us abundantly. God has called us to this holy Order for the salvation of the world. And He has made this contract between us and the world: that we give the world a good example and that the world provide us with what we need. So let us persevere in holy poverty. ..."

And after he had said those words, he gave them his blessing and went off to the cell by the beech tree. And his companions stayed in the Place with the firm intention of obeying the orders of St. Francis.

A few days later St. Francis was standing beside that cell, gazing at the form of the mountain and marveling at the great chasms and openings in the massive rocks. And he began to pray, and then it was revealed to him by God that those striking chasms had been made in a miraculous way at the hour of Christ's Passion when, as the Gospel says, "the rocks split." And God wanted this to be manifested in a special way here on Mount La Verna in order to show that the Passion of Christ was to be renewed on that mountain in the soul of St. Francis by love and compassion and in his body by the imprinting of the Stigmata.

Retained from Marion A. Habig, ed. *St. Francis of Assisi: Omnibus of Sources* [Chicago: Franciscan Herald Press, 1973], 1436.

THOMAS OF CELANO, FIRST LIFE 94–95

How the crucified seraph imparts the Stigmata onto Francis

While he was staying in that hermitage called La Verna, after the place where it is located, two years prior to the time that he returned his soul to heaven, he saw *in the vision of God* a man, *having six wings like a Seraph, standing over* him, *arms extended and feet joined*, affixed to a cross. *Two of his wings* were raised up, *two were stretched out over his head as if for flight*, and *two covered his* whole *body*. When the blessed servant of the most High saw these things, he was filled with the greatest awe, but could not decide what this vision meant for him. ...

His hands and feet seemed to be pierced through the middle by nails, with the heads of the nails appearing on the inner part of his hands and on the upper part of his feet, and their points protruding on opposite sides. Those marks on the inside of his hands were round, but rather oblong on the outside; and small pieces of flesh were visible like the points of nails, bent over and flattened, extending beyond the flesh around them. On his feet, the marks of nails were stamped in the same way and raised above the surrounding flesh. His right side was marked with an oblong scar, as if pierced with a lance, and this often dripped blood, so that his tunic and undergarments were frequently stained with his holy blood.

Sadly, only a few merited seeing the sacred wound in his side during the life of the crucified servant of the crucified Lord. Elias was fortunate and did merit somehow to see the wound in his side. Rufino was just as lucky: he *touched it with his own hands*. For one time, when the same brother Rufino put his hand onto the holy man's chest to rub him, his hand slipped, as often happens, and it chanced that he touched the precious scar in his right side. As soon as he had touched it, the holy one of God felt great pain and pushed Rufino's hand away, crying out *for the Lord to spare him*.

He hid those marks carefully from strangers, and concealed them cautiously from people close to him, so that even the brothers at his side and his most devoted followers for a long time did not know about them.

THE LEGEND OF THREE COMPANIONS 69–70

Francis' receipt of the Stigmata

While he was still alive in the flesh, the Lord adorned him with a wonderful prerogative of a unique privilege, wishing to show the whole world the fervor of love and the incessant memory of the Passion of Christ which he carried in his heart.

For when he was taken above in the seraphic ardor of desires into God and into Him, he who, by a boundless love, wanted to be crucified, was transformed by a compassionate sweetness. One morning, around the feast of the Exaltation of the Holy Cross, while he was absorbed in prayer on a slope of Mount LaVerna, two years before his death, a seraph with six wings appeared to him. Within its six wings there was the form of a very beautiful, crucified man, whose hands and feet were extended after the manner of a cross, and whose features were clearly those of the Lord Jesus. Two wings covered his head, two, the rest of his body down to the feet, and two were extended as if for flight.

When the vision disappeared, a marvelous glow of love remained in his soul, but, even more marvelous, an impression of the stigmata of our Lord Jesus Christ appeared in his flesh. Until his death, the man of God, unwilling to divulge God's sacrament, concealed it to the best of his ability, although he was unable to cover it completely since it became known to at least his intimate companions.

After his most happy passing, all the brothers who were present, as well as many seculars, clearly saw his body unmistakably adorned with the wounds of Christ. They saw in his hands and feet, not just the holes of the nails, but the nails themselves formed by his own flesh, taking shape from it, and showing the dark color of iron. His right side appeared as if pierced with a lance, covered with a red scar from a very

real and very visible wound, which, even while he was living, frequently poured out sacred blood.

The undeniable truth of those stigmata appeared most brilliantly through sight and contact not only in his life and in death, but also after his death, the Lord revealed their truth even more brilliantly by many miracles shown in different parts of the world. Through these miracles, the hearts of many who did not look kindly on the man of God and doubted the stigmata were also moved to a great assurance of faith. Thus, those who had been his detractors, by God's active goodness and the undeniable weight of evidence, became faithful heralds and promoters of his fame.

A DESCRIPTION OF LA VERNA
L'Alter Christus

The succession of days began, distinguishable only by the rising and the setting of the sun, by the blazing and the dimming of the stars.

A great silence prevailed.

At evening, when the mountains reddened in the sunset, from his cell Francis heard the falcons cry as they wheeled in the cobalt sky. Then a shadow began to creep downward from La Penna; slowly it veiled the forest and filled the distant valley.

One of the falcons became his friend. ... In the heart of the night, at the hour of matins, it came to awaken [Francis] by repeating its cry and beating its wings nor would it leave until Francis had gotten up. At dawn it "would very gently sound the bell of its voice" to call Francis to prayer.

But this, says Thomas of Celano, was Francis's victory, because his love was being repaid with love; "little wonder if all other creatures too venerated this eminent love of the Creator."

At the hour of matins when Brother Leo came, earth and sky were linked in harmony and from the woods came the sharp odor of cyclamens. The woodlands were immobile in a light of dream, wrapped in the whiteness of the full moon. Dark tree trunks stood straight as the lances of an army of giants. The breeze would rise and a long murmur, like the sighing of the sea, pass over the tops of the trees.

On one of those nights Brother Leo came to the brink of the gorge and said the words agreed upon, "Lord, open my lips."

No one replied. He crossed the log and looked in the cell. Francis was not there. He went further and walked through the woods.

At last he saw Francis on his knees, his face and his hands raised to the sky. Over and over he said, "Who are you, my dearest God? And what am I, your vilest little worm and useless little servant?" In the still night was a man overcome by his own insignificance as he confronted the immensity of God.

Later, Leo and Francis interrogated the Gospels, as Francis had done in the church of San Nicolò, after the night he spent with Bernardo di Quintavalle. And each of the three times they sought God's will, the book opened of itself to the Passion of Christ.

On this night, it seems that the lamentations of the Holy Week in Greccio fill the silence and make it a night of anguish. Francis and Leo hear all the pain in the world rising like a tide against the side of the mountain.

And he who was the father of all wants to bear the cross of all. Francis has a vision of Jesus rising before him. He comes forward on pierced feet, uncovers his lacerated heart, stretches out his nail-marked hands, and repeats the words of the Last Supper: "This is my blood. Drink all of it."

He has the tender face of those who suffer and endure more than their share of pain and abuse, who must drag crosses too heavy for them up exhausting hills. They collapse under the beatings life deals out to them, get up and go on, fall again. The mountain seems to be trembling under the blows of the hammers nailing them to their crosses. It echoes with the sounds of imprecations, everlasting derision, torture and grief. Jesus becomes every suffering creature; life, an immense Calvary.

And Francis, kneeling before his cell, lifts up this fervent prayer:

"My Lord Jesus Christ, I pray you to grant me two graces before

I die. The first is that during my life I may feel in my soul and in my body, as much as possible, that pain that you, dear Jesus, sustained in the hour of your most bitter Passion. The second is that I may feel in my heart, as much as possible, that great love with which you, O Son of God, were inflamed in willingly enduring such suffering for us sinners."

Francis's prayer is answered. The life that began with a kiss to a leper, the life that has in it leper hospitals, prisons, battlefields in Arce and Perugia and Damietta, and all the places he found pain and suffering, has now led to this moment in the night before the feast of the Exaltation of the Cross.

He saw the mountain covered by light, the heavens open, and a burning seraph swiftly descend. Light blazed everywhere. Every blade of grass was clear and distinct in the dazzling light.

Francis raised his eyes. The angel had his arms open, his feet stretched out. He was nailed to a cross. A living cross with six flaming wings, two raised over his head, two covering his body, and two spread out in flight.

Then he was over Francis and rays darted from the wounds in his feet, his hands, his side, to pierce Francis's hands, feet, and heart.

Francis's soul was caught up in a vortex of fire. An infinite joy filled him, and also infinite pain. He raised his arms toward the living Cross, only to fall unconscious against the stone.

The whole mountain of La Verna seemed to be burning, as if the sun were high. Shepherds, taking their flocks to the pasture-lands of the sea, were awakened. Muleteers got up, thinking it was dawn, and set out on the road again.

They travelled on in what seemed bright daylight. And then they saw that immense light fade and vanish. Night returned, alive with stars.

Arnaldo Fortini, *Francis of Assisi* [New York: Crossroads Publishing Co., 1981], 555–558. Used with permission.

DONATION OF LA VERNA (1274)

In this deed, the sons of Count Orlando of Chiusi ratify the oral donation of La Verna to Francis and his brothers, made by their father in 1213.

In the name of God, Amen. In the year of our Lord 1274, while Pope Gregory was reigning and the throne of the Roman Empire was vacant, on Monday, the ninth of July, in the presence of the priests, Giles, rector of the church of Trameggiano, and John, rector of the church of Campo; and of Cambio Catozzi of Chitignano; the Lord Guidone, son of Lord Rainerio of Gufaria, and Bernadino his son; and many other witnesses who were summoned for this purpose; etc. Orlando dei Caetani, son of the late Lord Orlando; Count of Chiusi; and Cungio, Bandino, and Guglielmo, brothers and sons of the said Lord Orlando; by his word and authority, and some of these from certain knowledge, and not through some error of law or fact, admitting that they live by Roman law, and are more than twenty-five years of age, acknowledged that the said Lord Orlando, Count of Chiusi, a most valiant knight of the Emperor and father of the above, in the year of our Lord 1213, on the eighth day of May, solely for reason of devotion, orally gave, bequeathed, and conceded, freely and without any restriction, to Brother Francis and his companions and to the brothers both present and future, the mountain of La Verna, so that the said Father Francis and his brothers might live there. And by the said mountain of La Verna we understand, and the said witness also understand, [to include] all the land, whether wooded, rocky, or meadow, without any exception, from the brow of the said mountain to the bases surrounding it on every side, together with everything attached to them. And because this gift was made to the blessed Father Francis and to his companions by word of mouth only and without anything in writing, therefore the said Orlando, most loving father of the younger Orlando and his brothers, when on his deathbed charged and ordained his said sons to renew the gift [of the said mountain] to the said brothers. Wherefore, desiring to carry out each and every command of their late beloved father, so that everything might be done according to his mind, with none of them dissenting or of a different opinion, they have now approved, confirmed, and ratified through this present document each and every thing bequeathed by their father. And they will and declare that the said fathers shall always live there, and that no one shall be able to turn them out or molest them, so that the said bequest of the said mountain [of La Verna] with its approaches shall be valid for all time and that [through this deed] it will stand as valid forever.

Further, by order of the said Lord, the elder Count Orlando, they gave to these same brothers the following items: a cloth, which the said Father Francis used at the table with the Lord Count Orlando and his children whenever he was staying with them; also a certain wooden cup or bowl, in which the said Father Francis used to prepare his bread and wine; also a leather belt that belonged to their most beloved father, the Count of Chiusi, which the said Saint Francis blessed and with which he himself girt the same Count Orlando when he received the habit, which has also shown miraculous powers for women in labor pains. The Lord Count Orlando dei Caetani and his brothers have bequeathed and handed over in perpetuity this mountain and every single thing mentioned above, not by force, fraud, or fear, but freely and willingly, and they have confirmed and do confirm these things as conceded and handed over, etc., renouncing etc., promising that they, their heirs and successors, will give heed to and observe in perpetuity each and every thing contained therein without any exception etc. The foregoing negotiations took place at the Rocca di Chiusi, in the palace of the aforesaid Count Orlando and his aforesaid brothers, on the day and year stated above.

Found in *Francis of Assisi: Early Documents*, Volume 3, 802–803.

FRANCIS: THE JOURNEY AND THE DREAM
Of Seasons and Weather

Looking back on his life in Jesus, Francis saw that in the life of the Spirit, as in nature itself, there was a rhythm, a plan that his Father in heaven had ordained. Jesus Himself spoke in little parables of seasons and weathers, and Francis saw in his own soul that they were true. The bright summer sun of his conversion and the heat of the days of his first fervor melted into the mellow fruitfulness and warmth of autumn days when he would walk the fields of Umbria through the mulberry patches, through the harvested wheat and corn fields and up the red and gold hillside of Mount Subasio to his little hermitage.

Then came the long winter of the spirit when the old temptations returned to chill his soul and the green hope of Umbria lay buried in a blank silence of snow, and the only voices he heard were the complaints of the brothers which sounded like the wailing of the Israelites taunting Moses for leading them into the wasteland. And the moan of the wind through the gnarled olive trees threatened these symbols of peace with rumors of war that shook the tranquility of Francis' soul.

How long the winter seemed! Even when he had grown more mature, and he knew that this cycle would be repeated over and over again as it was in nature, Francis always dreaded winter because spring would seem like some phantom dream when December gripped his soul.

But it was in winter that the passion of Jesus was most clearly in his mind. Just as the winter winds cleared the ever-present haze from the Umbrian valley and brought out the clear outlines of things, so winter in his soul cleared away everything misty, and the suffering face of Jesus shone bright and clear against the white snow of Francis' loneliness and desolation.

He had begun to feel lonely toward the end when the Dream was being challenged by so many of the brothers and when no one seemed to believe that the Gospel life could in fact be lived in its entirety. Many brothers feared that the Rule of Life of the Lesser Brothers was too rigid, and they threatened to leave the brotherhood. Others were wandering about the countryside outside of obedience and some were even insulting Lady Poverty by constructing buildings for the brothers to live in. It was when this terrible weather was blowing through Francis' soul that the radiant spring of La Verna suddenly appeared.

The suffering face of Jesus had been deeply imprinted in his mind ever since that day in San Damiano when his Lord had spoken from the crucifix. All of his days from that time were spent in meditation on the suffering Christ and in being present to Jesus in His suffering. He wished with all his heart to stand beneath the cross of Christ, assuring Him of his love, that he would be there with Him, ever present on the hill of Calvary throughout the ages till the Risen Christ returned in all His glory and the cross would be no more!

It was with such an intention that Francis had made his final journey to the top of La Verna, that holy mountain far to the north of Assisi, La Verna, his mountain retreat. Even now in retrospect the miracle of La Verna filled his eyes with tears and his heart with affection and love for Jesus. There on that mountain, in preparation for the Feast of St. Michael the Archangel, he had asked in fear and trembling that Christ would let him experience and share some of His suffering on the cross. What followed was more than a poor sparrow should or could expect.

La Verna

He remembered that strange anticipation of his last journey up the long trail to La Verna, of his thinking of the woman with the hemorrhage in Mark's Gospel, and how she felt through her whole being her healing, as from some ecstatic touch of Jesus' hand that sent shivers up and down her body. The touch, the ecstasy of flesh on flesh, was all he could remember of that moment before he felt the stab of the wounds burning in his hands and feet and side. And after that there was about La Verna and even about the sounding of the name in his ears an almost unbearable feeling of peace, as if his whole life had begun and ended there.

La Verna was the impossible Dream and the eternal Journey of every [one] come true. And yet it remained only as a memory, except for the wounds of Jesus in his feet and hands and side. And they, of course, made all the difference between the poor man who walked up the mountain and the poor man who limped down.

A Hymn to La Verna

La Verna. Let the song of her praise sound across the mountains for all the earth to hear. For there on the cold mountain top, so far from all human busyness, Francis had ended the Journey, and the Dream became a standard emblazoned on his own flesh.

When you live with the Dream so long, how do you know that it is true? How do you know that the road you took is the right one for the Quest? La Verna. Let the mystery of what took place upon those holy slopes be proof of what the brothers so longed to know: that the Journey had in fact been worth the love it cost them.

La Verna. Let the song be sung that the Journey is an inner one, and its mountaintop is in the heart. Francis, sick and weary in his bones, climbed the staggering heights of La Verna in order to scale the sheer cliffs of his own mind and heart. From La Verna he could see the breadth of Italy, eastward to the Adriatic and westward to the Mediterranean. ...

Francis saw all of this only in his heart and with the eyes of Brother Leo and Brother Masseo, for his own vision was blurred and could distinguish only the outline of what was there in front of him. But in his heart he saw much grander vistas than this peak of the Apennines opened up for the eyes of his body. He saw there that the voices and the visions were as real as the nails that pierced the flesh of Christ.

La Verna. Let every brother of the dream rest quietly in the knowledge that Jesus had set his seal of approval upon the flesh of little Brother Francis, their father and brother and standard-bearer in the Quest! Oh my brothers, my sons. Lift up your eyes to the mountains. La Verna is in your own hearts. Climb there and let your vision be blurred to all the kingdoms of the earth. The Kingdom of Heaven ... is within you.

La Verna is! And once that knowledge is there, you must leave La Verna, for the Journey goes on. Let the message of La Verna be that you must leave the mountaintop and shoulder your cross on the plain for the next Journey to the Summit where you will hang with Christ upon your own cross. And one day you will not descend but soar from atop your own La Verna to the sky. That day you will be with your Lord in paradis.

Murray Bodo, O.F.M., *Francis: The Journey and the Dream* [Cincinnati: St. Anthony Messenger Press, 1998], 96–99, 100–101. Used with permission.

OTHER READINGS

1C 91–93—Francis' spirituality of Gospel suffering
LMj XIII:1–4—Account of the Stigmata
DBF IX—The finding of Mount La Verna
Fioretti (found in Habig's *Omnibus*)—The Stigmata

EUCHARIST

PROCLAMATION OF THE STIGMATA OF ST. FRANCIS

ST. BONAVENTURE, MAJOR LEGEND XIII:1, 3–5

Reader 1:

[T]wo years before he returned his spirit to heaven,
after a variety of many labors,
he was led by divine providence
to a *high* place *apart* called Mount La Verna.
When according to his usual custom
he had begun to fast there for forty days
in honor of Saint Michael the Archangel,
he experienced more abundantly than usual
an overflow of the sweetness of heavenly contemplation,
was on fire with an ever intense flame of heavenly desires,
and began to be aware more fully of the gifts of heavenly
entries.

Proclamation—All

Lord Jesus, this is where you signed your servant, Francis, with the marks of our Redemption.

Reader 2:

On a certain morning about the feast of the Exaltation of the Cross, while Francis was praying on the mountainside, he saw a Seraph having six wings, fiery as well as brilliant, descend from the grandeur of heaven. And when in swift flight, it had arrived at a spot in the air near the man of God, there appeared between the wings the likeness of a man crucified, with his hands and feet extended in the form of a cross and fastened to a cross. Two of the wings were raised above his head, two were extended for flight, and two covered his whole body. Seeing this, he was overwhelmed and his heart was flooded with a mixture of joy and sorrow. He rejoiced at the gracious way Christ looked upon him under the appearance of the Seraph, but the fact that He was fastened to a cross *pierced his soul with a sword* of compassionate sorrow.

Proclamation—All

Lord Jesus, this is where you signed your servant, Francis, with the marks of our Redemption.

Reader 1:

As the vision was disappearing,
it left in his heart a marvelous fire
and imprinted in his flesh a likeness of signs
no less marvelous.

For immediately the marks of nails began to appear in his hands and feet just as he had seen a little before in the figure of the man crucified. His hands and feet seemed to be pierced through the center by nails, with the heads of the nails appearing on the inner side of the hands and the upper side of the feet and their points on the opposite sides. The heads of the nails in his hands and his feet were round and black; their points were oblong and bent as if driven back with a hammer, and they emerged from the flesh and stuck out beyond it. Also his right side, as if pierced with a lance, was marked with a red wound from which his sacred blood often flowed, moistening his tunic and underwear.

Proclamation—All

Lord Jesus, this is where you signed your servant, Francis, with the marks of our Redemption.

Reader 2:

After true love of Christ
transformed the lover *into His image*,
when the forty days were over that he spent in solitude
as he had desired,
and the feast of St. Michael the Archangel
had also arrived,
the angelic man Francis
came down from the mountain
bearing with him
the likeness of the Crucified,
depicted not on *tablets of stone* or on panels of wood
carved by hand,
but engraved on parts of his flesh
by the finger of the living God.

Proclamation—All

Lord Jesus, this is where you signed your servant, Francis, with the marks of our Redemption.

PERIOD OF SILENCE

READING: GALATIANS 6:14–18

A reading from the letter of Paul to the Galatians

May I never boast of anything except the cross of our Lord

Jesus Christ, by which the world has been crucified to me, and I to the world. For neither circumcision nor uncircumcision is anything; but a new creation is everything! As for those who will follow this rule—peace be upon them, and mercy, and upon the Israel of God. From now on, let no one make trouble for me; for I carry the marks of Jesus branded on my body. May the grace of our Lord Jesus Christ be with your spirit, brothers and sisters. Amen. **The word of the Lord.**

RESPONSE: I have been crucified with Christ.

GALATIANS 2:16, PHILIPPIANS 1:20–21

We know that a person is justified
not by the works of the law
but through faith in Jesus Christ. **R.**

And we have come to believe in Christ Jesus,
so that we might be justified by faith in Christ,
and not by doing the works of the law,
because no one will be justified by the works of the law. **R.**

It is my eager expectation and hope
that I will not be put to shame in any way,
but that by my speaking with all boldness,
Christ will be exalted now as always in my body,
whether by life or by death.
For to me, living is Christ and dying is gain. **R.**

ALLELUIA: I have been crucified with Christ. The life I live now is not my own; Christ is living in me.

GOSPEL: LUKE 9:23–26

A reading from the holy Gospel according to Luke

Then [Jesus] said to them all, "If any want to become my [followers], let them deny themselves and take up their cross daily and follow me. For those who want to save their life will lose it, and those who lose their life for my sake will save it. What does it profit them if they gain the whole world, but lose or forfeit themselves? Those who are ashamed of me and of my words, of them the Son of Man will be ashamed when he comes in his glory and the glory of the Father and of the holy angels. **The Gospel of the Lord.**

COMMUNION REFLECTION

THE PRAISES OF GOD

You are the holy Lord God *Who does* wonderful things.

You are strong. *You are great.* You are the most high.
> You are the almighty king. You *holy Father*,
> King of *heaven and earth*.

You are three and one, the Lord *God of gods*;
> You are the good, all good, the highest good,
> Lord God *living and true*.

You are love, charity; You are wisdom, You are humility,
> *You are* patience, You are beauty, You are meekness,
> You are security, You are rest,
> You are gladness and joy, You are our hope, You are justice,
> You are moderation, You are all our riches to sufficiency.

You are beauty, You are meekness,
> *You are the protector*, You are our custodian and defender,
> *You are strength*, You are refreshment. You are our hope,
> You are our faith, You are our charity,
> You are all our sweetness, You are our eternal life:
> Great and wonderful Lord, Almighty God, Merciful Savior.

A BLESSING FOR BROTHER LEO

May the Lord bless you and keep you.
> *May He show His face to you and be merciful to you.*

May He turn His countenance to you and give you peace.

May the Lord bless you, Brother Leo.

UMBRIAN LIGHT

It may have been the light, the way
it blinds at noon in the valley.
The sun's haloed disc pulses fast as
a laser's drill fixed on the soul.
St. Francis in ecstasy, that
stare that blinds anyone who
looks up with ordinary eyes.
Was that why he went blind? His eyes
bleed as he walks the wilderness
to Mount La Verna. The burning
Seraph opens his flesh like eyes;
all creation's a dazzling wound.

Murray Bodo, O.F.M., June 2001. Used with permission.

ST. FRANCIS' FAREWELL TO LA VERNA

Once a year, on the evening of 30 September, a letter is read aloud in the refectory at La Verna. It is the letter in which Brother Masseo handed down the very moving "Farewell to La Verna" uttered by St. Francis on His final departure from the Holy Mountain (30 September 1224). In commemoration of this date, which also marks the celebration of the Feast of St. Jerome, doctor of the Church, the religious, in honour of that saint, include his name in their prayers during the daily procession to the Chapel of the Stigmata.

"Brother Masseo, sinner, unworthy servant of Jesus Christ, companion of Brother Francis of Assisi, a man very pleasing to God, peace and well-being to all the Brothers and sons (and daughters) of the Great Patriarch Francis, standard-bearer of Christ. The Great Patriarch, being resolved to take a last farewell of this Sacred Mount on the 30th of September, 1224,

the day of the feast of St. Jerome, and Count Orlando of Chiusi having sent an ass for Him to ride (He being unable to put foot to the ground by reason of the wounds made by the nails), and having heard Mass at Santa Maria degli Angeli early in the morning as was His custom, all being summoned into the Oratory, He bade us live together in charity, devote ourselves to prayer, care diligently for the place and sanctify it with our prayers day and night. He further entrusted to our care the whole of the Sacred Mount, exhorting all his Brothers, future as well as present, never to permit this spot to be profaned, but always to require that it be venerated, bestowing His benediction upon all who should live there and render it honour and reverence. 'Should it be otherwise,' He said, 'be they confounded who shall lack respect for this place, and let them await from God the punishment they merit.' To me He said, 'Brother Masseo, know it to be my intention that in this place shall live Religious, God-fearing and of the flower of my Order; that, therefore, the Superiors shall strive to assemble here the best of the Brothers. Ah! Ah! Ah! Brother Masseo, I say no more.'

"He ordained and required of us, Brother Angelo, Brother Silvestro, Brother Illuminato and Brother Masseo, that we exercise special care over the spot where occurred that great wonder of the imprint of the Sacred Stigmata. Having spoken thus, He said, 'Farewell, farewell, farewell, Brother Masseo!' Then turning to Brother Angelo, He said, 'Farewell, farewell, farewell, Brother Angelo!' And He spoke similarly to Brother Silvestro and Brother Illuminato. 'Dwell in peace, beloved sons; may God bless you, most dear sons. Farewell! I depart from you in my person, but my heart I leave with you. I go with The Little Sheep of God (Brother Leo) to Santa Maria degli Angeli, and I shall return here no more. I leave you. Farewell, farewell, farewell, each one of you! Farewell, mountains! Farewell, farewell, Mount Alverna! Farewell, Mount of the Angels! Farewell, beloved, most dear falcon! I thank you for the charity you have shown toward me. Farewell, farewell, Projecting Rock!

No more shall I come to visit you. Farewell, great rock! Farewell, farewell, farewell, rock that received me into your vitals, leaving the devil mocked! We shall see each other no more. Farewell, Santa Maria degli Angeli! To you I entrust these my sons, Mother of the Eternal Word.'

"While our beloved Father was speaking thus, tears welled from our eyes, and He departed, also weeping, bearing away our hearts and leaving us orphans by the departure of one who was so truly a Father.

I, Brother Masseo, have written all. May God bless us."

B.N. Marconi, *The Shrine of La Verna* [Genoa: Fotocolor Realizzazone Stampa], an English guidebook. Out of print.

REFLECTION

DISTRIBUTION OF SYMBOLS

ASSISI: BASILICA OF SAN FRANCESCO

FRANCISCAN PILGRIMAGE PROGRAMS

ASSISI: BASILICA OF SAN FRANCESCO

TOMB OF ST. FRANCIS

EVENTS

Francis was buried here, May 25, 1230.

Brother Elias and many early companions lived here.

SPIRITUALITY

Francis' body is encased in a stone crypt below the lower and upper churches. It is a fine setting in which to ponder the power of his spirit, still alive in our time, a spirit that seems to leap out from the stones that surround him and into our spirit.

Assisi is sometimes called a New Jerusalem, a city set on a hill. The massive structure of this basilica can give one that sense and see in it a source of grace and new life for people of all backgrounds and cultures.

A legend records the dying Francis expressing a wish to be buried in the most despised spot near Assisi. This was the hillside known as the *Colle dell'Inferno* ("Hill of Hell"), because criminals were executed here. When the canonized Francis was brought for burial to this place it became known as the *Colle del Paradiso* ("Hill of Paradise"), a transformation effected through a simple presence.

REFLECTION

Consider how your Franciscan life transforms the world as you journey through it.

Reflect on Brother Elias: What did Francis think of him? How do the biographies deal with him?

This massive basilica was built as a monument to the faith of the people. Church buildings are to inspire and deepen one's faith.

Return to the tomb of Francis again and again. Let his spirit break into your heart and break down whatever keeps you from living the Gospel.

BASILICA OF SAN FRANCESCO

HISTORICAL NOTES

Francis of Assisi died at the little church of the Porziuncola, on the outskirts of Assisi, on the evening of October 3, 1226. He was forty-four.

St. Bonaventure, in his *Major Legend,* tells us that "God had brought him renown in a wonderful fashion during his life, but he made him more renowned than ever in death." The enormous flow of pilgrims to Assisi suggested that a large sepulchral church should eventually be constructed. Thus, on March 30, 1228, Pope Gregory IX was offered a piece of land on which to build an oratory for the blessed remains of St. Francis.

The land on which the church was built stood on the lower slopes of Monte Subasio, outside the city walls. The place was known locally as the "Hill of Hell," most probably because of its association as a place of public execution. By virtue of the papal bull *Is qui ecclesiam suam,* dated April 22, 1230, the Hill of Hell was transformed into the "Hill of Paradise."

Gregory IX himself laid the foundation stone of the church on July 17, 1228, the day after the solemn canonization of St. Francis at Assisi. The body of the *Poverello* (the "little poor man") was transferred to the new church built in his honor during the Pentecost Chapter of the friars two years later on May 25, 1230.

According to Ubertino of Casale, Blessed Giles of Assisi maintained that the sepulchral church of the saint ought to be constructed and embellished in such a way that the people would be instructed and edified by the holiness of Francis.

The lower church, built in the Romanesque style, so evocative of mystery, forms a Latin cross. The present entrance with its vestibule extending into the St. Catherine's chapel, together with the various side chapels, are all later additions.

Entering the church, looking up at the first arch, the visitor will see a fresco painted by Cesare Sermei, which shows Francis greeting the pilgrims. Two popes, Sixtus V and Paul V, kneel at the saint's feet. A long Latin inscription offers welcome: "Slow down your step and be joyful, O Pilgrim; you have already reached the Hill of Paradise." The next inscription concludes: "Ever resonant with praise and gladdened with holy choirs, this church is a true paradise of spiritual joy. Enter: you will see greater things."

The art form in both the upper and lower church in Assisi is quasi-sacramental. It represents and symbolizes a meeting between heaven and earth. This iconographic style of art opens up a window onto the eternal: It is a "calculated trap for meditation," a prismatic glass through which we may catch sight of things otherwise invisible.

After numerous unsuccessful attempts to find the actual tomb of St. Francis, it was finally discovered in January 1818, after fifty-two nights of digging. The body was found beneath three heavy blocks of travertine, where it had been hidden by Brother Elias some six hundred years before. A small chapel existed here until 1476 when Pope Sixtus IV ordered the small passageway leading to the funerary cell walled in so that the body could not be stolen and transported to some other place. Leo, Rufino, Angelo, and Masseo are buried around the tomb of Francis.

In the lower church, frescoes on the vault of the transept are by an unknown painter of the school of Giotto. Above the altar are other frescoes of the same school exemplifying poverty, chastity, obedience, and the triumph of Francis. Cimabue painted St. Francis; Lorenzetti, the Madonna of the Sunset and the Crucifixion.

In the upper church along the nave, under the gallery, is the famous series of twenty-eight frescoes depicting the life and miracles of Francis by Giotto and his pupils (1296).

Among the relics found here are the original bull of Honorius III approving the *Rule*, and the blessing written to Brother Leo in Francis' own handwriting.

FRANCISCAN READINGS

A LETTER ON THE PASSING OF SAINT FRANCIS ATTRIBUTED TO ELIAS OF ASSISI

On the occasion of Francis' death

To Gregory, his beloved brother in Christ, the minister of the brothers who are in France, together with all his brothers and ours, Brother Elias, a sinner, sends greetings.

Before I begin to speak, *I sigh,* and rightly so. My groans *gush forth like waters in a flood. For what I feared* has overtaken me and has overtaken you. *And what I dreaded has happened* to me and to you. *Our consoler has gone away* from us and *he who carried us in his arms like lambs had gone on a journey to a far off country. He who was beloved of God and of man, who taught Jacob the law of life and of discipline,* and *gave to Israel a covenant of peace* has been received into the most resplendent dwellings. We would rejoice exceedingly on his account, yet for our own part we must mourn, since in his absence darkness *surrounds us* and *the shadow of death covers us.* It is a loss for all, yet it is a trial singularly my own, for he has left me *in the midst of darkness,* surrounded by many anxieties and pressed down by countless afflictions. For this reason I implore you. Mourn with me, brothers, for I am *in great sorrow* and, with you, in pain. For *we are orphans without our father* and bereaved *of the light of our eyes.*

In truth, in very truth, the presence of our brother and father Francis *was a light,* not only *for us who were near,* but *even to those who were far from us* in calling and in life. *He was a light shed by the true light to give light to those who were in darkness and sitting in the shadow of death, to guide our feet into the way of peace.* He did this because *the true Daystar from on high* shone upon his heart and enkindled his will with the fire of His love. By *preaching the kingdom of God* and *turning the hearts of fathers to their children* and the rebellious *to the wisdom of the just, he prepared for the Lord a* new *people in the world.* His name reached distant coasts and *all lands* were in awe *at his marvelous deeds.*

For this reason, sons and brother, do not mourn beyond measure. *God, the father of orphans, will give us comfort by his* holy *consolation.* And if you weep, brothers, *weep for yourselves* and not for him. For "in the midst of life, we are caught in death," while *he has passed from death to life.* Rejoice, for, like another Jacob, he blessed all his sons *before he was taken from us* and forgave them all the faults which any one of us might have committed, or even thought of committing, against him.

And now, after telling you these things, *I announce to you a great joy* and the news of a miracle. Such *a sign* that *has never been heard of from the dawn of time except in the Son of God, who is Christ the Lord.*

Not long before his death, our brother and father appeared crucified, *bearing in his body* the five wounds which are truly *the marks of Christ.* His hands and feet had, as it were, the openings of the nails and were pierced front and back revealing the scars and showing the nails' blackness. His side, moreover, seemed opened by a lance and often *emitted* blood.

As long as his spirit lived in the body, *there was no beauty in him for his appearance was that of a man despised.* No part of his body was without great suffering. By reason of the contraction of his sinews, his limbs were stiff, much like those of a dead man. But after his death, his appearance was *one of great beauty* gleaming with a dazzling whiteness and giving joy to all who looked upon him. His limbs, which had been rigid, became marvelously soft and pliable, so that they would be turned this way and that, like those of a young child.

Therefore, brothers, *bless the God of heaven and praise Him before all, for He has shown His mercy to us.* Hold fast *the memory* of our father and brother, Francis, *to the praise and glory* of Him *Who made him so great* among people and gave him glory *in the sight of angels.* Pray for him, as he begged us, and pray to him that God may make us share with him in his holy grace. Amen.

On the fourth day before the nones of October, the Lord's day, at the first hour of the preceding night, our father and brother went to Christ. I am sure, dearest brothers, that when this letter reaches you, you will *follow the footprints* of the people of Israel as they mourned the loss of their great leaders, Moses and Aaron. Let us, by all means, give way to tears for we are deprived of so great a father.

Indeed, it is in keeping with our love for him that we rejoice with Francis. Still, it is right to mourn him! It belongs to us to rejoice with Francis, for he has not died *but gone* to the fair in heaven, *taking with him a bag of money and will not return until the full moon.*

At the same time it is right for us to weep for Francis. *He who came and went* among us, as did Aaron, who *brought forth from his storehouse both the new and the old* and *comforted us in all our afflictions, has been taken from our midst.* Now we are like *orphans without a father.* Yet, because it is written, "the poor depend on you and you are the helper of orphans" all of you, dearest brothers, *must earnestly pray that, though this earthen jar has been broken in the valley of Adam's children,* the Most High Potter will deign *to repair and restore* another of similar honor, who will rule over the multitude *of our race* and go before us into battle like a true Maccabee.

And, because *it is not useless to pray for the dead, pray to the Lord* for his soul. Let each priest say three Masses, each cleric the Psalter, and the lay brothers five Our Fathers. Let the clerics also recite in common the vigil office. Amen.

Brother Elias, Sinner.

Found in *Francis of Assisi: Early Documents,* Volume 2, 489-491. Used with permission.

PRAYER SERVICE

REMEMBERING FRANCIS

OPENING PRAYER

Let us pray:
Loving God, we give you thanks and praise
 for the light of this day.
We also give you thanks and praise for gifting us
  with Jesus, your Son
  whose light reveals your ever-abiding presence.
We gather, Almighty God,
  as sons and daughters of Francis of Assisi,
  to recall the flame of his spirit.
He mirrored Jesus for us
  and opened a new gospel way to you.
Help each of us capture his spirit, which is your spirit,
  so that we may praise and glorify you all days.
We ask this through Christ our Lord. Amen.

LIGHTING OF THE CHRIST CANDLE

Oh blazing fire so strong aglow;
  let joy and power from thee flow.
Alleluia! Alleluia!

Oh fire so masterful and bright;
  that give to us both warmth and light.
Oh praise God. Oh praise God.
Alleluia! Alleluia!

LIGHTING OF THE SEVEN CANDLES

FIRST CANDLE IS LIGHTED

Reader:
The first flame is the flame of the sun. How well Francis knew the flame of the Son burning ceaselessly in his soul. Francis was filled with "light." All creation became brighter, more alive, by his presence, just as the sun does the same to the created universe. Filled with light, Francis sang out: "All praise be yours, my Lord, through Brother Sun, who brings the day and light you give us through him. How beautiful is he, how radiant in all his splendor. Of you, Most High, he bears the likeness."

REFRAIN: G 30 "Song of Thanksgiving"

Silent Reflection

SECOND CANDLE IS LIGHTED

Reader:
The second flame is the flame of language. Francis had a wellspring of glowing fiery words that spoke plainly and simply of the Lord God. Thomas of Spoleto, once hearing Francis preach, wrote: "Nearly all the citizens of Bologna had gathered to hear him. He spoke of angels and people and devils, and with so much great exactness and eloquence that many learned scholars were filled with wonder, hearing such words from so simple a man. Yet he had not the manner of a preacher, rather his style was that of one who holds intimate contact with God and all people."

REFRAIN: G 30

Silent Reflection

THIRD CANDLE IS LIGHTED

Reader:
The third flame is the flame of passion. St. Francis was so

filled with the flame of passion that his body became alive. On Holy Mount La Verna he prayed: "O Lord, I beg of you two graces before I die: to experience in myself in all possible fullness the pains of your cruel passion, and to feel for you the same love that made you sacrifice yourself for us." And with his heart aflame with love and pity, Francis' body took on the image of our Crucified Savior.

REFRAIN: G 30

Silent Reflection

FOURTH CANDLE IS LIGHTED

Reader:
The fourth flame is hunger and thirst. In speaking to his sisters and brothers, Francis taught that a person is filled only when he knows the meaning of being truly empty, thirsty, and hungry. Francis saw the need to be empty, to be poor without possessions. For it is when persons find their hands open and empty, when they hunger and thirst, that they reach out to take in what is offered. Francis loved trees, which gave him shade; water, which quenched his thirst; fire, which gave him warmth; and his brothers and sisters, who loved him. Francis loved them because he hungered and thirsted.

REFRAIN: G 30

Silent Reflection

FIFTH CANDLE IS LIGHTED

Reader:
The fifth flame is the flame of music. A Christian is a person given to song. It is with hope and thanksgiving that one lives. Francis was such a person. He would sing of the Father, Son, and Spirit; of trees, hills, and birds; and of all his sisters and brothers. Though without possessions, Francis was never

without song. His life was a liturgy to the Father. Thus, in him burned the flame of music, a flame by which he listened and sang and played and danced.

REFRAIN: G 30

Silent Reflection

SIXTH CANDLE IS LIGHTED

Reader:
The sixth flame is the flame of hope. Francis, after a life of full dedication, was still a wanderer, a child, a prophet, a pilgrim in an ever-deepening search. Only the flame of hope could keep him in pursuit, a flame well expressed in his words: "Brothers and sisters, let us begin to serve the Lord, for up till now we have done very little."

REFRAIN: G 30

Silent Reflection

SEVENTH CANDLE IS LIGHTED

Reader:
The seventh flame is God. Without doubt Francis knew the God who sends out sparks into everything that lives. We hear him praise this God, a God who dwells within and yet apart from him: "You are holy, Lord, your deeds are wonderful; You are strong, great; You are Father, all Good, supreme Good. You are wisdom, love, humility, rest, peace, joy and gladness, and our riches. You are beauty, gentleness. You are courage, our haven and hope. You are our faith, eternal life, great and wonderful, almighty, merciful Savior." This is the prayer of one who knew God well, and in whom the flame of God was much alive.

REFRAIN: G 30

Silent Reflection

LIGHTING OF INDIVIDUAL CANDLES

Leader calls forth representatives from each continent represented and each branch of the Franciscan family. These representatives light the individual candles present on the altar.

Candles distributed to each person.

CLOSING PRAYER

Therefore,

let us desire nothing else,

let us want nothing else,

let nothing else please us and cause us delight

except our Creator, Redeemer and Savior,

the only true God,

Who is the fullness of good,

all good, every good, the true and supreme good,

Who alone is good,

from Whom, *through Whom* and in Whom

is all pardon, all grace, all glory

of all penitents and just ones,

of all the blessed rejoicing together in heaven. (ER XXIII:9)

EUCHARIST

TOMB OF ST. FRANCIS

READING I: SIRACH 50:1–4, 6–7

A reading from the book of Sirach

[Behold him] who in his life

repaired the house, and in his time fortified the temple. He laid the foundations for the high double walls, the high retaining walls for the temple enclosure. In his days a water cistern was dug, a reservoir like the sea in circumference. He considered how to save his people from ruin, and fortified the city against siege.

Like the morning star among the clouds, like the full moon at the festal season; like the sun shining on the temple of the Most High, like the rainbow gleaming in splendid clouds. **The word of the Lord.**

RESPONSE: O God, you are my portion and my cup.

PSALM 16

Protect me, O God, for in you I take refuge.
I say to the LORD, "You are my LORD;
I have no good apart from you." **R.**

The LORD is my chosen portion and my cup;
you hold my lot.
The boundary lines have fallen for me in pleasant places;
I have a goodly heritage.
I bless the LORD who gives me counsel;
in the night also my heart instructs me. **R.**

I keep the LORD always before me;
because he is at my right hand,
I shall not be moved.
Therefore my heart is glad, and my soul rejoices;
my body also rests secure. **R.**

For you do not give me up to Sheol,
or let your faithful one see the Pit.
You show me the path of life.
In your presence there is fullness of joy;
in your right hand are pleasures forevermore. **R.**

READING II: GALATIANS 6:14–18

A reading from the letter of Paul to the Galatians

May I never boast of anything except the cross of our Lord Jesus Christ, by which the world has been crucified to me, and I to the world. For neither circumcision nor uncircumcision is anything; but a new creation is everything! As for those who will follow this rule—peace be upon them, and mercy, and upon the Israel of God. From now on, let no one make trouble for me; for I carry the marks of Jesus branded on my body. May the grace of our Lord Jesus Christ be with your spirit, brothers and sisters. Amen. **The word of the Lord.**

ALLELUIA: Francis poor and lowly enters heaven rich in virtue, greeted with celestial hymns.

GOSPEL: MATTHEW 11:25–30

A reading from the holy Gospel according to Matthew

At that time Jesus said, "I thank you, Father, Lord of heaven and earth, because you have hidden these things from the wise and the intelligent and have revealed them to infants; yes, Father, for such was your gracious will. All things have been handed over to me by my Father; and no one knows the Son except the Father, and no one knows the Father except the Son and anyone to whom the Son chooses to reveal him. Come to me, all you that are weary and are carrying heavy burdens, and I will give you rest. Take my yoke upon you, and learn from me; for I am gentle and humble in heart, and you will find rest for your souls. For my yoke is easy, and my burden is light." **The Gospel of the Lord.**

TRANSITUS OF ST. FRANCIS OF ASSISI

Leader:
Each year on October 3, at sunset, Franciscans all over the

world gather to commemorate a poignant event in the life of our brother Francis of Assisi. The commemoration is called the *Transitus*, his passage from earthly life to everlasting life. After listening to a passage from the Gospel and a recitation of his favorite psalm, Francis embraced "Sister Death" on the evening of October 3, 1226.

Our service, deeply rooted in Franciscan tradition, is structured in its original sense: that of a vigil, a keeping watch, and is conducted in a spirit of remembering.

INTRODUCTION

Narrator:

"In truth, in very truth, the presence of Francis, our brother and our father, was a light, not only to us who were close to him, but also to those who were more removed from us in calling and in life. He was a light sent forth from the true Light, to enlighten those who sit in darkness and in the shadow of death, that he might guide their feet into the way of peace. He did this even as the true Daystar from on high enlightened his heart and inflamed his will with the fire of His love. When he preached the Kingdom of God, when he turned the hearts of fathers to their sons, when he brought the foolish to the prudence of the just, he made ready for the Lord a new people throughout the whole world."

Damien Isabel, O.F.M., "Encyclical Letter of Brother Elias Announcing the Death of Francis," in *Workbook for Franciscan Studies* [Chicago: Franciscan Herald Press, 1979]. Used with permission.

SERVICE OF LIGHT

As a bell tolls, the Christ candle is lit by Lady Jacoba, and the other candles by Leo and Angelo.

REMEMBERING FRANCIS

Narrator:
The forty-day fast and retreat that Francis made at La Verna when he had received the Stigmata left him utterly exhausted. It was now time to make the long, tiring journey back home to Assisi. The journey was to be made with Brother Leo and Brother Angelo. The saint, hardly able to walk, rode on a donkey lent to him by the solicitous governor, Count Orlando. Francis bid his last farewell.

Francis:
Goodbye my brothers, my dearest children. Remain in this sacred sanctuary in peace. May God bless you all. Goodbye. I leave you in the body, but I also leave you my heart. I go to our home at St. Mary of the Angels, and Brother Leo will accompany me. Never shall I come back to this place. Mother of the Eternal Word, I put my children in your care.

Narrator:
At length, Francis, Leo, and Angelo reached their Porziuncola home. Though nearly blind and desperately tired, Francis was not at ease. He desired to once more work among the poor and the lepers. His broken health and the changes he found at home depressed and troubled him. No longer did he see and live the simple peace and joy that had characterized the early years.

The winter was setting in, and the hills were already beginning to be covered with snow. In the dampness and cold of the Porziuncola chapel, it seemed impossible that Francis could long survive. So the brothers arranged to take him to a little hut near the church and convent of San Damiano. This seemed to give him new strength despite the overpowering burden of his sickness. Clare sent her greetings to Francis and awaited his response.

Francis:

Tell our Sister Clare what I have always told her. I thank God for her. She has understood me perfectly. Brother Leo, write my last will for Lady Clare. Write: "I, little Brother Francis, wish to live according to the life and poverty of our most high Lord Jesus Christ and his most holy Mother and to persevere in this to the last. And I beg you, my Ladies, and I exhort you to live always in this most holy life and poverty. Keep close watch over yourselves so that you never abandon it through the teaching or advice of anyone." (Ult Vol. Adapted)

(PAUSE)

Since I soon must die, Leo and Angelo, please sing *The Canticle of the Creatures* for me.

SONG OR RECITATION: F 2 "Canticle of The Creatures", verses 1–8

Angelo:

Though it was most difficult to do so, we sang the Canticle that our dear Brother Francis had composed. We knew it by heart, having sung it many times during our visits to the villages around Assisi. The melody haunted us long after Francis died ... and the words have become immortal.

Narrator:

Now close to death, Francis asked Brother Leo to write a letter to his dear friend, Lady Jacoba dei Settesoli, who lived in Rome. He desired to see her one last time.

Leo:

Francis told me to write this: "Dearest Lady, I know how faithful and devoted you have been to me and the brothers, and to the life we have preached to all the people. I send you this letter, knowing that you would want to know about my condition and would have need of consolation. I ask you to bring some cloth for a tunic the color of ashes, like the cloth made by Cistercian monks in the region beyond the Alps. Also bring some of your sweet cookies made of almonds and honey." (AC 8—adapted)

Narrator:
At the same time these words were being written, this noblewoman was already on her way to Assisi, accompanied by her sons Giovanni and Graziano, along with members of her household. When she appeared at the door, the brothers hesitated to let her in since Francis had cautioned against the presence of women in the cloister. But Francis immediately said to them:

Francis:
This command need not be observed in the case of this lady whose faith and devotion made her come here from so far away. Let our "Brother Jacoba" in.

Jacoba:
Dear Francis, while I was praying, a voice within me said "Go, visit your father, blessed Francis, without delay, and hurry, because if you delay long you will not find him alive. Moreover, take such and such cloth for his tunic, as well as the ingredients for making his favorite sweet confection. Take with you also a great quantity of wax and incense." (AC 8—adapted)

I have indeed brought the cloth you desire, and the almond cookies you love so much. But in addition, I have a pillow for your head, a cloth for your face and many candles whose fire you love. Accept these gifts with my love and my promise to live all you have taught me about loving God wherever I am, and in whatever I am doing for my family and for those in need."

Narrator:
Then Francis asked to be laid on the barren ground ... and those gathered around him recited the last verse of the Canticle he had composed.

SONG OR RECITATION: F 2, verses 9–11

Narrator:
Francis then raised his eyes to heaven and giving his entire attention to that glory, he said to all:

Francis:
I have done what was mine to do. May Christ teach you what you are to do.

Narrator:
After this, Francis glorified his Lord, for he was going to him a free man. And since he was a true imitator in all things of Christ, he loved to the end the brothers and sisters whom he had always loved. The time that remained before his death, Francis spent in prayer saying:

Francis:
I am hurrying to God, to whose grace I entrust all of you. Bring the book of the Gospels to me and read a passage from John.

Leo:
A reading of the holy Gospel according to John 13:1–9, 12–15

Now before the festival of the Passover, Jesus knew that his hour had come to depart from this world and go to the Father. Having loved his own who were in the world, he loved them to the end. The devil had already put it into the heart of Judas son of Simon Iscariot to betray him. And during supper Jesus, knowing that the Father had given all things into his hands, and that he had come from God and was going to God, got up from the table, took off his outer robe. ...

Angelo:
[He] tied a towel around himself. Then he poured water into a basin and began to wash the disciples' feet and to wipe them with the towel that was tied around him. He came to Simon Peter, who said to him, "Lord, are you going to wash my feet?"

Jesus answered, "You do not know now what I am doing, but later you will understand." Peter said to him, "You will never wash my feet." Jesus answered, "Unless I wash you, you have no share with me." Simon Peter said to him, "Lord, not my feet only but also my hands and my head!"...

Jacoba:
After he had washed their feet, had put on his robe, and had returned to the table, he said to them, "Do you know what I have done to you? You call me Teacher and Lord—and you are right, for that is what I am. So if I, your Lord and Teacher, have washed your feet, you also ought to wash one another's feet. For I have set you an example, that you also should do as I have done to you.

Narrator:
After hearing this passage, Francis, as best he could, broke out in response, reciting his favorite psalm, Psalm 142, all the way through to the end. Those present joined him, saying:

Side One:
With my voice I cry to the LORD;
    with my voice I make
        supplication to the LORD.
I pour out my complaint before him
    I tell my trouble before him.
when my spirit is faint,
    you know my way.

Side Two:
In the path where I walk
    they have hidden a trap for me.
Look on my right hand and see—
    there is no one who takes notice
        of me;
no refuge remains to me;
    no one cares for me.

Side One:
I cry to you, O LORD;
    I say, "You are my refuge,
      my portion in the land of the living."
Give heed to my cry,
    for I am brought very low.

Side Two:
Save me from my persecutors,
    for they are too strong for me.
Bring me out of prison,
    so that I may give thanks to
        your name.
The righteous will surround me,
    for you will deal bountifully
        with me.

Narrator:
            At last,
    when all of the mysteries were fulfilled in him,
  and that most holy soul was released from the flesh
     and absorbed into the abyss of the divine light,
    the blessed man *fell asleep in the Lord.* (LMj XIV:6)

DEPARTURE IN SILENCE

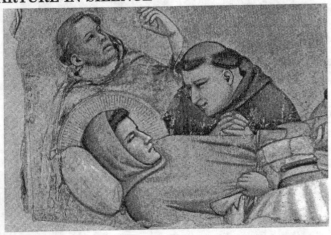

ASSISI:
BASILICA OF
SANTA
CHIARA

FRANCISCAN PILGRIMAGE PROGRAMS

ASSISI: BASILICA OF SANTA CHIARA

EVENTS
This basilica surrounds the remains of San Giorgio, the little parish church where Francis received his elementary education and was introduced to the basic teachings of the faith.

Francis was buried in San Giorgio 1226–1230.

Clare was also buried initially at San Giorgio and later in her crypt within the basilica, after it was completed in 1260.

SPIRITUALITY
This place, Santa Chiara, symbolizes the end of one era and the beginning of another in the Franciscan story. With Clare's death and burial in 1253, the initial chapter of Francis' dream comes to an end. Clare was the last of those who internalized the original vision. With the building of the basilica and the transfer of her sisters to Santa Chiara, a new chapter began. It is the task of the current generation of Franciscans to take up the inspiration of Francis and Clare and make it come alive for our time. Santa Chiara symbolizes this part of the journey for us and calls us to enflesh it in our day.

Santa Chiara houses the original San Damiano crucifix. Christ's message to Francis was perhaps lived out most fully by Clare herself. The crucifix became one of Clare's chief rebuilding tools as she gazed upon it each day, contemplated its mystery, and eventually became what she gazed upon.

REFLECTION
Francis was schooled in the book of the Psalms. He composed his own *Office of the Passion*. Slowly pray one of these Psalms. What theology do you find?

"Journeys Ended, Journeys Begun" is the title of a contemporary religious song. Francis said: I have done what was mine to do. May Christ teach you what is yours. What is yours to do in this era of Franciscan history?

BASILICA OF SANTA CHIARA

HISTORICAL NOTES

The Basilica of Santa Chiara stands on the site of the former San Giorgio parish church, which was administered by the canons of the Cathedral of San Rufino at the time of Francis and Clare. Next to it at that time was a hospital for the poor, outside the city walls.

Francis learned to read and write at San Giorgio, and he preached for the first time in this church. Francis' body was buried in the crypt of the church in 1226, and on May 24, 1230, it was transferred to the new basilica erected in his honor by Elias.

When Clare died in 1253, her body was first placed in the crypt of this same church (San Giorgio). After her canonization in 1255, Pope Alexander IV negotiated with the canons to have the property become the place for the basilica that would be the focus for the pilgrims coming to Clare's tomb. By his decree in 1259, the few Poor Clares staying with Clare's body, and those who remained at San Damiano, became united as one community with residence at the protomonastery built on the south side of the new basilica. In 1260 St. Bonaventure was present for the celebration of the completion of the basilica, at which time Clare's body was placed in a safe burial spot beneath the high altar.

The original San Damiano crucifix was brought by the sisters to the protomonastery when they left San Damiano, and it is now revered by the public in a side chapel. Behind the crucifix is sacred space that was part of the church of San Giorgio in the 13th century. The crucifix has been treasured by the Poor Clares and pilgrims throughout the centuries.

Clare's body was exhumed in 1850 and is maintained in a glass coffin beneath the main altar. Also in this place are other treasures from the early years of the Franciscan movement: Francis' breviary with an introduction probably written by Leo, and Francis' and Clare's habits.

FRANCISCAN READINGS

THOMAS OF CELANO, FIRST LIFE 23

On Francis preaching penance at San Giorgio

He then began to preach penance to all with a fervent spirit and joyful attitude. He inspired his listeners with words that were simple and a heart that was heroic. His word was like *a blazing fire*, reaching the deepest parts of the heart, and filling the souls of all with wonder. He seemed entirely different from what he had been, and *looking up to heaven* he refused to look down upon earth. It is truly amazing that he first *began to preach* where he had learned to read as a little boy, and where at first he was reverently buried.

Thus;
a blessed beginning was confirmed
by a more blessed end.
Where he learned, there he also taught;
and where he began, there he blessedly ended.

In all of his preaching, before he presented the word of God to the assembly, he prayed for peace saying, *"May the Lord give you peace."*

ST. BONAVENTURE: MAJOR LEGEND XV:5

Laid to rest in the church of San Giorgio

His brothers and sons, who had been called to their father's passing, with *the whole multitude of people*, spent that night in which the blessed confessor of Christ departed, in the divine praises. They did this in such a way that it seemed to be a vigil of angels, not a wake for the dead. *When day was breaking, the crowds that had assembled took branches from the trees* and carried his sacred body to the city of Assisi, with a blaze of many candles and hymns and songs. As they passed the church of San Damiano, where the noble virgin Clare, now glorious in heaven, was then living enclosed with the virgins, they stopped for awhile so that those holy nuns could see and kiss his sacred body, adorned with its heavenly pearls. Finally reaching the city with great rejoicing, with all reverence they placed the precious treasure they were carrying in the church of Saint George.

There as a boy he learned his letters,
there he later preached for the first time,
and there, finally, he received his first place of rest.

THE BLESSING OF CLARE OF ASSISI

Clare's last hours

The Legend of Saint Clare, 45, describes the last hours of the saint's life and tells how she blessed the sisters of San Damiano as well as those of the other monasteries and those who would come in the future. This is possibly the source of the special blessing that has been traditionally attributed to Saint Clare: The tradition of the Poor Clare has always cherished this text as a precious remembrance of their foundress which echoes that blessing given by Saint Francis to Brother Leo while they were on La Verna.

The Blessing

In the name of the Father and of the Son and of the Holy Spirit (Mt 28:19).

May the Lord bless you and keep you.

May He show His face to you and be merciful to you.

May He turn His countenance (cf. Num 6:24–26) to you, my sisters and daughters, and give peace to you, and to all others who come and remain in your company as well as to others now and in the future, who have persevered in every other monastery of the Poor Ladies.

I, Clare, a servant of Christ, a little plant of our most holy Father Francis, a sister and mother of you and the other poor sisters, although unworthy, beg our Lord Jesus Christ through His mercy and the intercession of His most holy Mother Mary and blessed Michael the Archangel and all the holy angels of God, of our blessed Father Francis, and all men and women saints, that the heavenly Father give you and confirm for you this most holy blessing in heaven and on earth (cf. Gen 27:28). On earth, may He multiply you in His grace and His virtues among His servants and handmaids in His Church Militant. In heaven, may He exalt you and glorify you among His men and women saints in His Church Triumphant.

I bless you during my life and after my death, as I am able, out of all the blessings with which *the Father of mercies has* and does *bless* His sons and daughters *in heaven* and on earth (2 Cor 1:3; cf. Eph 1:3) and a spiritual father and mother have blessed and bless their spiritual sons and daughters. Amen.

Always be lovers of your souls and those of all your sisters. And may you always be eager to observe what you have promised the Lord.

May the Lord always be *with you* (cf. 2 Cor 13:11; Jn 12:26; 1 Thess 4:17) and may you always be with Him. Amen.

PRAYER SERVICE

CLARE AND FRANCISCAN WOMEN

INVITATION TO PRAYER

Leader:
Let us begin our celebration together by worshipping God, our Mother and Father, the Ground of our being, the Source of our life, the Spirit who sets us free.

All:
In memory of all women who have sung praise to God before we were born, and in union with all women living today, we join to praise the Spirit of God in our midst.

Leader:
To worship is to open our beings to the power of God's truth and love. To worship is to heighten our awareness of the core of existence, the meaning of life.

All:
Let us celebrate with joy in the hope that our awareness and openness will bear the fruit of increased union with God's Spirit in each of us.

READING: "PILGRIMS IN SPIRIT"

She had known almost at once that she would follow him. The first time she heard Francis preach, his words pierced her heart with love for Jesus, and his soul was one with hers. She soon learned that they could never be together, for then they would not be free, they would not be who they really were, two pilgrims in love with the Lord, two souls who were closer apart than they could ever be together. Together they might end up loving each other more than the treasure they had found in one another's heart.

She had heard the echo of her own voice in Francis' words, and he had found in her the incarnation of every word he spoke. They were pilgrims in spirit, poor and wandering hearts in love with God; and knowing they loved each other, they were never lonely.

Clare drew her ideals from Francis' words, and Francis, she felt, drew his words at times from the inspiration of her life. She made it possible for him to believe that what he spoke was livable, that the gospel life brought joy indeed, and that every word that Jesus uttered could be lived by those who heard his words with open hearts.

Clare hoped that she would become the living proof of everything Francis believed in. And that was why she had to follow him the moment she heard him speak. They had been fashioned for each other out of the solitude of the ages. And they had known each other longer than they knew.

Murray Bodo, O.F.M., *Clare: A Light in the Garden* [Cincinnati: St. Anthony Messenger Press, 1979], 11–12. Used with permission.

SILENT OR MUSICAL REFLECTION

LITANY OF NAMING

Leader:
Let us begin by **remembering** the stories of our foremothers and praying that their courage to name, claim, and move with their visions may be shared by women and men of our time and **spark** us to be a people **moving with the church**.

We come here as daughters and sons of the **women** in our own families who have gone before us and have given us life. Let us share the names of these women now as we name ourselves as their descendants.

Mothers in our families, you have named us and have given us life. **Our mothers, move here with us.**

Lady Pica, you gave birth to Francis and taught him the way of a mother of tenderness. **Lady Pica, move here with us.**

Ortolana, you gave light to the daughter you named "light" Clare, the light in your garden. **Ortolana, move here with us.**

Clare Favarone, you had the courage to respond wholeheartedly to the call of God in your life and became the first woman to compose a Rule of Life approved by the church.

Clare Favarone, move here with us.

Agnes of Assisi, sister of Clare, you followed Clare into the solitude of San Damiano and later to lead the monastery of Monticelli as abbess. **Agnes of Assisi, move here with us.**

Lady Jacoba, you befriended Francis and walked with him in lasting friendship until the day of his death. **Lady Jacoba, move here with us.**

Angela of Foligno, daughter of Francis in the Third Order, you shared your mystical journey in the writings of your spiritual director. **Angela of Foligno, move here with us.**

Agnes of Prague, daughter of royalty, you "chose most holy poverty ... [and] united yourself to a Spouse of more noble lineage, the Lord Jesus Christ." (1LAg 6–7) **Agnes of Prague, move here with us.**

Angelina of Montegiove, you were the first woman of our order to gather with other women in community outside the enclosure and care for the sick, poor, widows, orphans. **Angelina of Montegiove, move here with us.**

Rose of Viterbo, you were one of the earliest women of our order to preach to people in the streets. **Rose of Viterbo, move here with us.**

Louise Albertoni, secular Franciscan in love with the poor, you generously gave of your income, often hiding money in the bread you gave. **Louise Albertoni, move here with us.**

Margaret of Cortona, you focused your tender love of Jesus on the poor and the sick. **Margaret of Cortona, move here with us.**

(Other names can be mentioned and prayed for.)

PRAYER

Spirit of God,
you are the life-giving Spirit who sets us free.
You are both promise and uncertainty,
poverty and hope, comfort and challenge.

Inspire us with courage to proclaim the truth
and strength to work for justice and peace.
Waken in us a spirit of joy that we may celebrate all
that is good and human,
and, especially today, all that is woman.

To the women whose names we have just spoken,
to all the special women in our lives,
and to each person here,
send your Spirit, O God,
to make us whole,
to make us know that you have created us in your image,
and that you are our mother and father,
our sister and brother,
our friend. Amen.

FINAL BLESSING AND EMPOWERMENT

Leader:
Bow your heads and pray with me.

In blessing our foreheads, we claim the power of reason, to know that path that leads to fulfillment of our hopes for a liberated humanity.

In blessing our eyes, we claim the power of vision, to see clearly the forces of life and death in our midst.

In blessing our ears, we claim the power to hear the Spirit of God as God speaks to us within.

In blessing our lips, we claim the power to speak the truth about our experience; we claim power to name ourselves and our God.

In blessing our hands, we claim our powers as creators of a new humanity liberated from fear, ignorance, and oppression.

In blessing our feet, we claim the power to walk the paths of our courageous foremothers and to forge new paths where they are needed.

In blessing each other, we claim the creative power that rests collectively in our shared struggle as women and men. We choose to extend this power in service to a world in need.

May our lives be blessings to each other.

All:
Amen.

EUCHARIST
TOMB OF ST. CLARE

READING: SONG OF SOLOMON 8:6–7

A reading from the Song of Solomon

Set me as a seal upon your heart, as a seal upon your arm; for love is strong as death, passion fierce as the grave. Its flashes are flashes of fire, a raging flame. Many waters cannot quench love, neither can floods drown it. If one offered for love all the wealth of his house, it would be utterly scorned. **The word of the Lord.**

RESPONSE: I will bless the Lord at all times.

PSALM 34

I will bless the LORD at all times;
his praise shall continually be in my mouth.
My soul makes its boast in the LORD;
let the humble hear and be glad. **R.**

O magnify the LORD with me,
and let us exalt his name together.
I sought the LORD, and he answered me,
and delivered me from all my fears. **R.**

Look to him, and be radiant;
so your faces shall never be ashamed.
This poor soul cried, and was heard by the LORD,
and was saved from every trouble. **R.**

The angel of the LORD encamps around those who fear him,
and delivers them.
O taste and see that the LORD is good;
happy are those who take refuge in him.
O fear the LORD, you his holy ones,
for those who fear him have no want. **R.**

ALLELUIA: Come, bride of Christ, receive the crown, which the Lord has prepared for you.

GOSPEL: JOHN 20:1–9

A reading from the holy Gospel according to John

Early on the first day of the week, while it was still dark, Mary Magdalene came to the tomb and saw that the stone had been removed from the tomb. So she ran and went to Simon Peter and the other disciple, the one whom Jesus loved, and said to them, "They have taken the Lord out of the tomb, and we do not know where they have laid him." Then Peter and the other disciple set out and went toward the tomb. The two were running together, but the other disciple outran Peter and reached the tomb first. He bent down to look in and saw the linen wrappings lying there, but he did not go in. Then Simon Peter came, following him, and went into the tomb. He saw the linen wrappings lying there, and the cloth that had been on Jesus' head, not lying with the linen wrappings but rolled up in a place by itself. Then the other disciple, who reached the tomb first, also went in, and he saw and believed; for as yet they did not understand the scripture, that he must rise from the dead. **The Gospel of the Lord.**

TRANSITUS OF ST. CLARE

The setting is the dormitory above the little church of San Damiano. Clare is lying on her bed of straw. She is surrounded by the Poor Ladies of San Damiano, some weeping, some praying, some staring in disbelief that their mother will soon be taken from them by Sister Death. Gathered together with the Poor Ladies are some of the brothers—Juniper and Leo. Memories of Clare are filling those around her bed. Memories are not logical, chronological, coherently arranged as they flow. Using our imagination let us enter this stream of consciousness and experience the flood of memory flowing through Agnes, Leo, Juniper, and Benedetta.

Sister Agnes, Clare's Sister:
Oh my mother, my sister. Are we really at the hour of your death, your passing from us? 1253: It's been so many years— so many years that I have been away from San Damiano at Monticelli and other monasteries that follow our form of life— and just returning this year only to have you leave me so soon. I already ache with the pain of separation once again. So many years, my sister, since we lived together in the home of our parents. I vividly remember our years there together. Even then you were living differently than most young women of nobility. You dressed differently; I watched you, not in all the

finery of the styles women wore, but in a very simple garb I saw you wearing around the house. It was almost like the dress of the penitents. And I watched you giving food to the poor people constantly at our door—food from your own dish, food that was extra (and there was much of that) from our own kitchen. And when you gave your food away, I knew you were fasting, but I never said anything about it to you. I worried that you would not eat enough to keep you going, to keep you strong. But this you seemed to do. And yes, remember our arrangement that I was to cover your absence from the household when you and Bona di Guelfuccio would go off to meet with Francis. Oh, Clare, I was so afraid these visits would be discovered! But they weren't!

And our Palm Sunday plan worked so well. I recall Mother wondering why Bishop Guido came down to you with the palm branch. She even questioned me about it. I told her to ask you why you never moved from your place. That day you were dressed so beautifully—like a bride adorned to meet her spouse. I never told you, but all that Palm Sunday I worried about your departure that evening. I was especially concerned about the door from which you would escape. All our furniture, old toys, and tools were stored by that exit. Yet, somehow—with the strength of God, I suppose, because you forbade me to help you for fear of being caught—you managed to get out. I didn't sleep the whole night.

You weren't home the next morning to witness all the confusion, anger, questioning to which Uncle Monaldo subjected every one of us. Then they found out, I don't remember from whom, that you were in Bastia with the Benedictines. When they returned to the house late that evening, I was expecting to see you with them. When I didn't, I went to our large reception room in which they were gathered and listened by the door. We were not invited to this family discussion. I heard Uncle Monaldo say you were wearing a coarse, smelly garb with head completely covered. He said he attempted to take you away, but you grabbed the altar and pulled the covering off your head to display your shorn hair, and he angrily backed away.

By this time God was stirring my own soul and spirit to come join you. It was very difficult for me to get away from the house, but God gave me an opportunity, and before I knew it, I was on my way to you. How happy I was to see you again, my sister. I never expected the family to search for me. I remembered what they said you did as I listened to them near the reception room door. I was all ready to do the same—you even prepared me for it; however, we both were unprepared for such vehement anger and the violent response they made. During all the physical violence they inflicted on my body, I, like the martyr St. Agnes, was preparing my soul to meet God, trying to pray myself when my body became so rigid and heavy. I thought death was upon me. Yet, I could still hear their voices, barely audible. I hadn't realized they had departed until I found myself resting in your arms as you cleansed and attended to my injured body. In all the pain I was so happy to be with you. I recall you telling me you heard Uncle Monaldo call off the attempt to "rescue" me because he said it was impossible to lift me. God again came to our aid! Always God, my sister, always God!

Brother Leo:
O Clare, my sister, little plant of St. Francis. "Little plant" you were when you joined our order, but a most mature plant for these twenty-seven years since Sister Death took Brother Francis. You became the new vine and we the branches. As I kneel here at your bedside, so many memories of these maturing years flood my being.

I remember Palm Sunday night, 1212, waiting for you at the

city gate to escort you to St. Mary of the Angels. You had already made arrangements with the gatekeeper to let you exit after the curfew hour. I was accompanied by your cousin Rufino,

who could easily recognize you since I had never met you before then. As Rufino spoke of Uncle Monaldo, I found myself a bit nervous as the hour of our rendezvous approached. The hour's walk from the city to St. Mary of the Angels passed quickly. Next thing I remember was your long, beautiful hair lying on the floor of the Porziuncola. And before long you were whisked away to Bastia.

How perfectly you followed in the footsteps of St. Francis regarding poverty. I recall your joy living in your Privilege of Poverty. Yet, I remember your concern as the Lord Cardinal Hugolino tried to get you to mitigate this privilege, the sadness you experienced when his own version of a Rule was given you for San Damiano. How you ever convinced him as Pope Gregory IX to reconfirm this privilege for you is amazing! How good you were to me when I came running to you the day I destroyed Brother Elias's collection box to build a basilica for St. Francis. He had me flogged and thrown out of the city. How soothing a balm you were for my wounds you'll never know.

And you know, dearest Clare, how hard I tried to get Brother Francis to come to you at San Damiano. To convince him to share that one meal with you as happened at St. Mary of the

Angels, I had to elicit the aid of the entire fraternity. I remember the radiant joy on your face as you sat opposite him and the meager fare set before you as he spoke to all of us of the love of God.

I recall one more "successful" visit that became a lengthy stay with you. When he could no longer bear the effect of daylight on his eyes, he was talking of staying somewhere to ease his pain. Being unable to travel very far, I convinced him to come to San Damiano, where you so lovingly served his needs for many weeks. I never saw him as happy and creative as he was then. His *Canticle of the Creatures* was composed during that time. I remember us singing it for you and the smile you had on your face as we did so.

O my Lady Clare, to whom shall we turn after you've gone. Remember me, my lady, when Sister Death embraces you!

Brother Juniper:
Mother Clare, how I long to make you laugh once again at this moment. But everyone seems so very sad, so somber, right now. We should be rejoicing. What is it in our being that's not preparing us for that final yielding? Why are we afraid of meeting the One to whom we've given our lives in a love relationship? I guess that's the reason why I want to make you laugh, to rejoice that such a glorious moment has arrived.

Your hidden life has meant so very much to me, for I like to look at the hidden, little things in life and to rejoice in them. You know how simple I am. I remember the time one of the brothers was summoned to the quest for oil for your kitchen. You had the container placed on the windowsill waiting to be filled by the quest. I smiled as the brother explained to us all on his return that he didn't understand why he was summoned because the container was filled. He said he enjoyed his walk to and from San Damiano. I almost laughed aloud as I realized what God had done for you. See, that's what I mean, little things.

Like the time a mother brought her child to you who had a pebble lodged in his nose. Your simple directive: Bring him to my mother. Such an easy directive, but you knew the secret power of your mother's prayer. So he was healed.

But you also handled the larger and more pressing aspects of life just as well. I recall the day St. Francis had died. He promised you would see him once more, and he kept his promise. For we carried that precious body from St. Mary of the Angels up hill to San Damiano. At the grill it was hard for you all to see. So we brothers took turns holding up this precious body on our shoulders for one hour before the grill. Even that day I wasn't sad for me nor for you, for I believed we had a more powerful Francis in heaven than here on earth. He'd take care of you, me, and all the brothers and sisters. I guess that makes the awesome moment of death "little," doesn't it?

I just remembered the time when the Saracens and mercenary soldiers were ready to attack Assisi. I think it was 1240, only thirteen years ago. They were rumored to be advancing up the slopes toward the city when they came upon San Damiano. I would have panicked, I think. How you ever thought of the Blessed Sacrament as protective cover, I'm amazed. Yet that is so simple and true—Jesus is our ark, protector, shelter from all harm. And it worked. I smiled as I imagined all those soldiers scrambling to flee—not from a formidable army,but from Jesus and you women of San Damiano. God does marvelous things for us little ones.

So, dearest Clare, I smile in my being. I rejoice within because I know you are in the most beautiful moment of existence— awaiting the embrace into the arms of Sister Death, who in turn will dance you into the arms of your lover, Jesus Christ. What a wonderful moment!

Sister Benedetta, Abbess after Clare:

My dearest Clare, most resplendent light, the enlightening power of your being shines even more splendidly than the stars this night. You taught me much, dearest Clare, so very much. I feel ready but unsteady to take your place as abbess. I remember so very well the day Francis trudged up our hill after his arrival from Rome and the Lateran Council. We were only four years old as a community. He came to tell you about the council. And like the literal obedient son that he always was, he came to tell you that you were to assume the role of abbess. I knew your feeling about this because we talked about your days with the Benedictines very often, especially why you felt God wanted you elsewhere. And now comes a Benedictine influence you were reluctant to accept. Yet in loving trust for St. Francis, you assented—just like Mary said yes. I was so touched by your obedience, and time has proven you to be the abbess that God wanted, that Francis needed, and under which we, poor ladies, flourished. I was so happy you said yes!

And I watched you serve as abbess. I learned. I recall the episode when one of our questing sisters returned from Assisi. You sat her down, and began to wash her feet, and when she resisted, moving her foot from your grip. The quick motion caused her unintentionally to strike your face, your nose bleeding. She was so upset, yet you continued this loving gesture, completing your task before attending your injury. I wanted to run to you and keep the blood away. Yet, your action gave me pause.

And when any of us was ill, you hovered over the sick one as Mother, solicitous for her daughter's healing. And if warm drink and ointment didn't work fast enough for you, your prayer and gentle touch of your hands healed. We were so safe with you around. What will we do now? I know, I've learned—the same things you did for us. Help me, Clare, to remember all you've taught me!

I'm thinking again of your obedience to Francis, and I shudder a bit as I remember your encounter with Pope Gregory IX in our refectory. You were so excited over his visit that you instructed much bread to be prepared for the pope to bless. Having entered the room in all his regalia, I awaited the solemn blessing. Then the two of you began the exchange of words I'll never forget. "Clare, please bless the bread." "Holy Father, I cannot do that with you here. The honor comes from you to us, Your Holiness." "Clare, I command you under holy obedience to bless the bread." And bless you did. And I recall the outcome: each loaf signed with the cross of holy obedience. But I remember my amazement that you would at first resist the pope's request.

But this denial taught me again. For I remember the turmoil that ensued in our community when another pope, Innocent IV, gave us a new Rule. You knew and we knew it wasn't what our order was all about; it wasn't what Francis set down for us in his form of life when we began at San Damiano. You not only got the pope to rescind this Rule but began to write one of your own. No woman ever before in the life of the church wrote a Rule. And, miracle of miracles, you lie before us now clutching his seal of approval to your breast. What a gift God gave you and us at this very hard, yet glorious moment. I choke back my tears. I don't want you to go, my teacher, yet, I say go. You have our leave, our permission to go to your Beloved. For I am certain that you will be with us even more powerfully than these past forty-one years. Go, Clare! Go in peace!

EUCHARIST
SAN DAMIANO CRUCIFIX

READING: PHILIPPIANS 2:5–11

A reading from the letter of Paul to the Philippians

Let the same mind be in you that was in Christ Jesus, who, though he was in the form of God, did not regard equality with God as something to be exploited, but emptied himself, taking the form of a slave, being born in human likeness. And being found in human form, he humbled himself and became obedient to the point of death—even death on a cross. Therefore God also highly exalted him and gave him the name that is above every name, so that at the name of Jesus every knee should bend, in heaven and on earth and under the earth, and every tongue should confess that Jesus Christ is Lord, to the glory of God the Father. **The word of the Lord.**

RESPONSE: Rest in God alone, O my soul!

PSALM 62

For God alone my soul waits in silence;
from him comes my salvation.
He alone is my rock and my salvation, my fortress;
I shall never be shaken. **R.**

How long will you assail a person,
will you batter your victim, all of you,
as you would a leaning wall, a tottering fence?
Their only plan is to bring down a person of prominence. **R.**

They take pleasure in falsehood;
they bless with their mouths,
but inwardly they curse.
For God alone my soul waits in silence,
for my hope is from him. **R.**

He alone is my rock and my salvation, my fortress;
I shall not be shaken.
On God rests my deliverance and my honor;
my mighty rock, my refuge is in God. **R.**

ALLELUIA: Whoever believes in me will not die but will have eternal life.

GOSPEL: JOHN 3:13–17
A reading from the holy Gospel according to John

[Jesus said to his diciples:] "No one has ascended into heaven except the one who descended from heaven, the Son of Man. And just as Moses lifted up the serpent in the wilderness, so must the Son of Man be lifted up, that whoever believes in him may have eternal life. For God so loved the world that he gave his only Son, so that everyone who believes in him may not perish but may have eternal life. Indeed, God did not send the Son into the world to condemn the world, but in order that the world might be saved through him." **The Gospel of the Lord.**

ASSISI: FAREWELL

FRANCISCAN PILGRIMAGE PROGRAMS

CLOSING EUCHARIST

CLOSURE OF THE PILGRIMAGE: THANKSGIVING

READING: COLOSSIANS 3:12–17

A reading from the letter of Paul to the Colossians

As God's chosen ones, holy and beloved, clothe yourselves with compassion, kindness, humility, meekness, and patience. Bear with one another and, if anyone has a complaint against another, forgive each other; just as the Lord has forgiven you, so you also must forgive. Above all, clothe yourselves with love, which binds everything together in perfect harmony. And let the peace of Christ rule in your hearts, to which indeed you were called in the one body. And be thankful. Let the word of Christ dwell in you richly; teach and admonish one another in all wisdom; and with gratitude in your hearts sing psalms, hymns, and spiritual songs to God. And whatever you do, in word or deed, do everything in the name of the Lord Jesus, giving thanks to God the Father through him. **The word of the Lord.**

RESPONSE: The Lord is kind and merciful.

PSALM 138

I give you thanks, O LORD,
with my whole heart;
before the gods I sing your praise. **R.**

I bow down toward your holy temple
and give thanks to your name for your steadfast love
and your faithfulness;
for you have exalted your name
and your word above everything. **R.**

On the day I called, you answered me,

you increased my strength of soul.
All the kings of the earth shall praise you, O LORD,
for they have heard the words of your mouth.
They shall sing of the ways of the LORD,
for great is the glory of the LORD. **R.**

ALLELUIA: Go home and proclaim the Good News to all; tell them what God has done for you.

GOSPEL: MARK 5:18–20

A reading from the holy Gospel according to Mark

As [Jesus] was getting into the boat, the man who had been possessed by demons begged him that he might be with him. But Jesus refused, and said to him, "Go home to your friends, and tell them how much the Lord has done for you, and what mercy he has shown you." And he went away and began to proclaim in the Decapolis how much Jesus had done for him; and everyone was amazed. **The Gospel of the Lord.**

FRANCISCAN READINGS

ASSISI COMPILATION 5

Francis' blessing of Assisi as he is carried to St. Mary of the Porziuncola

Francis, realizing that he was getting sicker by the day, had himself carried on a litter to the church of Saint Mary of the Porziuncola. ... Raising himself up slightly on the litter, he blessed the city of Assisi. "Lord," he said, "just as I believe that at an earlier time this city was the abode of wicked and evil men, with a bad reputation throughout all this region; so now I realize that, because of Your abundant mercy and in Your own time, You have shown an abundance of mercies to it. Now it has become the abode of those who acknowledge

You, give glory to Your name, offer the fragrance of good life, doctrine, and good reputation to the whole Christian people. I ask you, therefore, Lord Jesus Christ, Father of mercies, not to consider our ingratitude. May it always be mindful of the abundant mercies which You have shown to it, that it always be an abode for those who acknowledge You, and glorify Your name blessed and glorious throughout the ages. Amen."

After saying these things, he was carried to Saint Mary of the Porziuncola.

CIAÒ FRANCESCO

Ciaò Francesco of Assisi
whose bloody footprints in winter
(like carnelians cast upon snow)
can still disrupt Assisi ...

Ciaò Francesco of the Porziuncola
that blessed door too narrow
for me to enter, but led by you
I asked three things ...

Ciaò Francesco of San Damiano
who led me along that same
road of renunciation
(while the silver olive trees wept)
and showed me that we
leave all our fathers ...

Ciaò Francesco of the Carceri
whose food was to do the
will of God, and when I
saw this—too true—I ran
all the way down Mount Subasio ...

Ciaò Francesco of the Chiesa Nuova

your lively friar-son showed me
the prison where your father
tried to keep you and then
sensing my sins he let down
his cape for me to walk on
—this still hurts ...

Ciaò Francesco who fought the devils
and guarded my own room with
Leo's cherished blessing—while the
shutters rattled from the nightmare
howls, and the dark dreams
threatened to turn me back ...

Ciaò Francesco of La Verna
(my dearest home)
you climbed those rocks
to bemoan your sins and
left that mountain so transfigured,
so holy, that in that place
I could scarcely breathe ...

Ciaò Francesco of the Basilica
your body is the Feast of Fools,
parades, endless masses, cameras, dances,
songs, candles, and those weeping
because they have put you so high,
we can't even touch you
for healing anymore ...

Ciaò Francesco wounded-winter light
you are stricken with love
by God's smallest creatures ...
Ciaò Francesco of the Via Crucis
winter in Assisi is more harsh, silent
and bitter than I ever imagined,
and as I complained and nagged you

for comfort, you walked with me,
(like Jesus at Emmaus, wounds aglow)
and taught me the grace of
compassion ...

Ciaò Francesco of Assisi,
guide books, tapestries, and paintings
say you are dead,
but you still lead
the angels in song
at the Little Portion.

CIAÒ CHIARA

Ciaò Chiara of San Damiano
you led me up stone stairs
to the upper room and unbolted
the door to ancient visions,
and showed me how love

and the Holy Eucharist
put invaders to flight ...

Ciaò Chiara, Lady Poverty,
you are on display as some
venerable mummy;
your skeleton still observing
stark humility and holy poverty ...

Ciaò Chiara who cried the Passion
every day (hope against hope)
and who bathed our father's
wounds and kissed them when
he went home ...

Ciaò Chiara di Favarone
the Spirit hovers in the mist

outside your basilica and
sits like manna on the olive trees
and the Spirit and the Bride say:
"God is enough."

Both poems written by William Hart McNichols, S.J., S.F.O. Used with
permission.

CLOSING RITUAL
FOR FRANCISCAN PILGRIMAGE

SONG: G 4 "City of God," verse 1 and refrain

READING: ADAPTED FROM *LIVING THE INCARNATION*

[Clare] and Francis considered it a corollary of being brother
and sister that they only took what they needed from the soil;
after that, it must be left to sing its own song about the glory
of God. They were not addicted to "usefulness" and had no
problem with tracts of land not being productive. Wild flowers,
butterflies, and mice shared the world with Friars and Poor
Ladies. ... Francis sensitively discerned the hidden nature of
things; ... [Clare knew] that God is in everything, the source
and origin which we all share. [It was their] contemplative
stance, or attitude, which accepted and honored the
individuality of each creation, open to know it in its depths
and eager to learn about God from everything that is made.

[It was their awareness of shared beginnings which made them
brother and sister to all.] [T]he hallmark of true prayer appears,
not in ecstasy or rapture, but in daily life. In their daily life,
[Francis and Clare] were always open to the mystery of God
present in their midst. God was around them like the air, and
no matter how preoccupied their minds, their hearts were
aware; ... They never ceased to adore and be amazed ... by the
music within them playing in harmony with the music they

heard around them. ... They were brother and sister to everything and everyone, and as they lived this out in daily life, Clare and Francis worshipped the God who is Father and Mother of all that is.

Sister Frances Teresa, O.S.C. *Living the Incarnation* [Quincy, Ill.: Franciscan Press, 1996], 91–93. Used with permission.

RESPONSE

All:
Go home to your family and make it clear to them how much God's mercy has done for you.

One:
Because you are God's chosen ones, holy and beloved, clothe yourselves with heartfelt mercy, with kindness, humility, meekness, and patience.

All:
Go home to your family and make it clear to them how much God's mercy has done for you.

One:
Bear with one another. Forgive as God has forgiven you. Over all these virtues put on love, which binds the rest together and makes them perfect.

All:
Go home to your family and make it clear to them how much God's mercy has done for you.

One:
Christ's peace must reign in your hearts, since as members of the one body, you have been called to that peace. Dedicate yourselves to thankfulness.

All:

Go home to your family and make it clear to them how much God's mercy has done for you.

One:
Let the word of Christ, rich as it is, dwell in you. In wisdom made perfect, instruct and admonish one another. Sing gratefully to God from your hearts in psalms, hymns, and inspired songs.

All:
Go home to your family and make it clear to them how much God's mercy has done for you.

One:
Whatever you do, whether in speech or in action, do it in the name of the Lord Jesus. Give thanks to God through Him.

All:
Go home to your family and make it clear to them how much God's mercy has done for you.

SONG: G 4, verse 2 and refrain

RITUAL OF SENDING FORTH

The Tau has its roots as a symbol in the Hebrew Scriptures, particularly the book of Ezekiel: "Go through the city, through Jerusalem, and put a mark on the foreheads of those who sigh and groan over all the abominations that are committed in it" (Ez 9:4).

Moreover, the last letter of the Hebrew alphabet represented the fulfillment of the entire revealed word of God.
Francis would have heard the Tau proclaimed as a symbol of a "triple Passover renewal" in the church by Innocent III at the Fourth Lateran Council. The Crusaders were to bear this emblem, and Innocent encouraged them to be "champions of the Tau."

The Brothers of St. Anthony the Hermit, who cared for lepers, also wore this sign.

So Francis adopted it as his own symbol for willingness to be in continuous conversion of heart. Francis told his brothers that their religious habit was in the same shape as the Tau, meaning that they were called to be "walking crucifixes," models of a compassionate God and examples of faithfulness until their dying days.

RITUAL PRESENTATION OF THE TAU

Each pilgrim approaches a staff member and receives the symbol with appropriate words of commissioning.

SONG: G 4, verse 4 and refrain

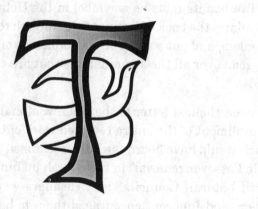

MUSIC

FRANCISCAN PILGRIMAGE PROGRAMS

MUSIC TABLE OF CONTENTS

MASS SETTINGS

OTHER EUCHARISTIC PROCLAMATIONS

SONGS OF FRANCIS

See also:

SONGS OF CLARE

See also:

CHRISTMAS MUSIC

E 1

Kyrie

Cantus Missae

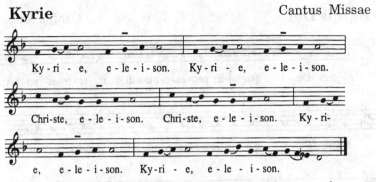

Ky - ri - e, e - le - i - son. Ky - ri - e, e - le - i - son.

Chri - ste, e - le - i - son. Chri - ste, e - le - i - son. Ky - ri -

e, e - le - i - son. Ky - ri - e, e - le - i - son.

E 2

Sanctus

Cantus Missae

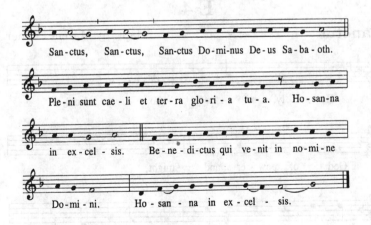

San - ctus, San - ctus, San - ctus Do - mi - nus De - us Sa - ba - oth.

Ple - ni sunt cae - li et ter - ra glo - ri - a tu - a. Ho - san - na

in ex - cel - sis. Be - ne - di - ctus qui ve - nit in no - mi - ne

Do - mi - ni. Ho - san - na in ex - cel - sis.

E 3

Agnus Dei

Cantus Missae

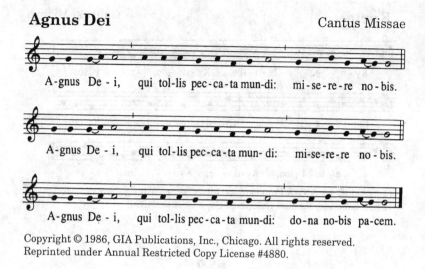

A-gnus De - i,   qui tol-lis pec-ca-ta mun-di: mi-se-re-re no-bis.

A-gnus De - i,   qui tol-lis pec-ca-ta mun- di: mi-se-re-re no-bis.

A-gnus De - i,   qui tol-lis pec-ca-ta mun-di: do-na no-bis pa-cem.

E 4

Sanctus

Adapt. by Marcia Pruner

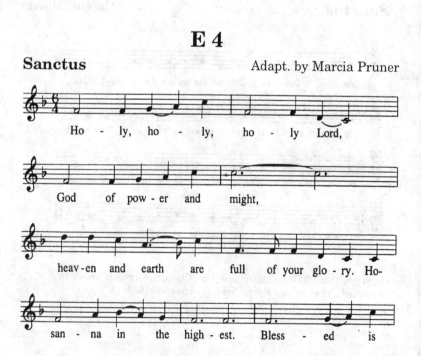

Ho - ly, ho - ly, ho - ly Lord,

God   of pow - er   and   might,

heav - en and earth   are   full   of your glo - ry. Ho-

san - na   in   the   high - est.   Bless - ed   is

...Sanctus

he who comes in the name of the Lord. Ho - san - na in the high - est, ho - san - na in the high - est.

E 5

Memorial Acclamation   Adapt. by Richard Proulx

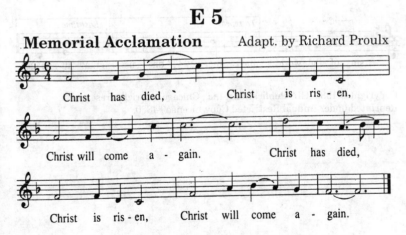

Christ has died, Christ is ris - en, Christ will come a - gain. Christ has died, Christ is ris - en, Christ will come a - gain.

E 6

Amen

Adapt. by Richard Proulx

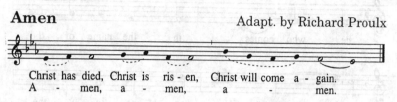

Christ has died, Christ is ris - en, Christ will come a - gain.
A - men, a - men, a - men.

E 7

Agnus Dei

David Clark Isele

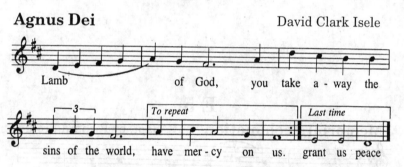

Lamb of God, you take a - way the

sins of the world, have mer - cy on us. grant us peace

E 8

Sanctus Marty Haugen

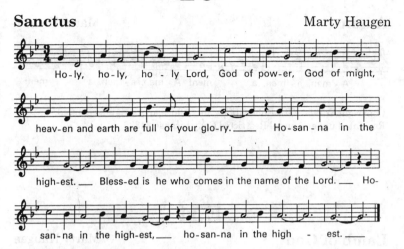

Ho-ly, ho-ly, ho-ly Lord, God of pow-er, God of might, heav-en and earth are full of your glo-ry. ___ Ho-san-na in the high-est. ___ Bless-ed is he who comes in the name of the Lord. ___ Ho-san-na in the high-est, ___ ho-san-na in the high - est. ___

E 9

Memorial Acclamation Marty Haugen

Christ has died, Christ is ris-en, Christ will come a - gain.

E 10

Amen

Marty Haugen

A - men, a - men, a - men! A - men, a - men, a - men!

E 11

Lamb of God

Marty Haugen

Cantor/Choir — All

1. Je-sus, Lamb of God; ____
2. Je-sus, Bread of Life; ____
*3. Je-sus, Prince of Peace; ____
} you take a-way the sins of the

(Repeat as needed)

world, ____ have mer - cy on __ us.

Final

world: grant us your __ peace.

E 12

Holy ("St. Louis Jesuits")

Robert Dufford, SJ
and Daniel Schutte

Ho-ly, ho-ly, ho-ly Lord, God of pow'r and might.

Heav-en and earth are_ full of your glo - ry. Ho - san-na, ho -

san-na on high.____ Bless-ed is he who comes in the

name of the Lord. Ho - san - na in the high - est. Ho -

san - na in the high-est. Ho-san-na, ho-san-na on high.____

E 13

Memorial Acclamation C ("St. Louis Jesuits")

Robert Dufford, SJ
and Daniel Schutte

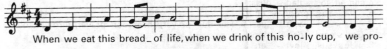

When we eat this bread_ of life, when we drink of this ho-ly cup, we pro-

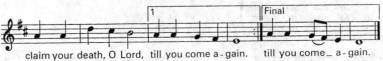

claim your death, O Lord, till you come a-gain. till you come_ a-gain.

E 14

Amen ("St. Louis Jesuits")

Robert Dufford, SJ

A - men, al-le-lu - ia, for - ev - er and_ ev - er, for - ev - er, al-le - lu - ia, for-ev-er and ev-er. A-men. ___

E 15

Jesus, Lamb of God

Bernadette Farrell

1. Je - sus, Lamb of God, bear - er of our sin;
2. Je - sus, Lamb of God, bear - er of our pain;
3. Je - sus, Lamb of God, bro - ken as our bread,
4. Je - sus, Lamb of God, poured out as our wine,
5. Je - sus, Word of God, dwell - ing with the poor;
6. Je - sus, Word of God, dwell - ing in our midst;
7. Je - sus, Word of God, speak - ing in our hearts
8. Je - sus, Word made flesh, touch - ing each one's need;
9. Kneel - ing by your friends, wash - ing each one's feet;
10. Hope be - yond de - spair, dawn of frag - ile light;
11. Tomb of se - cret hope, o - pen to the dawn;

REFRAIN: All

1. Je - sus, Sav - ior:
2. Je - sus, heal - er:
3. here a - mong us:
4. shared in glad - ness:
5. Je - sus, proph - et:
6. Je - sus with us:
7. God's com - pas - sion:
8. Je - sus, lov - er:
9. Je - sus, ser - vant:
10. Je - sus, ris - en:
11. Je - sus, liv - ing:

Hear our prayer, hear our prayer; through this

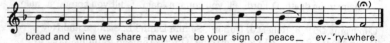

bread and wine we share may we be your sign of peace_ ev - 'ry-where.

E 16

Holy, Holy

Jan Michael Joncas

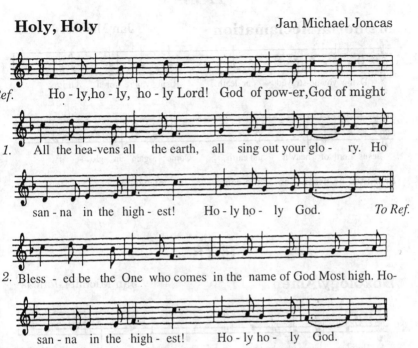

Ref. Ho - ly, ho - ly, ho - ly Lord! God of pow-er, God of might

1. All the hea-vens all the earth, all sing out your glo - ry. Ho

san - na in the high - est! Ho - ly ho - ly God. *To Ref.*

2. Bless - ed be the One who comes in the name of God Most high. Ho-

san - na in the high - est! Ho - ly ho - ly God.

Reprinted by permission of the composer, Jan Michael Joncas.

E 17

Memorial Acclamation Jan Michael Joncas

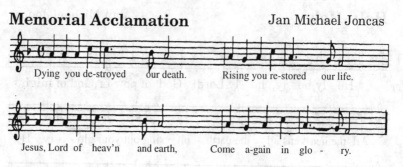

Dying you de-stroyed our death. Rising you re-stored our life.

Jesus, Lord of heav'n and earth, Come a-gain in glo - ry.

Reprinted by permission of the composer, Jan Michael Joncas.

E 18

Doxology/Amen Jan Michael Joncas

Through him with him and in him in un-ion with the Spi - rit, all

praise be to the Fa - ther, for ev - er. Amen.

Reprinted by permission of the composer, Jan Michael Joncas.

E 30

Alleluia A. Gregory Murray OSB

Al - le - lu - ia, al - le - lu - ia, al - le - lu - ia.

E 31

Alleluia

Howard Hughes, SM

Cantor: Al - le - lu - ia. Assembly: Al - le - lu - ia. Cantor: Al - le - lu - ia.

Assembly: Al - le - lu - ia. Cantor: Al - le - lu - ia. Assembly: Al - le - lu - ia.

E 32

Alleluia

William H. Monk

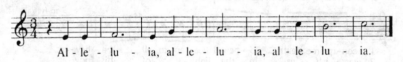

Al - le - lu - ia, al - le - lu - ia, al - le - lu - ia.

E 33

Celtic Alleluia

Fintan O'Carroll,
Christopher Walker

E 40

Christ has Died, Alleluia

Joe Wise

Christ has died, al-le-lu-ia. Christ is ris-en, al-le-lu-ia. Christ will come a-gain, al-le-lu-ia, al-le-lu-ia.

E 41

Jesus Christ Has Died

Tune - African
American Spiritual

Je-sus Christ has died, Je-sus Christ is ri-sen Je-sus Christ will come a-gain. Oh deep in my heart, I do be-lieve, that Je-sus Christ will come a-gain.

E 42

Keep In Mind

Lucien Deiss, CSSp

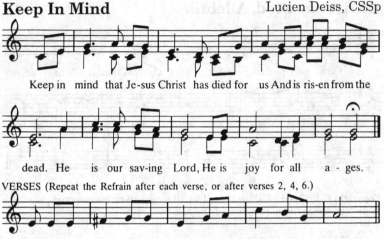

Keep in mind that Je-sus Christ has died for us And is ris-en from the

dead. He   is our sav-ing Lord, He is   joy for all   a - ges.

VERSES (Repeat the Refrain after each verse, or after verses 2, 4, 6.)

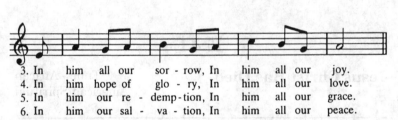

1. __ If   we   die with the   Lord, We   shall live with the   Lord.
2. If we en - dure with the   Lord, We   shall reign with the   Lord.

3. In   him   all our   sor - row, In   him   all our   joy.
4. In   him   hope of   glo - ry, In   him   all our   love.
5. In   him   our re - demp - tion, In   him   all our   grace.
6. In   him   our sal - va - tion, In   him   all our   peace.

E 43

We Remember

Marty Haugen

REFRAIN

We re-mem-ber how you loved us ___ to your death,   and still we

cel-e-brate, for you are with us here; ___   And we be-lieve_ that we will

...We Remember How You Loved Us

see you __ when you come in your glo-ry, Lord. __ We re-mem-ber, __

__ we cel-e-brate, we be-lieve. __ *Fine*

Ps 16

Center of My Life

Tune and refrain text: Paul Inwood
Text for verses: The Grail

O Lord, you are the cen-ter of my life: I will al-ways praise you,

1-3 to Verses | **Final** *Fine*

I will al-ways serve you, I will al-ways keep you in my sight. 1. (⅄) sight.
2. (⅄)
3. And

...Center of My Life

VERSES 1-3:

1. Keep me safe, O God___ I take ref-uge in you.__ I say to the
2. I will bless the Lord who gives me coun - sel, ____ who ev - en at
3. So my heart re - joic - es, my soul is glad; ___ (7) ev - en in

1. Lord, "You are my God._____ My hap - pi - ness _____
2. night di - rects my heart.___ I keep___ the Lord____
3. safe - ty shall my bod-y rest. For you will not leave___ my

to Refrain

1. lies in you a - lone; my hap-pi-ness ____ lies in you a - lone."_
2. ev - er in my sight: since he is at my right_hand,_ I shall stand firm.
3. soul a-mong the dead, nor let_ your be-lov-ed know de-cay. _____

VERSE 4:

4. You will show_me the path of life,_ the full-ness of joy_ in your pres-ence,_

to Refrain

Ps 19

Lord, You Have the Words

David Haas

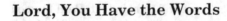

Lord, you have the words ____ of ev - er-last - ing life.

VERSE 1

1. The law of the Lord is per-fect, re-fresh-ing the soul; the

to Refrain

1. Lord's rule is to be trust-ed, the sim - ple find wis-dom. _____

...Lord You Have the Words

VERSE 2

2. The fear of the Lord is ho-ly, a-bid-ing for ev-er;__

2. the de-crees of the Lord are true, all of them just._____ *to Refrain*

VERSE 3

3. The pre-cepts of the Lord are right, __ they glad-den the

3. heart, the com-mand of the Lord is clear, giv-ing light to the eye.__ *to Refrain*

VERSE 4

4. They are worth more than gold, than the fin - est gold, __

4. sweet-er than hon-ey, than hon-ey from the comb._____ *to Refrain*

Ps 23
My Shepherd Is the Lord

Joseph Gelineau

Ps 23

Shepherd Me, O God

Marty Haugen

REFRAIN

Shep-herd me, O God, be-yond my wants, be-yond my fears, from

death in - to life. _____ life.

VERSES 1-3

1. God is my shep-herd, so noth-ing shall I want, I
2. Gen - tly you raise me and heal my wea - ry soul, you
3. Though I should wan-der the val - ley of death, I

1. rest in the mead-ows of faith - ful - ness and love, I
2. lead me by path-ways of right-eous-ness and truth, my
3. fear no e - vil, for you are at my side, your

1. walk by the qui - et wa - ters of peace._____
2. spir - it shall sing the mu - sic of your Name._____
3. rod and your staff, my com-fort and my hope._____

...Shepherd Me, O God

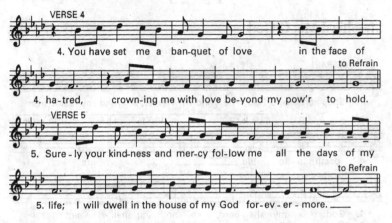

VERSE 4

4. You have set me a ban-quet of love in the face of

to Refrain

4. ha-tred, crown-ing me with love be-yond my pow'r to hold.

VERSE 5

5. Sure-ly your kind-ness and mer-cy fol-low me all the days of my

to Refrain

5. life; I will dwell in the house of my God for-ev-er-more. _____

Ps 25

To You, O Lord

Marty Haugen

Refrain

To you, O Lord, I lift my soul, to you, I lift my soul.

Verses

1. Lord, make me know your ways, teach me your paths
   and keep me in the way of your truth, for you are God, my Savior.

2. For the Lord is good and righteous, revealing the way to those who wander,
   gently leading the poor and the humble.

3. To the ones who seek the Lord, who look to God's word, who live God's love,
   God will always be near, and will show them mercy.

Ps 25

I Lift Up My Soul

Timothy Manion

REFRAIN: 1st time: Cantor, All repeat; thereafter: All

Fine

To you, Yah-weh, I lift up my soul, O my God.

VERSES 1, 3: Cantor/Choir

1. Yah - weh, show your ways to me.
3. All day long I hope in your good-ness. Re -

1. Teach me your paths, and keep me in the ways of your
3. mem - ber your love, the love that you prom-ised long a -

1. truth, for you are the God that
3. go, and the kind-ness that you gave from of

1. saves me.
3. old.

to Refrain

VERSE 2: Cantor/Choir

2. The Lord is so good, so ho - ly; sin-ners find the

2. way, and in all that is right he guides the hum-ble. The

2. poor he leads in his path-ways.

to Refrain

Ps 63

As Morning Breaks

Michael Joncas

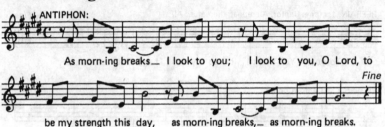

ANTIPHON:

As morn-ing breaks__ I look to you; I look to you, O Lord, to

be my strength this day, as morn-ing breaks,__ as morn-ing breaks.

1. O God, you are my God,
     for you I long;
   for you my soul is thirsting.
   My body pines for you
   like a dry, weary land
     without water.
   So I gaze on you in your
     holy place
   to see your strength and
     your glory. ℟.

2. For your love is better than life,
   my lips will speak your praise.
   So I will bless you all my life,

in your name I will lift up
     my hands.
My soul shall be filled as with
     a banquet,
my mouth shall praise you
     with joy. ℟.

3. On my bed I remember you.
   On you I muse through the night
   for you have been my help;
   in the shadow of your wings
     I rejoice.
   My soul clings to you;
   your right hand holds me fast. ℟.

Ps 84

How Lovely Is Your Dwelling Place

Michael Joncas

Ps 100

**All the Earth
Proclaim the Lord**

Lucien Deiss, CSSp

REFRAIN

All the earth, pro - claim the Lord. Sing your praise to God.

VERSES

1. Serve you the Lord, heart filled with glad - ness. Come
2. Know that the Lord is our cre - a - tor. Yes,
3. We are the sheep of his green pas - ture, For
4. En - ter his gates bring - ing thanks - giv - ing, O
5. Our Lord is good, his love en - dur - ing, His
6. Hon - or and praise be to the Fa - ther, The

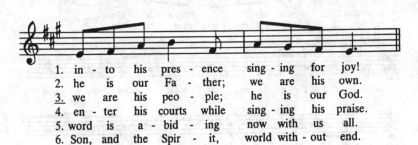

1. in - to his pres - ence sing - ing for joy!
2. he is our Fa - ther; we are his own.
3. we are his peo - ple; he is our God.
4. en - ter his courts while sing - ing his praise.
5. word is a - bid - ing now with us all.
6. Son, and the Spir - it, world with - out end.

Ps 103

The Lord Is Kind and Merciful

Marty Haugen

Refrain

The Lord is kind and mer-ci-ful, the
Lord is kind and mer-ci-ful.

Verse 1 *mf*

1. Bless the Lord, O my soul, and all my be-ing
bless his name; bless the Lord, and forget not his ben-e-fits. *rit.* **To refrain**

Verse 2 *mp*

2. He par-dons all your in-iq-ui-ties, and com-forts your
sor-rows, re-deems your life from de-struc-tion and
crowns you with his kind-ness. **To refrain**

...The Lord Is Kind and Merciful

Verse 3

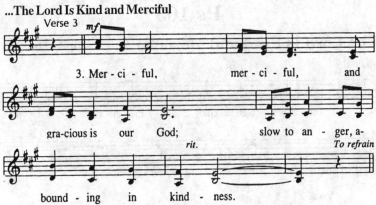

3. Mer - ci - ful, mer - ci - ful, and

gra-cious is our God; slow to an - ger, a-

rit.

To refrain

bound - ing in kind - ness.

Ps 122

We Shall Go Up With Joy

Joseph Gelineau

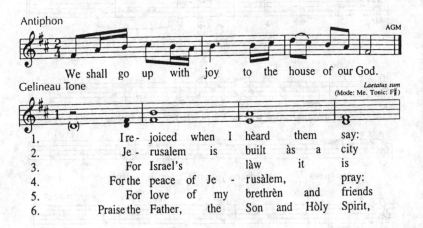

Antiphon

AGM

We shall go up with joy to the house of our God.

Gelineau Tone

Laetatus sum
(Mode: Me. Tonic: F♯)

1.	I re -	joiced when I	hèard	them	say:
2.	Je -	rusalem is	built	às a	city
3.	For Israel's		làw	it	is
4.	For the	peace of Je -	rusàlem,		pray:
5.	For	love of my	brethrèn	and	friends
6.	Praise the	Father, the	Son	and Hòly	Spirit,

...We Shall Go Up With Joy

1. "Let us go tó God's house."
2. stronglý com - pact.
3. there to praise thé Lord's name.
4. "Peace be tó your homes!
5. I say: "Peace úpon you!"
6. both now ánd for ever,

1. And now our fèet are standing
2. It is there that the trìbes go up,
3. There were set the thrònes of judgment
4. May peace reign ìn your walls,
5. For love of the house òf the Lord
6. the God who is, who was and ìs to come

1. within your gates, Ó Je - rusa - lem.
2. the tribes óf the [————————————] Lord.
3. of the hóuse of Da - vid.
4. in your paláces, [————————————] peace!"
5. I will ask fór your [————————————] good.
6. at the end óf the a - ges.

Ps 145

I Will Praise Your Name

David Haas

Refrain

I will praise your name, my King and my God.

I will praise your name, my King and my God.

G 1

Ave Maria

Gregory Norbet

G 2

Be Not Afraid

Robert Dufford, SJ

VERSE 1

1. You shall cross the bar-ren des-ert, __ but you shall not die of
1. thirst. You shall wan-der far in safe-ty__ though you do not know the
1. way. You shall speak your words in for-eign lands and all will un-der-
1. stand. You shall see the face of God and live. _____

to Refrain

REFRAIN

Be not __ a-fraid. I go be-fore you al-ways. Come fol-low
me, __ and I will give you rest. __

1, 2 to Vss 2, 3 | Final 2 Fine

VERSE 2

2. If you pass through rag-ing wa-ters in the sea, ____ you shall not
2. drown. If you walk a-mid the burn-ing flames, you shall not be
2. harmed. If you stand be-fore the pow'r of hell and death is at your
2. side, know that I am with you _____ through it all. ____

to Refrain

G 3

Christ Be Our Light

Bernadette Farrell

VERSES

1. Long - ing for light, ____ we wait in dark - ness.
2. Long - ing for peace, ____ our world is trou - bled.
3. Long - ing for food, ____ man - y are hun - gry.
4. Long - ing for shel - ter, man - y are home - less.
5. Man - y the gifts, ____ man - y the peo - ple,

1. Long - ing for truth, ____ we turn to you.
2. Long - ing for hope, ____ man - y de - spair.
3. Long - ing for wa - ter, man - y still thirst.
4. Long - ing for warmth, ____ man - y are cold.
5. man - y the hearts that yearn to be - long.

1. Make us your own, ____ your ho - ly peo - ple,
2. Your word a - lone ____ has pow'r to save us.
3. Make us your bread, ____ bro - ken for oth - ers,
4. Make us your build - ing, shel - ter - ing oth - ers,
5. Let us be ser - vants to one an - oth - er,

1. light for the world to see. ____
2. Make us your liv - ing voice. ____
3. shared un - til all are fed. ____
4. walls made of liv - ing stone. ____
5. mak - ing your king - dom come. ____

REFRAIN

Christ, be our light! Shine in our hearts.

Shine through the dark - ness. Christ, be our light!

Shine in your church gath - ered to - day. ____

G 4

City of God

Daniel Schutte

VERSES 1, 2

1. A-wake from your slum-ber! __ A - rise from your
2. We are sons of the morn-ing; __ we are daugh-ters of

1. sleep! A new day is dawn-ing __ for all those who weep.
2. day. The One who has loved us __ has bright-ened our way.

1. The peo - ple in dark-ness __ have seen a great light. The
2. The Lord of all kind-ness __ has called us to be a

1. Lord of our long-ing __ has con-quered the night. __
2. light for his peo - ple __ to set their hearts free. __

REFRAIN

Let us build the cit-y __ of God. May our tears be

turned in - to danc - ing! For the Lord, our light and our

Fine

love, _____ has turned __ the night in - to day!

VERSE 3

3. God _____ is light; _____ in him there is no dark-ness.

3. Let us walk _____ in his light, _____ his chil - dren,

3. one and all. _____ O com-fort my

...City of God

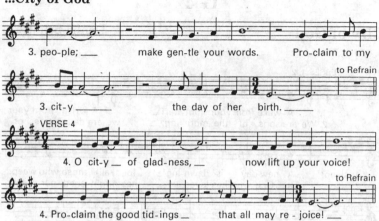

3. peo-ple; ___ make gen-tle your words. Pro-claim to my

to Refrain

3. cit-y _____ the day of her birth. _____

VERSE 4

4. O cit-y __ of glad-ness, __ now lift up your voice!

to Refrain

4. Pro-claim the good tid-ings __ that all may re - joice! __

G 5

Come and Journey With Me
David Haas

1. Come to the song, come to the dance. Bring all you are.

Bring all you be. Come with your voice, come with your heart

Come and Jour - ney with me.

Come and Jour - ney with me.

2. Come let the sun fill up your eyes. Take the time.

...Come and Journey With Me

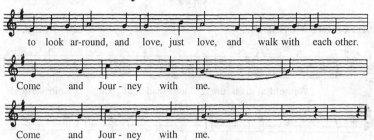

to look ar-round, and love, just love, and walk with each other.

Come and Jour-ney with me.

Come and Jour-ney with me.

G 6

Drink Living Water

Colleen Fulmer and
Rufino Zaragoza, OFM

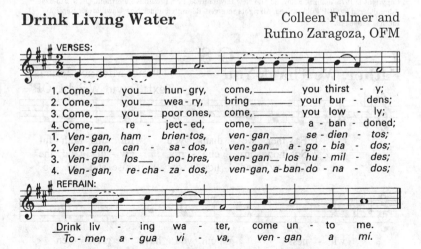

VERSES:

1. Come,__ you__ hun-gry, come,_____ you thirst - y;
2. Come,__ you__ wea-ry, bring_____ your bur - dens;
3. Come,__ you__ poor ones, come,_____ you low - ly;
4. Come,__ re - ject-ed, come,_____ a - ban - doned;
1. Ven-gan, ham - brien-tos, ven-gan____ se - dien - tos;
2. Ven-gan, can - sa-dos, ven-gan__ a - go - bia - dos;
3. Ven-gan los__ po-bres, ven-gan__ los hu - mil - des;
4. Ven-gan, re-cha - za-dos, ven-gan, a-ban-do - na - dos;

REFRAIN:

Drink liv - ing wa - ter, come un - to me.
To - men a - gua vi - va, ven - gan a mí.

G 7

Earthen Vessels

John Foley, SJ

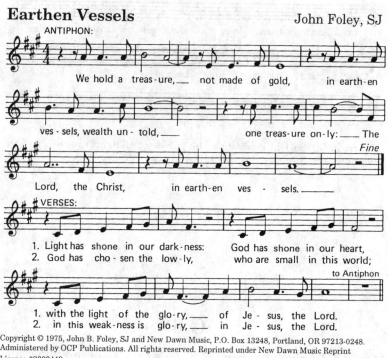

ANTIPHON:

We hold a treas-ure,___ not made of gold, in earth-en ves-sels, wealth un-told,___ one treas-ure on-ly:___ The

Fine

Lord, the Christ, in earth-en ves - sels.___

VERSES:

1. Light has shone in our dark-ness: God has shone in our heart,
2. God has cho-sen the low-ly, who are small in this world;

to Antiphon

1. with the light of the glo-ry,___ of Je - sus, the Lord.
2. in this weak-ness is glo-ry,___ in Je - sus, the Lord.

G 8

Father, We Thank You

Tune: Michael Joncas
Text: David Wright, OP

1. Fa - ther, we thank you for this faith - ful wit - ness
2. So now in cho - rus, giv - ing God the glo - ry,
3. Glo - ry and hon - or, praise and ad - o - ra - tion,

1. Whom you have giv - en
2. We sing his/her prais - es,
3. To you we of - fer,

...Father, We Thank You

ho - li - ness and wis - dom; For this we
tell - ing of his/her teach - ing, That in his/her
Fa - ther, Son, and Spir - it. Teach us to

praise you, source of light and know - ledge,
tri - umph we may be par - tak - ers
fol - low what in life s/he taught us,

Lord God al - might - y.
Here and here - af - ter.
Lord God al - might - y.

G 9

Food for the Journey

Colleen Fulmer and
Rufino Zaragoza, OFM

REFRAIN: All

Food for the jour-ney flows from a love di - vine;

1-7 to Verses | Final Fine

Je-sus, bro-ken liv-ing bread, Je-sus, out-poured wine. wine.

VERSES: Cantor

1. As manna fell from the starry heaven
   behold, my bread for you, my chosen, my beloved. (to Refrain)

2. I am the bread of life; whoever believes in me
   will never thirst again. All who come will never hunger. (to Refrain)

...Food for the Journey

3. I long to hold you through all pain, nourish you along the uphill road;
so I entrust this simple food, my own self I give to you. **(to Refrain)**

4. Each broken life is called to form this body,
this sacred cup all share; I laden with the outcast. **(to Refrain)**

5. Come, my people who gather as one;
feed on my love, then go forth and feed the world. **(to Refrain)**

6. My body broken, my blood shed, goes before you showing the way.
Give of your body, risk your blood, that the kingdom of God may
reign. **(to Refrain)**

7. In all the poor perceive this humble banquet;
and the lowly shall arise to guide you on your journey. **(to Refrain)**

G 10

Gather Us In

Marty Haugen

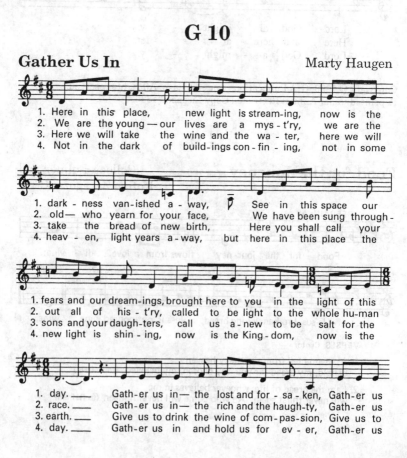

1. Here in this place, new light is stream-ing, now is the
2. We are the young — our lives are a mys-t'ry, we are the
3. Here we will take the wine and the wa-ter, here we will
4. Not in the dark of build-ings con-fin-ing, not in some

1. dark-ness van-ished a-way, See in this space our
2. old— who yearn for your face, We have been sung through-
3. take the bread of new birth, Here you shall call your
4. heav-en, light years a-way, but here in this place the

1. fears and our dream-ings, brought here to you in the light of this
2. out all of his-t'ry, called to be light to the whole hu-man
3. sons and your daugh-ters, call us a-new to be salt for the
4. new light is shin-ing, now is the King-dom, now is the

1. day. ____ Gath-er us in— the lost and for-sa-ken, Gath-er us
2. race. ____ Gath-er us in— the rich and the haugh-ty, Gath-er us
3. earth. ____ Give us to drink the wine of com-pas-sion, Give us to
4. day. ____ Gath-er us in and hold us for ev-er, Gath-er us

...Gather Us In

1. in— the blind and the lame;   Call to us now, and   we shall a-
2. in— the proud and the strong;   Give us a heart so   meek and so
3. eat   the bread that is   you;   Nour-ish us well, and   teach us to
4. in   and make us your own;   Gath-er us in— all   peo-ples to-

1. wa-ken,   we shall a-rise at the   sound of our   name. ___
2. low-ly,   give us the cour-age to   en-ter the   song. ___
3. fash-ion   lives that are ho-ly and   hearts that are   true. ___
4. geth-er,   fire ___ of love in our   flesh and our   bone. ___

G 11

Gift of Finest Wheat

Text: Omer Westendorf
Refrain: Robert E. Kreutz

You sat-is-fy the hun-gry heart With

gift of fin-est wheat; Come, give to us, O

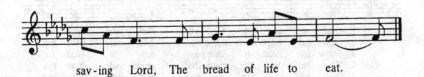

sav-ing Lord, The bread of life to eat.

...Gift of Finest Wheat

1. As when the shep - herd calls his sheep, They
2. With joy - ful lips we sing to you Our
3. Is not the cup we bless and share The
4. The mys - t'ry of your pres-ence, Lord, No
5. You give your-self to us, O Lord; Then

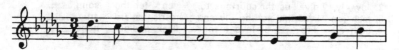

1. know and heed his voice; So when you call your
2. praise and grat - i - tude, That you should count us
3. blood of Christ out - poured? Do not one cup, one
4. mor - tal tongue can tell: Whom all the world can -
5. self - less let us be, To serve each oth - er

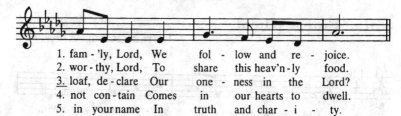

1. fam - 'ly, Lord, We fol - low and re - joice.
2. wor - thy, Lord, To share this heav'n - ly food.
3. loaf, de - clare Our one - ness in the Lord?
4. not con - tain Comes in our hearts to dwell.
5. in your name In truth and char - i - ty.

G 12

God of Day and God of Darkness

Text: Marty Haugen

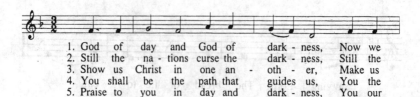

1. God of day and God of dark - ness, Now we
2. Still the na - tions curse the dark - ness, Still the
3. Show us Christ in one an - oth - er, Make us
4. You shall be the path that guides us, You the
5. Praise to you in day and dark - ness, You our

...God of Day and God of Darkness

stand be - fore the night; As the shad - ows stretch and
rich op - press the poor; Still the earth is bruised and
ser - vants strong and true; Give us all your love of
light that in us burns; Shin - ing deep with - in all
source and you our end; Praise to you who love and

deep - en, Come and make our dark - ness bright. All cre -
bro - ken By the ones who still want more. Come and
jus - tice So we do what you would do. Let us
peo - ple, Yours the love that we must learn, For our
nur - ture us As a fa - ther, moth - er, friend. Grant us

a - tion still is groan - ing For the dawn - ing of your
wake us from our sleep - ing, So our hearts can - not ig -
call all peo - ple ho - ly, Let us pledge our lives a -
hearts shall wan - der rest - less 'Til they safe to you re -
all a peace-ful rest - ing, Let each mind and bod - y

might, When the Sun of peace and jus - tice
nore All your peo - ple lost and bro - ken,
new, Make us one with all the low - ly,
turn; Find - ing you in one an - oth - er,
mend, So we rise re - freshed to - mor - row,

Fills the earth with ra - diant light.
All your chil - dren at our door.
Let us all be one in you.
We shall all your face dis - cern.
Hearts re - newed to King-dom tend.

G 13

God, You Are Good

Cathy Tisel Nelson

God, You are good,
God, You are love.
* Taste___ and see,
Taste___ and see.

You are the source of my joy!___
Feast on the good-ness of God!___

God, You are good,
God, You are love.
Taste___ and see.
Taste___ and see.

You are the source of my life!___
Feast on the good-ness of God!___

G 14

Heal Me, O God   Gregory Norbet

REFRAIN:

Heal me, O God; cre-ate a new heart in me. Save me, O God, with light of your pres-ence. Heal me, O God, and raise me to new life: you a-lone are my hope.

Fine

VERSES:

1. Deep in the night re-veal your wis-dom; teach me to live a life that is ho-ly.
2. Save me, O God; you are my ref-uge; put in my heart a faith strong and search-ing.
3. Be with me now, lift-ing each bur-den; you are my hope, my strength for the jour-ney.
4. As you have shown mer-cy and kind-ness, so may I grow in liv-ing com-pas-sion.
5. Strength-en my faith, melt my in-diff-'rence; set me a-fire with Spir-it's a-noint-ing.
6. Help me ex-tend peace and for-give-ness, know-ing so well my fail-ings for-giv-en.

to Refrain

G 15

Here I Am, Lord

Daniel Schutte

1. I, the Lord of sea and sky, I have heard my peo-ple cry.
2. I, the Lord of snow and rain, I have borne my peo-ple's pain.
3. I, the Lord of wind and flame, I will tend the poor and lame.

1. All who dwell in dark and sin my hand will save. I who
2. I have wept for love of them. They turn a - way. I will
3. I will set a feast for them. My hand will save. Fin-est

1. made the stars of night, I will make their dark - ness bright.
2. break their hearts of stone, give them hearts for love a - lone.
3. bread I will pro - vide till their hearts be sat - is - fied.

1. Who will bear my light to them? Whom shall I send?___
2. I will speak my word to them. Whom shall I send?___
3. I will give my life to them. Whom shall I send?___

REFRAIN: a tempo

Here I am, Lord.___ Is it I, Lord?___ I have heard you

call-ing in the night.___ I will go, Lord,___ if you

lead me.___ I will hold your peo-ple in my heart.___

G 16

How Great Thou Art

Text: Stuart K. Line

Vs 1: O Lord my God! When I in awesome wonder
Consider all the worlds thy hands have made.
I see the stars, I hear the rolling thunder,
Thy pow'r throughout the universe displayed,

REFRAIN
Then sings my soul, my Savior God to thee;
How great thou art, how great thou art!
Then sings my soul, my Savior God to thee;
How great thou art, how great thou art!

Vs 2: When through the woods and forest glades I wander
And hear the birds sing sweetly in the trees;
When I look down from lofty mountain grandeur
And hear the brook and feel the gentle breeze;

REFRAIN

Vs 3: And when I think that God, his Son not sparing,
Sent him to die, I scarce can take it in;
That on the cross, my burden gladly bearing,
He bled and died to take away my sin;

REFRAIN

Vs 4: When Christ shall come with shout of acclamation
And take me home, what joy shall fill my heart!
Then I shall bow in humble adoration
And there proclaim, my God how great thou art!

REFRAIN

G 17

In the Footprints of Jesus

Cathy Tisel Nelson

May we fol-low in the foot-prints of Je - sus Christ as we make our way — to You. In-ward-ly cleansed and en - light-ened, on fire with the Spir - it, may we

To Verses

fol - low in the foot-prints of Je - sus.

After final refrain

sus. May we fol-low in the foot-prints of Je - sus.

Verses:

1. Feed-ing the hun-gry, shelt-'ring the home-less, set-ting the pris-on-er free.
2. Friend to the strang-er, hope for the hope-less, car-ing for all those in need.
3. Sim-ple our liv-ing, few our pos-ses-sions, trust-ing in You for our needs.
4. With liv-ing wa-ters, You have re-freshed us; now we are filled with Your fire.
5. As we move for-ward in - to the fu-ture, led by Your Spir-it, O God,

To Refrain

1. Bring-ing Your jus-tice to all the earth, to all the earth, O God. *ritard*
2. Bring-ing Your jus-tice to all the earth, to all the earth, O God.
3. May we re-mem-ber how we are called to serve You all our days.
4. May we have cour-age, wis-dom and grace, to do Your will, O God.
5. Grant us a vis-ion, show us the way that brings us all to You.

G 18

Jesus, Remember Me

Music: Jacques Bertheir
(1923-1994)

Je-sus, re-mem-ber me when you come in-to your King-dom.

Je-sus, re-mem-ber me when you come in-to your King-dom.

G 19

Jubilate Deo

Gregory Norbet

1. Ju - bi - la - te De - o! Ju - bi - la - te De - o!
2. Peace of God, be in us, take a - way all dark - ness;
3. Light of God, be with us; shine for those de - spair - ing.
4. In all self - less serv - ing, with your Spir - it guid - ing,

1. Ju - bi - la - te De - o! Al - le - lu - ia!
2. seeds of love sow free - ly, ban - ish greed and hate.
3. Give them your com - pas - sion through our hands of care.
4. may your love bring heal - ing, ev - er faith - ful God.

G 20

Lord, You Have Come

Cesáreo Gabaráin, English
trans. by Robert C. Trupia

G 21

Lumen Christi

Gregory Norbet

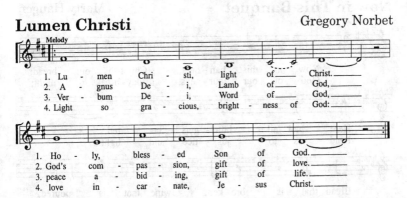

1. Lu - men Chri - sti, light of___ Christ.___
2. A - gnus De - i, Lamb of___ God,___
3. Ver - bum De - i, Word of___ God,___
4. Light so gra - cious, bright - ness of God:___

1. Ho - ly, bless - ed Son of God.___
2. God's com - pas - sion, gift of love.___
3. peace a - bid - ing, gift of life.___
4. love in - car - nate, Je - sus Christ.___

G 22

Magnificat

Music: Jacques Bertheir (1923-1994)

Ⓐ Ma - gni - fi - cat, ma - gni - fi - cat, Ⓑ Ma - gni - fi - cat a - ni - ma

me - a Do - mi - num. Ⓒ Ma - gni - fi - cat, ma - gni - fi - cat,

Ⓓ Ma - gni - fi - cat a - ni - ma me - a!

G 23

Now in This Banquet
Marty Haugen

Now in this ban-quet, Christ is our bread;
God of our jour-neys, day-break to night;

Here shall all hun-gers be fed.
Lead us to jus-tice and light.

Bread that is bro-ken, wine that is poured,
Grant us com-pas-sion, strength for the day,

Love is the sign of our Lord.
Wis - dom to walk in your way.

Verses 1, 2

1. You who have touched us and graced us with love,
2. Let our hearts burn with the fire of your love;

D.C.

make us your peo-ple of good-ness and light.
o - pen our eyes to the glo-ry of God.

G 24

Only This I Want
Daniel Schutte

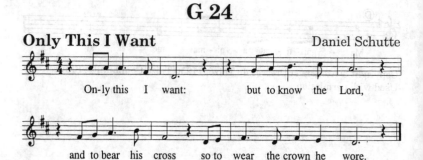

On-ly this I want: but to know the Lord,

and to bear his cross so to wear the crown he wore.

...Only This I Want

Verses

1. All but this is loss, worth-less ref-use to me,
2. I will run the race; I will fight the good fight,
3. Let your heart be glad, al - ways glad in the Lord,

D.C.

for to gain the Lord is to gain all I need.
so to win the prize of the King-dom of my Lord.
so to shine like stars in the dark-ness of the night.

G 25

Prayer of Peace

David Haas

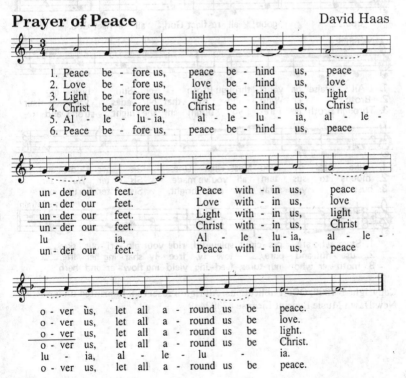

1. Peace be - fore us, peace be - hind us, peace
2. Love be - fore us, love be - hind us, love
3. Light be - fore us, light be - hind us, light
4. Christ be - fore us, Christ be - hind us, Christ
5. Al - le - lu - ia, al - le - lu - ia, al - le -
6. Peace be - fore us, peace be - hind us, peace

un - der our feet. Peace with - in us, peace
un - der our feet. Love with - in us, love
un - der our feet. Light with - in us, light
un - der our feet. Christ with - in us, Christ
lu - ia, Al - le - lu - ia, al - le -
un - der our feet. Peace with - in us, peace

o - ver us, let all a - round us be peace.
o - ver us, let all a - round us be love.
o - ver us, let all a - round us be light.
o - ver us, let all a - round us be Christ.
lu - ia, al - le - lu - ia.
o - ver us, let all a - round us be peace.

G 26

Sacred Creation

Rufino Zaragoza, OFM

REFRAIN:

Sa-cred the land, sa-cred the wa-ter, sa-cred the sky, ho-ly and true.

Sa-cred all life, sa-cred each oth-er; all re-flect God who is

1-3 to Verses | Final   Fine

good.____   good; all re-flect God, all re-flect God.

VERSES:

1. All praise be yours through Broth - er Sun, bear - ing a
2. Broth - er Wind and Air that per-vades, var - y their
3. Through Broth-er Fire you bright-en the night, strong and ro-

1. like - ness of you Most High One. Sis - ter Moon and
2. moods to sus - tain all you've made. Sis - ter Wa - ter,
3. bust yet play - ful and bright. Sis - ter Earth, our

to Refrain

1. Stars who are pre-cious, splen-did, ride your glo - ri - ous sky.____
2. use - ful and pure,____ low - ly, free - ly shar-ing her life.____
3. moth - er who nur-tures, feed-ing, yield-ing flow - er and herb.____

G 27

Salve Regina

Trans. by John C. Selner

...Salve Regina

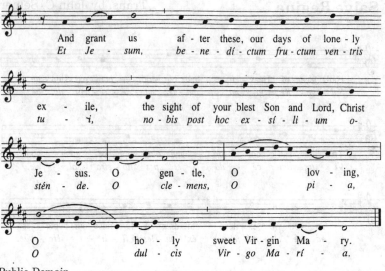

And grant us af - ter these, our days of lone - ly
Et Je - sum, be - ne - dí - ctum fru - ctum ven - tris

ex - ile, the sight of your blest Son and Lord, Christ
tu - i, no - bis post hoc ex - sí - li - um o-

Je - sus. O gen - tle, O lov - ing,
stén - de. O cle - mens, O pi - a,

O ho - ly sweet Vir - gin Ma - ry.
O dul - cis Vir - go Ma - rí - a.

Public Domain.

G 28

Seek Ye First   Karen Lafferty

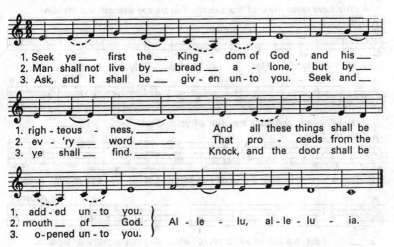

1. Seek ye __ first the __ King - dom of God and his __
2. Man shall not live by __ bread __ a - lone, but by __
3. Ask, and it shall be __ giv - en un - to you. Seek and __

1. righ - teous - ness, _____ And all these things shall be
2. ev - 'ry __ word _____ That pro - ceeds from the
3. ye shall __ find. _____ Knock, and the door shall be

1. add - ed un - to you.
2. mouth __ of __ God.   Al - le - lu, al - le - lu - ia.
3. o - pened un - to you.

G 29

Sing to the Mountains   Robert Dufford, SJ

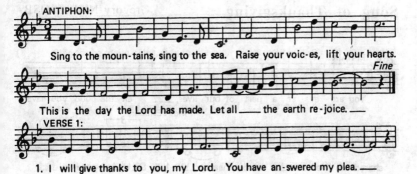

ANTIPHON:

Sing to the moun - tains, sing to the sea. Raise your voic - es, lift your hearts.

Fine

This is the day the Lord has made. Let all ____ the earth re - joice. __

VERSE 1:

1. I will give thanks to you, my Lord. You have an - swered my plea. __

...Sing to the Mountains

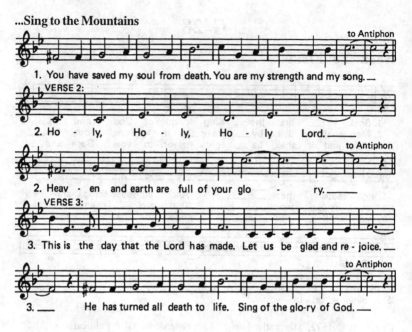

1. You have saved my soul from death. You are my strength and my song.

2. Ho - ly, Ho - ly, Ho - ly Lord.

2. Heav - en and earth are full of your glo - ry.

3. This is the day that the Lord has made. Let us be glad and re - joice.

3. He has turned all death to life. Sing of the glo-ry of God.

G 30

Song of Thanksgiving Gregory Norbet, OSB

You are ev - er a part of our lives, all the good you have

shared will live on in our heart. 1.-5. Let us be grate-ful

...Song of Thanksgiving

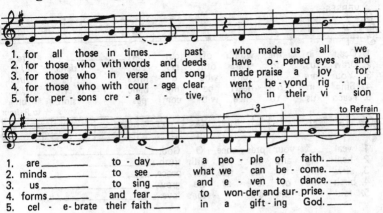

1. for all those in times____ past who made us all we
2. for those who with words and deeds have o - pened eyes and
3. for those who in verse and song made praise a joy for
4. for those who with cour - age clear went be - yond rig - id
5. for per - sons cre - a - tive, who in their vi - sion

1. are____ to - day____ a peo - ple of faith.____
2. minds____ to see____ what we can be - come.____
3. us____ to sing____ and e - ven to dance.____
4. forms____ and fear____ to won-der and sur - prise.____
5. cel - e - brate their faith____ in a gift - ing God.____

Copyright © 1975 from *Winter's Coming Home*, The Benedictine Foundation of the State of Vermont, Inc. Weston Priory, Weston, Vermont. Used with permission.

G 31

Spirit Come

Gregory Norbet

Spir - it, come, trans-form us. Come, be our breath, be our hope.__

__ Spir - it, come, trans-form us. Come, be our breath, be our

1-5 **Final**

Fine

hope.____ __ Come, be our breath, be our hope.

...Spirit Come

VERSES:

1. Deep in the womb of our heart _____ re-
2. Draw us to share oth - ers' bur - dens, (♪)
3. You are the one who u - nites us in
4. Sing in our heart, be the danc - er, (♪)
5. Teach us to live with com - pas - sion, un-

to Refrain

1. veal ____ your pres - ence, O God. ____
2. heal - ing and lov - ing with truth. ____
3. striv - ing for jus - tice, for peace. ____
4. birth - ing our love as we grow. ____
5. fold - ing cre - a - tor's love. ____

G 32

Stay With Me (Bleibet hier)

Music: Jacques Bertheir (1923-1994)

Stay with me, re - main here with me, watch and pray, watch and pray.

G 33

Stewards of Earth

Text: Omer Westendorf
Tune: Jean Sibelius

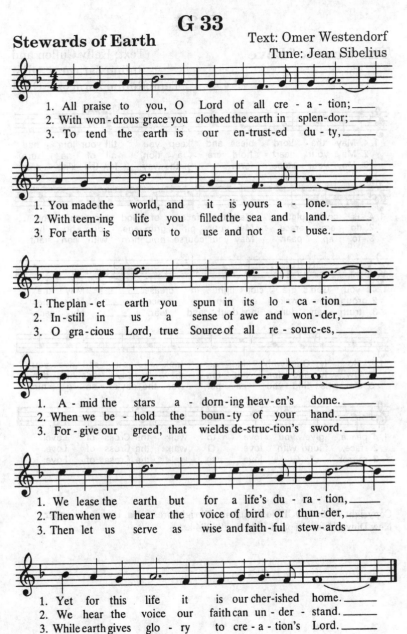

1. All praise to you, O Lord of all cre - a - tion;
2. With won - drous grace you clothed the earth in splen-dor;
3. To tend the earth is our en-trust-ed du - ty,

1. You made the world, and it is yours a - lone.
2. With teem-ing life you filled the sea and land.
3. For earth is ours to use and not a - buse.

1. The plan - et earth you spun in its lo - ca - tion
2. In - still in us a sense of awe and won - der,
3. O gra - cious Lord, true Source of all re - sourc-es,

1. A - mid the stars a - dorn-ing heav-en's dome.
2. When we be - hold the boun - ty of your hand.
3. For - give our greed, that wields de-struc-tion's sword.

1. We lease the earth but for a life's du - ra - tion,
2. Then when we hear the voice of bird or thun-der,
3. Then let us serve as wise and faith - ful stew-ards

1. Yet for this life it is our cher-ished home.
2. We hear the voice our faith can un - der - stand.
3. While earth gives glo - ry to cre - a - tion's Lord.

G 34

The Cross of Love

Text: Kelly Cullen and
Rufino Zaragoza, OFM
Tune: Rufino Zaragoza, OFM

1, 4. May the Lord bless and keep you till your jour - ney
2. May your heart hold cre - a - tion, all of na - ture
3. May your steps form a path - way for the king - dom

1, 4. is com - plete. May the face of God come shine on
2. do em - brace. May your pil - grim - age on ho - ly
3. to ap - pear. May your course hold firm with con - stant

1, 4. you; God's gra - cious light in - crease. _____ May the
2. ground a - wak - en you to grace. _____ May the
3. truth en - dur - ing doubt and fear. _____ May each

1, 4. Ho - ly One with kind - ness look on you and give you
2. low - ly and for - got - ten show our Sav - ior's hid - den
3. sun - rise find you ea - ger, for the day's an o - p'ning

1, 4. peace, give you love, to walk the Cross of Love.
2. face, found with love. O walk the Cross of Love.
3. mirror of God's love; so walk the Cross of Love.

G 35

The Cry of the Poor

John Foley, SJ

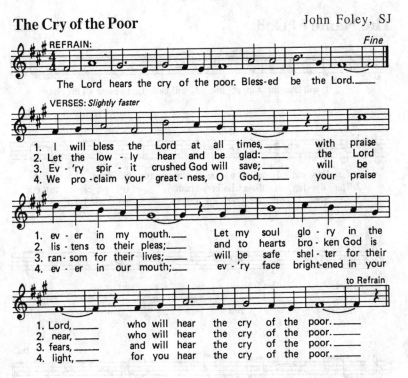

REFRAIN:

Fine

The Lord hears the cry of the poor. Bless-ed be the Lord.___

VERSES: *Slightly faster*

1. I will bless the Lord at all times,___ with praise
2. Let the low - ly hear and be glad:___ the Lord
3. Ev - 'ry spir - it crushed God will save;___ will be
4. We pro - claim your great - ness, O God,___ your praise

1. ev - er in my mouth.___ Let my soul glo - ry in the
2. lis - tens to their pleas;___ and to hearts bro - ken God is
3. ran - som for their lives;___ will be safe shel - ter for their
4. ev - er in our mouth;___ ev - 'ry face bright-ened in your

to Refrain

1. Lord,___ who will hear the cry of the poor.___
2. near,___ who will hear the cry of the poor.___
3. fears,___ and will hear the cry of the poor.___
4. light,___ for you hear the cry of the poor.___

G 36

The Name of God

David Haas

Refrain

I will take the cup of life, I will call God's name all my days.

Verses

1. How can I make a re - turn for the good - ness of
2. The dy - ing of those who keep faith is pre - cious to our
3. To you I will of - fer my thanks and call up - on your

God? This sav - ing cup I will
God. I am your ser - vant called
name. You are my prom - ise for

bless and sing, and call the name of God!
from your hands, you have set me free!
all to see. I love your name, O God!

D.C.

G 37

The Harvest of Justice

David Haas

(Refrain) May we find rich - ness in the har - vest of jus -
1. Gath-er with pa - tience for those who have noth -
2. For to have mer - cy on those for - got -
3. For to have lit - tle is to be in a - bun -

tice which Christ Je - sus has rip-ened for
ing. Leave them your rich - es, and you will re -
ten, this is my true law, this is my com -
dance. To give what re - mains, to give all we

us. Bread for the jour - ney,
ceive. Make room for the poor ones,
mand: Clothe the na - ked,
have, is to walk with the poor ones,

bread for the hun - gry, all for the
make way for the stran - ger; for I am the
be home for the or - phan, be hope for the
and be - come the stran - ger, one with the

glo - ry and praise of God.
Lord, the Lord your God.
wid - ow, and wel - come the lost.
Lord, the Lord our God.

G 38

Ubi Caritas Music: Jacques Bertheir (1923-1994)

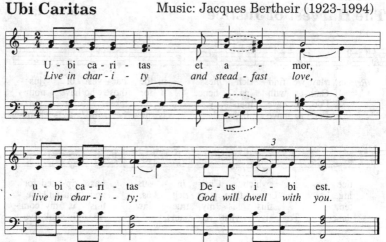

U - bi ca - ri - tas   et a - mor,
Live in char - i - ty   and stead - fast   love,

u - bi ca - ri - tas   De - us i - bi est.
live in char - i - ty;   God will dwell   with   you.

G 39

Water of Life David Haas

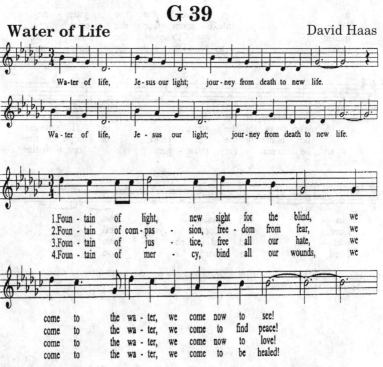

Wa-ter of life,   Je - sus our light;   jour-ney from death to new life.

Wa - ter of life,   Je - sus our   light;   jour-ney from death to new life.

1. Foun - tain   of   light,   new   sight for   the   blind,   we
2. Foun - tain   of com - pas - sion,   free - dom   from   fear,   we
3. Foun - tain   of   jus - tice,   free   all   our   hate,   we
4. Foun - tain   of   mer - cy,   bind   all   our   wounds,   we

come   to   the wa - ter,   we   come   now   to   see!
come   to   the wa - ter,   we   come   to   find   peace!
come   to   the wa - ter,   we   come   now   to   love!
come   to   the wa - ter,   we   come   to   be   healed!

G 40

Where Charity and Love Prevail

Tune: Paul Benoit, OSB
Trans. by Omer Westendorf

1. Where char-i-ty and love pre-vail, There God is ev-er found; Brought here to-geth-er by Christ's love, By love are we thus bound.
2. With grate-ful joy and ho-ly fear His char-i-ty we learn; Let us with heart and mind and soul Now love him in re-turn.
3. For-give we now each oth-er's faults As we our faults con-fess; And let us love each oth-er well In Chris-tian ho-li-ness.
4. Let strife a-mong us be un-known, Let all con-ten-tion cease; Be his the glo-ry that we seek, Be ours his ho-ly peace.
5. Let us re-call that in our midst Dwells God's be-got-ten Son; As mem-bers of his Bod-y joined, We are in him made one.
6. No race nor creed can love ex-clude, If hon-ored be God's name; Our fam-i-ly em-brac-es all Whose Fa-ther is the same.

G 41

You Are Near Daniel Schutte

ANTIPHON:

Yah-weh, I know you are near,— stand-ing al-ways at my side.— You guard me from the foe, and you lead me in ways ev-er-last-ing.—

Fine

VERSES:

1. Lord, you have searched my heart, and you know when I sit and when I stand. Your— hand is up-on me pro-tect-ing me from death, keep-ing me from harm.—
2. Where can I run from your love? If I climb to the heav-ens you are there; if I fly to the sun-rise or sail be-yond the sea, still I'd find you there.—
3. You know my heart and its ways, you who formed me be-fore I was born in the se-cret of dark-ness be-fore I saw the sun in my moth-er's womb.—
4. Mar-vel-ous to me are your works; how pro-found are your thoughts my— Lord. E-ven if I could count them, they num-ber as the stars, you would still be there.—

to Antiphon

G 42

You Are the Voice

David Haas

Refrain

You are the voice of the liv-ing God,

call-ing us now to live in your love, to be

chil-dren of God once a-gain!

Verses

Cantor:

1. Praise for the light that shines through the night, from
2. Praise for the wa-ter that springs from the sea, the
3. Praise for the sing-ing and praise for the dance, with

dark-ness to light, from death to new life, and
seed that gives life to all who be-lieve, God's
new heart and voice, all raise the song of

praise to the morn-ing that brings forth the sun, to
love o-ver-flow-ing, our hearts know the joy to be
praise to cre-a-tion; all heav-en and earth, come

All:

o - pen our eyes to the Lord!   To
daugh-ters and sons of the Lord!   To be
sing of the glo-ry of God!   Come

D.C.

o - pen our eyes to the Lord!   For
daugh-ters and sons of the Lord!   For
sing of the glo-ry of God!   For

F 1

All Creatures of Our God and King

Text: Francis of Assisi
Trans. by William H. Draper

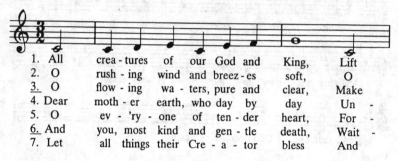

1. All   crea - tures of our God and   King,   Lift
2. O   rush - ing wind and breez - es   soft,   O
3. O   flow - ing wa - ters, pure and   clear,   Make
4. Dear   moth - er earth, who day by   day   Un -
5. O   ev - 'ry - one of ten - der   heart,   For -
6. And   you, most kind and gen - tle   death,   Wait -
7. Let   all things their Cre - a - tor   bless   And

1. up your voice with us and   sing: Al - le -
2. clouds that ride the winds a - loft: Oh, ___
3. mu - sic for your Lord to   hear.   Oh, ___
4. folds rich bless - ings on our   way,   Oh, ___
5. giv - ing oth - ers, take your   part,   Oh, ___
6. ing to hush our fi - nal   breath,   Oh, ___
7. wor - ship God in hum - ble - ness.   Oh, ___

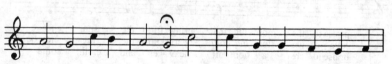

1. lu - ia! Al - le - lu - ia! O   burn - ing sun with gold - en
2. praise him! Al - le - lu - ia! O   ris - ing morn, in praise re -
3. praise him! Al - le - lu - ia! O   fire so mas - ter - ful and
4. praise him! Al - le - lu - ia! The   fruits and flow'rs that ver - dant
5. praise him! Al - le - lu - ia! All   you who pain and sor - row
6. praise him! Al - le - lu - ia! You   lead to heav'n the child of
7. praise him! Al - le - lu - ia! Oh,   praise the Fath - er, praise the

...All Creatures of Our God and King

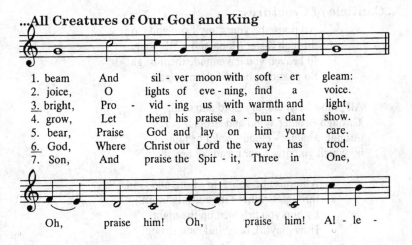

1. beam	And	sil - ver moon with	soft - er	gleam:
2. joice,	O	lights of eve - ning, find	a	voice.
3. bright,	Pro -	vid - ing us with	warmth and	light,
4. grow,	Let	them his praise a - bun - dant		show.
5. bear,	Praise	God and lay on	him your	care.
6. God,	Where	Christ our Lord the	way has	trod.
7. Son,	And	praise the Spir - it,	Three in	One,

Oh, praise him! Oh, praise him! Al - le -

lu - ia, al - le - lu - ia, al - le - lu - ia!

F 2

Canticle of the Creatures

Text: Benet A. Fonck, OFM

Most High, almighty, gracious God,
All glory, honor, praise is yours.
To you alone do they belong;
No one can utter your great name.

All praise be yours, my Lord and God,
through all the creatures you have made;
Especially Sir Brother Sun
who is the day, the source of light.

How beautiful, how radiant
How filled with holy splendor!
He bears the likeness of your face,
Most High, almighty, gracious Lord.

...Canticle of Creatures

All praise be yours, my Lord and God,
through Sister Moon and all the stars.
In heaven you have made them bright,
So precious, beautiful, and clear.

All praise be yours, my Lord and God,
Through Brother Wind and Brother Air,
through weather - cloudy, calm or fair -
by which you give your creatures breath.

All praise be yours, my Lord and God,
through Brother Fire burning bright;
by him you brighten up the night.
How playful, beautiful, and strong!

All praise be yours, my Lord and God,
through Sister Earth, our Mother fair,
who feeds us in her sovereignty
with fruits and herbs and colored flow'rs.

All praise be yours, my Lord and God,
through those who pardon in your love,
who bear their pain with holy peace;
for by you, Lord, they shall be crowned.

All praise be yours, my Lord and God,
through Sister Death of human limb.
No one among the human race
Shall ever flee from her embrace.

Woe to those dead in mortal sin!
Blest those she finds who do your will!
The second death can do no harm
to those who love you to the end.

Praise, bless, my Lord, and give him thanks
and serve him with humility.
Most High, almighty gracious God,
All glory, honor, praise is yours.

Melody: Praise God From Whom All Blessings Flow
Creator of the Stars of Night

F 3

Canticle of the Sun

Marty Haugen

REFRAIN

The heav-ens are tell-ing the glo-ry of God, ____ and all cre-
-a-tion is shout-ing for joy. ____ Come, dance in the for-est, come,
play in the field, ____ and sing, sing to the glo-ry

1-6 / **to Verses** / **Final**

of the Lord. ____ Lord. ____ Sing,

Fine

sing to the glo-ry of the Lord! ____

VERSES

1. Praise for the sun, the bring-er of day, he car-ries the
2. Praise for the wind that blows through the trees, the seas might-y
3. Praise for the rain that wa-ters our fields, and bless-es our
4. Praise for the fire who gives us his light, the warmth of the
5. Praise for the earth who makes life to grow, the crea-tures you
6. Praise for our death that makes our life real, the know-ledge of

1. light of the Lord in his rays; the moon and the stars who
2. storms, the gen-tl-est breeze; they blow where they will, they
3. crops so all the earth yields; from death un-to life her
4. sun to bright-en our night; he danc-es with joy, his
5. made to let your life show; the flow-ers and trees that
6. loss that helps us to feel; the gift of your-self, your

to Refrain

1. light up the way un-to your throne. ____
2. blow where they please to please the Lord. ____
3. mys-t'ry re-vealed springs forth in joy. ____
4. spir-it so bright, he sings of you. ____
5. help us to know the heart of love. ____
6. pres-ence re-vealed to bring us home. ____

F 4

Francis Now　　　　　　　Text: Robert M. Hutmacher, OFM
Adorned in Glory

Francis now adorned in glory, [we Franciscans] honor you.
In your life we see the life of Christ, Redeemer crucified.
We acclaim our father's fame, for all in heaven sing his praise;
We rejoice and sing in union with their voices glorified.

Taken up from earth to heaven, all his works reveal his life.
Francis lives on high forever; Christ has graced him endlessly.
God of everlasting kindness, prayerful hearts we offer you.
For this man adorned and honored shares your glory radiantly.

Many follow, many join with him who traveled holy lands.
Francis took the Gospel message as a light that dazzled all.
Francis bears the wounds of Jesus in his hands, his feet, his side.
Daylight breaks and night recedes: a new star shatters earthly pall.

Faithful leader, shining star, enlighten us who journey through
Constant challenge to your Rule and show us joys of Paradise.
Gently lead your followers in overcoming human bonds.
Gather us and guide us to the banquet that the Lamb provides.

Melody: Ode to Joy

F 5

Hymn: In a Dream Robert M. Hutmacher, OFM

1. In a dream Fran - ces - co saw the
2. In the Gos - pels Fran - cis heard three
3. While in prayer he re - cog - nized the
4. With the cross we sign our - selves, we

1. gleam - ing arms of the cross. He
2. times the pow'r of the cross; three
3. cross of Christ as his life. He
4. share its grace and its pain; we

1. heard the Cru - ci - fied say to him:
2. times the sac - red text did pro - claim:
3. saw and heard for him - self a course:
4. seal the bo - dy and mind with Christ,

1. "Now count all else as loss."
2. "This is your gain, your loss."
3. wounds would he bear, and strife.
4. heirs of the 'ter - nal reign.

1. In the cross he came to see a
2. In his con - tem - pla - tion, Fran - cis
3. Marked now with the stig - ma - ta he
4. Praise to you, O Source of Life, to

...Hymn: In A Dream

1. pow - er, re - fuge, re - pose; he
2. of - ten the cross em - braced; his
3. suf - fered, yet he en - dured; his
4. Je - sus, cru - ci - fied Lord, to

1. would be clothed in ar - mor now,
2. great de - sire to mir - ror Christ
3. heart, his flesh were pierced, he was
4. gen - tle Spir - it, Tri - une God,

1. fight - ing a - gainst all foes.
2. filled him with joy - ful grace.
3. mir - ror of Christ, the Lord.
4. for - ev - er loved, a - dored.

F 6

Hymn to St. Francis I
Text: Benet A. Fonck, OFM

Most High almighty Godhead
we praise you for yourself.
You made us out of nothing
through your most holy Word.
You made us in your image,
You gave us your own life,
You opened up your kingdom,
You called us to yourself.

We thank you, God, most faithful,
for through your holy love,
you sent your Son among us,
as human and divine,
to demonstrate your wonders,
to free us from our sins,
to be the way of pilgrims
that we may come to you.

We thank you, Lord of glory,
for all your saints above,
especially Saint Francis
who modeled Christ your Son;
with poverty and preaching,
with pray'r and tender love
he lived the holy Gospel
and built the Church anew.

For Francis of Assisi
we therefore praise your name:
You grant him wondrous blessings
and through him you proclaim
your gospel way of living,
your riches to the poor,
your grace to be at one with you
when we the cross endure.

Melody: The Church's One Foundation
All Glory Laud and Honor

F 7

Hymn to St. Francis II Text: Benet A. Fonck, OFM

Come be with us, St. Francis,
the model of our Lord.
You followed in his footsteps
and showed us God's reward
for living one with Jesus,
the poor and crucified,
revealing heaven's treasures
and shining as our guide.

The way of Christ engulfed you,
the Gospel was your way.
Your poverty of spirit,
your kind and gentle sway,
your lofty contemplation,
your purity of heart,
your oneness with Christ's Body
to you God's life impart.

In spirit and in body
you carried high the cross.
The poor and humble Savior
your mirrored without gloss.
You called souls back to Jesus
in whom all glories lie.
You witnessed all creation
as signs of God Most High.

Your faithfulness we honor,
your life we imitate,
your legacy we cherish;
to you we dedicate
our loving one another
as instruments of peace,
our simple, pray'rful living
where joy will never cease.

Melody: The Church's One Foundation
All Glory Laud and Honor

F 8

Hymn to St. Francis III   Text: Benet A. Fonck, OFM

Blessed Francis, holy father,
now our hearts to thee we raise
as we gather 'round the altar
pouring forth our hymns of praise.
Bless thy children, holy Francis,
who your mighty help implore.
For in heaven thou remainest
still the father of the poor.

By thy love so deep and burning
for the Savior curcified;
by the tokens which he gave thee
on thy hands and feet and side:
Bless thy children, holy Francis
with those wounded hands of thine
from thy glorious throne in heaven
where resplendently they shine.

Humble follower of Jesus
likened to Him in thy birth,
in thy way through life despising
for his sake the goods of earth:
Make us love the priceless virtue
by our hidden God esteemed,
make it valued, holy Francis
by the souls of the redeemed.

Teach us also, dear Saint Francis,
how to mourn for ev'ry sin;
May we walk in thy dear footsteps
till the crown of life we win.
Bless thy children, holy Francis
with those wounded hands of thine.
From thy glorious throne in heaven
where resplendently they shine.

Melody: Ode to Joy or Alleluia Sing to Jesus

F 9

I Am a Poor One

Composer unknown

I am a poor one, nothing do I own. I give you my heart.

F 10

In Perfect Charity

Randall DeBruyn

1. O most high and glorious God, cast your light into the darkness of my heart. Give me right faith, and certain hope, and perfect, perfect charity. Give me true insight, Lord, and wisdom, that I may always live within your ever holy will. Lord, may your light

2. O most high and glorious God, open wide the door that leads me to your love. Give me your firm, yet gentle strength; may I live that perfect charity. Lord, may your peace be ever in me, that I may always seek to serve your children here on earth; that I may find

3. Then most high and thankful praise I will sing unto the glory of your name: To Father, Son, and Spirit bright, Living Presence, Perfect Charity. Praise to the Love that shines in splendor, that lights the pathways of my heart, and brings me close to you. O Holy One,

...In Perfect Charity

1. with - in me burn, shin - ing out in per - fect char - i - ty.
2. my home with you, and ___ live in per - fect char - i - ty.
3. in - vite me in, where you live in per - fect char - i - ty.

F 11
My God and My All

David Haas

REFRAIN

My God and my all, how I long to love You, and give You my heart, and give You my soul. (To Verses)

1. Show me the way to love, and give of my life for you;
1. then will I live, then will I rise. My

3. And I will live with you, and I will die with you;
3. weep - ing for love, weep - ing for joy! My

F 12

My God and My All

Rufino Zaragoza, OFM

1. Je - sus, my on - ly de - sire. _____ Je - sus, my
2. Je - sus, the hope of my soul. _____ Je - sus, the
3. Je - sus, the mer - cy of God. _____ Je - sus, the
4. Je - sus, my life - giv - ing Lord. _____ Je - sus, my
5. Je - sus, the wis - dom of God. _____ Je - sus, the

1. on - ly de - sire. _____ Je-sus, my love; Je-sus, my
2. hope of my soul. _____ Je-sus, my strength; Je-sus, my
3. mer - cy of God. _____ Je-sus, my truth; Je-sus, my
4. life - giv-ing Lord. _____ Je-sus, my joy; Je-sus, my
5. wis - dom of God. _____ Je-sus, my light; Je-sus, my

1. beau-ty. _____
2. ref-uge. _____
3. jus-tice. _____ Je-sus, my God and my all! _____
4. glo - ry. _____
5. vi - sion. _____

F 13

Peace Prayer

John Foley, SJ

1. Lord, make me a means of Your peace. _____ Where there's
2. Lord, make me a means of Your peace. _____ Where there's
3. Lord, make me a means of Your peace. _____ When there's
4. Lord, grant me to seek and to share: _____ less to
5. Lord, grant me to seek and to share: _____ to re -
6. Lord. grant me to seek and to share: _____ to for -

...Peace Prayer

```
1. ha - tred    grown, let me sow Your love._____      Where there's
2. doubt and    fear,  let me sow Your faith._____     In this
3. sad - ness   here,  let me sow Your joy. _____      When the
4. be   con -   soled than to help con - sole,_____    less be
5. ceive love   less  than to give love free,_____     just to
6. give  in     Thee, You've for - giv - en me;_____   for to

1. in - jury,   Lord, let for - give -ness be my sword.
2. world's des - pair, give me hope in You to share.
3. dark - ness  nears, may Your light dis - pel our fears.
4. un - der -   stood than to un -der-stand Your good.
5. give  in     Thee, just re - ceiv -ing from Your tree.
6. die   in     Thee, is e - ter - nal life to me.

1.—6. Lord, make me a means of Your peace._____
```

F 14

St. Francis
Image of the Lord

Text: Benet A. Fonck, OFM

St, Francis, image of the Lord,
We sound our praise to you today.
You revelled in the Gospel life,
Inspiring us to walk your way.

Forsaking every base desire,
The poor one's crown you wore with pride;
The love of God became your home,
The wealth of all you laid aside.

...St. Francis, Image of the Lord

Your theme is one of unity,
Your mission is to humankind,
By being instruments of peace
Your way of life becomes a sign.

We ask you, Francis, hear our prayer,
To guide us in our earthly strife,
To lead us home to Jesus Christ,
Who is our Way, our Truth, our life.

Melody: Praise God From Whom All Blessings Flow

Copyright © 1960, Franciscan Press, Quincy University, 1800 College Ave.,
Quincy, IL, 62301-2699. All rights reserved. Used with permission.

F 15

The Praises of God   Robert M. Hutmacher, OFM

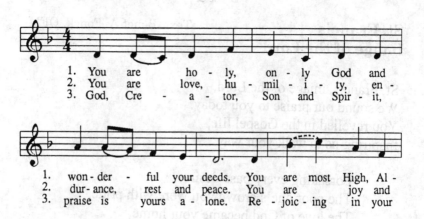

1. You are ho - ly, on - ly God and
2. You are love, hu - mil - i - ty, en -
3. God, Cre - a - tor, Son and Spir - it,

1. won - der - ful your deeds. You are most High, Al -
2. dur- ance, rest and peace. You are joy and
3. praise is yours a - lone. Re - joic - ing in your

...The Praises of God

1. might - y   the   king of   heav'n and   earth.
2. glad - ness,   our   cour - age,   wis - dom,   hope.
3. Pres - ence here   we   sing and   glo - ri - fy.

1. You   are   three and   one Lord,   the   liv - ing and true
2. You, Lord,   are   the   ha - ven,   pro - tec - tor   of our
3. With   our   Fa - ther   Fran - cis,   the   mir - ror   of your

1. God.   You   are   all   Good,   the   Lord Su - preme,   cre -
2. lives.   You   are   faith,   e - ter - nal   life,   our
3. love,   we   join   to - geth - er   in   one   voice,   and

1. a - tor   of   all   life.
2. lov - ing   Sa - vior.
3. sing: my   God,   my   All.

C 1

Blessing of St. Clare

Cathy Tisel Nelson

C 2

Clare Speaks to Her Soul

Sr. Helen Weier, OSC

Go in peace! Go, my blessed soul for the Guide is good who leads you on your way. Go forth my soul, for the one who has cre-a-ted you has al-so made you ho - - ly. God loves you, watches with a mother's tender care for the child of her love. May you be blessed, my Lord, who have created me.

C 3

Gaze Upon Christ

Cathy Tisel Nelson

Gaze up - on Christ, Con - si - der Christ.

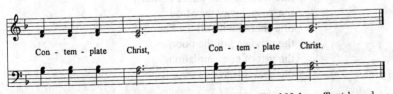

Con - tem - plate Christ, Con - tem - plate Christ.

C 4

Hymn of Clare I

Text: Benet A. Fonck, OFM

Most High almighty Godhead,
we praise you for yourself.
You made us out of nothing
through your most holy Word.
You made us in your image,
You gave us your own life,
You opened up your kingdom,
You called us to yourself.

We thank you, God, most faithful,
for through your holy love,
you sent your Son among us,
as human and divine,
to demonstrate your wonders,
to free us from our sins,
to be the way of pilgrims
that we may come to you.

We praise you, Lord, most loving,
for holy virgin Clare,
the mother of our Family
defending poverty,
the "little plant' of Francis
endowed with healing gifts,
the mirror of Christ Jesus
reflecting his own Light.

For Clare, our holy mother,
we thank you, Lord our God.
She walked with father Francis;
the gospel way they trod.
She shared with all the Family
the privilege of the poor,
the gift of contemplation,
the heav'nly way assured.

Melody: The Church's One Foundation or All Glory Laud and Honor

C 5

Hymn of Clare II

Text: Benet A. Fonck, OFM

Look down upon us kindly,
Assisi's holy Clare,
the light of gospel living,
a brightness we all share.
The fire of loving Jesus
burned deep within your heart;
you left your family's treasures
and set yourself apart.

You journeyed down the valley
to join the brothers' way
you traveled up the mountain
to find a place to pray.
The chapel of St. Damian
became your loving home
where with your sister pilgrims
you gazed on God alone.

You healed the sick with blessings,
you wrote a rule of life,
you mirrored gospel living,
you fought off earthly strife.
You showed the way to Jesus
through pray'r and poverty;
In union with your sisters
you loved God faithfully.

Your faithfulness we honor,
your life we imitate,
your legacy we cherish;
to you we dedicate
our work of prayer and service,
as Christ would have us do,
to wash the feet of others
and make the world anew.

Melody: The Church's One Foundation or All Glory Laud and Honor

C 6

What You Hold

Cathy Tisel Nelson

REFRAIN: What you hold, may you al-ways hold. What you do, may you al-ways do and nev-er a-ban-don, nev-er a-ban-don. *To Verses* Last Time and nev-er a-ban-don nev-er a-ban-don.

But with swift pace,
light step,
unswerving feet,
so that even your steps stir up no dust.
Go forward securely, joyfully and swiftly,
on the path of prudent happiness. **(Refrain)**

Believing nothing
agreeing with nothing
that would keep you from this resolution
or that would place
a stumbling block for you on the way. **(Refrain)**

So that you may offer your vows
to the Most High
in the pursuit of that perfection
to which the Spirit of God has called you,
called you,
called you. **(Refrain)**

C 7

With the Saints and Lights of Heaven

Text: Officium
Antiquum S. Clarae
Trans. by Robert M.
Hutmacher, OFM

With the saints and lights of heaven Lady Clare beams radiantly:
Joined in marriage with her Chosen, welcomed to eternity.
Clare is noble, source of riches, brilliant works her legacy.
Ever imitating Francis, earthly pow'r she did deny.

In a cloister poor and humble, Clare, espoused to Christ alone,
was to all a perfect model, mirror of her God enthroned.
Fruitful founder, to her daughters, she was teacher, gentle, kind.
Clare led many to the Savior by her holy strength of mind.

Christ was central in the heart and daily life of Lady Clare.
She embraced the cross of Christ in order to its glory share.
How she clothed herself in virtue! Ev'ry sister she impressed.
Those outside San Damiano recognized her holiness.

Stories told us are delightful: how the bread was multiplied,
how the sick she healed were grateful, how the oil: by heav'n supplied.
Legend, truth? it matters not for Clare is honored still today
as a woman, ill, yet still who healed through Christ our Light, our Way.

Heav'nly vision on her deathbed: virgins in procession came;
to the realm of lights ascended Clare, now blest among the same.
"Luce claret vocitata!" Lady Clare in heav'n is crowned.
And the Church on earth has gained a flower brilliant and renowned.

Virgo Clara tuis para devotis hospitia.
Per te data sint optata salus, quies, gloria.
Virgin Clare prepare for your devoted ones a haven blest;
In the reign of lights and glory may they share eternal rest.

Melody: Ode to Joy

CM 1

A Child Is Born

Lucien Deiss, CSSp

Un-to us a Child is born, Un-to us a Son is giv-en. E - ter-nal is his sway.

CM 2

Angels We Have Heard on High

Angels we have heard on high,
sweetly singing o'er the plain,
and the mountains in reply
echoing back their joyous strains.

REFRAIN
Gloria in excelsis Deo, Gloria in excelsis Deo.

Shepherds, why this jubilee?
Why your joyous strains prolong?
Say what may the tidings be,
which inspire your heav'nly song.

REFRAIN

...Angels We Have Heard on High

Come to Bethlehem and see
him whose birth the angels sing:
Come adore, on bended knee,
Christ, the Lord, the newborn King.

REFRAIN

See him in a manger laid,
Whom the choirs of angels praise;
Mary, Joseph, lend your aid,
while our hearts in love we raise.

Public Domain

CM 3

Joy to the World

Joy to the world! The Lord is come:
Let earth receive her King;
Let ev'ry heart prepare him room,
and heav'n and nature sing,
and heav'n and nature sing,
and heav'n, and heav'n and nature sing.

Joy to the world! The Savior reigns:
Let us, our songs employ;
while fields and floods, rocks, hills and plains
repeat the sounding joy,
repeat the sounding joy,
repeat, repeat the sounding joy.

No more let sin and sorrows grow,
nor thorns infest the ground;
he comes to make his blessings flow
far as the curse is found,
far as the curse is found,
far as, far as the curse is found.

He rules the world with truth and grace,
and makes the nations prove
the glories of his righteous,
and wonders of his love,
and wonders of his love,
and wonders, wonders of his love.

Public Domain.

CM 4

O Come, All Ye Faithful

O come all ye faithful, joyful and triumphant,
O come ye, O come ye to Bethlehem;
Come and behold him, born the King of angels;

REFRAIN
O come, let us adore him, O come let us adore him,
O come, let us adore him, Christ, the Lord.

Sing, choirs of angels, sing in exultation,
Sing all ye citizens of heav'n above!
Glory to God, all glory in the highest;

REFRAIN

Yea, Lord, we greet thee, born this happy morning,
Jesus, to thee be all glory giv'n;
Word of the Father, now in flesh appearing;

REFRAIN

Adéste fidéles, laéti triumphántes,
Veníte, veníte in Béthlehem.
Natum vidéte, Regem angelórum
Veníte adorémus, veníte adorémus,
veníte adorémus Dóminum.

Public Domain.

One in Royal David's City

CM5

Text: Vs. 1 Cecil F. Alexander
Text: Vs. 2 Brother Justus, SSF
Tune: Henry John Gauntlett

Once in roy-al Da-vid's ci-ty stood a
And a-gain in Grec-cio's stab-le was the

low-ly cat-tle shed, where a
Word of God made flesh, when the

mo-ther laid her ba-by in a
ho-ly Fa-ther Fran-cis gave the

man-ger for his bed; Ma-ry
world the Christ-mas creche. Hel-ping

was that mo-ther mild, Je-sus
all the world a-dore God's own

Christ her lit-tle child.
Son whom Ma-ry bore.

CM 6

Silent Night

Silent night, holy night, all is calm, all is bright.
Round yon Virgin, Mother and Child,
Holy Infant so tender and mild,
sleep in heavenly peace, sleep in heavenly peace.

Silent night, holy night, shepherds quake at the sight;
glories stream from heaven afar,
heav'nly hosts sing alleluia;
Christ the Savior is born, Christ the Savior is born.

Silent night, holy night, Son of God, love's pure light.
Radiant beams from thy holy face,
with the dawn of redeeming grace,
Jesus, Lord, at thy birth, Jesus, Lord, at thy birth.

Public Domain.

CM 7

The First Nowel

The first Nowell, the angel did say,
was to certain poor shepherds in fields as they lay
In fields where they lay keeping their sheep,
on a cold winter's night that was so deep.

REFRAIN
Nowell, Nowell, Nowell, Nowell,
Born is the King of Israel.

...The First Noel

They looked up and saw a star
shining in the East, beyond them far.
And to the earth it gave great light,
and so it continued both day and night.

REFRAIN

And by the light of that same star
three wise men came from country far;
to seek for a king was their intent,
and to follow the star wherever it went.

REFRAIN

Then entered in those wise men three
full rev'rently upon their knee,
and offered there, in his presence,
their gold and myrrh and frankincense.

REFRAIN

Public Domain.

CM 8

Tu Scendi Dalle Stelle   Afonso M. Liguori

1. Tu   scen - di dal - le stel-le.   O Re   del cie   lo,   E-
vie - ni in u - na grot - ta Al   fred - do, al ge - lo.   E-
vie-ni in u - na grot-ta Al fred do al ge - lo.   O Bam bi   no mi -o di-

...Tu Scendi Dalle Stelle

vi - no, I - o ti ve - do qui a tre mar O Di - o be -a -

to, Ah quan - to ti co- sto L'a ver - mia-ma

to! Ah quan-to ti co-sto L'a- ver - mia - ma - to!

2. A te che sei del mondo il Creatore,
Or mancan panni e fuoco, o mio Signore.
Caro eletto
        Pargoletto:
Quanto questa povertà
Più m'innamora
Giacchè to fece amor
Povero ancora.

Found in the Nella Casa del Padre Hymnal. Public Domain.

CM 9

What Child Is This

What child is this, who, laid to rest,
on Mary's lap is sleeping?
Whom angels greet with anthems sweet,
while shepherds watch are keeping?

REFRAIN
This, this is Christ the King,
whom shepherds guard and angels sing;
haste, haste to bring him laud,
the babe, the son of Mary

...What Child Is This

Why lies he in such mean estate
where ox and ass are feeding?
Good Christian, fear; for sinners here
the silent Word is pleading.

REFRAIN

So bring him incense, gold and myrrh,
come peasant, king to own him;
the King of kings salvation brings,
let loving hearts enthrone him.

REFRAIN

INDEXES

FRANCISCAN PILGRIMAGE PROGRAMS

SCRIPTURE TEXTS

New Testament

FRANCISCAN SOURCES

WRITINGS OF ST. FRANCIS

OTHER SOURCES FOR THE LIFE OF ST. FRANCIS

Thomas of Celano, First Life

The Legend of Three Companions

Bonaventure, The Major Legend of Saint Francis

Second Mirror of Perfection (Sabatier Edition)

The Little Flowers of Saint Francis

NB: All references can be found in *Francis of Assisi: Early Documents, Volumes I, II, and III;* edited by Regis J. Armstrong, O.F.M. Cap., J.A. Wayne Hellmann, O.F. M. Conv., and William J. Short, O.F.M.

WRITINGS OF ST. CLARE

OTHER SOURCES FOR THE LIFE OF ST. CLARE

NB: All references can be found in *Clare of Assisi: Early Documents,*
translated and edited by Regis J. Armstrong, O.F.M. Cap.

ACKNOWLEDGEMENTS

Franciscan Pilgrimage Programs sincerely thanks authors, music composers, publishers, and holders of copyrights who have kindly granted permission to reprint their material. Every attempt has been made to properly acknowledge resources used in *Pilgrim's Companion to Franciscan Places*. All oversights will be corrected as information is received. **Because of copyright agreements, permission to photocopy materials from this book cannot be granted.**

Special thanks to **Lisa Biedenbach** and the staff at St. Anthony Messenger Press for donating time and personnel for a professional editing of our texts; to **Sr. Malinda Gerke, F.S.P.A.**, and **Sr. Kathy Cairns, O.S.F.**, who incorporated all music into disk format; to **Patrick Markey** of New City Press for his support and invaluable assistance in making texts available from *Francis of Assisi: Early Documents*; and to **Maurizio Zubboli**, editor, publisher, and owner of the *Editrice Minerva* in Assisi, who printed this edition with artistic skill and generosity. Finally a very special thank you to **Sr. Elizabeth Christensen, S.D.S.**, and **Georgia Flanagan** of the Pilgrimage Office without whom this project would not have been completed.

Committee for revision:
>   **Fr. André Cirino, O.F.M.**
>   **Sr. Roberta McKelvie, O.S.F.**
>   **Sr. Joanne Schatzlein, O.S.F.**
>   **Br. Joseph Wood, O.F.M. Conv.**

WRITTEN TEXTS

THE FRANCISCAN INSTITUTE, St. Bonaventure University, St. Bonaventure, NY 14778, for texts used from *Clare of Assisi: Early Documents,* translated and edited by Regis J. Armstrong,

O.F.M. Cap.; *Clare Centenary Series, Volume 8,* edited by Ingrid Peterson, O.S.F.; and *The Cord,* a periodical edited and published by the Franciscan Institute.

NEW CITY PRESS, 202 Cardinal Rd., Hyde Park, NY 12538 (www.newcitypress.com), for texts used from *Francis of Assisi: Early Documents, Volume I: The Saint; Volume II: The Founder; Volume III: The Prophet;* edited by Regis J. Armstrong, O.F.M. Cap., J.A. Wayne Hellmann, O.F.M. Conv., and William J. Short, O.F.M. Copyright 1999, 2000, 2001 Franciscan Institute of St. Bonaventure University, St. Bonaventure, NY.

NATIONAL COUNCIL OF CHURCHES OF CHRIST IN THE USA, P.O. Box 1209, Minneapolis, MN 55440, for the use of scripture texts from the *New Revised Standard Version of the Bible*, copyright © 1989 by the Division of Christian Education. Used with permission. All rights reserved.

ST. ANTHONY MESSENGER PRESS, 1615 Republic St., Cincinnati, OH 45210-1298, for materials used from *Francis: The Journey and the Dream* and *Clare: A Light in the Garden,* by Murray Bodo, O.F.M.

FRANCISCAN PRESS, 915 N. Eighteenth St., Quincy, IL 62031-2670, for use of texts from *Man with a Song,* by Francis and Helen Line; *Living the Incarnation: Praying with Francis and Clare of Assisi,* by Sister Frances Teresa, O.S.C.; *Assisi Dawn*, by Francis and Helen Line; *St. Francis of Assisi, Writings and Early Biographies: English Omnibus of the Sources for the Life of St. Francis,* edited by Marion Habig, O.F.M; *True Joy from Assisi* by Raphael Brown; and *Workbook for Franciscan Studies (Second Edition) by* Damien Isabel, O.F.M.

THE CROSSROAD PUBLISHING COMPANY, 481 Eighth Ave., New York, NY 10001, for texts used from *Francis of Assisi,* by Arnaldo Fortini.

EDIZIONI MESSAGGERO PADOVA, Via Orto Botanico, 11, 35123 Padova, Italy, for texts used from *The Little Flowers of Saint Clare* by Piero Bargellini, translated by Edmund O'Gorman, O.F.M. Conv.

UNITED STATES CATHOLIC CONFERENCE, 3211 Fourth St. NE, Washington, DC 20017-1194, for texts titled "Jubilee Pledge" and "Nine Ways to Live Jubilee and Be a Holy Person," published in the Year 2000.

FRANCISCAN FEDERATION THIRD ORDER REGULAR OF THE BROTHERS AND SISTERS OF THE UNITED STATES, P.O. Box 29080, Washington, DC 20017, for use of texts from *The Rule and Life of the Brothers and Sisters of the Third Order Regular of St. Francis and Commentary.*

SR. FRANCES TERESA DOWNING, O.S.C., and her Poor Clare Sisters in Arundel, England, for use of her private translation of *The Four Letters of Saint Clare to Saint Agnes of Prague* and for her poem "Clare, the Light."

FOREST OF PEACE, 251 Muncie Rd., Leavenworth, KS 66048, for copyright permission to reprint texts from *Prayers for the Domestic Church* by Fr. Edward Hays.

MURRAY BODO, O.F.M., for use of unpublished poems.

WILLIAM HART McNICHOLS, S.J., S.F.O., for use of unpublished poems.

MUSIC

OREGON CATHOLIC PRESS, 5536 NE Hassalo, Portland, OR 97213, for use of music published under license #2393449.

GIA PUBLICATIONS, 7404 S. Mason Ave., Chicago, IL 60638, for use of music published under license #4880 and for assistance in obtaining copyright permission from other composers.

WORLD LIBRARY PUBLICATIONS, 3825 N. Willow Rd., Schiller Park, IL 60176-9936, for use of music published under license #AL0419011.

CATHY TISEL NELSON, 4512 Stratford Ln., NW, Rochester, MN 55901, for use of music from *What You Hold*, published in 1996 and available for purchase directly from the composer.

ATELIERS ET PRESSES DE TAIZÉ, 71250 Cluny, France, for use of music composed by Jacques Berthier.

WESTON PRIORY PRODUCTIONS, 58 Priory Hill Rd., Weston, VT 05161, for use of music composed by Gregory Norbet.

SOCIETY OF ST. FRANCIS, P.O. Box 389, Mount Sinai, NY 11766, for use of music text related to Greccio composed by Brother Justus, S.S.F.

THE FRANCISCAN INSTITUTE, St. Bonaventure University, St. Bonaventure, NY 14778, for use of music from *Clare and Francis: O Let the Faithful People Sing,* by Robert M. Hutmacher O.F.M.

FRANCISCAN PRESS, 915 N. Eighteenth St., Quincy, IL 62031-2670, for use of music texts by Benet A. Fonck, O.F.M., published by Franciscan Herald Press.

ARCHDIOCESE OF PHILADELPHIA, Office of Worship, 222 N. Seventeenth St., Philadelphia, PA 19103, for use of *Gift of Finest Wheat.*

G. SHIRMER, INC, 257 Park Ave. So., 20th Floor, New York, NY 10010, for permission to use *All Creatures of Our God and King.*

BENET A. FONCK, O.F.M., for use of music texts related to various Franciscan themes.

HELEN WEIER, O.S.C., for use of *Clare Speaks to Her Soul.*

JAN MICHAEL JONCAS, for use of his unpublished Mass texts set to Christmas songs.

ARTI GRAFICHE ANTICA PORZIUNCOLA
S. MARIA DEGLI ANGELI - ASSISI

COLASANTO

Finito di stampare nel mese di giugno 2006
presso lo stabilimento di Cannara (Perugia)